DOGS ON THE WEB

DOGS ON THE WEB

Audrey Pavia
Betsy Sikora Siino

A Subsidiary of
Henry Holt and Co., Inc
New York

MIS:Press
A Subsidiary of Henry Holt and Company, Inc.
115 West 18th Street
New York, New York 10011
http://www.mispress.com

ISBN: 1-55828-559-8

First Edition—1997

10 9 8 7 6 5 4 3 2 1

Associate Publisher: *Paul Farrell*

Managing Editor: *Shari Chappell*   **Production Editor:** *Gay Nichols*
Editor: *Andy Neusner*   **Copy Editor:** *Bert Shankle*
Technical Editors: *Paul Rutner*   **Copy Edit Manager:** *Karen Tongish*

For all the dogs who have ever touched our lives, and taught us about nature, laughter and love.

Acknowledgments

As much as we hate to admit it, we had a lot of help with this book, and feel compelled to thank the following people and animals for their assistance:

Our editor Andy Neusner for contacting us with this great idea and helping us turn it into something tangible; research assistant Paul Rutner, who stayed up late at night aiding us in our never-ending search for Web sites; dog lovers and experienced Net surfers Rosemarie Craver and Lexiann Grant-Snider for providing us with scores of addresses that met with their own experienced approval; Gina Spadafori for her encouragement and support; our families, which together included two husbands (Randy and Michael), one child (Christopher), two cats (Murray and Simba), one dog (Rebel), and one horse (Rosie) for their infinite patience while we sat glued for hours to the computer; Michael Siino for his ability to upgrade a computer at a moment's notice; and Doug Kraus for his expertise at Macintosh troubleshooting. We couldn't have done it without you all.

Audrey Pavia and Betsy Sikora Siino

CONTENTS IN BRIEF

Part I: Dog Basics

Chapter 1: The Breeds 1
Chapter 2: Health Care 43
Chapter 3: Training 63
Chapter 4: Behavior 81
Chapter 5: Nutrition 89

Part II: Getting A Dog

Chapter 6: Purebred Dog Breeders 105
Chapter 7: Protection, Rescue, and Adoption ..131

Part III Active Dogs

Chapter 8: Dog Clubs and Associations 159
Chapter 9: Dog Shows 181
Chapter 10: Canine Sports and Competition 193
Chapter 11: Working Dogs 217

Part IV: For Dog Owners

Chapter 12: Services 251
Chapter 13: Publications 271
Chapter 14: Products 283

Part V: Puppouri

Chapter 15: Individual Dogs 313
Chapter 16: Dogs in Culture 327
Chapter 17: Wild Dogs 341
Chapter 18: Miscellaneous Dog-Related Sites ...367
Chapter 19: All About Dogs 383

CONTENTS

Part I: Dog Basics

Chapter 1: The Breeds 1

The Official Jack Russell Terrier Site 2
Information Exchange 4
Akbash Dog Home Page 5
Akita Inus 6
Alaskan Malamute 6
American Bulldog Outpost 7
The American Eskimo Dog Home Page 8
Australian Cattle Dog Web 8
Australian Kelpies 9
Beagles on the Web 10
Belgian Shepherd Dogs 11
SitStay Presents Belgian Shepherd Dogs 11
Bernese Mountain Dog Home Page 12
All About Border Collies 13
Border Terriers 13
The Boxer Home Page 14
Bull Terrier WWW Home Page 15
Cairn Terrier Home Page 15
The Chihuahua Home Page 16
Donna Patz' Cocker Spaniel Home Page 17
The Collie Connection 17
The Dachshund Zone 18
The Dal-l Homepage (Dalmatian) 19
The Realm of the Doberman
    (Doberman Pinscher) 20
English Setters on the World Wide Web 21
English Springer Spaniels—Field Bred 21
The German Shepherd Dog Web Site 22
Golden Retrievers in Cyberspace 23

Ragtym's Golden Retriever Information Page 24
The Great Dane Home Page 25
Great Pyrenees 25
The Labrador Retriever Home Pages 26
Leonberger World 27
Maltese Only 28
Newf-L Homepage (Newfoundland) 29
The Pomerama: Informational Pomeranian Web Site 30
The Wonderful World of Poodles 31
The Pug Dog Home Page 32
Rottweiler Home Page 32
Saint Bernard Dog 33
Samoyed Dogs 34
Schnauzer Ware 35
The SHAR-PEIges (Shar-Pei) 36
The Sheltie Page (Shetland Sheepdog) 36
The American Shih-Tzu Club Home Page 37
Tibetan Mastiff Home Page 38
Tibetan Spaniel Home Page 39
The Welsh Terrier Web Page 40
Westies Home Page 40
Yorkshire Terriers 41

Chapter 2: Health Care 43
AVMA Online 44
Virtual Veterinary Center 46
AltVetMed Homepage 47
Canine Eye Registration Foundation 47
Orthopedic Foundation for Animals, Inc. 48
Canine Hip Dysplasia 49
Control of Genetic Disease 49
PennHip Method of Diagnosing Hip Dysplasia ...49
FDA Center for Veterinary Medicine 50
Institute for Genetic Disease Control in Animals .51
Pet Health News 52
Veterinary Ophthalmology Info Centre 53
VetGen 53
Veterinary Information Network 54

National Animal Control Poison Center 55

NetVet Veterinary Resources 55

Pets Need Dental Care Too 56

Rec.Pets.Dogs Health Care Issues 57

Deaf Dogs Web Page 57

Deafness in Dogs and Cats 58

DLM's Canine Page 59

Canine Vaccination Schedule 60

Eliminating Genetic Disease in Dogs:
  A Buyer's Perspective 60

The Virtual Veterinary Center 61

Chapter 3: Training 63

Raising Your Dog with the Monks of New Skete 64

The Dog Obedience & Training Page 66

Hawaiiana Canine School 66

Dr. P's Dog Training Library 67

Waltham Pet Foods World of Pet Care 68

West Virginia Canine College 69

Canines of America's World of Dog Training 70

Don't Shoot the Dog! 71

All About Dogs: Obedience Training 72

American Dog Trainers Network 73

Brunton Canine Training Services 74

The Greyhound Project 75

Flying Dog Press 76

Dog Owner's Guide 77

Dog Training Weekly 78

Chapter 4: Behavior 81

Campbell's Pet Behavior Resources 82

The Association of Pet Behaviour Counsellors
  (England) 84

Dog-Play: Behavior, Socialization, and Training ..85

Doggie Door to Canine Behavior 85

Dog Bite Prevention 86

Chapter 5: Nutrition 89

The Iams Company Home Page 90

Purina Pet Care Center 92
Ralston Purina Company 93
Pet Corner: Feeding and Basic Nutrition 93
Dogs UK — Nutrition Listing 94
Waltham World of Pet Care 94
Doggie Drive-Thru 95
The Dog's Kitchen 96
The Pomerama's Dog Biscuit, Treat, and
    Food Recipes 96
Veterinary Nutritional Formula 97
Pet Products Plus 97
Heinz Pets Unleashed 98
Dog Owner's Guide: Food and Nutrition 98
Barley Dog and Barley Cat: The "Original"
    Barley Grass Nutritional Supplements 99
Solid Gold Health Products for Pets 100
Our Pets Inc. Home Page 100

Part II: Getting A Dog

Chapter 6: Purebred Dog Breeders 105

Domino Chow Chows 106
Responsible Breeders 108
Puppy Buyer's Checklist 109
BreederLink Home Page 110
Dog Breeders Online Directory 111
A-1 Dog Breeders Showcase 112
Tamaron Collies 113
Timberline Retrievers (Golden Retrievers) 113
Draper Kennel (Golden Retrievers) 114
Superstar Irish Wolfhounds 115
Bear Paw Kennels (Karelien Bear Dogs) 116
Walkoway Beardies (Bearded Collies) 117
Carla's Toy Dog Home Page 117
Kinlayke Kennels (Lakeland Terriers and
    Chesapeake Bay Retrievers) 118
Welcome to the Merikaez Home Page (Italian
    Greyhounds, Lhasa Apsos) 119
Hot Pursuit Jack Russell Terriers 120

Covy-Tucker Hill Kennels
(German Shepherd Dogs) 121
Nadelhaus German Shepherds 122
Nuez Kennels (Xoloitzcuintli) 123
Szeder Pulik 123
Ravenwood Dalmatians 124
O'Serenity Shetland Sheepdogs 125
Katwala Australian Cattle Dogs 126
Stone Fort Rottweilers 127
Thai Ridgebacks in America 128

Chapter 7: Protection, Rescue, and Adoption ..131

The Humane Society of the United States 132
Alaskan Malamute Protection League 134
Best Friends Animal Sanctuary 135
Canine Connections Breed Rescue Information .136
Animal Protection Institute 137
Dallas/Ft. Worth Sheltie Rescue Inc. 138
The Fund for Animals 138
Samoyed Rescue 139
Pro Dog Breed Rescue Network 140
All Pets Yellow Pages: Rehabilitation and
Humane Shelters 141
Animal Welfare Information Center 141
Bide-A-Wee 142
All For Animals 143
The American Society for the Prevention of
Cruelty to Animals 143
Austin Humane Society and SPCA 144
Greyhound Rescue & Adoption Inc. 145
Little Shelter Animal Rescue 146
San Francisco Society for the Prevention of
Cruelty to Animals 146
The American Humane Association 147
New Yorkers for Companion Animals 148
Siberian Husky Rescue 149
Massachusetts Society for the Prevention of
Cruelty to Animals 149
Golden Gate Labrador Rescue and
Placement Service 150

Doris Day Animal League 151
Companion Animal Rescue and Education Service 152
People for the Ethical Treatment of Animals 153
Golden Retriever Rescue Groups 153
Animal Rescue and Adoptable Pets 154
The Marin Humane Society 155
Boxer Rebound, Inc. 156

Part III: Active Dogs

Chapter 8: Dog Clubs and Associations 159

American Kennel Club 160
The Kennel Club 162
American Canine Association 163
Continental Kennel Club 164
Pennsylvania Federation of Dog Clubs 165
Jack Russell Terrier Club of America 166
The American Rescue Dog Association 167
Frontier Belgian Shepherd Dog Association 168
ARF! 168
The Ottawa Kennel Club 169
Dog Writers' Association of America 170
The Guide Dog Association 171
California Rescue Dog Association 171
National Association of Dog Obedience
   Instructors 172
Delta Society 173
World Protection Dog Association 174
North American Versatile Hunting Dog Page 175
United Schutzhund Clubs of America/German
   Shepherd Working Dog Club 176
United States Rottweiler Club 177
Old Dominion Kennel Club 177
American Rare Breeds Association 178

Chapter 9: Dog Shows 181

The Virtual Dog Show 182
Crufts Dog Show 184
Info Dog 185

Onofrio Dog Shows 187
Actual Dog Show Working Dogs 217
Higham Press Show Printers 189
Show Dogs West 190
Newport Dog Shows 190

Chapter 10: Canine Sports and Competition 193
The Dog Agility Page 194
Dog Agility 196
Finnish Agility Pages 196
Flyball Home Page 197
Flyball 197
The United States Canine Combined Training
    Association 198
The Tracking Page 199
Schutzhund.Com 199
DVG America 200
Dog-Play 200
Carting With Your Dog 200
International Weight Pull Association 201
The Obedience Home Page 201
Lure Coursing 202
Mushing Internet 203
Mush With Pride 204
Iditarod Trail Sled Dog Race 204
Skijoring 205
Mary Jo's Frisbee Dog Page 205
Dallas Dog & Disc Club 206
National Capital Air Canines 206
Canine Cycle Freestyle 207
American Working Dogs Association 207
Stockdogs 208
The American Herding Breed Association 208
Belgian Games 209
French Ringsport 209
Workingdogs.Com 210
Earthdog/Squirrel Dog Hunting Homepage 210
Wellington Hurricanines Flygility 211

Back Packing With Your Dog 212
How To In-Line Skate With Your Dog 212
Bird Dog News 213
PAWS Working Dog Evaluation 213
Organization for the Working Samoyed 213
American Working Collie Association 214
Airedale Terrier Club of America Hunting and
    Working Committee 215

Chapter 11: Working Dogs **217**
National Disaster Search Dog Foundation 218
Black Paws Search, Rescue & Avalanche Dogs
    International 220
The California Rescue Dog Association, Inc. 221
Avalanche Rescue Dog's World 221
Avalanche Dogs! 222
Alaska Search and Rescue Dogs 223
National Association for Search and Rescue 224
RiverBend Search and Rescue Dog Association
    Home Page 224
RCMP Civilian Search and Rescue Service
    Dog Program 225
West Virginia K-9 Search and Rescue 226
Puppyraiser Email List Web Site 226
Service Dogs 227
Wolf Packs Service Dog Directory 227
The Seeing Eye 228
The National Education for Assistance Dog
    Services, Inc. 228
Independence Dogs, Inc. 229
Guiding Eyes for the Blind 229
Canine Working Companions, Inc. 230
Delta Society National Service Dog Center 231
Hearing Dogs for the Deaf 231
Paws with a Cause 232
Tails of Joy Therapy Dog Program 232
Delta Society Pet Therapy Pages 233
Lyn Richards' Therapy Dog Page 233
Furry Friends Pet Assisted Therapy Services 234

Livestock Guardian Dogs 234
On Guard!!!: Livestock Guarding Dog Magazine ...235
USDA-APHIS on Livestock Guarding Dogs 235
Livestock Guarding Dogs of the United
    Kingdom Homepage 236
Vietnam Dog Handlers Association 236
Scout Dogs and Their Handlers 237
North American Police Work Dog Association .238
RCMP Police Dog Services 238
The Police K-9 Home Page 239
The Police Dog Homepage 240
British Columbia Municipal Police Dog
    Training Standards 240
K9 Sweden 241
Australian Police & Service Dogs 241
Virginia Police Work Dog Association 242
National Police Bloodhound Association 242
Austrian K9-Handler Section 243
Texas K9 Police Association for Certification
    & Standards 243
Responsible Protection Dog Ownership 244
Bo's Nose Knows 244
USDA Beagle Brigade 245
WORKINGDOGS.COM: International
    Cyberzine for Working Dogs 245
Working Dogs 246
PAWS Working Dog Evaluation 246
American Working Dog Association 247
Dog-Play 247

Part IV: For Dog Owners

Chapter 12: Services 251
Camp Gone to the Dogs 252
American Boarding Kennel Association 254
Home Away From Home 255
Waldenway Canine Camp 255
Cactus Pryor's Canine Hilton (A Kennel) 256
Animal Resorts 256

Positive Power Kennels 257
RSPCA Australia—Operation of Boarding
    Establishments for Cats and Dogs 257
National Association of Professional Pet Sitters ...258
The Circle of Cybersitters 259
Pet Sitters International 259
American Dog Trainers Network—Dogwalkers
    & Petsitters 260
Pet Nannies 260
Pet Sitters Yellow Pages 261
Everything You Always Wanted to Know About
    Grooming... But Were Afraid to Ask 261
ABDog Grooming School 262
The Grooming Page from The Wonderful
    World of Poodles 263
Perfect Touch Grooming 263
Autumn Winds Dog Agility and Training Center ...264
Camp Dances With Dogs 264
Animal Camp: An Awesome Experience for Kids 265
Top Dog Training School 265
International Association of Pet Cemeteries 266
Bubbling Well Pet Memorial Park 267
The Hartsdale Pet Cemetery and Crematory 267
National Pet Registry, Inc. 268
Lorna Barkey, The Pet Coach 269
Dog Show Photography (Tom Di Giacomo) 269

Chapter 13: Publications 271

Dog Fancy Magazine 272
Canine Review 274
Dogs in Canada 274
Hoflin Publishing Dogs Online 275
Dog Lover's Bookshop 276
Our Dogs 277
Pet View Online Magazine 278
Howell Book House 279
Dog World Magazine 279
Dog Owner's Guide 280
Amazon.Com 281

Good Dog! 281
Mushing Online 282
Chapter 14: Products 283
DOGZ! 284
Telemark Productions Home Page 286
Dog Saver 286
AHEAD Graphics 287
Wizard of Dogs 287
Corsini Original Dog Figurines and Art Gallery
    of Limited Edition Prints 288
Doggie Diamonds 288
Dog Lover's Gallery 288
Animal Krackers 289
Dog Figurines Online Catalog 289
Attic Treasures Dog Collectibles Page 289
Raining Cats & Dogs 290
Pegasus Originals 290
Dannyquest 291
Golden Wonders Home Page 291
P.M.L. Prints Home Page 292
The Little Dog Laughed Home Page 292
Welcome to the World of Kong! 293
Diamond Dogs 293
Planet Pet Naples Florida 293
Captured by B. Walker—Litter I.D. Collars 294
Changing Horizons Premier Dog Collar 294
Wolf Packs Limited Slip Dog Collars 295
Fox & Hounds Collar and Leashes 295
Canine Collars & Leashes at the Acmepet
    Marketplace 295
Ruff Wear Home Page 296
BowWow Fits 296
Personalized Retriever Clothing 296
Petoria's Secret: Fashion Apparel For Dog Lovers ..297
Tucker & Company Dog Biscuits 297
Canine Country Kitchen 297
Whiskers Holistic Products for Pets 298
Program 298

PetSage 298
Home of Dog Stuff 299
Gone to the Dogs Home Page 299
SBM Products 300
Critters Choice Dot Com 300
Fuzzy Faces 301
Bernard Basics 301
Petmarket.com 301
All Creatures Pet Supplies 302
K9 World 302
Brown Kennel Supply, Inc. 303
L.L. Bowsers 303
DOGalogue 304
Canine Cryobank 304
Paul's Obedience Shop 305
Chihuahua Kingdom 305
Artistic Lasering's Tibetan Mastiff Catalog 305
Dachshund's Delights Badger Burrow
     Home Page 306
Dalmatian Delights 306
The Dal House 307
Ortho-Bean Pet Beds Home Page 307
A Dog's Best Friend 307
Canvasback Pet Supplies 308
Pet Supply Catalogs 308
Pooch Pouch 309
Jones Trailer Company 309
No Ants My Doggy 309

Part V: Puppouri

Chapter 15: Individual Dogs 313
Beau's Home Page 314
Yahoo! Individual Dogs 316
Foxbriar's Home Page 316
Caesar's Home Page 317
The Beau Page 317
Pictures of Our Dogs 318
You Talking to Me? 318

Jeff and Teresa's Home Page 319
Auggie's World 319
Sara's Story 320
Maui, Sabu & Trace's Homepage:
    The Three Dachshund Darlings 320
Ella the Dog 321
The Alaskan Husky Homepage 321
Dino the Basset Hound 322
Dog Agility: Fun for Man & Beast 322
Maggie's Homepage 323
The Amazing Jessie Home Page 323
Emma's Place 324
Murphy's World 324
Holly's Six Border Collies 325
Pepper's Page 325
Ludvick's Homepage 326
Labs in the Neighborhood 326

Chapter 16: Dogs in Culture **327**
Nipperscape 328
Index of Famous Dogs 330
The Fame and Glory Hounds 330
Jim's Puppy Quotes 330
James Herriot Home Page 331
William Wegman on the World Wide Web 331
Snoopy's Doghouse 332
Katharine Farmer: Dogumentary 333
Official Blue Dog Site 333
The National Bird Dog Museum 334
Rin Tin Tin 334
2 Stupid Dogs 335
Wiener Dog Art 335
101 Dalmatians Home Page 336
Wishbone 337
Wile E. Coyote Page 337
Q&A with Eddie the Dog 338
Snow Dog Festival (Inukko Matsuri) 338
Big Dog Sportswear 339
Domestic Dogs on Stamps 339

Chapter 17: Wild Dogs 341

Defenders of Wildlife 342
International Wolf Center 344
The Wolf Homepage 345
National Wildlife Federation 345
Kiopa's Side of the Jungle 346
African Wild Dog Conservation Fund 347
Adam's Fox Box 348
Wildlife Waystation 348
Wolf Haven International 349
The Ethiopian Wolf Home Page 350
The Virtual Zoo 351
Wolf Education & Research Center 351
The Wolf's Den 352
CoyoteHowl 353
WCSRC—The Wolf Sanctuary 353
Timber Wolf Information Network 354
Wolves of India 355
Sinapu—Returning the Wolf to Colorado 356
Urban Fox Ecology 356
U.S. Fish & Wildlife Service World Wide
    Web Site 357
Desert Moon's Wolf Page 358
Cochrane Ecological Institute (Swift Fox) 359
World Wildlife Fund 359
WWF Global Network 360
The Searching Wolf 361
Dingo Farm 362
The Predator Project 362
Swift Fox: Vulpes Velox 363
Vulpinification 364
Nebraska Wildlife—Coyotes 364
Ralph Maughan's Wolf Report 365

Chapter 18: Miscellaneous Dog-Related Sites ..367

Choosing a Dog Breed 367
Loss & Rainbow Bridge 368
Bad Dog Chronicles 370
Bad Dog Humour Collection 370

Traveldog 371
Dean's Dog House 371
Signs You Have a Dumb Dog 372
NewPet.Com 372
The Dog Run/Dog Park Reporter 373
You Know You've Gone to the Dogs When... ...374
Stupid Pet Photos 374
The Dog Poo Page 375
The Dog Hause 375
Kiva's Dog House 376
Pets in the White House 377
Allergic to Dogs? 377
Cassie's 3-Legged Dog Club 378
Canine Image Archives 378
Pet Name Pages 379
Tale Waggers 379
A Dog's Prayer 379
Hotel Search 380
Why Dogs are Better Than Men 380
Dogs Down Under 381

Chapter 19: All About Dogs 383
Acme Pet 384
WWW.Woofs 386
Kahoos K-9 Line 386
All Pets Com 387
Pet Station/Dog Domain 389
The Pet Channel 389
Rec.Pets.Dogs FAQ Home Page 390
Cyberpet 390
Canadian Animal Network 391
Adognet 392
Healthypet 392
PetNet 393
DogNet 394
Just Pets 394
Professional Dog Networks 395
Purina Pet Care Center 396
Talking Dogs 397
The Dogpatch Doghouse 398

World Wide Woof 399

Pet Path 399

K9NetUK 400

K9 Web 401

The Pet Project 401

Dog-e-Zine! 402

Dogs Northwest 402

Canine Home Page 403

Kirby's Korner 403

Bestdogs.com 404

NetPets 405

Pet Vet 406

INTRODUCTION

Since the dawn of history, the dog has been our best friend, which is evident from the ancient images carved and painted onto the walls of the caves we once called home. Images of our canine partners have followed us through the ages, from cave walls to canvas to books to film and television. And now, we have discovered a new arena in which to pay tribute to the dog: the Internet, which for the purposes of this book means the same thing as the World Wide Web.

In a phenomenally short period of time, the Internet has mushroomed into a great web of information, and within that—tails wagging and tongues lolling—are dogs. Thousands of dogs. We had the opportunity to meet and learn about many of these dogs as we began our journey into the Web to see what kind of sites are dedicated to this beloved animal. And what a journey it was. While we somewhat expected to find great devotion reflected in the sites that comprise the canine Internet, we never imagined we would discover such artistry, such energy, such unabashed affection, and even such genius, within those sites and pages.

We reviewed thousands of these sites in search of the 500 or so that we would christen the best of the bunch—and because the Internet is such a living, growing entity, even more sites have no doubt joined the party since this book went to press. No matter. View the book as your launching pad, as your starting point. We could not possibly include all of the Net's canine sites, nor could we even include all those deserving recognition. Yet from the sites you will find here, the entire canine Internet will open up to you.

Within the pages of this book, that world is broken down into 19 chapters devoted to all aspects of the dog world, from breeders to products to cultural icons to publications to rescue groups to therapy and service dog groups to wolves and their wild cousins to canine services to health and nutrition to large general sites that cover all canine topics. The sites chosen didn't necessarily make the cut because they were the most colorful, the flashiest or even the most user-friendly. Such elements help, of course, but we made our choices based on substance. Sometimes it is the plainest site, the one devoid of glitzy graphics and multimedia gimmicks, that turns out to be the gem, filled with sound advice, heart, humor, and an unmatched wealth of valuable information.

On its face, the huge and ever-growing World Wide Web can seem daunting to the newcomer. Yet from that great Web comes a close-knit community of dogs and their people, all linked together in a network, the members of which welcome all comers, both human and canine. It strives to fill computers, and the minds that use them, with information on the canine species. The good news is that you don't need to be an Internet expert to make the journey into the canine Web. We were simply dog lovers and journalists specializing in animal-related topics—anything but experienced Internet surfers—when we embarked on this project. If we can do it, anyone can.

While you need not be a veteran Internet surfer to put the information in this book to work for you, you will, of course, need a computer with ample memory. You must also sign up with one of the many services that allow you to access the Internet—either full-service commercial networks such as America Online and CompuServe or one of the many specialized Internet Service Providers that provide access via Web browser software (the two most popular software browsers being Netscape Navigator and Microsoft Internet Explorer). Once you have entered the Internet, the world is literally at your fingertips. With the click of a button, you have access to more information within your own home than was ever imagined ten, or even five, years ago.

The challenge here is navigating through that overwhelming morass of information. One method for locating dog-related Web sites is to employ search engines, such as Yahoo! or Excite. Type several keywords into the designated box, and the engine will probably come up with more information than you want, need or have time to sort through. A better method is to use this book. It provides the quickest access to canine sites, because the searching, the organizing, and even the reviewing have already been done for you.

You may access the book's listed sites in two ways. The more traditional method involves simply typing the site's address into your Internet service's designated address box. Of course, typing in those long, unwieldy, sometimes nonsensical Web site addresses can be tedious and frustrating, but there is an easier way. Our publisher, MIS:Press, has installed every site in the book as a live link within the MIS:Press Web site at www.mispress.com/dogs. Click on the site name of your choice, and you're there. Thanks to this added and probably unexpected bonus, you may tour the 500-plus sites covered in *Dogs on the Web* with ease.

As you will see in using this book, we have laid out each chapter as a guide, offering first an overview of the chapter—with background information on its particular subject—followed by a review of a featured site that we consider a stand-out. This is followed by shorter reviews of other related sites, each listed first by name, and then by address, or URL (Uniform Resource Locator). The reviews highlight the strengths and weaknesses of each site (mostly strengths; these sites were, after all, chosen for their excellence), and describe the elements that make them special.

You will find some Web sites listed in more than one chapter. A large, multifaceted site devoted to working dogs, for instance, may be of value to people seeking brass-tacks information on the training of livestock guarding dogs as well as information on herding trials. You would thus find the site included in the Working and Sports chapter and in the Competition chapter, with the respective reviews highlighting the pertinent sections.

In some cases, our reviews also explain how to get around within the site to make gathering information easier and more efficient. To the inexperienced, Internet navigation can be confusing at first. But after some practice, fledgling browsers learn that most sites begin with a main home page, from which browsers may choose from listed menu options, presented with illustrated icons and/or brightly colored text called hypertext. Move the cursor to your option choice, click on the mouse, and leap into the internal layers of the page for more in-depth information.

Keep in mind, however, that even the 500-plus sites you find here and the many layers of information they provide are only the beginning. The canine Web is unique because in many cases the most effective method of searching for more in-depth information can be done within the various sites themselves: the vast majority offer extensive lists of hypertext links, or hyperlinks, to other canine Web pages. Move the cursor to the chosen hyperlink, and with a click, the computer will transport you instantly to that site. From there you may find easy access to yet more pages that interest you, and so on and so on and so on. Before you know it, it is 3:30 in the morning, you are addicted to this game, and you have become a veritable expert on everything canine—and have probably met some new friends along the way.

As you pursue this quest, you may be in for a surprise, especially if this is your first intensive foray into the Internet. While the Internet is often seen as cold and impersonal, you will find just the opposite within those sites devoted to dogs.

The canine Net offers dog lovers the opportunity to meet others who share their passions from all over the world: breeders, police officers who work with K-9 units, the human partners of search-and-rescue dogs, pet product manufacturers, writers, veterinarians, groomers, kennel operators, artists, trainers, behaviorists, animal advocates, physically disabled individuals who work with service dogs, animal control officers, or just devoted pet owners. Even the simplest sites are invariably presented with a friendly, welcoming tone, all inspired by a love for the canine species. The Internet offers newcomers an easy way to become a part of a unique cyberspace community, but also invites browsers to join the canine community beyond the computer, as well. Many people who so enthusiastically devote their computer time to dogs also spend a great deal of time participating in noncomputer activities with their pets, a fact that will become evident from the first few sites you explore on the canine Internet.

We hope that you enjoy reading and using this book as much as we have enjoyed researching and writing it. We have attempted to make it not only a useful guide to the canine Internet, but an informative canine resource in its own right. In addition to reviews of the sites, we have provided background information to help you view the Web sites and pages within the broader context of the dog world at large. The Internet offers a whole new glimpse into that world, a whole new canvas on which to honor the images of these wonderful animals and to proclaim our respect and affection for them. While the Internet can be a dog's best friend in that it helps disseminate information worldwide that can improve our care and understanding of the canine species, so may it also become the dog lover's friend—second to the dogs, of course. So enjoy the journey. And most of all, enjoy the dogs.

Audrey Pavia and Betsy Sikora Siino
Orange County, California
May 1997

EASY ACCESS

Live links to all the Web sites mentioned in this book can be accessed at the following page from the MIS:Press Web site:

http://www.mispress.com/dogs

Add this address to the 'favorite addresses/bookmarks' section of your Web browser, then use these links to jump to any sites that sound enticing.

At our site, the author and publisher invite readers to make suggestions about future editions of *Dogs on the Web*. The Internet is ever-changing and expanding, and your suggestions will help us make later editions even more comprehensive.

PART I

Dog Basics

The Breeds

Once upon a time a single type of dog roamed the earth—or at least we think that was the case. We presume the first dog probably resembled the feral dogs now found in every corner of the globe.

A population of dogs—all different sizes, shapes and types—that breeds freely will ultimately produce what has been named "the natural dog." This is a dog of medium size with pricked ears, a slenderish muzzle, short brown hair, and a slightly curling tail. We assume that this animal probably resembles those early dogs which bred not according to a blueprint for the design of dogs for specific jobs and appearances, but according to the laws of survival of the fittest and natural selection.

Times have changed dramatically, however, since that first dog's era many thousands of years ago. From that original animal has sprung not only humankind's best friends, but a family tree of breeds, all of which share an identical physiological makeup that makes them members of the same species. But members within the same species vary so significantly in appearance, temperament and talent, that within that same family you can find a tiny 4-pound Pomeranian genetically equal to a 200-pound Mastiff. Chalk this diversity up to human tampering. As history progressed and humans recognized that dogs could enhance their lives significantly, they began to breed these animals for specific characteristics: pricked ears, floppy ears, speed, strength, companionability, a soft mouth for retrieving, an intimidating eye for herding—the list goes on. The results are the many breeds that share our lives today.

continued after the feature section

1

The Official Jack Russell Terrier Site

http://207.69.134.171/index.shtml

Get to know the Jack Russell Terrier (JRT), a feisty little dog that makes a habit of outwitting and exasperating its owners on a daily basis, and you will fully appreciate the tone and content of the Official Jack Russell Terrier Site.

The primary problem that faces this breed is that too many people, thanks to this small pooch's image featured so prominently in movies and television these days, believe that they do know the JRT and hanker to bring one of these canine tornadoes into their homes. This Web site aims to prevent such misguided impulses and the inevitable tragedies and misunderstandings they cause.

While this site is not particularly fancy in design, it is well-organized and easy to navigate. More importantly, it is rich with information so vital to the well-being of this small dog that was named for its British founder, John Russell, who in the 1800s succeeded in developing a premier terrier for fox hunting. Today the progeny of those dogs continue to embody the acute instincts, the tireless energy, and the intelligence that so delighted 19th-century hunters—and that can so overwhelm unprepared 20th-century pet owners.

This site, under the guidance of Webmaster Rick Hemsing, seeks to educate those who would assume a dog of this small size and attractive appearance is ideally suited to any pet situation, any home, or any owner. Wrong. Just click onto the many hyperlinks and section icons on the home page and beyond, and see that myth dispelled with a quick click of a button. Click on Breed on the home page's top menu bar, for instance, and then choose "Miscellaneous FAQs" at the next layer, and you will see painted in the informative JackFAQs section, the portrait of a dog that cannot live happily ever after as an apartment dog, that will be inclined to stalk and kill small pet animals with whom it is expected to coexist in the household, is prone to dog aggression, and simply must be offered an active, athletic lifestyle. This section, along with "The Bad

The Official Jack Russell Terrier Site

▶Home ▶Breed ▶JRTCA ▶Trials ▶How To ▶For Fun

Questions about us?

Jack Russell

Breed: Find out about the <u>Jack Russell Terrier</u>, it's History, the Breed Standard according to the JRTCA, <u>medical</u> information and more.

What's New?

Guided Tour
"Bad Dog" Talk
Guestbook
JackTalk! Q&A
Find a Breeder
JR Friends
Members Only
JR Stories
Training Tips
Lost Terriers
Search
Contact JRTCA
Survey

JRTCA Office
410) 561-3655

JRTCA

JRTCA: The **Jack Russell Terrier Club of America** is a non-profit organization dedicated to preserving the working ability, great intelligence, and sound physical structure of the Jack Russell.

Trials

Trials: Everything you wanted to know about Terrier Trials including the 1997 <u>Trial Schedule</u>, explanation of <u>Trial Events</u>, and a handy trial Survival Guide.

How To ...

How To: Information on <u>Adopting</u> a Jack Russell, <u>Joining</u> the JRTCA, buying and training a puppy, or <u>Registering</u> your terrier.

True Grit
JR Fun

Fun: Visit with <u>JR Friends</u>, read the <u>Stories</u>, ask questions in the new <u>JackTalk!</u>, or sign the <u>Guestbook</u>.

Dog Talk," which is accessible from the home page and offers an honestly presented worst-case scenario of JRT ownership, should be required reading for anyone even considering taking a JRT for a pet.

Also prevalent in this site is the concern among veteran enthusiasts over efforts to standardize the breed's broad standard, which currently focuses on working instincts and health rather than on appearance. Although standardization is an understandably emotional, not to mention political, issue among the ranks of the very passionate JRT enthusiasts, the information is presented here articulately and professionally—and is quite convincing to boot. The same may be said for the coverage of each challenge facing this breed, including that presented in the Russell Rescue section. Given that so many JRTs are given up, this site succeeds handsomely in informing this breed's very admiring public that JRTs "are not a dog for everyone."

Browsing through a large volume of dog breeds you will find a detailed history of the world, as dogs evolved in all corners of the planet, living intimately with people from all walks of life. They have been bred for every job imaginable, from hunting ducks to herding sheep to pulling sleds to finding lost travelers to looking beautiful in a wealthy aristocrat's lap. Regardless of calling, it is the dog's adaptable, flexible nature, coupled with its unexplained desire to spend its life with people, that have allowed it to evolve into so many different incarnations, each sharing the same fundamental qualities that make a dog a dog.

The following are Web sites devoted to individual breeds that, taken together, celebrate the dog's vast diversity. These sites, arranged alphabetically by breed, offer purebred dog lovers the opportunity to pay tribute to their chosen breeds, and to share what they have learned with each other and with interested visitors. With so many hundreds of breeds, such sites are many. We could not possibly include them all or recognize every breed. To make room for as many as possible, the reviews are brief. Consider them a stepping stone toward exploring the wonderful world of dog breeds.

Afghan Hound Database and Breed Information Exchange

http://ourworld.compuserve.com/homepages/
s_tillotson/menu.htm

There is nothing fancy about this impeccably organized site dedicated to a breathtaking sighthound with long flowing tresses and an overall appearance that screams aristocrat (it is indeed hard to imagine that a dog of such beauty was bred originally as a hunting hound). This site is rich with information. Hailing from the United Kingdom under the guidance of Steve Tillotson, this home page will literally take the browser through every aspect of the Afghan, from its history to rescue to Afghan care to in-depth coverage of showing and hound activities, all compiled with information gathered from enthusiasts all over the world.

The goal here is to present a truly global portrait of this beautiful hound from all different viewpoints, and it succeeds handsomely at its mission. Such variety in the presentation of ideas and opinions is refreshing. Also unique is the Monthly Debate, in which enthusiasts are encouraged to share their views on various issues prevalent in the Afghan world. All in all, this is an intelligent, thoughtful site that other Web-creating breed enthusiasts would be wise to emulate.

Akbash Dog Home Page
http://www.upei.ca/akbash.html

Frankly, few are familiar with the Akbash Dog, a large, white livestock guarding dog of probable Turkish origin that is as beautiful as it is devoted to its job. While this guardian angel is now called on more for the protection of home and family than herds of sheep alone on a mountainside, it remains virtually unchanged by recent decades that have so drastically altered its professional calling. This means it remains beautiful in appearance, and intelligent and headstrong in character, the latter traits critical for a working dog of this high caliber. Despite being in the livestock-guarding business and despite this breed's relative obscurity, the Akbash Dog is represented proudly by a contemporary Web site. Celebrating its wonderful gifts, this site strives to educate those interested in this dog, would-be owners and casual browsers alike, about the animal's true nature and character, and the challenges one must conquer to live with it peacefully and productively.

Enter this site and you are greeted first by a lovely portrait of an Akbash, perhaps the first representative of this breed many browsers will have ever seen. This affectionate, no-frills site proceeds to present a variety of home-page hyperlinks, including History of Akbash Dogs, Akbash Dogs International and Rescue Program, and links to information that enables prospective owners to evaluate whether the Akbash Dog is suited to their particular needs (for the Akbash, as this site emphasizes, is a dog suited to only certain types of owners). Rounding out the ample information provided here are lots of photos, as this site boasts not only the breed's brawn and brains, but its great beauty, too. So come on in and meet one of the dog world's best-kept secrets.

Akita Inus

http://www.zmall.com/pet_talk/dog-faqs/breeds/akitas.html

The product of several authors who are introduced at the beginning of this site, this is a page of information that is essentially a long article dedicated to the Akita. This increasingly popular dog was bred originally in Japan as a hunter and a fighter, and reached international prominence of late for its role in a certain Crime of the Century. Given the breed's history and its role in the shaping of this dog's character, any would-be owner should take the time to read and absorb the information within this site before inviting one of these potentially challenging animals into his or her household.

Opening with a detailed Table of Contents, the page proceeds to guide browsers through such topics as History, Training, and Health/Special Medical Problems, all presented in an abbreviated, reader-friendly format that invites the browser to take a look. The page concludes with a list of Frequently Asked Questions that delve into greater detail regarding the issues discussed in the previous sections. Taken as a whole, this page presents a valuable overview of this breed that certainly should not be seen as the perfect dog for every family or every living situation.

Alaskan Malamute

http://www.umdc.umu.se/~mmn/mal/malamute.html

Under the guidance of Maria Magnusson, this is an excellent site devoted to all things Malamute. A large and friendly, though headstrong, Arctic sled dog of ancient origin, valued more for its strength than its speed, this dog has long inspired the human imagination, a phenomenon that is reflected in the size and breadth of the material presented in this very informational and exhaustively researched Web site.

The available topics accessible from the site's home page include general breed information, rescue, the Alaskan Malamute Club of America, activities, and information on subscribing to the Malamute-L Listserver, all presented first in an Index bar along the top of the home page and vertically in a more detailed outline form down the page itself. Rarely will you find so much information from enthusiasts all over the world about Malamutes, and it's all here at your fingertips, all collected under one roof.

American Bulldog Outpost

http://www.primenet.com/~hinx/

Enter the American Bulldog Outpost site and you will be greeted by the graphic of an American Bulldog that leaps and chases a ball from one side of your screen to another. This fun, animated scene sets the tone of this site that is rich with dramatic graphics, color, and movement, but not so rich that it distracts the browser from the subject at hand: a breed with a rather violent past that this site suggests may make it inappropriate for novice dog owners.

The American Bulldog Outpost, managed by Christina Hinkel, offers an honest insight into the breed, easily accessible through its well-designed home page. Equally impressive is its attention to potential health problems, manifested in two newly added features promoted prominently on the home page: OFA Data Base for American Bulldogs, and Survey on Hip Dysplasia and Entropion in American Bulldogs. Only by communicating such issues can they be combated successfully. It would be refreshing if every breed site would make this type of information so accessible to their breeds' followers.

The American Eskimo Dog Home Page

http://ezinfo.ucs.indiana.edu/~hpassaue/eskie.html

A charming white dog nicknamed "The Dog Beautiful" certainly deserves its own home page, and now it has one. The American Eskimo Dog Home Page presents this intelligent creature to a world of admirers, many of whom find themselves enchanted after a single encounter with this beautiful, energetic companion that can take control of the household of an unprepared or less-than-committed owner.

Quite complete in content, this site provides browsers with access to Eskie books, breeders, rescue organizations, *The Eskie* magazine, the *Eskie Adventures* catalog, an Eskie FAQ (which, for the benefit of this breed, could include a bit more information on the potentially feisty nature of this incorruptible "alarm" dog), and the Eskie Owners Mailing List. Also unique to this site, which is maintained by Billy Passauer, is Owners and their Eskies. Click this option from the home page, and you will meet, as the name implies, people who can think of no more delightful canine companion than an American Eskimo. Should you be such an individual, the site also offers the opportunity for browsers to add their own names to this site that does its breed quite proud.

Australian Cattle Dog Web

http://www.idyllmtn.com/acd/acdhome.html

Few dogs are as keenly intelligent as the Australian Cattle Dog (ACD), a dog bred to control great herds of outback cattle with little or no direction. In keeping with this tradition of smarts, the Australian Cattle Dog Web, managed by Katherine Buetow, opens with the image of an ACD sitting at a computer. While these extraordinarily intelligent dogs probably could indeed understand how to surf the Internet on an unsuspecting owner's computer, the site is, of course, directed toward the people who live with these dogs. Exemplary for its fine organization and clean graphics, which include ACD silhouettes and barbed-wire borders, the clean presentation of this site meshes well with the breed it represents. The site, too, offers a great deal of information on the breed, offered with a snappy, reader-friendly delivery, all of which is easily accessible from the home page.

Also unique to this site is its emphasis on breeders and their responsibilities. It further strives to keep breeders honest by supplying browsers with a list of questions that would-be buyers should ask breeders (thus making this site valuable to anyone looking for any breed of dog). The Breeders section also lists not only ACD breeders, but the ACD Code of Ethics and the names of breeders who "have chosen to sign and abide" by them. What a good precedent.

Australian Kelpies

http://www.nethomes.com/kelpies/

Australia is known for smart herding dogs; the Kelpie is another of this illustrious family. Rumor has it that in its homeland, its handlers can go in for a spot of afternoon tea, while the dogs take care of business with the sheep on their own. Against a backdrop of Kelpie silhouettes, this site's home page welcomes the browser into a plethora of information on this medium-sized, savvy herder. It then proceeds to address any and all possible topics related to this breed, including Kelpies as Pets, Kelpie Pictures (of special value to those who many not be familiar with this breed), and The Working Kelpie Council (these dogs simply must have a job, or both they and their owners will go crazy).

The true newcomer to the breed should feel free to click on the home page link What is an Australian Kelpie? Here he or she will be greeted by a number of fascinating hyperlinks that answer this question handsomely and even include information on the Kelpie's relationship to Australia's wild dog, the Dingo. Deb Schneider is to be congratulated for maintaining so complete and informative a site on a dog that is somewhat unknown among the general dog-owning public, but deserves recognition and understanding for its great gifts.

Beagles on the Web

http://gdbdoc.gdb.org/~laurie/beagles.html

If you love Beagles, and most people do, you simply must check out Beagles on the Web, presented by Beagle enthusiast Laurie Kramer. Welcomed into a site that is, as the home-page introduction tells browsers, "dedicated to that noble little hound who loves to sniff and snack," you are in for a treat (and if there is anything Beagles are well-versed in, it's treats). The most well-known Beagle is the famed cartoon dog, Snoopy. They are a very popular breed both in pet households nationwide and apparently on the Internet, as well. This site provides a good insight into the breed's appeal. A small hound originally bred in Britain to hunt fox and rabbits, it now finds pleasure in eating virtually anything it can get its paws on and chasing after whatever interesting scents its nose picks up (hence the Beagle's propensity to find itself lost and pursued by frantic owners, who too often must learn the hard way about their Beagle's impetuous, inadvertent roaming behavior).

Respecting and celebrating the Beagle's unique take on the world, this home page, with its clean, contemporary design, places a great deal of emphasis on Beagle character and rescue, and on showcasing individual Beagles, both those that have their own Web sites (click on "The Pack" home-page hyperlink for this), and those that don't ("The Kennel" will take you here). While this page is fun, friendly, and easy to navigate, you can round out the experience with more serious information by clicking on the home-page hyperlink Beagle FAQ. This will transport you to a long, detailed, fact-rich document by Ellen Parr and Sharon Reid, located at http://www.zmall.com/pet_talk/dog-faqs/breeds/beagles.html. And finally, enrich your Internet Beagle experience even more by taking advantage of the direct access provided on the Beagles on the Web home page to i-barc, the Internet Beagle Aficionado Recreation Club e-mail list. Journey into all these distinct sites and pages, and you will come to know and experience all this sprightly hound has to offer.

Belgian Shepherd Dogs

http://snapple.cs.washington.edu/canine/belgians/

The Belgian Shepherd Dogs Web site, under the guidance of Terri Watson, dives right in and gets down to business from the moment you enter its home page. After first being greeted by the profile of this beautiful shepherd dog, you are then whisked into the body of the page to learn all about this treasured animal, which includes in-depth information on the four varieties of these dogs: the Belgian Groenendael, Tervuren, Malinois and Laekenois.

With a homespun, friendly feel from top to bottom, this page ushers you into the world of a dog that most members of the public know little, if anything, about, and it makes you feel right at home while doing it. It can also serve as inspiration for owners and would-be owners alike, as it provides a detailed listing of links that delve into the many activities in which this active, fun-loving dog can participate, including flyball, obedience, backpacking and, of course, herding. Thus both the dogs and their owners can benefit from a tour through the Belgian Shepherd Dogs Web site.

SitStay Presents Belgian Shepherd Dogs

http://www.sitstay.com/

Obviously the Belgian Shepherds have a passionate following guarding their interests, for here is yet another excellent site that celebrates their talents. Managed by Kent and Darcie Krueger, the SitStay Belgian Shepherd site deserves recognition for its dynamic though friendly presentation, all guided by an obvious affection for the breed.

Especially impressive here is the vast collection of subject choices on the site's home page that explain in detail exactly what you'll be getting when you click on to a given option. These options include, among many others, separate and distinct areas for the Groenendael, the Malinois, the Laekenois and the Tervuren, as well as the headings Medical, Training, Writings, and How to Learn More. There is even a home-page link, Create a Pedigree, that allows the browser to do just that for his or her dog with the promise that "It's never been easier." The eloquent, reader-friendly text throughout, coupled with colorful, lively graphics and a sensibly organized format, make touring the SitStay Belgian Shepherd site fun and easy as well as educational.

Bernese Mountain Dog Home Page

http://www.prairienet.org/~mkleiman/berner.html

If you were to poll the public about their knowledge of the Bernese Mountain Dog, it's a good chance that few would know much, if anything, about this large and rather beautiful Swiss native. Matthew Kleiman seeks to remedy this situation with the Bernese Mountain Dog Home Page, a site dedicated to a dog that is often mistaken for a Saint Bernard, though it is actually smaller, darker, and more svelte.

Check in to the breed's home page and you will find that this is indeed a distinct breed. Here you are treated to a colorful, easy-to-navigate, well-designed Web site that addresses such topics as the Berner-L Mailing List for those "devoted to Bernese Mountain Dogs"; Pictures, for those who want to bask in the beauty of these lovely animals; The Owners List, which "all past and present owners are invited to join"; Lost Dogs and Rescue; and Finding a Puppy. Each of these and more are accessible from the home page. Once you've completed the tour, you'll never again mistake a Bernese Mountain Dog for any other dog.

All About Border Collies

http://www.bordercollie.org/

Few dogs inspire as much fierce devotion and public adulation as the Border Collie, but this dog is also the subject of great controversy. Enter this graphically elegant, wonderfully organized site sponsored by the United States Border Collie Club (the club most vocally opposed to the recent recognition of the breed by the AKC) and be ushered into the fascinating world of an incredibly intelligent, hardworking stock dog from the border country between Scotland and England. It may take you weeks or even months to complete the journey.

Everything you need to know about this dog is presented on this site which is maintained by Heather Nadelman, beginning with an easy-to-navigate, fun-to-explore home page. In addition to access to in-depth information on herding, you will also learn just why this breed so often ends up in rescue situations (it's often too smart and too active for its own good), and why, on the other hand, some people just cannot imagine living with any other than this dog, which is frequently hailed as the most intelligent dog on the planet. The site's layers take the browser into FAQs, mailing lists, veterinary information, herding trial info, personal anecdotes, and literary references—the list literally goes on and on. This rather complicated breed is fortunate to be so well represented.

Border Terriers

http://www.oberlin.edu/~scarrier/Border_Terrier/Intro.html

While certainly not the most elaborate site you are likely to find on the Net, this site dedicated to the Border Terrier, a rather unsung member of the terrier family, is, like the dog it represents, low-key in presentation but rich in substance. Opening with a delightful portrait of these sweet-faced animals, the home page guides browsers through a variety of informational links that will educate them about a rather rare breed, but one with a devoted following.

You may begin your educational journey by clicking on the home-page hyperlink The Border Terrier Guide, which, like a tour book, carries you through a variety of topics first introduced by author Sam C. Carrier. This begins with a detailed Table of Contents that includes Characteristics and Temperament, History of the Border Terrier, and Frequently Asked Questions. Back on the home page, you will find access to even more layers of information on such topics as Finding the Right Border Terrier and Border Terrier Resources. This diminutive creature from the border country between Scotland and England deserves such recognition.

The Boxer Home Page

http://www.ice.eecs.uic.edu/~rsteven/

The Boxer Home Page, managed by Rob Stevenson, is a site dedicated to a dog who looks ferocious, but who in truth has the heart and soul of a pussycat. Simply ask any of the many children who have been raised by these good-natured pups and you will hear nothing but accolades. Those accolades are also precisely what you will find within this site that revolves more around the interactivity of Boxer lovers than around educating browsers to the whys and wherefores of this fascinating breed.

If such information is what you are seeking, before you dive into the world of the Boxer Home Page, click on Boxer Pages on the home page and you will find links to other sites that can provide you with that. Otherwise, take advantage of the unique info available on the home page itself, which includes Boxer Mailing List information, as well as an additional unique feature: The Boxer Ring, available from the home page and designated by illustrated Boxers in boxing gloves. This is a mailing list of sorts, which is actually, as its introduction states, "a community of Boxer lovers and their home pages."

Bull Terrier WWW Home Page
http://www.sarsen.demon.co.uk/bully/bully.html

Acknowledging that the Bull Terrier is an immensely popular breed on both sides of the Atlantic, the British-based Bull Terrier WWW Home Page offers fans on both sides of the pond the information they crave about this British native. The site opens with a gunmetal gray backdrop in which you see the profile of this tough little terrier. From this vivid welcome, you may then travel on to the various home-page hyperlink options, which include History of the Breed (bred originally for fighting but now bred for loyalty to their masters, gentleness with children, and tenacity in their quest for fun and activity), Rescue in the U.S. and the U.K., and the British and American breed standards.

Clean and crisp in its design with good color contrast, this site, which is maintained by Karen McGowan, is elegant, professional, and a joy to tour. For another special, not to mention unique, treat, click on the home-page hyperlink Bullies Around the World. Here you will understand why this dog has long been a media favorite, manifested in such images as Bullseye of Charles Dickens' Oliver Twist fame, to, more recently, beer mascot Spuds MacKenzie. Within this area you will meet Famous Bullies, Movie Star Bullies, Literary Bullies, and Famous Bully Owners. This site is unusual in it's international scope, offering breed information to both Americans and their British counterparts. How fortunate for the Bullies in their respective care.

Cairn Terrier Home Page
http://winnie.acsu.buffalo.edu/terrier/

Clean, crisp and to the point, this simple home page opens with the lovable mug of a Cairn Terrier, the breed made internationally famous by Toto of *Wizard of Oz* fame. It then invites you to choose a hyperlink from a long list of

Cairn Terrier choices. These include, among others, Cairn Pictures (a showcase of "almost famous" Cairns), Cairn Essays and Poetry (loving tributes to a much-loved terrier that can be as demanding as it is darling), and Terrier FAQ.

Yet this site offers more than just in-depth information on this diminutive "vermin-killing dog" from Scotland. It actually celebrates the entire Terrier family, offering after the initial Cairn home page choices a complete list of Terrier hyperlinks, arranged alphabetically from the American Pit Bull Terrier to the Yorkshire Terrier (the latter of which technically belongs in the AKC's Toy group). This unique focus on all Terriers makes this site an excellent source not only on Cairns, but on the entire Terrier clan.

The Chihuahua Home Page

http://www.icon-stl.net/~jbpeck/chp/chp.html

What is typically considered the world's smallest breed, the Chihuahua has an impressive Web page here, a page devoted primarily to the dog's history and character. Managed by Josh Peck, this site is actually one long page chock full of information on this diminutive native of Mexico. Though it's not fancy, it is easy to navigate and has much to offer those seeking to learn more about the breed.

The information presented is not of the run-of-the-mill variety; it is quite clever and full of interesting bits of trivia on such topics as Chihuahuas in the space program and Chihuahua images on ancient artifacts. If you so desire, you may also click on the hypertext words "squeals and yelps" that appear in Survivors of the Sand, and hear exactly what these potentially demanding little creatures can sound like when they seek to communicate with those they love. A quintessential companion because of its small size, the Chihuahua is well-represented by this site, which is delightful in character, educational in substance, and unique in focus.

Donna Patz' Cocker Spaniel Home Page

http://www.oia.ucalgary.ca/htm/patz/donna.htm

As one of America's most popular breeds, and thus prone to various health and temperament problems commensurate with popularity and the overbreeding it can inspire, the American Cocker Spaniel is not immune from a bad rap from time to time. But take a gander at this page devoted to this beautiful, lushly coated creature that was bred originally as a hunter in Britain and you will find a plethora of positives that seek to inspire and motivate as well as educate.

The journey begins with a collection of well-groomed Cockers in the perfect stack, as well as Donna Patz' greeting: "This page is dedicated to one of the great loves of my life … the American Cocker Spaniel." She proceeds to do that love a great service by presenting such a fine site dedicated to their breed.

After meeting Donna's own dogs, you are thrust into a page of choices arranged logically in outline form with the primary category names marked by a pawprint. As you begin what will prove to be an enjoyable tour, you will find home-page access to all things Cocker Spaniel. These include Cocker E-mail Lists (there are several from which to choose), About the Breed (which includes the AKC standard and a profile of this "merry" little dog from the Dog Owner's Guide), Rescue Organizations (various groups from around the country), and American Cocker Spaniels on the Net (photos and profiles of individual, and obviously much-loved, Cockers). Based in Canada, this site offers Cocker Spaniel enthusiasts everywhere a place where they can come to share and celebrate their deep affections for this breed.

The Collie Connection

http://jasmine.oit.gatech.edu/~ashley/collie-l/

There is no dog on this planet more famous than Lassie, and it is thus understandable that a Web site devoted to

Lassie's breed, the Collie, would invite much attention from those both in and out of the Collie fancy. As the Web site for the popular Collie-l discussion group, The Collie Connection actually serves two functions. On the one hand, it serves as headquarters for those who seek to commune with others who share their passions for rough and smooth Collies. Click on Welcome under the lovely Collie portrait that welcomes browsers into the home page, and you will learn all the rules and regulations of Collie-l, which is moderated by Ashley McLure. You may, of course, subscribe to the group if you so desire.

On the other hand, The Collie Connection offers a wealth of information on this beautiful herding breed. All you need to do is move down the home page a bit, and find hyperlinks to a Collie FAQ, the breed standard, the Collie Club of America, Collie publications, Collie rescue, and even links to Scotland sites (the Collie's homeland). One of the best of these links is The Collie Page (http://www.vlt.se/ingers/colliepage.html), an entirely different Web site available with a click from The Collie Connection home page. Within this well-illustrated site, highlighted by photos of this lovely dog, you will have access to such topics as History, Buying a Puppy, and the Featured Dog of the Month. Taken together, these two sites with a homespun tone, create a true community of Collie lovers, whose affection will no doubt prove quite contagious to the browser.

The Dachshund Zone

http://www.cybercom.net/~micetta/

The wiener dog, the sausage dog, the dog for whom the "hot dog" could have been named. Everyone knows the Dachshund, and not necessarily for reasons this adorable breed's passionate followers appreciate. But there is no denying that there is something irresistible about this long, skinny dog with short legs, floppy ears, and a feisty temperament. So too is there something special about The

Dachshund Zone, the Web site maintained by Jeannie Fazio, that playfully and musically (each area is accompanied by music) represents this unforgettable breed.

Enter the zone, and be greeted by music, an adorable Dachshund mug and a long home page of hyperlink options, beginning with those presented in a detailed Table of Contents. Here you will find quick access to, among others, Puppy Purchase Education, links to other Dachshund sites and Cybercom Cafe (an area of poetry dedicated to Dachshunds). Or click on to Wiener Stuff, a unique grab bag that invites Dachshund-loving browsers to ask questions, contribute tidbits of humor or information, or anything else of interest to the Dachshund world. As the intro to Wiener Stuff says, if you don't know where else it goes, "this is the place." At the end of the Dachshund Zone's home page, a sprightly Dachsie bids the browser farewell with a friendly, "Hope You Had Fun. Thanks for Stopping In!"

The Dal-l Homepage (Dalmatian)

http://www.io.com/~mbshick/dal-l.html

The Dalmatian world is ever being battered by popular images of their media darling of a dog. Movies and television cannot resist the black-and-white spots of this unique member of the dog family, the results of which inevitably dangerous population explosions that exacerbate temperament and health problems. In the wake of such events, far too many Dals end up in inappropriate homes, and far too many are subsequently relegated to animal shelters and rescue groups. This site, however, created by Matthew Hicks for the DAL-l electronic mailing list, which opens with a humorous image of a Dalmatian in devil horns, seeks to educate the public and prevent those tragedies.

Honest, warm, and affectionate in tone, this site welcomes Dal newcomers and veterans alike to explore this breed. It also invites browsers to subscribe to the DAL-l mailing list on the home page, but it then warns would-be subscribers of a three-month waiting list. Do we need any more evidence of this breed's popularity?

Work your way down the page, and you will find information on the breed, its health, and its rescue. You will also run across a hyperlink that asks "So, You Think You Want a Dalmatian? Consider This..." By all means click on this option, and you will find yourself in yet another excellent Dalmatian site: Dalmatian Plantation (http://www.magpage.com/~kdee/dal.html). Here you will receive brass-tacks information on the breed, clues to purchasing a Dal responsibly, and links to yet more Dalmatian-related sites. Together, Dalmatian Plantation combined with the Dal-1 Homepage to which it is linked, will provide you with all the information you need to understand this vibrant animal for what it is and what it is not.

The Realm of the Doberman (Doberman Pinscher)

http://www.execpc.com/~dober/

The Doberman Pinscher is an often misunderstood breed, presumed to be vicious and unpredictable by those who do not know it, known to be devoted and loyal to those who do. It is this latter group who invite browsers to "Enter the Realm of the Doberman," the Doberman Pinscher Web site, ushering them in to the strains of the song "Wind Beneath My Wings," an apt tribute to this guardian dog. From that welcome, you will probably assume that this site will be just as dramatic as the breed it represents. You will not be disappointed.

This site, which is owned by Louise Neumann, offers a most enjoyable, as well as educational, experience. Against a vibrant backdrop of blue and black, reminiscent of a gleaming black Doberman coat and with more music to highlight your journey, you will enjoy access to a pleasant mix of personal Doberman pages, as well as hard informational links to such topics as obedience training, ear cropping, Doberman history, and evaluating whether the Dobe is the right dog for you. To round out the picture, you may even access and subscribe to the Doberworld-l mailing list. Exemplary for its color, sound and drama, as well as its personal presentation, this is a site not to be missed.

English Setters on the World Wide Web

http://www.vvm.com/~dthacker/home.html

Not everyone is familiar with the English Setter, but check into English Setters on the World Wide Web, and you will be impressed not just by this graceful and very beautiful hunting breed, but also by the quality of this site that so vividly represents it. Maintained by David and Deborah Thacker, this site is dedicated, as its introduction tells us, "to the betterment of English Setters through the use of information on the Internet." It thus proceeds to use this resource to its best advantage, incorporating animation, color, and a dramatic presentation to capture the browser's attention and practically insist that he or she hear all about the English Setter.

The long and extraordinarily complete home page offers quick access to topics that run the gamut from English Setter health to breed clubs to field work, all presented in a boxed grid. Then it is on to specially featured hyperlinks to such areas as The English Setter Association of America, National Specialty News, English Setter Rescue, and Setters-L, the breed's mailing list. This site is as elegant and graceful as the English Setter itself.

English Springer Spaniels—Field Bred

http://pw2.netcom.com/~mnspring/ESS.html

The author of this site, Tom Radde, wishes to make clear from the moment the browser enters this domain that there is a distinct difference between show and field English Springer Spaniels. This site is primarily devoted to the latter.

What is identical between the two members of this same breed is their mutual need for companionship and attention, and it is Radde's emphasis of this and of humane training methods that make this site not only information-al, but uniquely warm in tone, as well. Rich with informa-tion about the field Spaniel and the many types of events in which it may participate, the site also addresses the show Springer, too, conveying in the process a deep respect for this very popular breed as a whole; making this site a place of value not only to field enthusiasts, but to anyone with an interest in the very popular dog that is the English Springer Spaniel.

The German Shepherd Dog Web Site

http://www.gdconsulting.com.au/GSD/

Most people believe they know the German Shepherd. They have encountered this dog on city streets and in parks accompanying police officers, the blind and regular run-of-the-mill pet owners, and they have met it repeatedly in movies and on television. But the German Shepherd Dog Web Site seeks to offer those interested in this breed—new-comers and veterans alike—the opportunity to meet the real German Shepherd, a dog introduced at the beginning of this Web site as the dog that, because of its versatility, is "the second best at all tasks."

Dedicated as it is to an immensely popular and far-too-often misunderstood and improperly bred breed, this site offers information that should help to educate those who dream of living with a Shepherd of the true nature and care of the dog. At the same time it also offers timely informa-tion on German Shepherd shows, events, and news from the Shepherd world. A logical place to begin your journey through this site is FAQs and Figures, accessible with a click from the home page. Here you will find hyperlinks to, among others, a traditional FAQ, as well as information on Selecting a Working Dog Puppy (as a working Shepherd may require different characteristics from one whose sole job will be that of companion), and breed standards in the United States and Britain. From this area, you may also subscribe to the GSD Mailing List. Pop in to this layer and learn all about the list and how to use it.

Not to be accused of a lack of humor, this area also includes hyperlink choices to Things Eaten by Loved GSDs and a survey on the GSD's Most Endearing and Annoying Habits. Personal and friendly in the site's delivery, yet serious about its mission, Webmaster Gareth Davies informs browsers that he owes his own inspiration for this site to his two GSD muses Zeus and Harley. Their influence shows.

Golden Retrievers in Cyberspace

http://www.rahul.net/hredlus/golden.html

No information on dog breeds could be complete without an entry devoted to the Golden Retriever, one of the world's, and it would appear, one of the Internet's, most beloved dog breeds. This site indeed stands out not only because of its impressive and extremely thorough coverage of this very popular breed, but also because it accomplishes this task with a tone that, like the breed at its heart, remains friendly and personal throughout. Once you begin to explore Golden Retrievers in Cyberspace, you get a sense of true community among the people who so love this breed, and you may just feel motivated to join them yourself.

It would be fruitless even to attempt to list all the topics available from this site's home-page Quick Find menu. Just rest assured that anything a browser could possibly need to research on this breed—clubs, rescue, chats, tips, e-mail lists, FAQs, training—is covered here, available with a quick click of a button. You will no doubt also be impressed by the coverage of both national and local issues within this page. It would indeed appear that Helen T. Redlus and her colleagues responsible for this site are aware of the needs and circumstances of every Golden Retriever and nearly every Golden club and rescue group in the nation, as all that information is subsequently presented right here. You will find detailed information on rescue clubs in need of volunteers and donations, the Golden events being sponsored by local clubs throughout the nation, and even an impressive collection of puppy referrals.

While popularity is never considered something positive for a breed, as it may attract people to the breed who are either ignorant of the breed's needs or who get involved for all the wrong reasons, it appears that those who love the Golden Retriever are making the best of it. If Golden Retrievers in Cyberspace is any indication, it would appear they are directing their energies toward turning that popularity into a community of caring for their lovely golden dogs.

Ragtym's Golden Retriever Information Page

http://www.alaska.net/~ragtym/

A breed of such popularity as the Golden Retriever is bound to inspire a great deal of creativity, and it has done just that with Ragtym's Golden Retriever Information Page, which is sponsored by Golden Retrievers of Ragtym. Dramatic, almost three-dimensional, in appearance, this site's home page, bordered as it is by photos of a sweet Golden puppy, seeks with all sincerity to educate the public about this wonderful dog in hopes that such knowledge will help every Golden land in a loving and permanent home.

Sadly, for the time being, a permanent home is not the fate of every Golden, evident in the number of sweet-tempered Goldens that end up in animal shelters or with one of the nation's many rescue groups. Acknowledging this fact, Ragtym's Golden Retriever Information Page gives prominent coverage to rescue from the very beginning of its home page. It then moves on to present a vast array of hyperlinks, arranged in an organized, easy-to-navigate configuration that carries browsers through all aspects of this golden breed and its care. No doubt its efforts will lead to salvation for many deserving Golden Retrievers.

The Great Dane Home Page
http://is2.dal.ca/~dcodding/dane.html

What a fabulous site to pay tribute to so elegant, so dignified, so giant a breed as the illustrious Great Dane. Enter The Great Dane Home Page and you are greeted first by a portrait of four lovely Danes against a backdrop of Dane silhouettes. This is then highlighted by an animated graphic of a Great Dane gaiting with a handler. You know from those first moments that you are in for something special.

Travel on through the home page and find that it offers you access to a variety of informational sources (the Great Dane Club of America Web Page and The National Animal Poison Control Center, to name two) and one of the most detailed option menus you are likely to find anywhere. Here you will find listed topics that cover virtually every aspect of this giant breed and its care, from the breed standard to rescue information to canine bloat to ear taping to breeding to feeding to news groups. But this isn't all. The home page, which is maintained impressively by Doug Coddington, is quite long and could keep one happily occupied in pursuing Dane expertise for hours and hours. Indeed a Great Dane enthusiast need look no further for an end-all source of information on this truly dynamic breed.

Great Pyrenees
http://www.pacifier.com/~jeffg/Pyrenees.html

This clean, text-heavy Web page is as simple and direct as the giant white livestock-guarding dog it represents. In getting to know this great white dog of gentle disposition and an acute guarding instinct, the browser will learn just why the desire to live with this dog transcends simply wishing to walk beside a dog that resembles a displaced polar bear.

Arranged essentially as one long page headed by a menu entitled Quick Index, this site presents all pertinent Pyrenees information and access to such areas as, among others, The Great Pyrenees Club of America, Rescue, Breed Info, Pictures, the Pyrenees mailing list, Breeder Listings, and Clubs. It also offers a detailed FAQ addressing such topics as canine bloat (a severe threat for large dogs), the Pyrenees with children (a relationship that should shine, assuming the child is taught to treat the dog gently), and the fact that the Pyrenees makes "an excellent house dog." An unexpected surprise is the vast roster of links presented at the end of the page, covering the gamut from personal Pyr sites to livestock-guarding-dog sites to sites devoted to other breeds. Indeed there is much value in simplicity and this site uses that fact to its best advantage.

The Labrador Retriever Home Pages

http://www.k9Web.com/breeds/l/labrador/

Few breeds are as well-known and well-loved as the Labrador Retriever. Enter The Labrador Retriever Home Pages, which bills itself as the "original online home of the Labrador Retriever emphasizing the amazing versatility of the breed," and you will be treated first to an artistic rendition of the breed's three color types: yellow, black, and chocolate brown. This site strives to provide Labrador-loving browsers with access to the wealth of information on Labs that exists on the Internet.

Clean and straightforward in its presentation, this valuable resource offers traditional information areas from its home page—Labrador Retriever FAQ, Breeders Directory, Labrador Rescue (quite a problem for this breed that too often proves too energetic for the run-of-the-mill owner), Health Issues for Labradors, Labrador Marketplace (a listing of Lab-related publications and products), and several

Labrador mailing lists to which browsers can subscribe. But as you peruse these choices, which are presented in a well-organized, large-print, often boxed format, you realize that this is quite a large home page managed to its optimum efficiency by Lisa Lee Miller, who also invites browsers for input on the job she is doing. Miller indeed has much to manage here for a dog that is consistently named in the AKC's Top Ten list of popular breeds, but she accomplishes this handsomely. In the long run, it is the very active, water-loving, people-loving Labrador who will benefit from the open lines of communication that exist here.

Take advantage, too, of the open lines of communication that can exist between Web sites. For example, this site offers you a link to another site—a Labrador FAQ written by Lisa Lee Miller and Cindy Tittle Moore at http://www.zmall.com/pet_talk/dog-faqs/breeds/labradors.html—that is incredibly complete in the topics it covers and the substance with which it does so. Check this site out by clicking on the hyperlink text "Labrador Retriever FAQ" at the beginning of The Labrador Retriever Home Pages.

Leonberger World
http://www.Webcom.com/~isberg/leonberger.html

What is a Leonberger? Well, check into the Leonberger World Web site, and find out. Once you do, you will discover a beautiful, lion-like dog from Leonberg, Germany, who, as this site proudly proclaims, "loves children, other animals, and water." Maintained by Caroline Isberg, this site celebrates these rare dogs, known affectionately as Leos, with a warm, friendly tone that reflects the character of these animals themselves. With an easy sense of humor throughout, the site proves welcoming to newcomers, while at the same time remaining a comfortable home for what are referred to as regulars. This is also one of the simplest sites to navigate that you are likely to find, as it practically takes you by the mouse and guides you step by step through either a quick overview of its pages or a leisurely tour.

Your best bet is first to take advantage of the home-page link to an excellent FAQ composed by Caroline Isberg that gets to the basics of the Leonberger and then propels you forward into learning more and more and more. Also available is home-page access to the LEOLIST discussion group, a group of Leonberger lovers from around the world who share their affections for this breed via computer. What you will glean from the various elements of this site is that love for the Leonberger crosses all borders and transcends all language barriers. Indeed, as far as this very international site is concerned, the Leonberger world has no barriers at all.

Maltese Only

http://www.greenepa.net/~jbianco/index.html

There is nothing cuter, nothing more lovable, nothing more irresistible than a soft, scruffy little Maltese puppy, a ball of white fluff with two shining ebony eyes and a black button nose. You'll be treated to three of these delightful toys when you enter Maltese Only, a site maintained by Jay and Bev Bianco that bills itself as "the most complete Maltese site on the World Wide Web." Spend a little time in this site, and you'll come to realize just how justified that claim is.

What sets this site apart from the pack is not only its dazzling design of black and just the right amount of color to contrast with the white of the dogs, nor is it the richness of the design and the ease in which you can move from place to place. No, what truly marks this site as special is the way it so successfully encourages interactivity among browsers while providing an extraordinary wealth of information on Maltese dogs and dog care.

The framed introduction, for example, highlights the Maltese Only Photo Album (of which a browser's dog can become a part), the Maltese Only Q&A Forum, and the Maltese Only Chat Room, which meets nightly. In the meantime, check out the framed menu of hyperlinks on the left side of the screen and you can't help but be impressed by the number of choices there. These options include, among many others, rescue, fleas and heartworms, aging, housebreaking, dental care, pet owner survey and what to ask a Maltese breeder. Click on to one of these choices and be struck by the reader-friendly professionalism with which each topic is addressed. This site covers Maltese dogs and their care, and ownership in general, so thoroughly that it is of great value to any dog owner. In other words, despite its name, this site is certainly not for Maltese only.

Newf-L Homepage (Newfoundland)

http://jasmine.oit.gatech.edu/~ashley/newf-l/

Those with a passion for the big, water-loving Newfoundland will be delighted to check in to the Newf-L Homepage and see two Newfies, a Landseer and a black, participating via individual computers in this site's sponsor organization, the Newf-L mailing list. Yet this site is more than a mailing list, and is rich as it is with information on Newfoundlands.

While you may indeed join Newf-L right on the home page, you will also find lists there of hyperlinks to areas devoted to Newf books, search-and-rescue Newfs, Newf memorials, Newf clubs, Newf breed information, and, of course, a Newf FAQ. Clean and well-organized, this site does the giant dog to which it is devoted proud. It is sure to delight the followers of this breed, who will find this site supportive of interaction within the Newfoundland community, while offering a plethora of information about this beautiful dog,bred originally to help fisherman and to rescue those who fell overboard into a freezing ocean.

The Pomerama: Informational Pomeranian Web Site

http://pages.prodigy.com/pomathon/pomerama.htm

Hailing proudly from Germany is the smallest member of what is known as the spitz family of dogs. The Samoyed, the Keeshond, the Wolf Spitz, the Alaskan Malamute, and the Pomeranian, too, all share the same thick double coat, the curled tail, the indomitable spirit, and the wolfy/foxy profile. The Pom is just the smallest of the clan, and here Susann Lilian Philbrook provides this wee animal with a dramatic Web site that reflects its nature quite appropriately.

Set against a backdrop of black, highlighted by the Pom's sprightly expression, the Pomerama home page welcomes browsers in with a friendly hello. What awaits is a great deal of information about Pomeranians, including a detailed FAQ list, dog-treat recipes, poetry, links to other Pom sites, and personal and fictional stories. You may even stop by Ye Ol' Pomeranian Gift Shoppe, which offers Pom enthusiasts a variety of collars, cleaning supplies, Pom-motif clothes, and gift items.

Indeed the choices available from the home page run the gamut from the fun to the serious and everything in between. Take a look at the Pomeranian FAQ List, for example, accessible with a click from the home page. This takes you to what is essentially a separate and distinct home page all its own, offering hyperlink access to General Information, Training, and Health, the latter area offering candid presentations of health conditions, such as luxating patellas (dislocated kneecaps), hair loss, and skin diseases, to which the Pom can be susceptible. The Pomerama enables browsers to become intimately acquainted with a small dog that, according to its new AKC breed standard, should be "cocky, commanding, and animated as he gaits," even though he weighs all of three to seven pounds.

The Wonderful World of Poodles

http://www.geocities.com/Heartland/2826

Tackling the world of the Poodle, one of the world's most popular dog breeds, may indeed be considered a daunting undertaking. But Patricia Gray meets that challenge handsomely with her Wonderful World of Poodles Web site. Fun, busy, and exuberant—much like the dog that it celebrates—this site succeeds in forging a community of Poodle owners from all walks of Poodle ownership, who can find a source here for all types of information and camaraderie. In the latter case, the site offers home-page access to information on pen pals and to The Haus of PoodleWeb Chat Room.

Giving equal time to all three types of Poodles—Toy, Miniature and Standard—this site is rich with clever graphics depicting all colors and all sizes of Poodles, simultaneously promoting the most lovable characteristics of this breed: its intelligence and its sense of humor. Anyone who has ever lived with a Poodle or has simply seen one prancing down the street as if it ruled the world, knows these traits well. Yet this site, like the Poodle itself, is not all fun and games. Rich in substance, it offers ample access to solid information, as well, with hyperlinks that carry browsers into informational areas that cover such topics as general care, grooming, breeders, books and magazines, Poodle pictures (to which you are invited to add your own), grooming (obviously an important issue in this glamorous, high-maintenance breed's life), and the especially impressive Poodle Health and Genetics Page.

The Wonderful World of Poodles strives to substantiate Poodle owners' claims that this breed is the ultimate companion. With its mix of light and serious information, presented with an energetic tone and design, rich with links to layers of material within its own pages and to other Web sites, it indeed paints this proud portrait of a dog that has long cherished the experience of living with and loving human beings.

The Pug Dog Home Page

http://www.camme.ac.be/~cammess/www-pug/home.html

You will receive a warm welcomeupon entering The Pug Dog Home Page. Two illustrated Pugs peer out to greet you, and you are made instantly at home. Well-designed in format, with Pug icon guides throughout, the site is easy to navigate and full of great information for its target audience: those who love Pugs.

From this site's home page you will find hyperlinks to a variety of topics, including History (the breed is Chinese in origin), Sounds (this, the largest of the toy breeds with its signature pushed-in nose, does boast a unique, shall we say, vocabulary), Curiosities (Pugs in art, books, movies, and TV), and The Pug Fan Club (only Pugaholics need apply). Indeed much imagination has gone into the creation of this site, both in its design and in the nature of the layers of information that lie beneath the home page. It thus stands as an example to other dog-site designers of what can be achieved in paying tribute to one's chosen breed and as a powerful testament from the passionate followers of Pugs to the dog they adore. Authors Jan Mylemans and Serge Scory are to be congratulated for their thorough and affectionate treatment of this sweet-tempered, downright irresistible member of the Toy family of dogs.

Rottweiler Home Page

http://members.tripod.com/~RottHome/

When you first enter the home page for this immensely popular working breed of German origin, you will no doubt be impressed by the many link subjects included on the detailed Table of Contents. These cover the gamut from Rott Rescue to Rott Standards to Training, to Health to detailed areas on local, national, and international breed clubs. All of these are of vital interest to the breed's ever-growing stable of fans, and to the well-being of the breed itself, which far too often winds up in the hands of people who are not capable of caring for it properly—as is the curse of any breed that captures the collective attention of a society. But such popularity, as Rottweiler enthusiasts know, can border on ruination when that breed is renowned for its protective nature, its muscle, and its fierce loyalty—a dangerous combination in the hands of those who are not pure of heart in their keeping of this dog.

In the face of such challenges, the Rottweiler Home Page paints a portrait of the well-bred Rottweiler as a decidedly special animal who can indeed be the ideal, and most loving, pet when its owner earns the right to claim such a partnership. Also unique to the site, which is managed by Kat Lakey, is the Rott Owners section, "Personal pages of people owned by the great rott-n-ones," and Jan's Breed Specific Legislation Page, an astoundingly well-researched and very detailed overview of state-by-state efforts to restrict the ownership of such large, potentially aggressive dogs as Rottweilers. Click on to this area, and learn how to get involved.

Saint Bernard Dog

http://www-nmbe.unibe.ch/abtwt/saint_bernard.html

For a quick, thorough overview of this legendary dog, check out Marc Nussbaumer's Saint Bernard Dog Web site. While it may not be fancy in organization or design, it does have much to offer in terms of information and historical artwork of this low-key, though much-celebrated, breed.

The site is essentially arranged in two parts. The first is its in-depth coverage of the breed's history, perhaps the most-emphasized element of this site. The home page opens, for example, with fascinating illustrations of old-time Saints searching for lost travelers in the snow of their Alpine home. This is then followed by photos of modern-day Saints in their more contemporary—and relaxed—role as full-time companion. Click on the accompanying hyperlink, History of the Saint Bernard Breed, to enter a new layer of information that harbors a fascinating eight-chapter history of the breed, complete with illustrations.

Meanwhile, back on the home page, you may explore the more traditional, technical aspects of the breed: its country of origin (Switzerland), an historical summary, the breed's temperament (friendly, gentle, and calm), its coat (short hair or long hair), its height (approximately 27–35 inches), etc. Although its attention to this gentle giant's history elevates this site to a level all its own, it provides a great deal of information on all aspects of the breed in a relatively limited space. This site glows with a special respect for a breed that for its life-saving heritage truly deserves to be called a saint.

Samoyed Dogs

http://www.samoyed.org/samoyed.shtml

Everything you ever wanted or needed to know about the Samoyed, the beautiful smiling white sled dog from the Siberian Arctic, can be found within the Samoyed Dogs Web site. This site, as you will learn from the home page, actually acts as headquarters to a variety of individual specialized sites devoted to the dog "with Christmas on its face." Visit this home page, as managed by Gregory Newell, and you will be presented with direct access to, as the illustrated menu bar informs you, the individual sites for Samoyed Rescue, Expedition Samoyeds, the Organization for the Working Samoyed, the Samoyed Club of America, and Samoyeds from Around the World.

Related to this site is the Samoyed Fanciers mailing list (at http://www.samoyed.org/samfans.html), known affectionately to its subscribers and to the Net at large as SAMFANS. Here you will find an enthusiastic community of Sammy lovers, all celebrating a breed that is amply equipped, with its silver-tipped coat, smiling face, and friendly disposition, to inspire much passion among its followers. That passion is evident in the information presented for subscribing to and participating in SAMFANS, as well as in the messages sent by the members themselves. Combine a tour of Samoyed Dogs and its various Sammy areas with a visit to the friendly environs of SAMFANS and you will enjoy the ultimate Samoyed experience.

Schnauzer Ware

http://www.schnauzerware.com/

The American Kennel Club recognizes three types of Schnauzer—the Miniature, the Standard, and the Giant. Now Schnauzer aficionados of any member of this illustrious German family may enjoy a celebration of them all together on the Schnauzer Ware Web site. No need to bop from site to site—all three are here and waiting for interested browsers.

Clever and colorful in design and tone, this site makes use of references to popular culture, a technique that helps it stand out from the pack. Click on The S Files home page option, for example, and participate in a Schnauzer Trivia contest or test your skills at a Schnauzer Word Search. Or maybe you're hankering for some Schnauzer News. Click on the Planet Schnauzer icon and you'll be faced with more news and informationally oriented choices than you ever thought possible for a single type of dog. From the Schnauzer Art & Literary Guild to The Schnauzer Cafe to The Schnauzer Ware Catalog, this is indeed a creative site that can't help but leave you impressed by the fact that it does such justice to three distinct breeds and that it accomplishes this task with such creativity. Webmaster Carey Bradley is to be congratulated on this effort.

The SHAR-PEIges (Shar-Pei)
http://www.teleport.com/~keller/sharpei.html

In the past 10 or 15 years, the Shar Pei, the wrinkled dog of China who seems too small for its coat, has taken the dog world by storm. Even those ignorant of canine subjects have taken notice at one time or another of this unusual creature sauntering down the street. The SHAR-PEIges carry on this breed's tradition of flash and panache.

Complete with animation and music, The SHAR-PEIges Web site guides browsers through its layers of information with cute home-page Shar-Pei icons that introduce such topics as Pei-People (profiles of "proud Shar-Pei families"), a Shar-Pei News Group, Pei-News, and Pei-Talk (an interactive chat). In addition to providing the necessary information on its breed (vital for a breed that may end up with people who are swept up in Shar-Pei fever but are unprepared to care for this potentially demanding dog properly), this site is devoted to creating a sense of community among those who share their lives with Shar-Peis, and it does this with a warm and welcoming tone throughout. Sponsors Dixon and Christine Keller of KellioPei Kennels in Oregon succeed in their mission to bring Shar-Pei owners together to share their love of those wrinkles. This is a fun site, a creative site, and a thorough site. Enjoy.

The Sheltie Page (Shetland Sheepdog)
http://www.dogpatch.org/sheltie.html

Though the Sheltie is often mistaken for a miniature Collie—a miniature Lassie, if you will—this native of Scotland's Shetland Isles, like the similarly diminutive cattle and ponies who share its island home—is a distinctive breed in its own right. The very colorful Sheltie Page does all it can to make that fact crystal clear to browsers. Welcoming veteran owners as well as casual browsers who simply want to know more about the breed, this site has something for everyone.

The Sheltie Page's warm and friendly home page offers links to Commonly Asked Sheltie Questions as well as The Sheltie FAQ, quick access to The Shetland Sheepdog Homepage, and hyperlinks to various Sheltie clubs in the United States and Canada. Check in to the Fluff 'n' Stuff Sheltie Page, and you will be treated to personal reflections on this adorable dog, presented in poems, stories, pictures, etc.—a nice addition and one to be expected of so complete a site dedicated to so attractive a dog. If you wish to contact breeders, those who are online are hyperlisted right on the home page, as is information on subscribing to the Sheltie E-Mail List. And nowhere does the page in any way insinuate this small dog is actually Lassie in a smaller package.

The American Shih-Tzu Club Home Page
http://www.users.intellinet.com/~kandyj.astc/

While the reason for most breed clubs' Web sites is to promote the activities and inner workings of their individual clubs, the American Shih-Tzu Club Home Page is a bit different. As soon as you enter its home page, you will realize that it exists primarily as an informational source for the Shih-Tzu itself. It strives to educate the public about this very popular, longhaired, wonderfully tempered toy breed. It does this with a fun, undeniably affectionate tone.

Designed by Kandice Jones, this site is vivid in color—lots of purple and lavender—so very appropriate for this glamorous little dog, which was bred originally in China to enhance life within the palace walls of royal families. To explore this breed, the site offers two menus, the first appearing on the home page along the left-hand side of the screen, which offers several general topics about the breed and the club. Once within one of these areas, you then have access to a menu bar along the bottom of the screen, which offers more detailed links to such topics as Photo Album, Ethics (always an impressive addition to a breed-club site) and Rescue. Grooming, too, is a helpful topic here, given this dog's long, silky tresses. That this site seeks to guide the pet owner in this department is even more evident here, because the grooming emphasis is on what is required for the Shih-Tzu companion, requirements that are far less daunting than those for the show dog.

Another fun area to explore is accessible quickly and easily from the home page. Click on the words "To learn a little more about us…" from the introduction and you will find yourself immersed in a delightful, very informational discussion on living with and caring for Shih-Tzu—all presented by the dogs themselves, the "us" in the hyperlink, in fun and friendly Shih-Tzu language and illustrated with adorable pen-and-ink-style illustrations. All in all, this is a valuable site for those who love the Shih-Tzu. It stands as a solid representative not only of the breed's club, but of the animal for which that club exists.

Tibetan Mastiff Home Page

http://www.tibetanmastiffs.com/

Against a backdrop of silhouettes of what you assume must be very large dogs, appears the Tibetan Mastiff Home Page. This backdrop, along with the portrait of an adorable Tibetan puppy and exuberant announcements of new developments in the breed, convey a true affection for this little-known breed and the genuine desire of Webmaster, Liz Bartlett, to share it. Bred in Tibet as a livestock-guarding dog, the Tibetan Mastiff boasts a small, though devoted, community of followers who know each other and each other's dogs, all of whom may share and benefit from a site like this. Easy to navigate and easy on the eyes, this site offers browsers a well-organized Site Index to guide them through the layers of information that await. On this grid of topics, Tibetan Mastiff icons represent such topics as the breed standard, health, pictures, clubs, litters and rescue, and owners.

A good place to begin your tour of the Tibetan Mastiff Home Page is the Introduction option on the Site Index.

This offers a good overview of the breed, from which you may then, now properly prepared, explore the more in-depth topics. However, this site also emphasizes repeatedly that a livestock-guarding dog of this caliber can be very strong willed and needs firm, consistent handling and proper socialization to thrive in a contemporary pet situation. Impressive in its combination of admiration for the breed and honest information, the Tibetan Mastiff Home Page is a winner. Every breed should be so well-served by the Internet.

Tibetan Spaniel Home Page

http://www.albritons.com/tibbies/

Tibet has an ancient tradition in dogs, yet few would expect that so cute and diminutive a creature as the Tibetan Spaniel would emerge, could emerge, from the towering Himalayan Mountains. But that is exactly where the Tibetan Spaniel came from, nurtured and cherished for an estimated 2,000 years by Buddhist monks and lamas. As the introduction to this site tells those who make the cyber pilgrimage to learn of this fascinating pup, historically Tibetan Spaniels were never sold. They were only given "as treasured gifts to esteemed friends."

That human affection for the Tibetan Spaniel continues to reign within the Tibetan Spaniel Home Page, a colorful site sponsored by the Tibetan Spaniel Club of America. The home page opens with a reader-friendly discussion of the breed's history and personality, and what one must know about living with Tibetans. This information is bordered on the left by a long list of hyperlinks that follow the browser throughout the many layers that lie ahead. These topics are divided logically into such categories as FAQs (all the basics), Owners & Breeders, Resources, and Fun Stuff (jokes, quotes, and chats). The Tibetan Spaniel Home Page invites browsers to "Discover the World of Tibbies." The site then proceeds to help them do just that.

The Welsh Terrier Web Page

http://alumni.caltech.edu/~slp/welsh.html

This lovely, well-organized site welcomes browsers at the very top of its home page with the delightful mug of The Welshie of the Month. After learning about this individual Welshie, you may then move on to find out all about its family, referred to here as "Britain's First Terrier." Click on those words from the homepage introduction and you are whisked away to a detailed profile of the breed written by Bardi McLennan.

Now fully educated on this playful, intelligent, often demanding dog—a classic member of the terrier family—you may then explore other environs of the site, including the Welsh Family Album, which features photos of beloved Welshies. You will also be offered direct access to both the Welsh Terrier Club of America and its rescue service, WTCARES. Completing this full-service Welsh Terrier site is the Welsh-L Discussion Group, which is conveniently accessible from the home page. From start to finish, this site emanates warmth and a true affection for this unique terrier breed.

Westies Home Page

http://mrdata.simplenet.com/westies/westies.htm

Enter the Westies Home Page and what you will learn from your very first moment within this very colorful, very lively site is that West Highland White Terriers are "lovable little canines with an attitude." The site then proceeds to invite both owners and would-be owners to explore this sprightly Scottish native.

Begin by touring the home page with its dog-treat backdrop and its many adorable portraits of these diminutive white pups that always appear to be having the time of their lives. From the home page you may visit such areas as Adopt a Westie, Frequently Asked Questions (impressively complete in its coverage of history as well as care basics),

Westie Clubs, Westie Bulletin Board, Audio/Video Clips, and even access to Other Terrier Home Pages. Once a terrier lover, always a terrier lover, and those who proudly claim this title, whether a Westie owner or not, will find this site not only inspirational, but a valuable—and fun—resource.

Yorkshire Terriers

http://www.zmall.com/pet_talk/dog-faqs/breeds/yorkies.html

This FAQ, dedicated to the diminutive Yorkshire Terrier and written by Sue James, is as articulate and reader-friendly as it is complete in the information it presents. Though this breed may be quite tiny in stature, it is well represented here in an attempt to ensure that it is properly understood and nurtured.

The browser is presented first with a detailed Table of Contents that will carry him or her through all aspects of this popular toy breed, from Breed History (both in the United States and the United Kingdom, the latter of which is home to both the Yorkie and to James) to Grooming (owners may wish to keep this dog's coat trimmed short to avoid the extraordinary attention a long coat requires) to Suitability as Pets (Yorkies can be quite possessive of their owners but adaptable to any environment) to Health and Longevity (the well-bred Yorkie should be healthy and long-lived). Rounding this information out is separate and quite valuable information on Choosing a Puppy, and a detailed list of books, magazines, and online Yorkie discussion groups.

The Northern Maremma Association Home Page

http://cedar.hud.ac.uk/nmapages/nma.htm

This is a beautifully designed and illustrated site devoted to an equally beautiful livestock-guarding dog of Italian origin, the Maremma Sheepdog. The site's home page opens with a menu set against a backdrop of Maremma silhouettes, a design element found throughout the site. The menu options, which are illustrated with photos of this large white dog that would be difficult to pick out of a flock of fluffy white sheep, offer browsers a unique opportunity to get acquainted with a rather rare animal. These options include What is a Maremma?, What is the Northern Maremma Association? (a U.K.-based breed club), Care of the Maremma, Breed News and Photo Gallery.

Another unique option is Problem with your Maremma?, which offers solid advice of value not only to owners of this dog, which, as we learn is not for everyone, but for owners of any dog. With layers and layers of information, presented in a thoughtful, reader-friendly style, this site is designed to help both owners and dogs, demonstrating just what a well-planned Web site can accomplish.

CHAPTER 2

Health Care

Few subjects are closer to the heart of dog fanciers than canine health care. People who love dogs make it their business to know as much about the health of their pets as they do any other aspect of dog ownership. They know that dogs depend on us for their very existence, and good veterinary care is a significant part of our responsibility to them.

Dogs are basically healthy creatures, as long as they are provided with good preventative medicine, decent nutrition, and plenty of exercise.

However, despite this, the health of the nation's purebred dogs has received a lot of attention in the media over the past decade. Numerous magazines and news programs have repeatedly brought to light the tragedy of genetic illnesses that plague nearly every breed of dog, from the very common ailment hip dysplasia to some of the rarer autoimmune disorders.

The purebred dog community has responded to charges that the health of their dogs has taken a back seat to appearance. A plethora of individuals and organizations, including a number of veterinary schools across the United States and Canada, are now working hard to control and eventually eliminate genetic disease in dogs.

Despite these efforts, there are still those dog owners who must live day to day with these debilitating diseases. Many members of the canine community, including breeders, veterinarians, and researchers, are striving to help these people and their dogs by disseminating information on how these diseases can be treated and managed.

continued after the feature section

AVMA Online

http://www.avma.org

It stands to reason that the American Veterinary Medical Association (AVMA) would have the largest veterinary presence on the Internet. This nonprofit national association of veterinarians basically serves as the veterinary community's governing body. Nearly every small-animal veterinarian in the country is a member of the AVMA.

One of the AVMA's many purposes is to "inform the public about matters of animal and public health." The AVMA Online was obviously created to help fulfill this goal. The site offers information on all types of animals, with particular emphasis on dogs, cats, and horses, and it is an excellent source for basic health care information.

The AVMA Online home page begins with Breaking News, an area that features short newsy articles on disease task forces, online conferences, and recent discoveries in animal health.

For pet owners, the huge Care for Pets area is the place to go. The first icon here, titled AVMA, presents background information on the organization, along with material on careers in veterinary medicine and how to choose a veterinarian.

The next area is Pet Loss. Dog owners facing the difficult decision of whether or not to euthanize an ailing pet, or those trying to cope with a recent loss will find these articles on euthanasia and coping with grief invaluable. A list of books and Pet Loss Hotlines around the country is especially helpful.

The Buying area covers the hows and whys of purchasing a healthy pet. There is plentiful information here on acquiring a dog, including breed basics and selecting a puppy or older dog.

Safety Tips covers first aid, health rules at home (keeping pets clean), safety tips for kids, poison control, seasonal health concerns, and taking your pet along (safety away from home).

The most serious, in-depth articles can be found in Animal Health Information, under Canine Health, and

WELCOME TO THE AMERICAN VETERINARY MEDICAL ASSOCIATION'S (AVMA) WEB PAGE ON ANIMAL HEALTH.

As the premier professional organization for veterinarians, AVMA is recognized as the voice of the profession and the authority on animal welfare. AVMA resources provide the latest and most advanced information on animal health care.

Our Commitment to Animal Welfare is Unsurpassed.

What does this all mean for you, the pet owner? It assures for you that the information provided constitutes the most informed and responsible approach to provide for the well-being of animals.

We hope you will become an active participant of our Web site. Visit us often. We will be updating our site regularly to provide new and useful information to you. For late breaking items of information on animal health you don't want to miss visiting Pet Health In The News, which contains reprinted articles and press releases of interest to pet owners.

If you have any comments or suggestions on our Care4Pets Web site, we hope you will share them with us in our "Tell Us About You and Your Pets" page.

If you have questions on any of the information you see or if you have specific concerns about the health of your pet, we urge you to talk with your local veterinarian.

Site Index   Disclaimer/Copyright ©AVMA 1996

Animal Illnesses and Diseases. Here, details on diseases such as distemper, parvovirus, cancer, heart disease, Lyme disease, toxoplasmosis, and rabies can be found.

Interactive areas make up the remainder of the AVMA Online site. The Tell Us area invites browsers to submit short stories about their pets, some of which are posted. Heroic Pets, included in the Pet Stories area, features stories of dogs who have risked their lives to save those of their owners. A section for kids allows young dog fanciers to print sections of the site for coloring and learning.

Finally, the Resources area lists veterinary organizations. State and local veterinary medical associations are included here, as are AVMA-allied organizations (such as the American Animal Hospital Association and the American Association of Food Hygiene Veterinarians) and specialty organizations (like the American College of Veterinary Behaviorists and American Veterinary Dental College). Addresses and phone numbers for each are included, but there are no links to Web sites or e-mail addresses.

This is where the Internet comes in. In addition to being a good source on basic health care for dogs, a number of solid Web sites offer not only information on how to treat genetic diseases but how to rid purebred dogs of these heartbreaking maladies.

Whether you want to research genetic problems that might be plaguing the breed of dog you are considering or just want to find out how to brush your dog's teeth, there is a health care site in this chapter for you.

Virtual Veterinary Center

http://www-sci.ib.uci.edu/~martindale/Vet.html

One of more than 40 centers relating to science and medicine on the University of California at Irvine server, the Virtual Veterinary Center provides links and a variety of other information pertaining to veterinary medicine.

Beginning with Veterinary Dictionaries and Glossaries, the Virtual Veterinary Center offers an online resource for medical, veterinary, and general dog terms. Available in eight different languages, the words can be browsed through alphabetically or by using the first letter of the word being sought.

In the Online Veterinary Journals area, lists of veterinary journals and newsletters can be found, containing technical articles and information on various canine health conditions. Publications from around the world are included in this list, which features a wide variety of periodicals.

If you want to look up information on veterinary schools around the world, the Veterinary Schools: Complete Curriculum hyperlink is invaluable. With connections to international veterinary school Web sites, this area offers a wide variety of data. Normally hard-to-find information like the names, phone numbers, and e-mail addresses of university faculty and staff appear in these sites.

For serious research, the section on Veterinary Courses, Textbooks, Modules, Cases, and Images gives you access to links to sites relating to the various biosciences, including animal genetics. Individual areas covering clinical sciences, diagnostic testing, and microbiology are also available for browsing.

AltVetMed Homepage

http://www.altvetmed.com/

Authored by two veterinarians with a strong interest in complementary and alternative medicine, the AltVetMed Homepage provides quite a bit of information on the area of alternative veterinary care.

The FAQs area introduces the site with a thorough explanation of what AltVetMed is and how it works. A section called Current News features breaking topics on the subject of alternative medicine, one of the hottest areas of veterinary medicine today.

To get to the meat of this site, you'll need to go to the Table of Contents, which begins with a list of U.S. and Canadian American Holistic Veterinary Medical Association members, organized by state. If you are looking for a holistic veterinarian, this is the place to be. Hundreds of veterinarians are listed here.

Also in this site are articles on allergic skin problems, arthritis, epilepsy, and other subjects, all written by a holistic veterinarian. A directory of associations containing addresses and phone numbers of organizations representing holistic practitioners is also included, along with links to other alternative medicine resources on the Web.

Canine Eye Registration Foundation

http://www.prodogs.com//chn/cerf/index.htm

This site is part of the Professional Dog Networks, but is worth mentioning on its own because of its in-depth information on the most well-known organization in the area of canine eye disease.

The Canine Eye Registration Foundation, also known as CERF, sponsors this no-frills page, which includes an explanation of the foundation's purpose and the importance of eye care in dogs. Dedicated to eliminating genetic eye disease, CERF is an invaluable aid to breeders and pet owners alike. Details on how to register your dog with CERF, how the foundation conducts research on eye disease, and the various services offered by the organization are featured on this page.

Orthopedic Foundation for Animals, Inc.

http://www.prodogs.com/chn/ofa/index

The Orthopedic Foundation for Animals (OFA) page is located within the massive Professional Dog Network site and is a simple and to-the-point page.

The OFA was started several decades ago by researchers who were looking for a way to evaluate dogs for the existence of canine hip dysplasia. It is the most widely accepted method of determining and keeping track of the incidence of hip dysplasia within canine breeding lines.

Since its inception, OFA has added several other registries designed to monitor other canine genetic diseases. Databases are currently maintained on elbow dysplasia, thyroid disease, congenital heart disease, and patellar luxation. All of these conditions are covered in this site, with a brief description of each disease, information on its prevalence, an explanation of how each registry works, and other pertinent facts.

One especially interesting area is called Correction of Anecdotal Misinformation, where popular yet inaccurate beliefs about hip dysplasia are addressed. For example, the often-talked about use of vitamin C to cure or prevent hip dysplasia is addressed here as a myth, as are other common suppositions about the disease.

An explanation of how to interpret the numbers given in OFA evaluations can also be found on this site, as can a list of books on each of the genetic diseases addressed by the registry.

Canine Hip Dysplasia

http://www.ool.com/hunting/hipdysplasia.html

Part of the Outdoors Online site, which is dedicated to outdoor sports, this page is included in the Hunting section, under Hunting Dogs. This makes sense since larger breeds such as retrievers and pointers are particularly susceptible to canine hip dysplasia.

A one-page site consisting of text only, Canine Hip Dysplasia gives good, solid information on this very common canine joint disorder. A detailed description of the condition, its clinical symptoms, possible environmental influences, treatment, prevention, and how to control the disease are also included here. In addition, there is a discussion of the role of breeding in the perpetuation of hip dysplasia, and well as advice on how dogs can live with this crippling ailment.

Control of Genetic Disease

http://workingdogs.com

A page on the Workingdogs.Com site, Control of Genetic Disease consists of information on inherited diseases in purebred dogs, collected from seminars presented by George A. Padgett, V.M.D., a pathologist at Michigan State University College of Veterinary Medicine with a special interest in canine genetics.

A simple site with no graphics, Control of Genetic Disease delves into the causes and effects of canine genetic disease. The responsibilities and obligations of breeders on this issue are covered in four points each, as are definitions of severity. Dr. Padgett's strong views on this subject are emphasized throughout the site.

PennHip Method of Diagnosing Hip Dysplasia

http://www.canismajor.com/dog/pennhip1.html

Detailed information on the newest method of diagnosing canine hip dysplasia can be found within the Dog Owner's Guide site for the PennHip method of diagnosing hip dysplasia.

Different from the standard OFA method of diagnosis, the PennHip method uses a new X-ray technology for assessing the health of canine hips.

Beginning with the Introduction, the site explains the University of Pennsylvania position that a new test was needed to more accurately diagnose hip dysplasia. According to the authors, the standard OFA X-ray method allows a 20–25% chance of producing a dog within a breeding that has canine hip dysplasia.

The test is then explained thoroughly in a section called A New Test, which describes the research done at the University of Pennsylvania by orthopedic surgeons that resulted in the unique PennHip method.

PennHip and OFA: A Comparison covers the difference between the two methods, including details on the requirements for a PennHip diagnosis. Common Questions are answered by veterinarians involved with the method, while the Conclusion discusses the applications of the method's findings and how breeders can use them to help breed better dogs.

FDA Center for Veterinary Medicine

http://www.cvm.fda.gov/

The Food and Drug Administration's Center for Veterinary Medicine (FDA CVM) regulates the manufacturing and distribution of drugs and feed additives for use on animals. If you want to keep up on the latest goings-on in this very important area of veterinary medicine, there is no better site to visit on a regular basis.

The first hypertext link you'll see here is the Important News area, which will take you to various articles on recent developments within the Center for Veterinary Medicine. Announcements on recent drug approvals, committee meetings, and other important happenings can be found here.

In the FDA CVM Documents and Databases area, there is a wealth of information on various topics relating to developments in veterinary drug approvals. Access to the Information and Resources Library, containing public CVM documents of interest to dog owners and those in the veterinary health profession, is here, as well as the FDA-Approved Animal Drug Products Searchable Database, maintained by the Virginia Tech Scholarly Communications Department.

A comprehensive area covering the administrative aspects of the FDA CVM can be found under FDA Center for Veterinary Medicine Offices, including names, address and phone numbers of staff, in addition to organizational charts, annual reports, and other information relating to FDA CVM Offices.

For an overview of the FDA CVM, the area titled For Further Information About the FDA CVM contains basic information about the organization, along with commonly used forms, job announcements and FAQS relating to the agency's work.

One of the handiest aspects of this site is the Related Links and Useful Resources area, which contains links to the *Federal Register,* veterinary resources, other government agencies, colleges of veterinary medicine, and other veterinary-related pages.

Institute for Genetic Disease Control in Animals

http://mendel.berkeley.edu/dogs/gdc.html

Describing itself as an "open registry," the Institute for Genetic Disease Control in Animals maintains a database of genetic history for all breeds of dogs. The registry enables owners, veterinarians, and researchers to trace back the genetic history of any particular dog, as well as study the background of any breed. The purpose of the institute is to help breeders and owners reduce and eventually eliminate genetic disease in purebred dogs.

Unfortunately, the database itself is not accessible from this all-text site, although information on the institute's function and how to obtain access to the registry is here. There is an e-mail link to the institute where interested dog fanciers can ask questions to get more information on this important service.

Pet Health News

http://www.newss.ksu.edu/WEB/News/NewsReleases/
pethealth.html

Part of the Kansas State University Web site, the Pet Health News area ties into the KSU School of Veterinary Medicine. Featuring a galloping Greyhound across the top of the page, Pet Health News strives to help educate people about issues affecting the health of their pets. Dogs feature prominently here, with cats a close second.

The site begins with an area called Pet Myths, where a KSU veterinarian assists pet owners in separating truth from fiction when it comes to medical issues. One question presented here, for example, asks whether the temperature of a dog's nose can indicate its state of health. The answer is that a KSU study of 75 dogs determined that a dog's nose does absolutely nothing to tell us anything about its physical well-being.

Pet Health News also contains information on Perpetual Pet Care, a program developed by the KSU School of Veterinary Medicine. Perpetual Pet Care is a scholarship program for veterinary students funded by the estates of pet owners who have become incapacitated or are deceased. A student cares for the owner's pet when the owner can no longer do so, and a scholarship is awarded in return.

Health care information is also provided in this site in the form of articles, under the areas of Canine Orthopedics, Winter-Time Pet Care, Kennel Cough Vaccine, Dental Care for Pets, Hip Dysplasia, Heat Exhaustion, *E. coli,* Flea Control, Ringworm, and others.

Veterinary Ophthalmology Info Centre

http://bay.netrover.com/%7Eeyevet/info.html

Authored by two veterinary ophthalmologists, this page is devoted strictly to the subject of animal eye care and disease. Because board certified veterinary ophthalmologists do not specialize on a particular type of pet but are required to practice on all creatures, everything from cats to horses is included here. However, there is considerable information relevant to dogs, an animal that is afflicted with a number of different eye disorders.

The first area on the Veterinary Ophthalmology page is Cataracts & Cataract Surgery. A description of cataracts, their types and causes, treatment, and the decision for surgery are all included here in several thorough articles on each subject.

Other areas of particular interest to dog owners include Corneal Ulcers, Prolapsed Gland of the Third Eyelid, Dry Eye, Progressive Retinal Atrophy, Eye Problems in Collies and Sudden Acquired Retinal Degeneration Syndrome (SARDS). All of these ailments are found in canines, and the information presented here emphasizes the conditions as they affect dogs.

VetGen

http://www.vetgen.com

VetGen is a company dedicated to the research and detection of genetic diseases in purebred dogs. Started by molecular geneticists from Michigan State University's School of Veterinary Medicine and the University of Michigan Department of Human Genetics, VetGen provides services in DNA profiling and storage, as well as in other areas of genetics.

The VetGen Web site offers information on the company's services, as well as data on the company's recent discoveries in genetic disease, in its Breakthroughs area. There is also detailed information on tests for conditions such as von Willebrand's disease, copper toxicosis, and phospho-fructokinase deficiency, along with details on DNA profiling, storage, and sample collection. Recommendations on how to use the results of VenGen testing in breeding programs are also included.

Under the Research link, details on current research projects, the company's goals, pedigrees being sought for research, and information for breeders and dog owners on how to get involved with genetic research in purebred dogs are all here. A list of traditional resources on subjects covered in the site is also featured in the References link.

Veterinary Information Network

http://205.138.228.126:80/jolasa/vetquest

The Veterinary Information Network (VIN) is a veterinarian-owned company working to provide information to veterinarians and pet owners on health-related issues. Authors of America Online's Pet Care Forum, VIN also maintains this Web site, which is geared primarily toward veterinarians. However, there is one service here for pet owners that is worth checking out.

On the VIN home page, amidst the varied topics for veterinarians, there is an option called Search. A click on this hyperlink brings up an area where pet owners can look for local veterinarians anywhere in the United States and Canada. Search options include city, state, and zip code of the pet owner, plus board-certified specialty or area of interest of the desired veterinarian.

The search is limited to veterinarians belonging to the Veterinary Information Network, but there are 25,000 veterinary hospitals and clinics listed in the VIN database.

The site also includes a limited section of links to other veterinary pages that can have value to pet owners.

National Animal Control Poison Center
http://www.prodogs.com//chn/napcc/index.htm

Before the College of Veterinary Medicine at the University of Illinois at Urbana–Champaign opened the National Animal Control Poison Center (NACPC) in 1978, pet owners had no centralized information center to turn to during poisoning emergencies. Now, the NACPC provides daily advice and information to dog owners and veterinarians on poison exposures in animals, the great majority of which are dogs.

The NACPC site itself does not offer specifics on poison treatments, but it does provide valuable information on how to contact the NACPC in an emergency. Details on how the center works, what to do if an animal is poisoned and where to get more information on the subject of poison are also included.

To speak with a veterinarian at the NACPC, contact must be made by telephone. Instructions on how to reach one of the veterinarians or board-certified veterinary toxicologists are given here. For general questions on the center, an e-mail address is also provided.

NetVet Veterinary Resources
http://netvet.wustl.edu

The NetVet Veterinary Resources page is authored by the same Webmasters who run the NetVet and Electronic Zoo Web sites. The purpose of the Veterinary Resources site is to organize veterinary and other animal-related information present on the Internet and make it accessible to veterinarians and pet owners alike.

As far as link sites go, this page is impressive. Starting with the What's New area, which contains sites that have been added in recent months, the list of veterinary links is incredibly thorough. Arranged first by the month the link was added to the site and then by subject, veterinary links appear first, with other animal sites following. A search option brings up a list of veterinary search links plus a long list of general search engines.

Other specific veterinary subject links found here are Career (becoming a veterinarian), Education (veterinary colleges around the world), Specialties (veterinary areas of specialization), Organizations (veterinary, animal science, animal welfare, commercial), Veterinary Meetings (conferences around the world), E-Lists (animal-related e-mail lists), Government (general government sites plus those specifically animal related), and several others.

Pets Need Dental Care Too

http://www.petdental.com

Sponsored by the American Veterinary Medical Association, the American Veterinary Dental Society and Hill's Pet Nutrition, the Pets Need Dental Care Too site was created as part of the Pets Need Dental Care Too campaign, a joint effort by the aforementioned organizations to help educate pet owners on how to care for their pets' teeth and gums. The Web site version of the campaign aims to teach pet owners as much about the importance of caring for the dental needs of their cats and dogs as possible. There is no separation of the dog information from the cat information here because dental requirements for both species are virtually the same.

The site begins with a short piece on basic dental care, and then opens up to a page bearing a list of topics from which to choose.

Pets Need Dental Care Too includes two separate information categories: one for veterinarians and one for pet owners. To get to the data for lay people, you must click on the Pet Owners hyperlink. Here, the reasons dental care is necessary are spelled out, and a dog and cat icon beckons browsers "Follow Us." A click on this cartoon pair takes you to a page bearing a three-step program for dental care, along with detailed information on visiting the veterinarian for a check-up and cleaning, dental care at home, and the importance of making a return visit.

Other parts of this site include Quick FAQs, answered by a veterinarian, as well as some fun spots like the Coloring Contest for kids and the Pet Name Poll. One very useful area is the Home Care Tips section, where instructions on how to brush a pet's teeth, the need for good nutrition to tooth and gum care, and other topics are discussed. While reading this, you will undoubtedly find yourself distracted by an entertaining live graphic of a cat and dog brushing their teeth at the top of the page.

Rec.Pets.Dogs Health Care Issues

http://www.zmall.com/pet_talk/dog-faqs/health-care.html

The Health Care Issues area of the Rec.Pets.Dogs page features an abundance of articles on canine afflictions and disease prevention. Written by the site's author, Cindy Tittle Moore, these pieces offer good, solid information for new dog owners or those wanting to learn more about the basics of canine health.

Subjects included here are administering medication, allergies, aging, bathing, dental care, disease transmission to humans, ear care, nutrition, incontinence, spaying and neutering, heat exhaustion, canine puberty, skin problems, taking a dog's temperature, trimming nails, vaccinations, vomiting, and worms.

Deaf Dogs Web Page

http://www.kwic.net/~cairo/deaf.html#BAER

The subject of whether deaf dogs make safe and suitable pets is a controversial one in the world of purebred dogs. Many breeders believe deaf puppies should be euthanized at birth to keep them from potentially passing their deafness along to another generation. Some are also concerned about the safety of humans in a home with a dog who cannot hear. On the other side, there are people who belief that deaf dogs can make good pets in the right home, whether the dog was born deaf or becomes deaf later in life as a result of illness or old age. The Deaf Dogs Web Page is for those dog lovers who fall in the latter category.

Labeled as a resource for people living with deaf dogs, this site provides a wealth of information on coping with canine deafness. While not fancy, it does contain material that is hard to find. Deaf Dog Myths and Information, Deaf Dogs in the Media, and Deafness Incidence Data are all areas worth exploring to learn more about the overall subject of deafness in dogs. For specific details on how to live with a nonhearing animal, areas entitled Training Information and Special Collars are provided. A section on the Brainstem Auditory Evoked Response (BAER), a hearing test used to test hearing in dogs, is also discussed at length.

Information on a deaf dogs e-mail list, plus stories about blind dogs and deaf owners also appear on the page.

Deafness in Dogs and Cats

http://www.lsu.edu/guests/senate/public_html/deaf.htm

For those who want to learn as much about the technical side of congenital hearing loss as they can, there is no better site than Deafness in Dogs and Cats. Filled with data generated by George M. Strain, professor of neuroscience at Louisiana State University, this site provides complete and thorough information on all aspects of deafness in dogs.

Papers and talks by Dr. Strain, who has done extensive research on the subject of canine deafness, make up the bulk of the information in this site. Starting with a list of dog breeds known to have congenital deafness in their backgrounds, a chart specifying the incidence of deafness in dog breeds and an excerpt from a paper by Dr. Strain on the prevalence and diagnosis of deafness in dogs and cats, Deafness in Dogs and Cats brings you into the silent and mysterious world of canine deafness.

There is weighty, scientific evidence available here, including the most recent data analysis on deafness, data analysis based on the hearing of parent dogs and the genetics of deafness. A significant amount of information on the Brainstem Auditory Evoked Response (BAER) test is also presented in a clear, understandable form.

Dr. Strain has authored a number of publications on the subject of canine deafness. The bibliography of his works presented at the end of the site can be a good start on the road to learning even more about this not-uncommon canine malady.

DLM's Canine Page

http://desmodus.biom.cornell.edu/~dlm/canine.html

This simple site is authored by Lab Animal Services employee Dennis L. Martinez, a breeder of Rhodesian Ridgebacks who believes the general public needs more health information about dogs. In this site, Martinez strives to provide answers to simple and commonly asked health questions.

The homespun look of this site contrasts greatly against many of the dryly written and text-heavy places in the canine health category. The opening page bears a large photo of two wolves underscored with the line "The Wolf—Granddaddy to Them All." Nice quotes about dogs from several famous people follow.

Once past this, the site gets serious with several articles on canine health topics. Starting with heartworm, the author discusses general information on this parasitic disease as well as ways to prevent infection. Similar coverage is given to hip dysplasia and urinary stones, and topics like when to vaccinate, spaying and neutering, and food-borne pathogenic microorganisms and natural toxins are also covered. An area called "Things to Ask a Breeder Before Buying," while somewhat out of place with the medical topics on this site, nonetheless provides good information to new puppy buyers.

After all the hard-hitting medical advice, the author has added some levity, showing photos of his dogs enjoying life in upstate New York.

Canine Vaccination Schedule

http://www.acmepet.com/canine/k9vacsch.html

This simple page is part of the overall Acmepet Dog Guide, but is worth mentioning here because it provides a quick and handy reference for canine vaccines.

Presented in chart form, all necessary vaccinations for dogs and puppies are given, including at what age each shot is required. The necessary frequency for each shot is also included. The standard inoculations are listed here in the main part of the chart, while data on other less commonly given vaccines like those for bordatella and Lyme disease are provided separately.

Eliminating Genetic Disease in Dogs: A Buyer's Perspective

http://www.teleport.com/~gback/cg-egdid-mason.html

This site was started by the owner of a Scottish Terrier, whose dog developed von Willebrand's disease, a genetic bleeding disorder. Because open discussions on genetic diseases are often hard to come by in the animal world, this concerned dog owner, who prefers not to use his or her name in the site, created this page as a means of discourse.

With the intention of providing assistance to other dog owners who are living with canine genetic disease and providing information to others interested in the subject, the author hopes to contribute to the ultimate elimination of genetic disease in dogs.

Brief discussions of various inherited diseases are present on this site, including von Willebrand's disease, Collie eye anomaly, portosystemic shunt, hemophilia, Scottie Cramp, hip dysplasia, Legg/Calv Perthes, medial patellar luxation, and craniomandibular osteopathy (CMO). The author also presents an approach to the problem of genetic disease, describes the need for basic education on this subject, and covers other topics relating to the control and elimination of genetic disorders. Lists of health organizations, references, and other materials for further research are also included.

The Virtual Veterinary Center
http://www.dvmedia.com/vetclinic.html

Dr. Jim Humphries is a well-known veterinarian and writer on the subject of dogs. He is also the author of the Virtual Veterinary Center, where he lends some of this expertise on various veterinary subjects for the benefit of Internet users.

In addition to a lot of information on Dr. Humphries and how to order his books and videotapes, there are articles here on flea control, canine maturity, melanoma, appropriate weight for dogs, parvovirus, and cancer, among others. The pieces are short, and the coverage of veterinary topics here is scattered, but there is some good basic information for those just starting out in the research of dogs-related topics.

CHAPTER 3

Training

It goes without saying that an untrained dog is not typically a very popular dog. What some may be surprised to learn is that the untrained dog is also not a very happy dog. Dogs thrive on direction. They feel more secure, more content, when they know their boundaries and when they know who's boss. If there is no one there to teach them their boundaries, to be their boss, they will take on that responsibility themselves. The results—a dog that roams wherever and whenever it pleases and indulges in any behavior it deems pleasant at the moment—can be annoying to the dog's owners and everyone around the animal, and it can be downright dangerous.

Dogs thrive on routine and the knowledge of what is what and who is who in theirenvironment. Training offers them that. Ideally both at home and in the class environment, beginning with the youngest puppies, training instills in dogs a confidence in themselves, in us, and in their place in the world. An added bonus to the training commitment is the bond that builds between an owner and his or her dog when the two work together to master the intimate communication that can exist between the human and canine species.

The following are Web sites representing people and organizations devoted to the fascinating subject that is canine training. Their ultimate goal is to improve the age-old relationship between dogs and their people. Using training in tandem with a knowledge of dog behavior (covered in the next chapter) can help prevent and heal problems that can arise in that relationship.

Raising Your Dog with the Monks of New Skete

http://www.dogsbestfriend.com/

One of the classic books of dog training is *How to Be Your Dog's Best Friend*, by the Monks of New Skete. This world-famous order of monks has dedicated itself to the raising of German Shepherds and to the vocation, if you will, of teaching the public how to train their dogs with love, compassion, patience, and understanding. This book has led to other New Skete training aids in both literary and video-tape format. Now the monks' Web site, which so succinctly reflects the tone that has made the New Skete training materials so phenomenally successful, is headed for that same classic status.

Beautifully illustrated with color photo collages that evoke a sense of mysticism surrounding the dog and the ancient bond we share with that animal, this site is a joy to explore. You may not even realize that you are learning from your journey. For instance, click on the What is New Skete? option from the home page, and you will learn about the monks of New Skete, their monastery, their farm, their dogs, and their "unique vision." You will also be treated to The Voices of New Skete, a fascinating section where the monks themselves speak of their way of life and the dogs with whom they share that life in a very personal and forthright manner.

Another unique feature within this site—and there are many—is the Contests section. Here you can enter contests online by writing four paragraphs or less directly into a space provided about "how your dog has made a positive impact on your life." With a click of a button, you e-mail your entry. Three monthly winners are awarded Monks of New Skete videos, dog biscuits, and books.

Once you have finished your essay, head over to the Questions Answered section of the site, which is essentially a FAQ produced by the monks in response to the questions so often sent their way. Here, via the real-life quandaries faced by dog owners each and every day—house training,

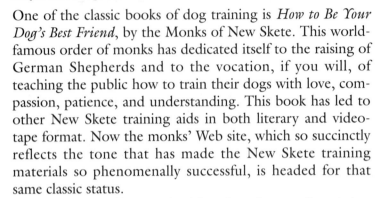

choosing a dog food, puppy biting, etc.—you get a taste of the holistic training methods practiced by the monks at the monastery and promoted in their books and videos. Virtually every dog owner, novice and expert alike, can pick up some valuable tips here, all presented in a gentle, yet clear and concise, manner.

For browsers inspired by the interactivity and philosophy (canine and otherwise) of the Monks of New Skete, the site offers ample information on what made the monks famous: the canine-inspired books and their new video series. Click on The Books, and you will find information on these classic volumes, along with quotes from experts in the field who praise their emphasis on positive and very humane methods. Newer additions to the monks' resume are three videos—The New Skete Way, In the Beginning..., and Obedience—presented with the gentle tone and collage graphics that follow the browser throughout this site.

The site's theme of friendship is evident in the monks' work with their dogs and in the warm and inviting tone of the Web site. The monks encourage the browser to be a dog's best friend, and to "become a friend of New Skete," by providing personal information on themselves and their dogs, and sending along comments and suggestions.

When it is time to leave what is a most unusual yet decidedly enjoyable site, you may feel as if you have made a mini-sojourn to the monastery.

The Dog Obedience & Training Page

http://www.dogpatch.org/obed.html

Mary Jo Sminkey has been busy. She maintains a massive site that is actually a collection of links to all things training.

Essentially one long, continuous home page filled from top to bottom with links to other home pages and to specific material within other sites, this is a one-stop shop for those seeking to enhance their knowledge of dogs and their behavior.

Category headings run the gamut from Advanced/ Competition Obedience Sites to Training Schools and Clubs on the Web, and each is rich with links. Consider for example the Basic Training/Behavior category. Here you will find, among others, "An Obedient Dog is a Happy Dog" from the Adopt a Greyhound Web site, "12 Tips for a Well Behaved Dog" from the American Dog Trainers Network, and "Puppy Biting" from Dog Owner's Guide.

Sites, articles, clubs, trials and events, schools and training products are all here in a site that may not be fancy, but could win awards for organization and bulk of information. It's a good thing that at the bottom of the page, amid yet more boxes of section options that include Agility, Frisbee, and Herding, there's a Search function to help you locate specific information. This is a valuable asset to a site that offers dog lovers everything they could ever need to know about training and behavior and from all different points of view.

Hawaiiana Canine School

http://www.jakenmax.com/~hawaiiana/hcshmpg.htm

When you access the address for Hawaiiana Canine School you know your journey will be different from most you have taken before. Your first clue is the fact that this sprightly, colorful site refers to its home page as the Dog House.

California's Hawaiiana Canine School is a multi-campus facility founded 20 years ago by Sam Alama Kuoha, that promotes the training of dogs with love, respect, and patience. This site, a companion to the schools, strives to put browsers at ease, to show them a good time, and to teach them a thing or two while they're at it. Designed both with fun and ease-of-travel in mind, and liberally decorated with cartoon bone and pawprint icons, this site leads its visitors through the dog house, helping them to learn about dogs and their behavior. The light tone and energetic design make this a great site for kids and adults alike.

Information presented within this site on the school itself is minimal. The majority of it is dominated by educational materials that are as interactive as they are fun to peruse. For example, click on the hyperlink Dog House Fun Facts, and you will be presented with several lively headings that suggest education but emanate fun. These include The Power of Positive Reinforcement, Who's the top dog at your house?, and If I Could Talk to the Animals.... The last of these is especially interesting in that it explains in simple terms the art of reading canine body language and challenges browsers to test their canine savvy.

The Hawaiiana Canine School Web site shines with creativity and energy: it's a great site with lots to offer those who stop by for a visit.

Dr. P's Dog Training Library
http://www.uwsp.edu/acad/psych/dog/library.htm

This site receives many accolades from other sites devoted to the subject of canine training and behavior.

The Dr. P in the site's title is Dr. M. Plonsky, a professor of psychology with expertise in animal behavior and a passion for dog training. As stated in the site's welcoming message, Dr. P's goal is to collect and organize all the information on the Internet pertaining to dog training and "give visitors easy access to it all." Given the current condition of this site, that goal is being met handsomely.

This library is at the outset a list of links and nothing but links to behavior and training information in other sites and to Dr. P's own material. In keeping with the true library spirit, Dr. P acknowledges that the ideas in many of the pieces contradict each other—and Dr. P even disagrees with some—but in this marketplace of ideas, there is room for all.

Designed in a clean, well-organized format (as befits the scientific mind behind it), the hypertext links are arranged in outline form, a simple border of pawprints "walking" up the left side of the screen. The topics presented cover problem diagnosis and solving, basic commands, puppy training, general training issues, housetraining, obedience competition, protection and police dog training, assistance dogs, working, playing, videos, books, events, e-mail discussion groups—the list literally goes on and on. Choose one of these topics and you are whisked away into "The Stacks" for more lists of materials, this time actual articles and sites you can access directly; each organized and properly attributed.

Simply describing Dr. P's immense collection cannot do it justice. It must be seen—and toured—to be believed.

Waltham Pet Foods World of Pet Care

http://www.waltham.com/pets/dogs/pdt.htm

Nestled within this site, sponsored by a major pet food manufacturer, is a detailed page on training. Either check in via the address given here or access it from the main Waltham page from the Pets section, under which you will find Training listed under Dogs.

It seems rather simplistic at first: simple text about training dogs. But within that text are hyperlinks that carry browsers even deeper into the subject matter.

Hidden behind that original text is in-depth information on, among other topics, canine socialization, vocalization, the senses, body language, and, given the sponsor of this site, feeding behavior. Take the time to explore these passages, all of which are directly accessible from the text of the original training page.

More direct hyperlinks on the training page take the browser into a detailed treatise on house training and obedience training. This latter section is especially impressive in that it first lists the commands. Choose "sit," for instance, and you will suddenly find yourself in a virtual training session, the basics of this command laid out in a lovely, step-by-step progression illustrated with soft line drawings. The user-friendliness of this information might entice some otherwise disinterested pet owners into implementing some of the training lessons learned here, and make life just a little bit easier for dog and owner alike.

West Virginia Canine College

http://www.wvcc.com/

Calling all would-be professional trainers: If a career guiding and molding the behavior of dogs is your dream, check out the Web site for West Virginia Canine College. While this site acts as a promotional tool for this school for dog trainers, it also presents a great deal of information on the career choice itself.

With a plain, simply designed home page that lists the link choices beneath the school's German Shepherd logo, it is easy to learn what you wish to learn. Link choices include a message from the president and in-depth information on the various courses of study, which include narcotic and police dog training. But of utmost value to those considering a career in dog training is the Introduction option. Here you will find an excellent essay on dog training as a career that covers all aspects of the field, from salaries to the need for dog trainers, to the pros and cons of the job to what the job actually entails. It is an excellent overview.

Elsewhere you will learn about the school's philosophy. While there are no state or national requirements for dog trainers to be licensed or certified, not surprisingly, this school believes in such training and qualifications. It also pursues, as we learn in the Institutional Philosophy section, a psychological approach to dog training, which typically requires some in-depth training of the trainers themselves.

All in all, this site helps ensure that people who enroll in their school are prepared and well-informed. These educators obviously take their vocation seriously and expect their students to do the same.

Canines of America's World of Dog Training

http://www.canines.com/index.html

It may take you a little while to figure out what Canines of America's World of Dog Training is all about, but once you do, you will find a great deal of valuable information waiting. Keep in mind that the bar of dog-bone options at the left of every screen is your key to getting through this rather large site.

Sponsored by Canines of America Center for Dog Training & Clinical Behavior Therapy, a large, full-service, New York dog training academy that was founded by behaviorist Bob De Franco (who is also the site's Webmaster), Canines of America is devoted to all aspects of dog training This covers the gamut from obedience training for competition to young puppy socialization to therapy dog training to behavior problem solving and beyond, all reflected in the logo that appears throughout the pages—a smiling hound in cap and gown, holding a diploma in its paw.

Because it represents an actual training facility which serves much of the northeastern United States, as well as efforts to impart information about behavior and training, you will find an abundance of promotional material within these pages. For example, click on Who We Are from the home page and you will learn all about the services offered at the training facility itself, including various training programs, the companion television program Companion Animal Network's Pet News, and the internship program where fledgling trainers can be trained and certified. You will find such information in many sections, but work your way down the dog-bone bar and you will ultimately find information from which all dog owners and their dogs can benefit.

Click on Dog Behavior, to learn about a large selection of behavior problems. Click on Digging, for example, and enjoy a concise, reader-friendly fact sheet that explains first that digging is a very natural behavior for a dog, followed by details on what to do (designate a spot in the yard where the dog is allowed to dig and reward it for doing so). A similar section is available for that age-old problem of house training, which subsequently offers you choices on teaching a dog to eliminate either outdoors or indoors on newspaper.

The training philosophy on this site is obviously one of redirecting energy in more positive directions via positive reinforcement. In pursuing this, it also promotes a holistic approach to living with dogs, offering browsers sections on Dog Care, Pet Loss, Dog Rescue, and even one on links to other dog-related sites. Take the time to move around this site and see why it is of value not only to those who take advantage of the services offered by Canines of America's training facility, but to the general population of dog owners as well.

Don't Shoot the Dog!

http://dontshootthedog.com/

First, you may be wondering about the title of this site. Don't Shoot the Dog! is the title of a dog training book written by the proprietor of this site, Karen Pryor. It refers to the sound idea that before you are driven to extremes by a misbehaving dog, training should be considered as an alternative.

That alternative is what this site and all of Pryor's work is all about. Pryor is an expert in the field of clicker training, which she describes at the head of her home page as "the new art of teaching and training." A method that shuns force and punishment, clicker training finds its roots in a psychological theory far too technical to explore here. That theory has resulted in Pryor's technique for communicating with dogs, employing a small hand-held clicker that acts as a "yes signal" to the dog as it obeys various commands.

This principal is outlined in Pryor's book and on this site as well. Not simply a promotional piece for Pryor, this site instructs browsers about the basics of clicker training and then offers them the tools to get started. This begins with the background information on the home page, which leads into a catalog of Pryor's instructional books and videos, as well as information on e-mail discussion groups and Pryor's seminars and newsletter.

Also available are home-page hyperlinks to brass tacks information. Click on Memos from Karen, for example, and take a fascinating tour through actual dated cases on which she has consulted, trains of thought, and questions and answers, all presented with a personal, friendly tone. Another hyperlink of interest is Fifteen Rules and Frequently Asked Questions. Here you are offered succinct information on getting started with clicker training, advice on avoiding frustrations along the way, a primer on how to clicker train, and words of encouragement. All of this is set against an attractive backdrop that makes a tour through Don't Shoot the Dog! a pleasant experience designed to remove any thoughts of firearms from the mind of even the most frustrated dog owner.

All About Dogs: Obedience Training

http://www.ptialaska.net/~pkalbaug/traindex.html

The Obedience Training page of the very large All About Dogs Web site, designed by P. Kalbaugh, is rich with hyperlinks to a variety of articles and home pages, all with an eye toward the behavior and training of dogs, and an allegiance to positive training methods.

Though graphics are minimal on this page, its tone in presenting its' many options is light and friendly. That's fortunate, because one could spend a very long time in this site, increasing his or her knowledge dramatically in the process. As this page is quite long—essentially one long home page with an incredible amount of information—take advantage of the two hyperlinks that appear directly beneath the home page opening greeting. They will convey you quickly and easily to the various sections of the home page.

The page is divided into sections, the first being Puppy and Basic Training, followed by the sub-category: Puppy Issues and Training. No doubt any new puppy owner would find this section of value as it presents articles on reinforcement, aggression, puppy development and a listing of professional associations for obedience instructors. Prospective puppy owners can best take advantage of this information by surfing this valuable collection of material **before** they become new puppy owners.

What sets this list apart from others of its kind is the fact that editorial comments appear with each hyperlink, informing the browser just why this particular article, this particular link, is of value. A FAQ from the Monks of New Skete, for example, receives a rousing thumbs up and the comment that this is a "Must see!" This simple feature indicates a dedication to the subject matter since someone is taking the time to ensure what is presented on this site is up to the high standards of positive training.

American Dog Trainers Network

http://www.inch.com/~dogs/

The mission of the American Dog Trainers Network (ADTN) is made clear from the moment you enter its home page: "Promoting humane education, responsible pet care, and positive motivational dog training."

First, choose one of the many section options presented for your review. Click on Dog Training, for instance—a logical place to start—and you will be treated to an extensive, reader-friendly, primer on what dog training is and the many ways in which it is pursued. Presented almost exclusively in bullet form, this section is fun to read and won't take all day. The site deserves accolades for this straight, no-nonsense presentation of what can be a rather complicated subject.

Once you begin to explore the choices offered, you will find that this site is not only rich with information, but well-designed and well-organized navigationally, faced with so many choices, you won't ever have to fear being lost among the hyperlinks. And speaking of links, this site boasts an excellent collection, arranged both by subject and alphabetically.

The Dog Owners' Helpline, a free telephone hot-line service you can read about here, is provided by the ADTN to dog owners nationwide who need help with their pets. Also special is the Articles section, accessible with a click from the home page. A grid of square color photos, each illustrating a topic, offer access to articles like Prevent Your Puppy's Destructive Chewing and Protect Your Pet from Being Stolen—and be impressed yet again at how much wonderful information is available within this site. And it's so easy to access. This site indeed provides a service in the truest sense of the word.

Seeking to make the ADTN site a valuable resource to dog owners, trainers and even the media, director Robin Kovary speaks personally to browsers and urges them to keep coming back, as the site promises to expand to meet the needs of dog owners.

Brunton Canine Training Services

http://www.thenerve2.com/silk/intro.htm

With a polite, straightforward introduction, British Columbia dog trainer Dennis Brunton welcomes you to the Brunton Canine Training Services home page. He lays out exactly what you can expect from this page—a discussion of "all aspects of owning a dog," which of course includes behavior—and invites browsers to offer their input.

The vehicle used to convey his information is an online monthly newsletter, accessible by clicking on the hypertext word *newsletter* in the Introduction. Devoid of graphics, except for a pawprint here and there on the menu bar, this is a text-heavy site, though its tone is warm. The newsletter articles are to the point and are obviously directed at pet owners, as it is pet owners and their dogs that Brunton specializes in training.

The newsletter acts as an excellent promotion for the hands-on training services provided at Brunton's facility and the philosophies that guide that operation. Information on the courses offered there are included on this site, in a quiet, reserved fashion. Click on Family Courses, for example, and you will learn about Brunton's Companion Concept Program, a step-by-step course designed to train both families and their dogs to cohabitate successfully.

For those who don't happen to live in Brunton's neck of the woods, click on the Training Video option on the menu bar and you'll find that Brunton also offers Video Assisted Training in his tape Dog Obedience Training...the Easy Way. But instead of offering the video for sale as one would expect, he instead offers a list of libraries in British Columbia, Alberta and Prince Edward Island from which the tape can be borrowed.

It is precisely this humility that makes this plain-looking site so attractive. It stands quietly as an example of substance over style, and there is much to be gained by taking a brief tour through its messages.

The Greyhound Project

http://csa.delta1.org/~greyhound/obeddog.html

We could all use some advice from time to time. The Greyhound Project offers valuable advice not only to those who live with Greyhounds, but those who live with any dog. Just come in to this page, which is accessible either directly with the address given here or from the Greyhound Project's home page (from which you click on the Some Advice option), and you will be presented with a lovely article, entitled "An Obedient Dog Is A Happy Dog," that illustrates, via examples from author Audrey A. Schneider's own four-dog household, that dogs are indeed happier when they know what is expected of them.

This is an important message. Far too many dog owners out there hold to the misunderstanding that training is somehow mean, that it squelches a dog's inner spirit. Wrong. Training can indeed be mean if it is carried out in a cruel fashion. But training conducted with positive reinforcement and respect can be a dog's best friend. The Greyhound Project knows this, as they, and other organizations across the country that take in retired racing Greyhounds and adopt them out to new homes, experience daily the miracles that a little compassionate training can do.

Inspired by the Project's success, perhaps you'll enjoy a tour of the other realms of their site, as well, which include an excellent link page to canine activities and organizations.

Flying Dog Press

http://www.flyingdogpress.com/articles.htm

Flying Dog Press is an online catalog company that offers various dog-related materials to the public. But nestled within this site is a rich font of information that, like Flying Dog Press itself, is devoted to the training and behavior of dogs.

Enter this site and you will find yourself immersed in information: a collection of articles written by celebrated dog trainer and Flying Dog Press owner Suzanne Clothier. These easily accessible, well-written, and informative articles are of great value to the general dog-owning public, given the articles' emphasis on positive interactions between dogs and people, and the how-to tips for achieving that noble goal.

Click on 10 Tips for Problem Behavior, for example, and you will receive some valuable tips on controlling the dog and the situation and allowing your dog to be a dog. Throughout the articles, Clothier exhibits a sound understanding of dog behavior and a respectful approach to dealing with it successfully. While the presence of these articles on this site acts as a public service, they also promote Clothier's mail-order booklets, and videos, etc. If you feel so inspired, access to the online catalog is available at the conclusion of each article.

Dog Owner's Guide

http://www.canismajor.com/dog/topic1.html#Manners

Everything you ever wanted to know about dogs: That is what is provided on this extensive list of hyperlinks within the Dog Owner's Guide Web site Topic List. Enter this page and you are greeted by an illustration of a smiling hound sitting at a computer.

The wealth of information represented within this scroll of subjects and articles is nothing short of astounding. Before you begin your journey, take a gander at the Topics Available list at the top of the page—a lifesaving tool for navigating what lies ahead. Of interest here are the Manners & Training, and Behavior and Aggression sections, each of which is accessible quickly and easily with a click on the hyperlink titles on the topics list.

First stop: Manners & Training. Interested in obedience training your dog (always a valuable activity for any dog)? You'll find plenty of well-written, in-depth articles to prepare you and encourage you to take that step. Wondering why all the fuss about dog crates? Click on "Dog crates" and "More on dog crates," and learn all you need to know about this very effective housetraining aid. Questions on kids and dogs, wildlife and dogs, biting dogs....virtually anything you're looking to explore on this very important subject—are answered here.

Now on to behavior and aggression. The topics of dog bites, canine aggression, the importance of socialization, canine dominance, viciousness and more are presented in clear, easy-to-read-and-navigate detail by a variety of qualified experts. This area addresses what can be a negative aspect of dog ownership by offering remedies and solutions. The first step is understanding these issues—what makes a dog tick and how to recognize when a screw is loose. The next step is learning what to do about them. Some hints? "Give that dog a job to keep him happy," advises a selection from this list. Or how about some "Canine Playtime." It's all here. Take advantage of it.

Dog Training Weekly

http://www.k9.co.uk/dog_training_weekly

Hailing from the United Kingdom is Dog Training Weekly, a site that is essentially an online newsletter, the official Journal of the Dog Training Clubs of Great Britain. American dog fanciers will certainly enjoy searching this site to see what's happening with their British counterparts and how the dog world there differs from that in the States, picking up some helpful tips along the way.

Designed for people with aspirations to competitive obedience, agility and working trials, this site is essentially one long page of text almost completely free of hyperlinks. Changed monthly, it is obviously meant for browsers to read, absorb and wait for next month's edition. Though it is not fancy in design, it is rich in information that includes articles on training trends, training tips and personal accounts from trainers and owners; veterinary information and advice; a diary of events; show reports; and information on commercially available training products.

Though this site's focus is on training, Dog Training Weekly is willing to address other aspects of living with dogs, as well, thus achieving an almost full-service informational status. But regardless of the subject matter presented in a given section, it remains informative and is ever willing to offer words of encouragement: Yes, you can teach an old dog new tricks; yes, training is critical to family harmony; and yes, any breed can be trained.

Behavior

Closely related to the subject of Chapter 3, Training, is canine behavior. The two are not necessarily one and the same: Training aims to teach a dog certain behaviors and responses, typically on command, and often performed in structured obedience competitions for various titles. Behavior, on the other hand, refers to the dog's innate responses to stimuli in its environment. Unpopular behavior is often the reason dogs are abandoned or given up to shelters.

Consider the case of a dog that suffers from a chronic inability to be separated from its owner. Such a dog may bite out of fear or aggression or chew and destroy everything in its owner's home. Now place this dog in the care of an individual who does not have the time, the knowledge or the inclination to work with the dog to mold its behavior in more positive directions. This situation will result in conflict. Behind virtually every identifiable canine behavior problem there exists a very good reason for that behavior: the dog is lonely, the dog is afraid, the dog has never been taught otherwise. The canine behaviorist is trained to recognize the problem, to find the problem's root, and, with the owner's help, to implement a program leading to a solution.

The Web sites in this chapter, devoted to canine behavior, will help owners to understand why their dogs are acting in a particular manner and offer solutions that will make both dog and owner happier.

Campbell's Pet Behavior Resources

http://www.Webtrail.com/petbehavior/index.html

With his simple, rather unadorned Web site, respected animal behaviorist William Campbell has accomplished something great. While information on canine behavior and training is meant to inspire interaction between owners and their dogs, Web sites and other written documents devoted to these topics are not always considered interactive in nature. Campbell's Pet Behavior Resources is a welcome exception.

Though on its face the rather plain, text-heavy home page that welcomes you into this site may appear purely informational, divided into sections with hyperlinks here and there, you soon discover that those sections and their corresponding hyperlinks will lead you into new territory that makes a journey through this site as fun as it is informative.

Oregon-based behaviorist Campbell, author of the books *Behavior Problems in Dogs* and *Owner's Guide to Better Behavior in Dogs*, is known primarily for his devotion to positive reinforcement in training and what he calls "the jolly routine." Campbell's program is designed to teach even the most severely troubled dog to turn his old troubles into positive additions to his environment.

The same respectful philosophy and approach that Campbell employs in his training pervades this site, which is the perfect complement to Campbell's quarterly *Pet BehavioRx Newsletter* (to which you may subscribe online). You may use the straightforward home-page hyperlinks, to access such informative articles as Guide to Selecting a Behavior Consultant and How Do Dogs Think?

When visiting the home page, you will notice two sections that are quite interactive in character.

The first of these, The Case of the Month, outlines real-life cases that have been sent to Mr. Campbell (old-age urination, poop eating, etc.), and you are offered the opportunity to figure out the cause and the solution.

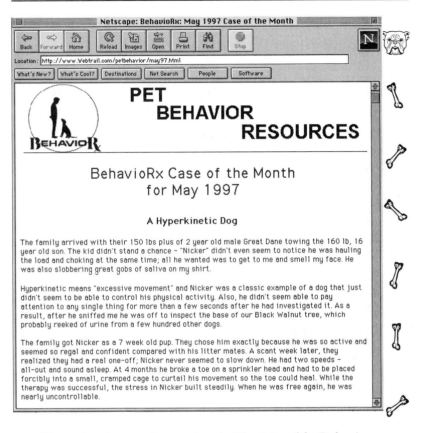

PET
BEHAVIOR
RESOURCES

BehavioRx Case of the Month
for May 1997

A Hyperkinetic Dog

The family arrived with their 150 lbs plus of 2 year old male Great Dane towing the 160 lb, 16 year old son. The kid didn't stand a chance - "Nicker" didn't even seem to notice he was hauling the load and choking at the same time; all he wanted was to get to me and smell my face. He was also slobbering great gobs of saliva on my shirt.

Hyperkinetic means "excessive movement" and Nicker was a classic example of a dog that just didn't seem to be able to control his physical activity. Also, he didn't seem able to pay attention to any single thing for more than a few seconds after he had investigated it. As a result, after he sniffed me he was off to inspect the base of our Black Walnut tree, which probably reeked of urine from a few hundred other dogs.

The family got Nicker as a 7 week old pup. They chose him exactly because he was so active and seemed so regal and confident compared with his litter mates. A scant week later, they realized they had a real one-off; Nicker never seemed to slow down. He had two speeds - all-out and sound asleep. At 4 months he broke a toe on a sprinkler head and had to be placed forcibly into a small, cramped cage to curtail his movement so the toe could heal. While the therapy was successful, the stress in Nicker built steadily. When he was free again, he was nearly uncontrollable.

The other interactive section is The Monthly Behavior Quiz, which also tests the browser's dog-behavior instincts with real-life cases from Campbell's clients. Don't be surprised if in the midst of your activities as virtual behaviorist, you realize, hey, you're really enjoying this—and learning something too.

As an added bonus, a journey through Campbell's Pet Behavior Resources can't help but motivate owners to get even more involved with their own dogs once they shut off the computer—and with far more confidence than they had before their cyber journey.

The Association of Pet Behaviour Counsellors (England)

http://Webzone1.co.uk/www/apbc/

In 1989, the Association of Pet Behaviour Counsellors (APBC), a network of animal behavior counselors committed to upholding a certain level of quality both in practice and ethics, was founded in England.

Given England's relatively advanced views on the humane treatment of animals (the practice of ear cropping, for example, is outlawed in that country), this was certainly the logical home for an organization of that kind.

With a dual mission in mind—to act as a communication tool for members and as an information source for pet owners—the APBC Web site achieves its goals handsomely. It employs a clean, simple, text-heavy design, enabling browsers to navigate its terrain quickly and efficiently, always with ready hyperlink access to the home page, which here is called the Main Index.

A logical place to begin is the code of conduct that appears in the About the APBC section. Reading through the stringent guidelines, you will see just how seriously this organization takes animal behavior and their own vocational role in helping pet owners deal with it successfully. They are portrayed in the process as a group of individuals at a level of professionalism on par with doctors, lawyers, and veterinarians.

Another valuable asset is the Pet Behavior Therapy FAQ accessible from the home page, an excellent document directed to the pet owner. It not only informs the user that a pet behavior counselor deals with the more serious problems that can arise in the pet and owner relationship, but also guides him or her through a visit with a counselor.

Click on the Articles section of the home page for a variety of documents contributed by APBC members and APBC news releases, all directed to the pet owner. Written in a lively, reader-friendly style, these seek to enhance the pet owner's understanding of the animals with whom they live. Typical issues covered include barking (it's natural but should be controlled), the "shocking truth" about shock collars (the APBC condemns them), and puppy socialization (why it's necessary, how to do it).

Dog-Play: Behavior, Socialization, and Training

http://www.dog-play.com/behavior.html

Within the expansive Dog-Play Web site, a guide to "Having Fun with Your Dog," there is a valuable page devoted to the subjects of behavior, socialization and training, which are the fundamental core to the success of any canine activity.

The site is led off by a message from Diane Blackman, author of all the original material here, and a woman who obviously takes her work very seriously. Following the introductory passage, you will come across some excellent links to other Web sites and to sections in other related regions of Dog-Play itself, such as Kids and Dogs and the Canine Good Citizen Test. Each of these has been reviewed and approved personally by Blackman, and she tells you why right there next to the hyperlink.

Personal and direct in its first-person presentation, this page provides not only links, but also sound, in-depth information from Blackman herself. In the course of your explorations, you may also be anxious to click on the link to "Dog Training—Fast and Simple." Do so, and you're in for a surprise.

All we can say here is remember that the force behind this site and the author of this particular piece is deeply devoted to sound training and long-term commitments.

Doggie Door to Canine Behavior

http://members.aol.com/brandynjoe/doggie/index.htm

It may take you a while, but with some practice you will figure out how to navigate the Doggie Door to Canine

Behavior Web site. Indeed doors are all over this site, and it's nice that it's proprietor and Webmaster, Brandy J. Lyle, provided visitors with ample instructions on how to navigate its various environs.

This is a fun, busy site (almost too busy when you're trying to figure out what's what) with adjustable framing and animated graphics and sounds. All of this comes together to celebrate the importance of canine training and behavior.

At the top of your screen, the home page boasts a long, multiscreen menu bar of iconed options—doggie doors—from which to choose. Click on About Doggie Door to Canine Behavior just to get your bearings and figure out where you want to go. Within this section you learn under the guidance of Brandy Lyle, who seeks to provide browsers with sound behavior information.

To discover how the site pursues this goal, take a trip through the menu bar, one icon at a time. My Doghouse, Your Doghouse, for instance, invites browsers to ask questions. Choose from the pertinent subject headings (Barking, Aggression at Dogs or People, etc.) that appear along the top of the screen, or check in to previous questions and answers also available.

Another section that garners much attention is The Puppy Place. Once you click this option the top menu bar transforms into icons of puppies eating, sleeping, playing, and peeing. Click on an icon and learn more about the particular subject it illustrates.

The home page menu options are abundant, as is the friendly feel to this site that is essentially presented from the side of the dogs. While these pages are devoted to Lyle's point of view, she invites comments and questions.

Dog Bite Prevention

http://www.ci/madison.wi.us/health/dogbites.html

Taken from information provided by the Humane Society of the United States, this site is more of a document than a

Web site, but it is a document of critical importance to dog and non-dog people alike.

Each year, more and more cases of dog bites are reported as society becomes increasingly urban and suburban in composition. Simply put, we are living closer and closer together, and the lack of space is leading to more clashes between dogs and humans. This results in the rise of dog bites as a public health problem and would-be death sentences for dogs.

The problem is that far too many adults don't know how to prevent dog bites, and far too many children are not taught how to behave around dogs. The two-pronged solution to this problem, then, is education and prevention, as spelled out here.

Of value to both children and adults, the document begins with the warning that "every dog has the capacity to bite." If you abide by the recommendations that follow, you need not become a victim of a dog bite or play a role in involving a dog in such an incident.

Laid out in simple bulleted-list form and written in clear, concise language, this multisectioned page presents all you need to know about this serious topic. The sections include When Dogs Bite, Do's and Don'ts Around Dogs, How To Tell When a Dog Might Bite, What To Do If You're Threatened by a Dog, What To Do If You Get Bitten, and How To Keep Your Dog from Becoming a "Problem" Dog. So read it, and pass it on.

Nutrition

Years ago, no one thought much about canine nutrition. Dogs eat meat. End of story. But that isn't the end of the story. Within the past 30 years or so, much has been learned about canine and general pet health. We now know that dogs require much more nutritionally than a slab of raw meat and a pat on the head.

Nutrition's new-found respect is evident in the attention it now garners in veterinary school curricula and in the hundreds of pet-food manufacturing companies that have cropped up, all in search of the optimum diet for canine health. One fact we have acquired is that dogs are not pure carnivores. They require some grain and vegetable material in their diets in addition to meat, and considerable research has gone into determining the perfect balance of nutrients.

We have also learned that there is no one optimal diet for dogs. As a dog grows and develops, its nutritional needs change. Developments in canine nutrition have ensured that as it reaches each new stage, the dog will have specialized foods available to satisfy its nutritional requirements. A puppy requires a high-energy food to accommodate growth. A moderately active, healthy adult will thrive on a high-quality maintenance diet, while a high-power canine athlete (e.g., dogs on a sled-racing team) or a pregnant or lactating female will require a special high-energy diet. An older dog may fare best on a diet that is lower in fat and calories (as will, of course, an overweight dog that can now diet without feeling deprived), and dogs with various ailments may benefit from one of the special prescription diets now on the market.

continued after the feature section

The Iams Company Home Page

http://www.iamsco.com/

One would expect a major pet food manufacturer to have a large, well-designed, multilayered Web site to promote its products and the importance of proper pet nutrition, and that is exactly what the Iams Company has done. From your first moment within this site's home page, you will sense its commitment to nutritional education when you see the collage of images of people and their pets and read the mission statement ("To enhance the well-being of dogs and cats by providing world-class quality foods.").

From there, the site moves on to present a variety of nutrition- and health-related menu options on a colorful menu bar on the left side of the screen and on a hyperlink list at the bottom. The topics offered provide information about the Iams Company and its products and general pet nutrition, all of which can come in handy for the pet owner.

For information about Iams itself, click on About Iams. You'll find an illustrated history of the company, which was founded a half a century ago by self-taught animal nutritionist Paul Iams, and information about the Paul F. Iams Technical Center and Animal Care Facility, which is where the company tests its foods on resident dogs and cats, referred to here respectfully as "our four-legged associates." The most efficient and accurate way to test foods is with genuine subjects, and all the major pet food companies test their products according to national guidelines to ensure that dogs and cats nationwide will receive proper nutrition. Also accessible from the Iams home page are sections on Products, Customer Service, and Employment.

For more general nutrition information, browsers may check out two other valuable sections, also accessible from the home page. One choice is the Food for Thought Fact Book. Essentially a miniature home page of its own, this section opens with four illustrated icons from which browsers are invited to choose. The question mark icon leads browsers into a section that explains the Fact Book

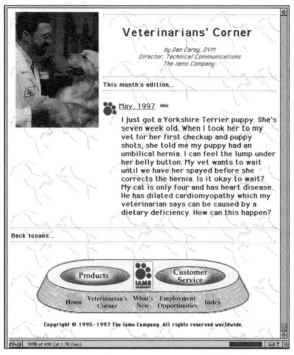

Veterinarians' Corner

by Dan Carey, DVM
Director, Technical Communications
The Iams Company

This month's edition...

🐾 <u>May, 1997</u> NEW

I just got a Yorkshire Terrier puppy. She's seven week old. When I took her to my vet for her first checkup and puppy shots, she told me my puppy had an umbilical hernia. I can feel the lump under her belly button. My vet wants to wait until we have her spayed before she corrects the hernia. Is it okay to wait? My cat is only four and has heart disease. He has dilated cardiomyopathy which my veterinarian says can be caused by a dietary deficiency. How can this happen?

Back Issues...

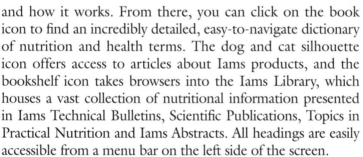

Products   Customer Service

Home   Veterinarian's Corner   What's New   Employment Opportunities   Index

99% of 49K (at 1.7K/sec)

and how it works. From there, you can click on the book icon to find an incredibly detailed, easy-to-navigate dictionary of nutrition and health terms. The dog and cat silhouette icon offers access to articles about Iams products, and the bookshelf icon takes browsers into the Iams Library, which houses a vast collection of nutritional information presented in Iams Technical Bulletins, Scientific Publications, Topics in Practical Nutrition and Iams Abstracts. All headings are easily accessible from a menu bar on the left side of the screen.

Another valuable section accessible from the home-page menus is the Veterinarian's Corner (listed as Ask the Veterinarian on the menu). Here you will find a list of nutrition questions that is updated monthly. This site is filled with information and answers to questions that pet-owning browsers probably didn't know they had. It is nice to know that the answers to those questions may be found in a site that is pleasantly designed and easy to navigate.

Regardless of which diet you choose, certain tenets of feeding apply to all dogs. Make sure the food is fresh and that it comes from a reputable source, divide the dog's daily ration into two or three feedings offered throughout the day if possible, supplement the diet with a constant supply of fresh clean water, and resist the temptation to offer the dog table scraps or other "people-food" treats, which can lead to obesity.

While advances in canine and pet nutrition have been made, you won't find pages and pages of nutrition sites on the Internet, nor will you find long lists of nutrition links scattered through the many dog-related sites on the Web. What you will find, however, is information on this important aspect of dog care tucked inside larger sites that address general dog care, and, of course, within sites sponsored by pet food manufacturers. The information is out there; it just requires a bit of browser effort to find it.

Purina Pet Care Center

http://www.purina.com/

One of best-known names in pet foods is Ralston Purina. Within its large Web site that covers all aspects of pet care, browsers can find extensive nutrition coverage. You may begin on the home page, where a welcoming passage laced with hyperlinks and an accompanying menu bar appear. Choose Pet Care, and then from another colorful menu, choose the Pet Nutrition option. This presents you with hyperlinks to The Story of Purina Nutrition Research, Comparing Pet Foods, Reading Food Labels, and What Not To Feed Your Puppy, all of which offer general nutrition information of value to all pet owners.

The Library/Conference section, also accessible from the homepage menu, boasts an abundant collection of articles on canine (and feline) health and nutrition, which may be located via a long list of hyperlinks presented after the introduction or through an in-house search engine that will help you locate specific topics. Once you have become a pet nutrition expert, you may want to take advantage of the easy access to the rest of the pet care information presented within this site.

Ralston Purina Company
http://www.ralston.com/pethome.html

For a more in-depth presentation of the Ralston Purina Company and its products, visit this more specialized site. Here you will find hyperlinks to areas devoted specifically to Purina pet products as well as to the company itself. While you're here, check out the Purina Farms Visitors Center (http://www.ralston.com/farm.html). This page is devoted to the unique facility where the various Purina foods are tested on live dogs and cats in an attempt to provide these animals with the best possible nutrition. According to the introduction to this section, 150,000 people visit this facility each year, and now browsers can do so via the Internet. The Visitor Center home page and hyperlinks provideaccess to articles about the center and its activities.

Pet Corner: Feeding and Basic Nutrition
http://www.pet-vet.com/10057.htm

Pet Corner is a large pet site devoted to all species of pet and all aspects of their care. One of those aspects, of course, is nutrition, and you will find the site's canine Feeding and Basic Nutrition page within the larger Dogs section. Authored by renowned veterinary dermatologist and author Dr. Lowell Ackerman, this page offers an abundance of detailed information presented in a no-nonsense style.

The main page, which offers a brief introduction to canine nutrition, opens with a list of hyperlink options to such topics as Food Selection and Feeding, Nutrition and the Health of Your Pet, and Obesity. Also covered are more technical topics, such as cardiomyopathy (heart disease), an introduction to essential fatty acids, and a carbohydrate overview. The combination of technical information and brass-tacks advice on feeding dogs right—which includes information about food types and feeding strategies—makes this site invaluable to all pet owners, both those who are already well-versed in canine nutrition and those who are just beginning to study the topic.

Dogs UK — Nutrition Listing

http://dspace.dial.pipex.com/willchapman/c4bnutri.htm

One of the few link listings you will find devoted solely to nutrition is located within the Dogs UK Web site, which offers browsers links to more than 1,600 dog pages. While the nutrition section is not lengthy, it is nevertheless rich in valuable topics pertaining to nutrition. These include, among others, Why do dogs eat grass?, Doggie Treat Recipes, Diet, Nutrients, and Preparing your dog's food. At the bottom of this link page, you are then offered easy access back to the Dogs UK home page just in case you are inspired to explore some of the other topics included here, as well. This entire site is definitely one that deserves to be bookmarked.

Waltham World of Pet Care

http://www.waltham.com/

You will find nutrition information scattered throughout the large, colorful Web site of UK-based Waltham Pet Foods. The brightly colored home page has a menu of cartoon-illustrated choices that will take you to sections on Waltham (maker of Kal Kan and Pedigree dog foods), Pets (general pet care, including thorough coverage of canine nutrition), Vets (emphasizing the company's commitment to encouraging veterinary interest and involvement in pet nutrition), and PetZone (a fun section for younger browsers).

In the Pets section you will find a page of lively text laced with hypertext phrases and a list of pet-care subjects, the first of which is Feeding. Here you will find out just how complicated this seemingly simple task can be. Once within the Feeding page, you will find yet another list of topics, including A balanced diet, Bones and milk, Puppies, Growing dogs, Working dogs, and Older dogs. Hyperlink access to the Waltham feeding guide, a detailed grid that should help pet owners determine how much their dogs should eat each day based on their size and activity levels, is also offered here.

As you travel through this site, make time for the virtual tour of the Waltham Centre for Pet Nutrition. As the introduction to this page explains, "The Waltham Centre is home to our pet dogs and cats which are lovingly cared for." Indeed, every pet food manufacturer requires the services of such animals as test subjects for their foods. Within this page you can meet those dogs, which represent 20 different breeds of all shapes and sizes, and get a look at the grounds. By the time you finish the tour, you'll no doubt have more respect for what it takes to make sure a dog eats right.

Doggie Drive-Thru

http://www.doggie-drive-thru.com/

In 1990, a drive-through restaurant catering to dogs opened in Indiana. That restaurant, the Original Doggie-Drive-Thru, attracted considerable media attention, and it became a rousing success. Today, it sponsors its own Web site that advertises not only the Doggie-Drive-Thru but the line of treats it inspired—Maggie's Biscuit Treats—which are available by mail. Light, browser-friendly, and well-illustrated with photographs of the restaurant and the cheese and whole wheat treats it features, this site is fun and easy to navigate. A menu bar on the home page (and on all subsequent pages) offers access to such sections as Menu, Pet Tips, and History. Should you feel inspired, click on the Order optionto find out how you can bring a little bit of Doggie-Drive-Thru home to your own pet.

The Dog's Kitchen

http://www.clever.net/chrisco/kitchen/dogskit.html

The Dog's Kitchen offers a different viewpoint on canine nutrition. While most experts agree that high-quality commercial pet food is best for most dogs, there are a few dog owners who prefer to cook for their dogs themselves. Of course, that can be dangerous if all the proper nutrients are not included in a home-cooked meal, and preparing such meals can be incredibly time-consuming. But those who take the time and make the effort to do it right can make a success of cooking for their dogs.

While The Dog's Kitchen is primarily a page that promotes Johnny Tom's how-to video on home cooking for canines, it also provides good background information on this concept for those considering the possibility. Covering such topics as What Kind of Diet Is It?, What Ingredients Should I Use?, Would This Increase My Dog's Performance? and Will My Dog Enjoy Long Life? Much research—and preferably a veterinarian's approval—is required before deciding to take on the responsibility of providing your dog's nourishment. This site can help.

The Pomerama's Dog Biscuit, Treat, and Food Recipes

http://pages.prodigy.com/pomathon/pomtreat.htm

If home-cooking sounds too intimidating, you might satisfy your desire to cook for your dog by making homemade treats. This page from the Pomerama Web site—which invites browsers to "Give Your Dog A Bone...And A Hug!—provides all the information dog owners need to prepare a vast selection of biscuits, treats, appetizers, and a variety of show-ring bait treats. The all-meat, veggie, and grain recipes were submitted by Ursula R. Taylor and Lynne Dauber and are presented in one long and very detailed home page. Also included are "A Word About

Ingredients" and succinct preparation instructions. So delectable and fresh do some of these treats sound, it's a safe bet that the humans who are preparing them will envy their pets.

Veterinary Nutritional Formula

http://www.vivanet.com/~drdog/index.htm

Trimmery Pet Care has developed a Web site that is not just a tool to promote its Veterinary Nutritional Formula (VNF) line of pet foods, but also to provide a quick, fun pet care education. While you will indeed find a great deal of information about its natural, preservative-free line of pet food (which you may order from this site), you will also find a list of options that complement the product-oriented data with information on pet care. This menu includes topics such as Dr. Dog's Cool Tips (how to keep pets cool in summer), Pet Food Information (which provides, in addition to information on the various VNF foods, general background information on pet nutrition), and Behavior Tips (a bulleted list of what owners can do to prevent behavior problems). Browsers can also take advantage of the Ask Dr. Dog option, where "the doctor is in" to answer owners' questions about their pets.

Pet Products Plus

http://www.pppinc.com/index.html

Recently, pet-food researchers discovered that the nutritional needs of large- and giant-breed puppies differ from those of smaller breeds because they are slower to mature and often more prone to bone and joint problems. This site, devoted to a food manufactured by Pet Products Plus, makers of Sensible Choice pet foods, addresses this situation both informationally and as a means of promoting a food they have developed to meet the larger puppy's needs. From the home page, click on ...read the full story to find a page that details the special dietary needs of "those breeds whose adult weight is approximately 70 pounds or more, and for breeds predisposed to bone and joint deformation."

Heinz Pets Unleashed

http://www.heinzpet.com/main/index.htm

As is to be expected, the subject of nutrition can be found throughout this Web site, sponsored by Heinz Pet Products, makers of well-known brands such as Cycle pet foods, Meaty Bone, Reward pet foods, and Jerky Treats. With a clean, attractive design, the Heinz Pets Unleashed home page offers browsers easy access to several areas, most of which provide nutrition information of one type of another. What makes this menu even more user-friendly is that each option provides not only the area name, but a brief synopsis of what you will find there.

While the About Heinz, Legal Information, and Petfood Pantry sections will fill browsers in on the Heinz Company, more general nutrition information is presented in the You and Your Pet section (a collection of articles of interest and value to pet owners). More specialized, browser-prompted information is available from the Ask A Vet section ("...your chance to get answers on-line—straight to your e-mail address from a certified veterinarian."). Upbeat in presentation and easy and convenient to navigate, the Heinz Pets Unleashed site encourages browsers to dive in and take a tour.

Dog Owner's Guide: Food and Nutrition

http://www.canismajor.com/dog/topic1.html#Food

Dog Owner's Guide, a full-service information site on everything canine, offers within its list of available topics a section on food and nutrition (the address listed above will take you directly to this heading's position on the topic list page). Here you will find hyperlinks to a variety of pertinent topics that address all facets of canine nutrition—Diet, Nutrients, Preparing your dog's food, Diet & more, and Obesity in dogs. Each topic area is well organized, beginning with an initial table of contents detailing what the page will cover, followed by a well-written, document. Dog Owner's Guide offers browsers an easily accessible overview of this important element of dog care.

Barley Dog and Barley Cat: The "Original" Barley Grass Nutritional Supplements
http://www.greenfoods.com/index.html

A fascinating and logical treatise on why dogs and cats eat grass—a phenomenon familiar to most pet owners—is presented in the Web site representing the nutritional supplements Barley Dog and Barley Cat from Green Foods Corporation. While supplements should be offered to a pet only with a veterinarian's approval, the information presented here on an animal's propensity to munch grass (and the often unpleasant aftermath of such a snack) is worth a read.

The home page of this large, well-designed site offers a long menu of hyperlinks to such topics as Ever Wonder Why Your Dog or Cat Eats Grass?, GFC Supplements to the Rescue, Ordering Information, How You Can Help Support Our "Best Friends," and Will My Dog or Cat Stop Eating Grass with GFC Supplements? Also available are sections that chronicle actual users of this product. Click on People Are Talking!, for example, to find a long list of testimonials from pet owners who have found success with Barley Dog and Barley Cat. For an even more personal account, click on The Story of Sara Bone's Skin, taken from an unsolicited letter sent to GFC from a very satisfied customer. Easy to navigate, interesting, and pleasantly designed with a sky-motif backdrop and cute cartoon dog and cat icons, this site is both fun and informative.

Solid Gold Health Products for Pets

http://www.solid-gold-inc.com/dod.html

Founded in 1974 by Sissy Harrington-McGill, Solid Gold Health Products for Pets uses its Web site to detail clearly and crisply why it believes its natural foods can enhance a dog's quality of life and lengthen its overall lifespan. This mini-lesson in natural pet nutrition (told from the owner/founder's point of view), begins with the clean, well-designed home page that offers browsers access, via a gold menu grid, to such topics as Do's & Don'ts (detailing what Solid Gold does use and doesn't use in its foods), Hot Topics (articles on Solid Gold foods and nutrition strategies), and Ingredients. Also included are links to areas that provide information about ordering Solid Gold products and special programs for veterinarians, dog clubs, kennels, and so on. Another unique feature of this site is the Who We Are section, which presents an engaging, reader-friendly story about how a trip to Germany inspired Harrington-McGill to found her own pet-food line when she noted how healthy and relatively long-lived German Great Danes were compared to their American cousins. This story is indeed an effective addition to a site such as this.

Our Pets Inc. Home Page

http://ourpets.com/

Through the Our Pets Inc. site, Edmund R. Dorosz, D.V.M. offers one of the most detailed collection of pages devoted to nutrition that you are likely to find. Though short on graphics, it is long on information, accessible from the home page, which offers a list of links to layers of nutritional information. The best place to begin is the Why a Pet Nutrition Site on the Internet? section. Here Dr. Dorosz explains why he has prepared this site, the many articles in it and how to navigate through it most effectively.

While Dr. Dorosz is a proponent of home cooking for pets (information on ordering books on that subject is available on this site), he provides an abundance of nutritional information of value to both those who do want to cook for their pets and those who prefer commercially prepared diets. Click on the Articles option on the home page to find an incredibly detailed index of articles that cover topics such as Which pet food to buy?, What are we buying?, Cooking for your pet, Cooked or raw food, Water, Obesity and overweight, Healthy hair and skin, Feeding the working dog, and Feeding your dog. From start to finish, the information within this site is presented in a style that makes the journey through these pages comfortable as well as informative.

P A R T   I I

Getting A Dog

CHAPTER 6

Purebred Dog Breeders

The vocation of dog breeding has received much media attention in recent years, attention sparked by controversies over mass breeding operations known as puppy mills, and the potential health and temperament problems of puppies from pet shops. In the wake of this debate, many potential puppy buyers have sought reputable, ethical breeders for purebred puppies.

In an ideal world, breeders get involved in dog breeding out of a genuine love of a given breed and a desire to reach the ideal outlined in the breed standard. In other words, breeders get involved out of a love of the breed and a quest for its perfection in both mind and body, not out of a desire to make money. In fact, if done properly, there is very little, if any, profit from the endeavor, as costs for proper nutrition, veterinary care, housing and all the ingredients in puppy breeding and care often exceed the price new owners are willing to pay for puppies.

The ethical breeder also enters the vocation understanding that a breeder is responsible for the puppies he or she produces for the rest of their lives. Contracts signed at the time of purchase address such issues as health guarantees and the requirement that pet puppies be spayed or neutered. Contracts should also mandate that, should future events prevent the owner from keeping the dog he or she has purchased, the dog must be returned to the breeder.

Finding such a breeder is the buyer's responsibility. He or she must do the necessary homework both about the breed and potential breeders. This requires reading; spending

continued after the feature section

Domino Chow Chows

http://www.chowchows.com/

The Chow Chow, the densely coated dog with a purple tongue that originated in China more than 2,000 years ago, is one of those breeds that is extremely popular and really shouldn't be. This is a dog that certainly is not appropriate for every owner. That is why it would be worthwhile for anyone with even a passing interest in the breed to check out the Domino Chow Chows Web site.

More than simply an advertisement for New York breeders Alex and Irene Cartabio, this colorful, musical, beautifully designed site (which was created and maintained by Alex Cartabio's Domino Video Company) stands as an example of what breeders can do for their kennels, their chosen breeds and the potential buyers of their puppies. This excellence is immediately apparent with its boxed menu options, which offer such section choices as Welcome!, Our Chows, What's New, Information, Chow Links and E-Mail Us! Given the style and panache with which these options are presented, the temptation to explore the layers that lie beyond is downright irresistible.

Extremely professional in presentation, this site is more of a general Chow breed site than simply a breeder site, and that is exactly what its proprietors intend it to be. While information on the kennel operation, which was founded in 1975, is included in detail, check into the Welcome! section and learn that "this site is not a marketplace to 'sell puppies.'" No, the main goal of this site is to celebrate the breed and inform browsers of its true nature and care. Only that way can the Chow Chow land in the hands of owners who understand what it needs to enjoy a long and healthy life.

The Cartabios not only celebrate their own Chows (which they do with much pride, particularly in the Our Chows section, featuring each dog prominently by name, photo, and pedigree), but also provide an abundance of information on their breed in an effort to prepare would-be

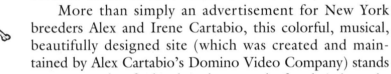

Chow buyers for this grand commitment. Obviously a great deal of energy and creativity went into their efforts.

The Information section takes on this mission handsomely, beginning with in-depth information on the breed and its history. From there, travel on down the Information page to a grid of boxed options entitled "Answers to Some Questions About the Chow Chow." Here you will find options ranging from Temperament?, Where to Buy?, Spay/Neuter?, and Questions to Ask? Replies are in-depth, designed to prepare the browser both for Chow Chow ownership (or not) and how to use that information in the choice of a breeder and a new pet.

This site, reflecting as it does a devotion to the health and well-being of the Chow Chow breed, equally reflects the responsibilities of any ethical purebred-dog breeder. It takes these responsibilities seriously, using the vast resource of the Internet to convey this. It does this with great pride in the featured dogs, as well as with a lively, fun, educational style that compels the browser to tour the whole site and emerge far more knowledgeable for the experience.

time with the breed in which you are interested; making calls; asking questions; and collecting referrals from other owners, veterinarians, dog trainers and perhaps even animal shelters and rescue groups. Find that perfect breeder, ask all the necessary questions, and meet the prospective parents, and you may then have to wait even longer on a waiting list for the new arrivals. Such legwork can take time, but if you approach this for what it truly is—the search for a new family member who will be with you for the next 10 to 15 years, perhaps even longer—then that time is well worth the investment.

The following are Web sites of individual purebred dog breeders, breeder-referral listings, and other breeder- and breeding-related subjects (many that offer information on individual breeds and dog care as well). While the presence of a particular breeder here does not guarantee responsible, ethical breeding, the sites offer an enjoyable and informational tour, and should at least help to launch would-be purebred puppy or dog buyers on the grand journey of procuring a new pet and family member. As for the rest, nothing takes the place of the necessary pet-choosing legwork. No matter how glowing a breeder's references, reputation, or recommendations, it is still the buyer's responsibility to do the proper research and ask the proper questions.

Responsible Breeders

http://www.iupui.edu/~ihls400/responsible_breeder.html

What Makes a Breeder Responsible? That is the title of this important document, which contains answers by several breeders. Anyone seeking a breeder should look here first to find out exactly what to look for.

The answers give us several characteristics to look for in a breeder: a breeder's openness about his or her breeding stock and willingness to discuss strengths as well as faults; an allegiance to genetic testing and to keeping dogs that don't pass muster out of the breeding program no matter how beautiful they are; a breeder who willingly supplies the puppy buyer with all the necessary paperwork; and a breeder who, as respondent Dianne Schoenberg put it, "cares about each and every pup." The response from respondent Robin Nuttall is worth noting. She divides her responses into definitions, outlining what makes a puppy mill, what makes a backyard breeder, and what makes a reputable breeder. The differences are distinct and seeing them laid out this way makes that point perfectly clear.

With most of the responses to the main question arranged primarily in bullet form, making for a fast and informational read, this is indeed a valuable site. There is nothing fancy about it, yet each respondent deserves thanks for taking the time to contribute thoroughly and passionately to a document that is not only must-see information, but also, in a sense, a tribute to breeders. This document's existence and the critical points it addresses, indicate that there are indeed breeders out there who meet this ideal. If nothing else, it may also be viewed as a breed standard, per se, for breeders themselves, outlining clearly to the dog-breeding community just what is to be aspired to and what can be accomplished.

Puppy Buyer's Checklist

http://is2.dal.ca/~dcodding/buyer.html

Just as it is critical to evaluate a breeder from whom you might purchase a puppy, it is equally critical to evaluate your own motivations for taking on a new pet. The puppy buyer is the other side of the equation that determines the fate of a dog.

To assist in this mission is Georgia Alyce Thomas's Puppy Buyer's Checklist, a document designed to take the prospective puppy buyer step by step through an exploration of why he or she wants a puppy and how to go about it correctly. Though the text is directed toward someone considering a Great Dane, you may substitute any breed name and the information remains pertinent.

This no-frills site first addresses the buyer's experience with the breed in question and his or her ability to provide a proper and permanent home. It instructs the buyer on how to locate potential breeders (and rescue groups, too, in case adopting an older dog is of interest) and the issues he or she should discuss, such as genetic testing and temperament evaluation of both puppies and parents. Buyers are advised to avoid any breeder who is not interested in interviewing potential buyers, as such a breeder is not concerned about the ultimate fate, and probably the health and quality, of the dogs he or she produces. Listing all the points this document addresses would take up several pages of this book, but rest assured that this is a valuable site for those seeking to choose a new pet wisely.

BreederLink Home Page

http://www.breederlink.com/index.htm

When a prospective puppy buyer decides that he or she would like to take the responsible route and find a reputable breeder to work with, the next step—finding that breeder—can be a challenge. BreederLink—an online directory of breeders—can help, billing itself as a service that seeks to help "consumers across America find the purebred dog they want, from a breeder they'll trust."

Those consumers are to be warned, however, that a breeder's presence on the BreederLink listing does not, as the site's own disclaimer (accessible from the home page) states, mean that breeders found here necessarily fit the mold of the responsible breeder. "We do not recommend, endorse, guarantee, or rate the breeders on this service," it says. They do make an attempt to prescreen the breeders, however, requiring that everyone on the service provide a written refund/return policy, a written health guarantee, and a kennel club affiliation and reference. Yet the consumer must still remain vigilant in his or her own evaluations of both breeds and breeders.

Such technicalities aside, this colorful, easy-to-navigate site is a valuable resource, evident from the extensive menu grid on its home page. From this grid you may access a variety of subject areas, including, of course, the list of breeders (some of which also do rescue) arranged alphabetically by breed name. Click on the breed, and when the list of breeders appears, click on a name, and you are whisked into a detailed page all about that breeder. This page includes a Breeder's Statement, which serves to personalize the entry even more.

You can also access an excellent discussion of evaluating breeders (click on the home-page hyperlink Tips on Breeders and Purchasing a Purebred Dog), and even directly access a site, sponsored by Our Dogs, that offers links to more than 1,600 other dog-related sites. This site offers the browser a great deal of information all under one roof.

Dog Breeders Online Directory

http://www.doggies.com/index.html

The choices presented to you are simple when you enter the Dog Breeders Online Directory home page. If you're looking for a breeder, click on the Search option, scroll down as instructed to your breed of choice and click the mouse. Then input your zip code and hit Fetch. This will access a grid listing of breeders and breed clubs in your area, so your search for that perfect breeder and that perfect dog or puppy may begin.

This is an impressive site for prospective dog owners who will be thrilled at the ease with which they may access pertinent information. But that's not all the Dog Breeders Online Directory offers. From the home page click on How to Find Your Dog (best done, of course, before contacting breeders), and you will be treated to a very informational, very educational discussion of the ins and outs of responsible puppy buying.

This begins with the big question: Do you really want a dog? Dogs can be quite demanding, expensive, and time consuming, and it is impressive to have this issue addressed in a site dedicated to matchmaking between dogs and people. Should your answer to this question be yes, travel on to a succinct, reader-friendly discourse on evaluating breeders (and the distinct differences between puppy-mill breeders, backyard breeders, and serious hobby breeders; this site, of course, recommends the latter), evaluating breeds, and, finally, choosing your new pet. Easy, fun to navigate and thorough in the information it provides, this is a valuable resource for both breeders and puppy buyers.

A-1 Dog Breeders Showcase

http://www.cyberpet.com/cyberdog/breed/

Prospective puppy buyers can find listings of breeders within the Web site sponsored by A-1 Dog Breeders Showcase. The site opens with an outer-space motif and a welcome by resident cartoon host, Cyber-Dog. What follows is a listing of breeds arranged alphabetically. Choose one and you're off.

As with any such site, the inclusion of a particular breeder here is not an endorsement of reputability nor of the quality of the puppies he or she sells. This is laid out clearly in the A-1 Dog Breeders Showcase disclaimer, which reminds prospective buyers that they must still do all the necessary research and ask all the necessary questions. Once you have accepted that as a given, you may explore this site and enjoy it.

Each breed section begins with a list of Featured Breeders, providing ample information and a photograph about each. Following this are the Classifieds, which also offer a great deal of information (the substance of which just might be a good clue to the operation's overall philosophy), and include photographs in some cases. The classifieds are organized by region, making them easy to search. Several breeder-referral sites link to this one on the Web. You simply cannot have too much information when seeking an animal that should remain with you as a beloved member of the family for a decade or more.

Tamaron Collies

http://home.sprynet.com/sprynet/tamaron/

Founded in 1988 in Alberta, Canada, by Trudy Taphorn, Tamaron Collies, producers of award-winning rough Collies, presents a Web site as lovely as the breed they represent. Beautifully organized and multilayered, the site opens with a soft profile of a Tamaron Collie and a grid of well-illustrated topic boxes including Showcase (a profile of Tamaron champions and wins), Care and Grooming, Fine Print (sample contracts), Facts (info about Tamaron Collies and the rough Collie itself), Puppies (litter announcements), and Canine Worlds (links to other dog and Collie sites).

Click on one of these options and you will be impressed, not only by this kennel, but by the information it provides on its Web site. Choose Fine Print, for example, and you are offered three distinct sample contracts: one for show pups, one for companion/pet pups, and one for stud services. Extremely thorough in content, the existence of these contracts in so public a venue is a great service to puppy buyers, to other breeders, and to dogs.

Equally impressive is the Facts section, which first presents information about Tamaron Collies and the kennel's breeding goals (you can get to know them, too, on the home page in a detailed discussion of the operation's accomplishments and special dogs). It then offers hyperlink access to information about Collies in general, Collie history, and the breed standard. With a lovely design and a wealth of Collie and general dog information, this site is of value not only to those who love Lassie, but to all dog owners seeking sound information about the business of breeding dogs responsibly.

Timberline Retrievers (Golden Retrievers)

http://www.goldens.com/

With the Golden Retriever having been elevated to the position of quintessential canine companion, what many people fail to remember is the fact that this dog was bred originally as a working field dog. That soft mouth was not designed strictly to carry stuffed animals around the house all day. It was made to retrieve and carry birds.

Douglas and Judy Spink, owners of Oregon's Timberline Retrievers, seek to remind the public, through their dogs, just why this dog came to be bred in the first place. Carrying on the tradition, they breed dogs for work and field, and boast a "25 year commitment to excellence in working Goldens." The Timberline Web site as a whole boasts this commitment both to the Timberline dogs and to the breed at large. While the primary focus of this site is on the kennel and its dogs, it also offers links to other Golden-related sites.

Consisting of several layers, the site is easy to navigate, offering a menu bar on the left and bottom of every screen. From this menu, browsers may visit such topic areas as Upcoming Litters (announcements of who is expecting and when), Stud Dogs (meet "the boys" who are all "free of standard genetic defects" or temperament problems), and More Info (which allows browsers to subscribe to the Retriever Field Trials Discussion list, trials-l). Also unique is the Kennels section. Here you are offered a full-fledged tour of the grounds, complete with photos and commentary, that allows you to meet the dogs and to visit their home as well.

Draper Kennel (Golden Retrievers)

http://www.american-research.com/draper-kennel/

Whether you are actually looking for a Golden Retriever as a new addition to the family or simply seeking information on the breed, the Draper Kennel Web site can serve both purposes. Sponsored by the Utah kennel's owners, Rod and Jennifer Stucker, who are striving "to provide a professional and responsible breeding program for Golden Retrievers," this site is clean and well-designed, and draped in gold from start to finish.

Beginning on the home page with a heartfelt testimonial to their breeding efforts, the Stuckers present in detail their breeding philosophy that includes their statement that "Our dogs are among the healthiest and most affectionate Golden Retrievers you will find in the Western United States." Topics on this site include: What is a Golden Retriever, Preparing for Your Puppy, Choosing a Puppy, House Training, Grooming, and Spaying and Neutering—the list simply goes on and on, making this site not only an excellent breeder site, but an all-around dog-care site as well.

Also impressive is the section on Hereditary and Medical Problems. Here you will find a thorough and very honest treatment of the various health problems to which Goldens may be prone, including hip dysplasia, various eye diseases, and hypothyroidism. Indeed everything about this site is impressive, from its easy-to-navigate design that provides the browser with constant access to the long golden menu bar, to the reader-friendly language that instructs its audience with a genuine affection for the canine subject at hand. So even if you are not necessarily seeking a Golden, consider this a valuable site to visit.

Superstar Irish Wolfhounds

http://www.bmts.com/~superstar/index.html

Enter the Web site for Superstar Irish Wolfhounds, and you will be greeted with splashy graphics, framing a hypertext Index that offers you access to such topics as Introduction, Achievement, Some of the Family, Appearance, Temperament, and What Are They Like?

The Introduction section is a logical place to begin. Here you will meet some Superstar dogs face to face, and learn that proprietor Connie Banks believes that dog breeding "is a science; doing it right is an art." Indeed you'll like what you see here, as those behind Superstar's success discuss online the fact that breeding must be done only by someone who is "totally committed to the welfare of every pup which may result." You will be impressed, too, to see the awards Superstar Wolfhounds have received in the conformation show ring as well as in field trials and obedience.

The site exudes a tone of warmth to visiting browsers and great pride in the gentle giants this Canadian kennel produces. A fine example of this exists in the What Are They Like? section, where a long bulleted list of attributes and owner requirements does a wonderful job of educating would-be owners about Irish Wolfhounds, the tallest of all dogs, and helping potential owners decide whether or not they are likely candidates for successful Irish Wolfhound ownership. Enjoy the energy, the color, and the ease of navigation in this site.

Bear Paw Kennels (Karelien Bear Dogs)

http://www.mtdirect.com/kbdog/

This site is devoted to a breed that is unknown to many Americans: the Karelien Bear Dog, a hunting breed from Russia and Scandinavia that is presumed to be approximately 3,000 years old. The Bear Paw Kennels site, therefore, is of interest both to those who are seeking one of these large, robust, spitz-type dogs for their very own, and to those simply seeking to increase their canine IQ. Check into the home page for this Montana kennel, which is owned and operated by Janet Yatchak, and you will learn much about a dog that is, as this site claims, "devoted, loving and playful," as well as "independent and courageous."

Several photos in the site show that the Karelian Bear Dog, also known as the Russo European Laika, is quite beautiful. Though the site itself is short and simple in format, it offers much information and an easy-to-navigate design. From the home page, for example, browsers may choose from several boxed options that include Sales, Traits, Genealogy, and History. As for the kennel itself, we learn that Bear Paw Kareliens all come from Russian- and Finnish-imported lines, and that they are bred according to the Russian standard. So impress your dog-loving friends. Check into the Bear Paw Web site, and learn all about a dog that few people stateside even know exists.

Walkoway Beardies (Bearded Collies)

http://home.revealed.net/walkoway/index.html

Bearded Collies are the resident passion of Illinois breeders Chris and Ed Walkowicz. With a cute design that features a pawprint backdrop coupled with light-hearted caricatures of Bearded Collies in various states of play, the home page includes a great deal of information on Walkoway Beardies (including introductions to each and every one), and on the books and articles Chris has written as a prominent dog writer.

Follow the home page down and you will be greeted by a wealth of information on both Beardies and on the Walkoway operation. What is a Beardie? takes you to a page of well-illustrated background information on this adorable Scottish breed that, according to an excerpt from Chris' book on the subject, is known for "almost overpowering friendliness." From the home page you will also have access to a Walkoway photo album; a list of titles won by Walkoway Beardies; and in keeping with Chris' involvement in breeders networks, a list of other breeders, litters available, and breed rescue resources, thus making this site a valuable all-around Beardie resource.

Carla's Toy Dog Home Page

http://www.magna.com.au/~gclarke/carla/homec.html

From Australia comes this unique site sponsored by Carla Timmins, a 22-year veteran breeder of Chihuahuas, Pekingese, and Pomeranians. It would seem that in that time, she has become quite expert in the care, feeding, and raising of tiny, orphaned, or otherwise compromised puppies, who, for whatever reason, are left without a mother's care.

Within this site, you will find fascinating information on how Carla takes the mother's place. From the Topics list presented on the home page, click on Hand Raising Toy Dogs, and you will find step-by-step instructions on how Carla helps the tiny ones, as well as her cautionary message that you must not expect miracles, and that sometimes, no matter how attentive you are, they just don't make it. She warns, too, that the puppies that do make it tend to be extraordinarily bonded to their surrogate moms, and may be extremely difficult to send off to new homes.

Those inspired by Carla's message, all conveyed with warmth and genuine affection for toy dogs, may order the necessary supplies from her by clicking on the My Handrearing Items option on the Topics list. These special items are readily available to her because they are frequently used for the hand-rearing of the orphaned and premature young of the unusual marsupials that are native to Australia. So if toys are your passion, this site is worth a look.

Kinlayke Kennels (Lakeland Terriers and Chesapeake Bay Retrievers)
http://www.lon.hookup.net/~sunrise/Kinlayke/

Two breeds in one site are found when you enter the home page for Kinlayke Kennels, a breeding operation located in Ontario, Canada. Playful and colorful in design, this site does not go into great detail about the dogs the kennel breeds, other than the fact that the dogs come with written health guarantees. Proprietors Pam and Schoot McKinlay prefer a more personal one-on-one approach with prospective Lakeland and Chessie buyers.

The site does offer information about the breeds, however. Kinlayke Lakelands, for example, are described on the home page as "big dogs" in their minds, and their pedigrees combine American, Canadian and English bloodlines. Click on the hyper-text breed name for a description of the breed, courtesy of *Dogs in Canada* magazine. The same format follows the Chesapeake Bay Retriever. The McKinlay's Chessies (under the kennel name Mossbank) are touted to be bred "for friendly and outgoing temperament as well as conformation and hunting ability." Again, click on the hyper-text breed name to learn more from *Dogs in Canada*.

Welcome to the Merikaez Home Page (Italian Greyhounds, Lhasa Apsos)

http://www.ozemail.com.au/~merikaez/

To the strains of the theme from the popular television drama The X-Files, you enter the home page for Merikaez Italian Greyhounds, presented by Adrian, Mary, and Alicia Keast. Based in Australia, this site offers information on Italian Greyhounds, Lhasa Apsos, Junior Showmanship, and a visit to the Keasts' Rouse Hill Boarding Kennel.

Unique to this site is The Merikaez Notice Board, which documents the goings on at Merikaez in diary form, in keeping with the site's friendly, personal tone. That same tone reigns in the various areas you may visit by clicking on the options at the bottom of the home page. Click on Italian Greyhounds, and you will learn all about this graceful breed, again presented in the friendly tone that makes browsers feel they are all part of the Merikaez family. Especially impressive here is that though the site seems light and fun, it deals with very serious issues in a very serious manner. For example, the Italian Greyhound section addresses the various genetic problems in the breed and offers discussions of the Merikaez breeding efforts to steer clear of them. We then move on to meet all of the Merikaez Italian Greyhounds.

Equally impressive are the areas devoted to Lhasas and the Rouse Hill Boarding Kennel—you'll wish you lived in Australia and could board your dog there. While a great deal of creativity went into the design of this multifaceted site, what shines even more is the genuine affection that went into its creation. The language is friendly, honest, and welcoming throughout. The messages about commitments and devotion to dogs are clear. The effect is to make you want to come back again sometime, and the proprietors invite you to do just that.

Hot Pursuit Jack Russell Terriers

http://home.ican.net/~hpjrt/

Billing itself at the top of its home page as "the Unofficial Canadian Jack Russell Terrier Site," this is another excellent Canadian entry that is chock full of information both about its own breeding operation and about the fascinating, often infuriating, Jack Russell Terrier (JRT) itself.

First, Hot Pursuit proprietors Reid Bannister and Mary Lea introduce themselves and their efforts to breed not show dogs, but "healthy terriers who are naturals in the field, with excellent family-oriented temperaments." Below this friendly intro, you will encounter two large menu grids: one for Hot Pursuit Jack Russell Terriers and one for The Jack Russell Terrier Club of Canada. It is the former that concerns us here, and its menu options include Hot Pursuit's Approach to Canine Nutrition, Visit Our Favourite Links, and Our Awards and Stories.

The Hot Pursuit site spends a great deal of time working to educate would-be owners about just what JRT ownership entails. This is especially true in the Hot Pursuit Philosophy section. Here you will learn that the dogs, which can be "feisty" critters, are home-raised and a warning is offered that not everyone who applies "will be approved for puppy placement." You also can't miss the message in the Getting a Jack Russell Terrier: What You Need to Know section and The Hot Pursuit Pack section, where you meet each dog personally and learn just how active these dogs must be to remain content. There is even a section, the Jack Russell Terrier Friends section, where you can add your own JRT's picture to an online photo album. It is precisely this combination of solid information presented with a friendly, personal tone that makes this a top site.

Covy-Tucker Hill Kennels
(German Shepherd Dogs)

http://www.scalesaz.com/cth/index.html

In 1987 the world was enthralled when a breathtaking German Shepherd Dog named Covy-Tucker Hill's Manhattan was crowned Best in Show at the Westminster Dog Show in New York City. That dog was bred by Gloria F. Birch and Cappy Pottle of Covy-Tucker Hill Kennels in California. What a treat to dog-loving Internet browsers to have access to a Covy-Tucker Hill Web site, maintained by Stacy J. Speer. Simple in design—it is one long informational page devoid of links or layers—this site radiates the Covy-Tucker Hill proprietors' dedication to their breeding program (evident in the quality Shepherds they produce) and their genuine affection for their chosen breed.

The page is divided into several sections, from About Covy-Tucker Hill Kennels, to Goals, to About the Owners, to Services (the kennel provides boarding and training services in addition to producing top-quality Shepherds). We are introduced first to a portrait of Birch and Pottle and several of their champion Shepherds, and then learn about these two well-known women and the kennel they founded in 1971. The resume of their kennel and the dogs at its heart could fill volumes, their dogs having earned almost every award possible, yet the track record is distilled here, topped by the impressive statement that they have bred and/or owned more than 200 champion German Shepherd Dogs.

Especially impressive is the information presented in the Goals section, which states the kennel's objective of breeding "the ideal German Shepherd Dog." This very successful breeding program, dedicated to an immensely, almost dangerously, popular breed that is often the subject of controversy, revolves around temperament and intelligence—mainstays of this breed that are too often disregarded in favor of appearance—that are as critical to Covy-Tucker Hill

Shepherds as structure and movement. This, Birch and Pottle contend, is the secret to true show-ring success.

Nadelhaus German Shepherds

http://now2000.com/nadelhaus/index.htm

According to the information presented on the Nadelhaus home page, if you get a German Shepherd from Nadelhaus German Shepherds in California, you will have a dog, with a written guarantee that has been "vet-checked, tatooed, socialized, wormed, vaccinated to date, temperament-tested by a professional dog trainer and, above all, very much loved." Such elements are critical for a dog as strong and intelligent as the Shepherd. It is refreshing to see a breeder's attention to such detail so explicitly broadcast.

Though this site is short in size, it is long on design (a black backdrop with white speckles that look like stars in space) and ease of navigation. After the initial warm welcome that informs the browser of this kennel's good intentions and its desire to produce Shepherds that are built to work, the home page proceeds to present the Nadelhaus Shepherds themselves. Along with a vivid color portrait of each dog in a stacked position is a very personal description about that dog, evidence that these dogs are well-known and, yes, "very much loved" by their handlers.

Complete your tour of Nadelhaus German Shepherds with a visit to the Bulletin Board, described as "an online forum for people around the world to interact and exchange information about German Shepherds." Take a gander and you'll see that the messages do indeed come from all over the world. It's interesting to see that German Shepherd enthusiasts are taking advantage of what is a rather unique element to have included within a breeder Web site.

Nuez Kennels (Xoloitzcuintli)

http://www.mylink.net/~rae/

The lead-in to the Nuez Kennels home page begins: "Where bald is beautiful." The Nuez Kennels are in fact breeders of Xoloitzcuintli, the unusual, typically hairless breed from Mexico. You will quickly see why this site opens with a comment about a love of baldness. While most people have heard at one time or another about the so-called "Mexican hairless," few know of its true background or even how to pronounce its official name properly (it is pronounced show-low-itz-quent-lee, and is often shortened to Xolo).

This is essentially one long well-illustrated page, presented by Georgia Xolo breeder Ramona Younts. Aside from stating that Nuez Xolos are Mexican and United Kennel Club registered, and "family raised with emphasis on sound temperament and type," this site is devoted not so much to introducing browsers to Younts' own breeding program, but to educating them about this exotic animal. From a discussion of the breed's historical role as a religious icon by the ancient people of Central America, to the very alert, courageous, family-loving creatures the dogs are today, you will no doubt find a tour of this site to be fascinating, and very informative.

Szeder Pulik

http://www.neca.com/~szeder/navgh1.html

A Puli, a unique Hungarian herding breed (pluralized as Pulik), simply cannot walk down the street without attracting attention with its long dark corded coat that hides its eyes and sometimes even disguises the front of the dog from its back. This site, sponsored by the Szeder Pulik Kennel in Connecticut, is attractive, fun to tour, and filled with valuable information.

From the home page, you may access a variety of areas devoted to both the Puli breed (the home page itself explains to browsers the importance of understanding "the Puli Soul before undertaking the task of making him happy"), as well as the Szeder kennel. In addition to the more traditional topics of grooming, puppy care, herding, the AKC standard, Puli FAQs, and the history of the breed, you will also find within this multilayered site a section of Puli Fan Mail that owners have sent, as well as the Candid Gallery, which features photos of Pulik from all over the world.

This site is a credit to what a breeder can do for his or her breed. While exuberant, it also stands up as a valuable educational piece devoted to the Puli, and indeed educating the public is the breeder's first duty.

Ravenwood Dalmatians

http://www.prodogs.com/dbn/ravenwood/index.htm

Like Cruella de Ville, many members of the public consider the Dalmatian extraordinary simply because of its unique spotted coat. But look beneath the surface of this dog, and you will find a hardy worker, a fun-loving companion, and a willing partner in virtually every family activity. Indeed with the Dalmatian, beauty is not skin deep.

It is precisely this message that Virginia Dalmatian breeders Kathy and Lee McCoubrey are attempting to broadcast in their Web site for their Ravenwood Dalmatians. Their goal is not simply to produce beautiful spots, but also to celebrate those spots with dogs that exemplify the best in health and obedience. Both content-heavy and well-illustrated and designed, this site is a joy to tour. The introduction on the home page warns that if you are simply interested in this breed because of the media hype, think before you leap because "a Dalmatian is not the right choice for everyone."

The text that follows is as interesting as it is reader-friendly. You are presented several browsing options on the home page menu; a good place to start is About Ravenwood Dalmatians. Here Kathy McCoubrey shares the tale of how she came to know and love Dalmatians, and what has guided her breeding and training efforts ever since. You will also learn of the Ravenwood commitment to health—this particular aspect of the Dalmatian has been sharply criticized of late thanks to the media attention this breed invites, especially because of movies that revolve around 101 of these vibrant animals.

From there you may travel on to such topics as "Is a Dalmatian Right for You? (which includes a detailed and very honest Pro-and-Con list) and Selecting a Breeder (of value to a purchaser of any breed). All are presented in the same personalized tone that permeates this site. These articulate elements make this a valuable informational site to would-be Dalmatian owners (of which there are many) and a tribute to the breed at large.

O'Serenity Shetland Sheepdogs

http://www.geomarket.com/sheltie/

The Web site of California Sheltie kennel O'Serenity Shetland Sheepdogs cuts right to the chase with the statement: "One of the goals of this Web page is to provide a public awareness about the Sheltie breed and general dog care." Though a tour of this site shows many details about the O'Serenity kennel operation, its stated mission of education about the breed is backed up with ample detail as well.

A true affection for the Sheltie, a small, very beautiful herding breed from Scotland's Shetland Isles that is frequently misidentified by those who know no better as a "miniature Lassie," is obvious in this site. Well organized and easy to navigate, it offers browsers direct access to such topics as Shetland Sheepdog History (extremely in-depth and written by Sue Ann Bowling), Meet O'Serenity's Shelties (a home page introduction to breeder Laurel Worth's goals and philosophies with links to greater detail about the kennel's dogs and their accomplishments), and Care of Your Sheltie Puppy. The site also offers a set of links to other related sites, including Shetland Sheepdog Rescue and Herding with Shetland Sheepdogs.

You will emerge from this site with much more knowledge about this breed than you had when you went in. You may also wish to give Worth your two cents' worth via a Sheltie Survey, in which browsers are encouraged to share their thoughts. This personalized element simply adds to the homespun tone that permeates this site.

Katwala Australian Cattle Dogs

http://www.idyllmtn.com/acd/katwala.html

Katwala Australian Cattle Dogs Web site, sponsored by kennel owners Katherine Buetow and Gary Loescher, is simple and to the point. There are photos of the breed—one of the world's premier working breeds—but what truly stands out is the affection with which the dogs are described and the obvious dedication of these breeders to their chosen breed.

During a tour of the Katwala home page, you will learn much about the ideals behind this Illinois breeding program. It outlines the basics: no breeding until there is a solid waiting list for puppies; no breeding in mass quantities; in-depth genetic testing for all breeding stock; and, because of this kennel's devout commitment to the production of family pets, rigorous socialization of all puppies with children, adults, and other animals. Each puppy comes with a lifetime guarantee, which, we learn, "includes not only health and temperament concerns, but also short-term 'babysitting' and full return and placement into a new loving home." It is indeed refreshing to see such a lifetime commitment on the part of breeders to the puppies they produce.

Also unique to this site is a home page link to the Katwala Questionnaire that every prospective puppy buyer must complete as part of the prescreening process, and a link to the Katwala sales contracts. These latter documents (separate Pet/Non-Breeding Contract, Show/Breeding Contract and Deposit Agreement) are, we are told, "written to insure the safety and well-being of our puppies—period." All breeders should be equally commited to protecting the puppies they produce and proclaiming that intention with such passion.

Stone Fort Rottweilers

http://www.gcstation.net/~im4rotts/stone.htm

It seems that just about everyone is breeding Rottweilers these days, thanks to the breed's burgeoning popularity. Unfortunately, this popularity has been to the detriment of the breed, which is now plagued with far too many dysplastic, ill-tempered members. In an attempt to remedy the misconception that virtually everyone is the ideal owner for these large, powerful dogs, Brenda K. Jones of Stone Fort Rottweilers in Louisiana presents this informative breeder site that is unique in its promotion of interaction.

The Stone Fort home page, a long page rich with links to underlying layers, is topped by an animated flying angel Rottweiler that also provides the image for the backdrop. We then meet, in all their show glory, the Stone Fort champions, whom 20-year Rottweiler veteran Jones refers to as the "Rott N Kids," the dogs that she "is owned by."

The interactivity emerges in the browser-friendly tone of the site, coupled with the many links to pages that encourage browsers to get involved. Sign the guest book, e-mail the Stone Fort proprietor, and, in a most unique feature, participate in Brenda's Rottweiler Message Forum, where browsers are invited to take part in a personal forum designed to address training, general care, and "any question that will help your Rottweiler." Jones does warn, however, that the forum will be moderated and any inapropriate postings—that is, Rottie bashing and flames—will be removed.

Also accessible from the home page are Dog Related Links, Photos and Pedigrees, Special Homes Needed, Litter Announcements, individual pages for each of the Stone Fort dogs, and Questions to Ask Breeders ("If you don't read anything else on this page," implores Jones, "please read this"). All in all, this is more than a breeder site. It is a unique informational source and a site for Rottie lovers everywhere.

Thai Ridgebacks in America
http://home.earthlink.net/~ll889/

If you're seeking information on rare and unusual breeds, check out this site devoted to the Thai Ridgeback Dog. While you may not necessarily want one of these dogs for your own, this is an excellent—not to mention graphically stunning—tribute to this unusual creature, presented by New York enthusiast and breeder Jack Sterling.

The long home page is actually a very personal article by Sterling beginning with how he came to encounter these dogs, which he says look "like something from the planet Mars," quite by accident on a trip to Bangkok and how, many imports and Sterling's own home-bred litters later, his dogs attract a great deal of attention in America. This vibrant torqouise-and-black site, festooned with photos, offers background on the breed itself, which is found indigenously only in Thailand, where it is believed to have existed in much the same form and temperament as we see today for 3,000 years or more.

A hunting, guard, and show dog, the intelligent, large-eared, extremely alert Thai Ridgeback is certainly not the perfect pet for everyone, but it is a pleasure to meet this unusual animalhere in this context and to share Mr. Sterling's admiration for his treasured breed. You may just find it contagious.

Protection, Rescue, and Adoption

Every year millions of dogs—puppies and adults, mixed-breeds and purebreds—find themselves homeless and in need of permanent, loving families because of abandonment, neglect, and overbreeding. Most will never find homes. It is to these animals that humane societies, animal shelters, and rescue groups are dedicated.

It takes a special type of person to take on the daunting, seemingly thankless task of finding new, loving homes for society's throwaway animals. The Internet has proven to be a boon to this task, providing a way to communicate instantly with other rescuers and with prospective adopters from coast to coast. A breed rescue, for example, will often use a national breed rescue Web site as headquarters for all the smaller rescue groups around the country. Tracking the dogs they have rescued and now have available for adoption is a breeze. At the same time, prospective adopters can check in and look over the available dogs for prospective pets.

The Internet has also proven to be a valuable tool for local and national animal-welfare organizations by enabling members and others who donate to these causes to keep in touch as never before. With the convenience of the computer, they can check in periodically to find out the latest happenings within the organization and to get information on current issues and how they might get involved. For instance, many people may be interested in writing to their elected officials on certain issues, but aren't sure how to go

continued after the feature section

131

The Humane Society of the United States

http://www.hsus.org

The Web site for the Humane Society of the United States (HSUS) opens with the statement "The Helping Hands for Animals." Framing the opening statement is a collection of hand-shaped icons, each holding a different animal in its palm, and overlaid with section names, such as What's New,

Current Campaigns, Feedback, and Photo Gallery, that direct browsers toward explanatory sections that demonstrate how to help animals in need of attention.

Representing as it does an organization that is deeply involved in just about every animal-welfare issue you can name, the emphasis here is on interaction, and all the issues are presented in an easy-to-navigate, no-nonsense format.

Wherever you are in this site, you always have access to those original hand icons that will take you home or to any other part of the site.

The journey begins with About the HSUS. Here, within the story of this national, nonprofit animal-protection organization that was founded in 1954 and now boasts more than 3.5 million members, you will find hypertext

links that will carry you even deeper into the subject matter. Click on Our nine regional offices, for example, and there they are, along with a United States map outlining the regions each of them serves. Or perhaps you are interested

in the HSUS Electronic Directory, which features hypertext e-mail addresses you may use to contact various HSUS publications, and other organizations with similar interests.

Where dogs are concerned, the material is rich. Click on the Current Campaigns icon, for instance, and find a list of several active campaigns that are aimed at helping dogs (and cats, too). The Until There Are None, Adopt One, campaign is one such choice. Launched in 1991, this campaign promotes the idea that pet overpopulation can be overcome by adopting pets from shelters. The Be A P.A.L.

campaign, begun in 1987, urges the public to "be a pal" to their pets and have them spayed or neutered.

"Until There Are None, Adopt One" Campaign

In 1991, The HSUS started the "Until There Are None, Adopt One" campaign as another step toward the goal of increased public awareness of dog and cat overpopulation. Specifically, this campaign urges responsible prospective pet owners to adopt dogs and cats from shelters instead of going to breeders or pet stores when looking for a companion animal.

In virtually every community across the United States, animal shelters are filled with dogs and cats. Some are lost pets whose owners cannot be found. Others are pets whose owners can no longer keep them. Each deserves a permanent and loving home. Unfortunately, there just aren't enough homes for them all. Dogs and cats have become victims of their own overabundance caused by human carelessness and irresponsible breeding. Through this campaign The HSUS is calling upon the strength of the consumer to change the way society thinks about its treatment of companion animals.

Our campaign slogan is "Choose a Pal for Life." Until there are no more healthy animals dying in shelters, adopt a shelter pet. The HSUS has produced many educational items, both for the general public and for shelter workers, on this campaign, such as posters, brochures, and a special issue of our *Shelter Sense* magazine.

For more information about the "Until There Are None, Adopt One" campaign, contact us at:

The Humane Society of the United States
2100 L Street, NW
Washington, DC 20037
(202) 452-1100

Home | About The HSUS | What's New | Joining The HSUS | Current Campaigns
Humane Living | Publications | Photo Gallery | Links to Other Sites | Feedback

This site offers another unique feature in the Photo Gallery section. Here you will see the faces of animals that benefit from the work the HSUS is doing—for example, the sad faces of dogs in a puppy mill. While not always pleasant, you may end your tour of the gallery by selecting a more uplifting, encouraging shot; say, a photo of a smiling dog, the ultimate goal of all this hard work.

Browsers may use this site to join the HSUS and order society publications and other products. In keeping with its focus on interaction, the site's Feedback section invites visitors to contact the HSUS about the issues, and offer suggestions on the site's content. By allowing browsers to be a part of the action—and part of the solution to the many problems facing our animals today—this site promises to be an ever-growing entity that can effectively channel help to the many animal welfare problems of concern to its members about it. Check in with a Web site involved with that issue, and information is available with a click of a mouse.

A well-organized Web site rich with information and timely updates can have an effect not only on the political processes that govern the well-being of the world's animals, but on the individual animals themselves. Perhaps there is a rescued dog in Southern California that would be ideal for a family in Northern California. That family sees a profile of this dog on a breed rescue Web site, contacts the group and makes the trek south to meet their prospective new pet. Five years ago, that family might never have even learned about this dog because of the complications of communicating succinctly as a rescue network.

This chapter covers Web sites for animal-welfare organizations as well as dog and all-animal rescue groups. While not every breed rescue site could be listed, several are given to illustrate what's out there. You will also find main home pages for universal breed rescue sites that offer you access to sites for virtually every breed you can imagine. From national animal-welfare organizations to local breed rescue groups, there is a dire need for all levels of rescue groups in today's companion-animal landscape. It is thus encouraging to know that the existence of Web sites like these increases the ways we can help animals more efficiently.

Alaskan Malamute Protection League

http://www.connix.com/~myone/ampl/ampl.htm

Enter the site for the Alaskan Malamute Protection League (AMPL), a nationwide network that is headquarters for the various Malamute breed rescue groups around the country and keeps track of homeless Malamutes, and you will be greeted by a howl. Howling is what most of these large, beautiful sled dogs do instead of barking, and it is a joy to hear that voice.

Also a joy is the dedication to the cause evident within this site, which is managed by Webmaster Martin Yonnone.

When dealing with a dog as large and as headstrong as the wolf-like Alaskan Malamute, it comes as little surprise that far too many people will obtain one who have no business doing so. AMPL and the rescue groups with which it is affiliated not only work to be the safety net for the canine casualties of such mistakes, but also work to remedy those dog/owner relationships that can be repaired, prevent problems from occurring in the first place through education, and provide funds for dogs that can be made adoptable with a bit of medical care.

You will find these details and many more during a visit to the AMPL home page, but that's not all. Also available are direct links to, among others, the Alaskan Malamute Club of America, a wonderfully informative FAQ, subscription information for the Alaskan Malamute Mailing List, and an Alaskan Malamute Rescue List of dogs up for adoption around the country. This latter list is presented in chart form, detailing such attributes as training, activity level, size, and age. Interested parties may then e-mail the site for further information.

Best Friends Animal Sanctuary

http://bestfriends.org/

Officially this site is titled Tomato's Home Page. Technically, however, it is the home of Best Friends Animal Sanctuary, the largest sanctuary of its kind for unwanted, abused, and neglected dogs and cats. So who is this Tomato? Tomato is a sprightly tabby cat who apparently runs this cyber show. His presence sets the tone for what is, thanks to Webmaster Don Bruce's guidance, a very fun, energetic, user-friendly site devoted to a very serious topic.

Designed for quick navigation and a pleasant tour, this site offers users a variety of easy-to-access options that tell them all they would ever want to know about this world-famous sanctuary, and even offers them a mini-tour of the grounds. While crowds of people do each year make the pilgrimage for a visit to Best Friends, choose the mini-tour option from the home page, and you can take a look for yourself.

The tour begins with a collection of graphics depicting the region that Best Friends and its 1500 resident animals call home—Southern Utah, north of the Grand Canyon—and of the facility itself. Here you will meet some beloved resident dogs, visit the on-site veterinary clinic, and even get a glimpse of Dogtown, 25 acres of dog houses and enclosed yards that accommodate as many as 700 dogs on a given day. Most of these dogs will eventually find new and permanent homes. Others deemed unadoptable will spend the rest of their days within the care of this no-kill shelter.

Canine Connections Breed Rescue Information

http://www.cheta.net/connect/canine/Rescue/

Amazing. Simply amazing. That is all that can be said about this immense network of breed rescue pages, all bound together under one main page. Almost every recognized breed is represented here, and those that aren't are encouraged to get themselves added to the list. Text heavy in what amounts basically to endless lines of blue hypertext on a field of gray, the material here isn't fancy in presentation, but it is rich in information that touches all realms of canine rescue.

First is the long list of breed names that appear on the main page. Click on the name Cocker Spaniel, Basset Hound, Labrador Retriever—even Caucasian Ovcharka—and you will be inundated with the names and addresses of numerous individuals and organizations dedicated to rescuing the homeless representatives of their breeds and placing them in new homes. You might even find some information on available dogs themselves and links to other related rescue sites. Of course this listing is a never-ending work in progress, as more names and numbers are being added all the time.

But that's not all you'll find here. You'll also find a wealth of information on breed rescue itself, including a four-part FAQ by Janice Ritter that lists various breed rescues alphabetically, and information on "Starting a Purebred Rescue," by Pam Bishop. All of this falls within the larger home page for Canine Connections Online Magazine and Information Service, which is easily accessible with a click from the Breed Rescue section.

Animal Protection Institute

http://www.g-net.com/api.htm

Lovely to look at, complete in presentation and efficient in design: That is the Animal Protection Institute's Web site in a nutshell. This site, under the guidance of Webmaster Gil Lamont, boasts a particularly detailed home page that offers the browser a quick synopsis of what API is (a national nonprofit organization founded in 1968 to promote humane treatment of animals and to work actively toward that goal), and gives a complete rundown on the many publications for which API is known. But it also wastes no time in getting down to business, moving on immediately to home-page icons and hyperlinks that get the browser involved in the issues.

Following that initial introduction, you may click on one of the vivid animal icons that illustrates a particular section (e.g., a Beagle for Companion Animals or a frog for Humane Education). There is even a capitol building icon you may choose for the Public Policy section. Within these sections you will find first some basic information on how and why API is involved in this area, and then a collection of hyperlinks that delve deeper into the subject matter. For example, under Companion Animals, you can learn all about adopting a pet from a shelter, gather tips on pet care, or even click on to the USDA's "Missing Pets" Web page. At the conclusion of each section, you are offered the e-mail address and telephone number of an API contact person for that subject. All very simple and to the point.

From the home page you may also access various Action Alerts, which are issues in dire need of public involvement. The page invites you to "Join the API Action Alert Team" by first reviewing the background of each Action Alert issue, and then contacting the individuals and entities listed at the end. For those browsers who really want to get involved in the protection of animals and the prevention of animal cruelty, this Web site, a site rich in information and calls to action, is a great place to start.

Dallas/Ft. Worth Sheltie Rescue Inc.
http://www.sheltie.org/dfw.sheltie.rescue/index.html

For those who love the Shetland Sheepdog—a diminutive pup from Scotland's Shetland Isles, where the ponies, the cattle, and even the dogs are small—and are seeking to adopt a rescue Sheltie, the perfect Web site is Dallas/Ft. Worth Sheltie Rescue.

While this is indeed a locally oriented site, which is maintained by Bob Wakefield, it also offers much of value for those who don't happen to live in the Dallas/Ft. Worth area. A home page directory box appearing at the top of each section offers access to sections on rescue, public education, rehabilitation, and, a rather unique choice: lost and found, which serves to reunite Shelties with their owners. This site also offers an incredible array of links to all things Sheltie. Gathered under the title Sheltie Internet Directory, these links fill out this site, making it a full-service Sheltie information site as well as a rescue site.

The Fund for Animals
http://www.envirolink.org/arrs/fund/

The Fund for Animals, founded in 1967 by celebrated author Cleveland Amory, takes its work very seriously. Their job, says Mr. Amory, is "to speak for those who can't," whether those animals be wild, in zoos, or living in human households. The Fund's Web site offers it yet another avenue through which those voices may be heard.

Clear, concise and easy to navigate, this site, under the direction of Mike Markarian, offers abundant information: section options include Welcome to the Fund, Current Campaigns, Sanctuaries and Services, and Kids' Corner. Each of these exemplifies the combination of interactivity and information that make this a truly valuable site. For instance, one home page option is Action Alerts, which presents a vast array of local and national issues that currently require public input. Choose one of these hypertext issues, and you will be treated to the background of the issue, followed by the names and addresses of those who need to hear from the public, as well as the e-mail address of a Fund representative who can offer more information.

Also of value are the detailed Fact Sheets accessible from the home page. Covering such topics as pet overpopulation and the fur controversy, these sheets not only offer a phenomenal amount of information, but also solutions and details on what the public can do to help. The mission of this organization is to encourage people both to get involved and to volunteer input on the Web site itself.

Samoyed Rescue
http://www.samoyed.org/samrescue.html

Few dogs are as loving as the fluffy white Samoyed with its indomitable smile, but even Sammys can find themselves abandoned, homeless, and in need of rescue. Nestled within the larger Samoyed Web site, the Samoyed Rescue site has been designed as a resource to help rescuers do the best job possible in finding new and permanent homes for the dogs in their care.

Gregory Newell maintains a site that is simple and direct, headed by a home page with several area options, all of which contain helpful advice and encouragement. For instance, click on Success and Horror Stories, and, while these stories focus on the bad as well as the good, they can essentially serve as group therapy for those rescuers in need of some encouragement and the message that they are not alone.

Also available on this site, under Samoyed Rescue Pages, are detailed links to various local and national Samoyed rescue and general animal-welfare organizations (the latter of which ideally work hand in hand with the former to prevent dogs from falling through the cracks), as well as a listing of "Samoyeds in need of caring homes." Here would-be owners may peruse a chart of dogs from around the nation, reviewing their vital statistics as well as such personality comments as "Excellent with kids...Good with other dogs...Spayed...All shots...Needs experienced owner." Obviously someone is taking the time to get to know these dogs, and that is the first step toward matching the right dog to the right family, the key to a permanent relationship.

Pro Dog Breed Rescue Network

http://www.prodogs.com/frmst5.htm

Once upon a time, when someone wanted to adopt a pure-bred rescue dog, locating the appropriate rescue group could be an impossible challenge. The Internet has changed all that, of course, and today finding that group is as easy as logging on to a computer. The huge and very popular Pro Dogs Networks has made it even easier by collecting many of these under one main home page called the Breed Rescue Network. Visit this site and when you read the opening welcome—"A Collection of Breed Rescue Organizations Dedicated to Saving Animals"—you'll know you're in the right place.

From that main home page you are guided on a tour that leads you first to a home-page option of Breed Rescue Stories from various breed rescue sites, and then to Janice Ritter's Rescue FAQs that are divided alphabetically by breed. You then arrive at the Breed Rescue Web Links, where you will find an alphabetical listing of local breed rescue groups as well as those sponsored by national breed clubs.

With a slick, professional presentation, this site is easy to see, read and navigate. Most of the sites to which this rescue network links are well-constructed, discussing first their individual breeds and their care, and then presenting lists of available rescue dogs. Represented in these sites you'll find Pomeranians, Dalmatians, Chows, and Kuvascek. In fact you'll find almost every breed, and as for those you don't find, just be patient. New breeds and new sites are joining all the time, so it's safe to assume that one day, they'll all be here. In the meantime, this remains an address no dog lover should be without.

All Pets Yellow Pages: Rehabilitation and Humane Shelters

http://member.aol.com/petpage/rehab.html

Given the information presented on the main home page of All Pets Yellow Pages, it seems the site has brought on a conflict of interest. This large, multifaceted page accepts ads from people seeking to buy and sell animals for various, often controversial, reasons, yet it also accepts ads for rescue and welfare organizations. Put this conflict aside, pay attention only to the Rehabilitation and Humane Shelters page of the Yellow Pages, and you will find a valuable resource.

You won't, however, find any fancy stuff here. Just start browsing through the long list of organizations, arranged alphabetically, and you'll see why. From breed rescue organizations for, among others, Fox Terriers, Afghan Hounds, Great Danes and Basset Hounds, to regional humane organizations all over the country—many of which include direct links to the listed sites—the mix you find here is truly unique.

Animal Welfare Information Center

http://www.nal.usda.gov/awic/

From the United States Department of Agriculture, the governmental branch assigned the task of overseeing the federal Animal Welfare Act, comes this site that presents a more technical and more political view of animal protection. This begins on the AWIC home page with a menu of boxed options including Legislation, Regulations, Policies and Guidelines (extremely detailed access to government policy pages and to the entire text of the Animal Welfare Act itself), AWIC Newsletters (timely information on changes to the Act, its enforcement and related issues, as well as a search feature to help browsers locate specific topics), AWIC Publications (bibliographies and fact sheets), News and Information, APHIS Animal Care, and Institute of Laboratory Animal Resources.

Simple, direct, and surprisingly easy to navigate considering its size and many layers, this site helps browsers see animal protection issues in a broader national context and understand what they can do to get involved. It is a valuable addition to the vast array of Web sites devoted to the often-controversial subject of animal protection.

Bide-A-Wee

http://www.inch.com/~bideawee/index.html

In Scottish, Bide-A-Wee means "stay awhile." On the Net, it means you have just entered the site for a New York animal-welfare organization with a national reputation that has operated no-kill animal shelters since 1903. While this organization was obviously ahead of its time when it was founded almost 100 years ago, it is also unique in its modern-day Web site.

Simple and nondescript, beginning with a table of contents (the hypertext for which appears periodically throughout the page), this site, with few exceptions, is essentially one long page. Simple to traverse, the page clearly divides its general pet care information from the description of the organization and the services it offers. These services include fostering available animals, adoptions, the Pets for People Program that assists senior citizens in keeping their pets, pet-assisted therapy, humane education, and bereavement counseling. It then concludes with a full list of staff names and services, and the numbers where they can be reached.

All For Animals

http://allforanimals.com

Serving the Santa Barbara, California, area, this is a site that is not only informative, but graphically attractive. Friendly, personal and polished, this site represents an organization dedicated to wildlife, pets, and nature. It boasts vivid photography and clean, contemporary graphics, the latter of which highlight the home page options: Animal Rescue, Animal Testing, Calendar of Events, and Goods and Services. Click one of these—Animal Rescue, for instance—and you will be inundated with pertinent addresses and resources.

Each section opens with an inspirational quote from the likes of Darwin and da Vinci. Indeed, a great deal of thought went into the design and execution of this site, making it a valuable resource to animal lovers in Santa Barbara and beyond. Resource value aside, this site is also a nice calming place for weary Web surfing animal-lovers to visit from time to time.

The American Society for the Prevention of Cruelty to Animals

http://www.aspca.org/

Founded in 1866, the American Society for the Prevention of Cruelty of Animals is one of the oldest animal-welfare organizations in the country. Its name suggests a national scope, and many of the issues with which it concerns itself are national, but because its shelter and services primarily serve the New York area, it is typically considered more of a local than national organization.

The ASPCA's Web site is highly informational, focused on the organization and the services it offers (i.e. Humane Law Enforcement, Bergh Memorial Animal Hospital, Behavior Helpline) and the products it has available (ASPCA Pet Care books, "Extend the Web" educational materials). Illustrated with cute, simplistic graphics, it offers a clean presentation and gets right to the point. For example, the home page opens with three illustrated section options: Pet of the Week, ASPCA Founding, and Why Spay or Neuter. The first of these choices features a photo and vital statistics of one animal currently available for adoption at the ASPCA shelter and then invites the browser to come on in and meet others also awaiting new homes. Click on one that seems to be to your liking, and you will learn about that dog's breeding, size, age, etc.—the basic information you need to launch the journey toward adopting that pet.

Another impressive home-page choice is Why Spay or Neuter? Here you will find a great deal of complete, concise, reader-friendly information on the many benefits of spaying and neutering pet dogs and cats. If we would all heed this message and take to heart the information available in this section, there would be far less need for such organizations as the ASPCA.

Austin Humane Society and SPCA

http://www.austinspca.com/homepage.html

With a clean, contemporary design it is the home page that stands out most prominently on the Austin Humane Society and SPCA Web site. Designed almost like a newsletter, this two-column page maintained by Russell Malone is packed with information. Here you'll find quick info about pets and a guide to the organization's services, and it won't take you all day to collect the facts.

Covering everything from the Texas group's Pet Loss Support Group to the Furry Friends Gift Boutique, the site provides easy access to the inner workings of this organization as well as to the sections within the site. From the home page, click on the Dog Database box, for example, and be whisked to a well-organized list of dogs available for adoption, as well as information on dog care and training, the latter of which shares the home page's newsletter format, ensuring that browsers can easily find and retain important tips on safety and care.

Greyhound Rescue & Adoption Inc.

http://206.160.225.6/greyhound/

One of the most organized breeds in breed rescue and adoption is the Greyhound, specifically, the racing Greyhound. From coast to coast, enthusiasts have joined together to take in retired racing Greyhounds, place them in foster homes, rehabilitate them to civilian life, and adopt them out to well-screened owners. Rarely will you find a more wonderful pet than one of these quiet, genteel animals, most of whom seem downright grateful to their owners for their new lives off the track. Indiana-based Greyhound Rescue & Adoption Inc. is one of the organizations that takes these animals under its wing, and its Web site reflects just how effective and efficient its efforts are.

On its home page, the site urges browsers to "care enough to save a life," but it does not strive to convince the public that this is the ideal pet for every owner. Heading a text-heavy site illustrated with lovely color photos, the home page offers a clean and very detailed directory with numerous options. These cover the gamut from information on how to adopt a Greyhound, the reality of Greyhounds as pets, a listing of available dogs, and a schedule of Greyhound picnics and reunions for adopters and dogs alike. Also accessible here is a detailed section on Greyhound care, which includes the warning that your new pet, being a veteran racer, may never have navigated stairs before. It thus gives advice on training the animal in how to traverse these new strange structures in its midst.

What makes this site even more valuable to anyone who has ever been captivated by this fastest of all dogs, is the home-page link option to other Greyhound Web sites. This is an incredibly detailed listing arranged by subject. It even includes a list of other Greyhound adoption organizations from all over the country in case a would-be adopter does not happen to live in GRA's service area. The link listing alone makes this site indispensable to Greyhound lovers nationwide.

Little Shelter Animal Rescue

http://www.516Web.com/animal/ls/menu.htm

At first glance, you might assume that the Web site for Little Shelter Animal Rescue is rather ordinary, but as you spend more time there, you come to recognize the special tone to the site that lends a friendly, warm, and humble feel to its atmosphere. The site represents a nonprofit no-kill shelter organization in Huntington, New York, that was founded approximately 70 years ago. In fact, you may wish to begin your journey through this site by clicking on the history option, which will take you back, via a detailed account, to 1926 when the concept of humane societies was virtually unknown, and a group of New York residents decided to make it their job to protect "the voiceless ones."

Today their efforts have culminated in the rescue and adoption of thousands of abused and abandoned animals each year, many of whom benefit from the group's use of the Internet. While the site could expand a bit on the information presented in the Pet Overpopulation section, it hits the nail on the head with its graphics and its presentation of information on its available dogs. The former are cute pen-and-ink line drawings coupled with great photos of the dogs up for adoption. And speaking of those dogs, their stories are told by the dogs themselves, a rather sweet element that simply adds to the overall comfort factor of this site.

San Francisco Society for the Prevention of Cruelty to Animals

http://www.sfspca.org/

The San Francisco SPCA is one of the nation's most successful animal welfare organizations. This fact is reflected in the statement at the opening of the SFSPCA Web site that "only one city currently guarantees that no adoptable dog or cat will be euthanized. That city is San Francisco."

Welcome to a site that, designed by Leslie Zemenek, is inviting, clean, and energetic. From the lovely graphics (American primitive renditions of dogs and cats) to the well-organized format, this site is user-friendly and rich with information. A variety of section options on the home page lead browsers on a pleasant journey through all that makes the SFSPCA such a unique organization. For instance, take a gander at the What's New section for a calendar of events and current news stories. Then travel on to Adoptable Cats and Dogs. Here you will find a listing of the available animals, complete with color photographs and detailed information on those animals' personalities and backgrounds.

But this is only half of the SFSPCA Web story. Also within this site is information on the many programs and services for which this organization is known. These include the Foster Care Program; the Cinderella Fund that pays for medical treatment that will make sick and injured animals adoptable; the Pet Grooming College, where grooming students practice by spiffing up prospective adoption candidates; Animal Behavior Counseling Services; the Hearing Dog Program; the Low Cost Spay/Neuter Clinic; and numerous programs that help people keep their pets. Given the hospitable feel of this site, which no doubt reflects the organization itself, it is no wonder the SFSPCA has enjoyed such great success both in its adoptions and in recruiting volunteers to keep their many programs running smoothly.

The American Humane Association
http://www.sni.net/aha/

The Web site for the American Humane Association, a national nonprofit animal-welfare organization founded in 1877 and headquartered in Englewood, Colorado, is targeted at the entire spectrum of those who seek to help animals and children. From individual citizens who would like to help to animal shelter personnel to kids just entering the world of animal protection, all will find something of value here.

Short on graphics but bright with color, the AHA home page invites browsers to explore a variety of options. Because the AHA is charged with the duty of monitoring the treatment of animals on television and movie sets, for example, you may find it interesting to visit the TV & Film section. Here you will get the lowdown on all the behind-the-scenes happenings on recent films that feature animals, as well as the messages imparted by such films and answers to inevitable questions regarding show-biz animals.

While this site could benefit from the addition of more information on the problems inherent in animal cruelty and advice on pet care, spaying, and neutering, etc., it is unique in its focus on both animals and children, as the two are invariably linked. In this site, the two converge in a very positive way with the "Be Kind to Animals Kid" Contest. You'll find information on this annual contest that rewards children who make a special effort to educate the public about the needs of animals and who act on their words.

New Yorkers for Companion Animals

http://tezcat.com/~rescue/rescuegrps/nyca.shtml

The high-profile New Yorkers for Companion Animals (NYCA) has never shied away from controversy and they are not about to do so on their Web site. This site accurately reflects the passions of this grass-roots organization, and in a professional, civilized manner, covers all that is vital to NYCA volunteers and the animals they are seeking to help.

Never shrill in its presentation, this site, under the guidance of Erin Miller, covers the vital rescue information presented in the home page's adoption information and policies, and the link to Animals Available. It also offers a home-page link to Special Reports for New Yorkers, which presents such reports as "New York's Secret Animal Crisis." Ever vigilant in monitoring the treatment of animals and the policies that affect animals in the Big Apple, NYCA's devotion to those animals is present in all they do.

Siberian Husky Rescue

http://www.breeders.com/html/rescue/siberian/sibrescu.htm

This site opens under the assumption that before one presents anything about rescue, it is best first to provide the browser with links that outline the pros and cons of Siberian Husky ownership. It is inevitably the dog purchased on impulse by someone who is unprepared for the challenge such an animal can present that winds up in rescue. This is certainly true of the intelligent, energetic, almost overly exuberant Siberian, a dog that was bred to race endlessly across the tundra of Alaska and who we now ask to reside in contemporary urban and suburban households.

So at the top of this home page, which is a part of the larger Pro Dog Networks, you will find direct links to such valuable topics as The Joys and Sorrows of Siberian Ownership, Siberian Husky FAQ, and Dog Owner's Guide to the Siberian Husky.

From there, you travel on to the brass tacks of Siberian rescue and the Siberian Husky Club of America Rescue Program. Click on to Regional Contacts and Listings of Available Dogs, and you will find just that in a clear, easy-to-navigate presentation that enables the browser to explore these resources both in and out of the United States. You will also find a whole new set of valuable and pertinent links to other sites, as well as information from the Siberian Husky Club of America on how to start a breed rescue. It is always refreshing to know that a breed's national club is willing to acknowledge the need for rescue and assist in that endeavor. Not every breed club does.

Massachusetts Society for the Prevention of Cruelty to Animals

http://www.mspca.org/

If you are looking for an animal-welfare site with flair, the site for the Massachusetts Society for the Prevention of Cruelty to Animals (MSPCA) is the place. Designed by

Rob Ansaldo, this site, from the opening of its home page, draws browsers in to what is a very pleasant place to visit.

Even newcomers to the Web will find this site easy to navigate, beginning with one unique feature: The Virtual Shelter. Here you will find a listing of the animals currently available for adoption at the MSPCA's Springfield Animal Shelter in Springfield, Massachusetts. Photos accompany detailed synopses of the featured animals, which are written as if narrated by the animals themselves. "I can walk beautifully on a leash," boasts a 7-month-old Rottweiler. "I am great with children," chimes in a 3-year-old Lab. The Virtual Shelter is a very effective feature of this site, reflecting the genuine concern this organization has for the animals in its care, and the creative lengths to which it will go to ensure that they are placed in loving, permanent homes.

Also included on this site is information on upcoming MSPCA events and pertinent animal welfare legislative issues as well as information on the organization itself and what browsers can do to further its success. You can even check in with some MSPCA alumni, animals that have been adopted from the organization and have returned to report on just how things are going with their new families. Also unique is the MSPCA Springfield Animal Shelter Bulletin Board, which invites the community to discuss the many issues involved in animal welfare.

Golden Gate Labrador Rescue and Placement Service

http://www.best.com/~doghouse/dogs.htm

What sets this site apart and makes it shine is the enthusiasm with which the San Francisco Bay Area's Golden Gate Labrador Retriever Club (GGLRC) approaches the rescue of their breed. Check in to the club's main home page in which this site is nestled and you will be greeted with the pronouncement that "The GGLRC supports Labrador Rescue!" Faced with the rescue crisis that invariably affects a breed of such top-10 popularity, it would be far easier just to ignore the many dogs that are lost, abandoned, thrown away, and thus fall through the cracks. But those involved in this fine rescue site will have none of that.

Rarely will you find a listing of dogs available for adoption that is this complete. This club obviously takes great pains to learn all they can about the dogs in their care, and they present that information with style. Yet the site also works to prepare would-be adopters by regaling them with detailed information on living with Labs, choosing the right pet, and the group's various adoption requirements. As for the beneficiaries of these efforts, what lucky Labs they are.

Doris Day Animal League

http://www.ddal.org/

For years actress Doris Day has made public her passion for animals. Several years ago she founded the Doris Day Animal League, and now the DDAL has a Web site of its own. Simple and well-organized in its design, this site's home page, festooned with a portrait of Ms. Day and two of her best four-footed friends, as well as pawprint icons that carry you through the site, invites you to explore a number of options.

For instance, learn about litigation involving laboratory animals and the DDAL's own attempts to stop inhumane puppy mills in the Animal Litigation section. Or click on Legislative Updates and get the details not just on bills being introduced on a federal level that affect animals, but specific state bills, as well. Or visit the Spay Day section, and learn all about this annual event that encourages the public to participate in some positive way to end pet overpopulation by having a pet spayed or neutered, or sponsoring a poster or essay contest on the subject for school kids. You'll find plenty of great ideas here.

Of particular value is the Action Letters section, which helps you to get personally involved with animal-welfare bills, policies, and issues by contacting your elected officials and letting your voice be heard. Beginning with tips on how to write to these officials, this section then takes you in to learn everything you ever needed to know about dealing effectively with your representatives. Included here is an incredibly detailed Congressional Directory, which helps you to "Find Your Member." Also available are details on the legislative process and even advice on how to visit your representatives personally. A great deal of work has gone into this site and this section alone makes it a truly valuable asset to animal advocates.

Companion Animal Rescue and Education Service

http://www.sluug.org/~wehner/rescue/

As the old saying goes, united we stand, divided we fall. The Companion Animal Rescue and Education Service (CARES) has obviously taken this missive to heart, bringing together a variety of animal welfare and rescue groups within the St. Louis, Missouri, area for the good of the animals in that region. Tour the CARES Web site, and you will learn just how effective such cooperation can be.

After a friendly welcome on a home page that is easy on the eyes, you are presented with a simple list of options. In the process, you will meet the network of volunteers who are helping abused and homeless animals in St. Louis. Here you'll find a detailed adoption policy, an adoption application, and, under the heading "Come See Who's Looking for a Good Home," the animals themselves. Another nice, and rather unique, feature is the "Look Who's Going Home!" section, which celebrates those dogs who have found new homes because of this collective. CARES proves that you need not be glitzy and well-financed to present a Web site that is effective as well as compassionate.

People for the Ethical Treatment of Animals

http://envirolink.org/arrs/peta/index.html

It's no secret that People for the Ethical Treatment of Animals (PETA) is one of the nation's most controversial animal organizations. You can be sure that it will be at the forefront of any current issue that in any way affects non-human animals. The PETA Web site carries on this tradition.

With a tone that is far from shy and retiring, this site gets right down to business, beginning with a clean, blue and black home page devoid of illustration but rich with options. Click the various option boxes and learn about Virginia-based PETA's mission ("that animals are not ours to eat, wear, experiment on, or use for entertainment"), history, and current projects. The choices and the information presented are immense, though the entire page is beautifully organized and you always know where you are and how to get where you want to be. The many departments available for exploration include Action Alerts, which inform the public on how they can get involved in various issues; News Releases; Research, Investigations & Rescue; and Factsheets. On a lighter side, and to assist browsers to practice what PETA preaches, are a Shopping Guide for Caring Consumers and even a large collection of vegan recipes.

Another unique feature within this site is the Search Engine. As a vehicle by which browsers can call up various subjects within the vast amount of material presented here, this feature is not only a convenience, it's a necessity. So whether or not one agrees with PETA's stand on the issues, it's difficult not to be impressed by the organization's Web site.

Golden Retriever Rescue Groups

http://golden-retriever.com/rescue3.html

As part of the larger Golden Retrievers in Cyberspace site, this is a giant collection of Golden Retriever rescue groups from almost all 50 states. Even a breed as immensely popular as the Golden, is often relegated homeless and alone to the care of breed rescue volunteers.

You will find most of those volunteers' organizations represented here, easily accessible and arranged alphabetically by state. If you would rather not peruse the entire list, simply click on the state abbreviation of your choice at the top of the home page . Poor color contrasts make reading difficult in some areas, but this does not detract from the effort that has gone into compiling these resources, most of which include e-mail addresses and telephone numbers, as well as addresses.

If you're looking for glitz and glamour, you won't find it here. You will find Goldens, and once you have found inspiration, and possibly a new pet, within the rosters of this rescue site, you may wish to click on the Golden Retrievers in Cyberspace home page and be treated to even more things Golden.

Animal Rescue and Adoptable Pets

http://www.access.digex.net/~rescue/

Serving the Washington, D.C./Baltimore, Maryland area is the Web site for Animal Rescue and Adoptable Pets. Under the guidance of Michael K. Heney and Amy Bleich, with the input of a network of local organizations and volunteers, this site provides information on various animal welfare and adoption events being held in the region, as well as informational resources. Right on the home page you will find hyperlinks to information on the Doris Day Animal League's Spay Day USA and Prevent-A-Litter Month sponsored by the Humane Society of the United States, as well as a schedule of adoption events at local pet supply stores.

Click on Adoptable Dogs from the home page, and you will be treated to a detailed list of dogs up for adoption, as well as an animated graphic of a running puppy for inspiration. The list is well-detailed with statistics on the individual dogs as well as notes regarding their personalities and situations, such as "big, sweet dog" and "needs special home." Also listed are the organizations from whom the dogs are available, as well as links to those organizations. What a boon such communication is for dogs in need.

The Marin Humane Society

http://www.marin-humane.org

The Web site for the Marin Humane Society (MHS) in Novato, California, boasts one of the most beautiful home pages you're likely to find on any dog-related site. It opens with a lovely pastel portrait of animals running against a backdrop of the rolling green hills of California's Marin County.

From there you can learn a great deal about this local organization, founded in 1907, and now considered one of the best in the nation. The options on the home page, cover everything from Behavior and Training to Rescue Services to featured Pets of the Week at the MHS Adoption Center. Before visiting the center in person, you may wish to stop first at the online Adoption Center, where you will meet the dogs currently available for adoption. This virtual center is accessible either from the home page or the Pets of the Week section. The Adoption Center is valuable because it introduces would-be adopters to prospective pets and takes great pains to educate them about what they are getting themselves into in case they choose to make this important commitment.

Such attention to detail is evident throughout this site. For instance, even within the Service sections—say, the Low Cost Spay/Neuter Clinic section—you will learn not only about the particular service, but also why spaying and neutering are important and how they are significant both to the individual animal and to the pet population at large. This site stands as a fine example of just what a local organization can accomplish for the animals in its community and beyond.

Boxer Rebound, Inc.

http://www.cl.ais.net/chipper/index.html

Colorful and lively: That is the impression one gets when entering the Boxer Rebound's Web site for the benefit of rescued Boxers in the Northern Illinois and Southern Wisconsin area. With colorful graphics this page is so skillfully executed that it no doubt is quite successful in getting its message across and finding its Boxers permanent homes.

This attention to design is not to say that this site does not mean business. Begin your exploration into what it means to own a Boxer—and to qualify as an adopter for this organization—and you may begin to feel a bit intimidated. This group's aim is not to place its Boxers as quickly as possible, but to take the necessary time to ensure placements will be permanent. This means careful evaluation of the dogs' health and personalities, long-term foster care of the dogs if necessary, a long, drawn-out application process for would-be adopters, and home visits of those would-be adopters in which every family member must be evaluated with the dog. This page convinces those who are seeking to adopt a dog from this organization that it is truly a privilege to be chosen.

Do not allow the fact that this site is local in focus to prevent you from exploring its environs. Acknowledging that the intensely personal nature of their adoption procedures preclude them from adopting out beyond their service area, this group does provide a detailed list of referral links to all regions of the country, as well as to Boxer information sites and the American Boxer Club home page. This feature makes this a valuable site to anyone seeking to live with a Boxer (or any dog), or to those who just want to satisfy a thirst for knowledge about the breed.

PART III

Active Dogs

Dog Clubs and Associations

Dog lovers are good at getting together and forming strong alliances—much like their pack-loving dependents. Consequently, just about every aspect of the dog world is represented by an organization of some sort.

Dog clubs and associations are places where dog lovers come together to share their common interests and goals. These groups are the source of considerable social interaction for their members, particularly local dog clubs that sponsor shows and other activities. Many dog-oriented groups represent strong opinions on various issues in the dog world, while others simply provide fun activities for their members.

Whatever the focus of each club or association, these organized groups clearly make up the backbone of the canine world. From powerful all-breed registries like the American Kennel Club to tiny, local dog groups with only a handful of members, these are the organizations whose dedicated participants and staff have made the dog community the political and social force that it is today.

Dog clubs and dog associations are slowly beginning to make themselves known on the Internet, although limited funds and manpower make it difficult for many volunteer-oriented groups to create and maintain their own Web sites. Even some groups who have more money than the smaller volunteer organizations have not rushed to put up Web sites. Important all-breed registries such as the United Kennel Club and States Kennel Club do not have a presence on the Net for instance, nor do many of the larger federations of

continued after the feature section

American Kennel Club

http://www.akc.org

The American Kennel Club (AKC) is the king of dog clubs, the premier registry and governing body in the North American dog world, and was founded in 1884 by an elite group of sporting dog fanciers.

The AKC's primary function is to register purebred dogs. There are 141 recognized breeds and varieties on the AKC roster, and the organization maintains stud books for each of these breeds. The club also sanctions dog shows and other canine events around the country.

In recent times, the AKC has become more involved in issues affecting the well-being of dogs, such as genetic disease, legislation, and animal welfare. This huge organization, once governed by an aristocratic group of dog fanciers, is now ruled by delegates representing hundreds of regional and breed-specific dog clubs.

The AKC site begins with a newsy section that highlights recent developments. Legislative news, the most recent breed registration statistics, and the details on the latest genetic health conference can all be found here.

The next section is Registration, which contains the club's guidelines regarding registration, record-keeping, suspensions from the club, artificial insemination, and more. Just about anything you'd want to know about registering a dog with the AKC can be found here, including a FAQ section and the option to download an application form.

The Dog Breeds area of the site includes information on buying a dog, choosing the right breed, living with a dog, selecting a breeder, and obedience training. A Breed of the Month is highlighted with several photographs and video clips from the breed's AKC videotape.

An explanation of the AKC's seven groups leads into the general breed section, where individual breeds are listed by group. Browsers can find photographs and descriptions of every AKC recognized breed of dog.

In addition to national breed club information, a listing of the National Breed Club Rescue Network can be found here with the name, address, and phone number of each rescue club coordinator.

Sanctioning events is a large part of the AKC's function, and the Rules and Regulations section includes all the club's rules dog shows, obedience trials, lure coursing events, herding trials, hunting tests, and other AKC activities.

The AKC publishes the *AKC Gazette,* a monthly magazine with a circulation in excess of 50,000. Browsers can take an abbreviated look at the most recent issue of the magazine. The cover and table of contents are featured here, along with subscription information.

The remainder of the site includes an explanation of how the AKC is governed, along with a list of delegates and board members; an area to purchase AKCmaterial; details on how to reach each department in the organization; and a complete listing of all upcoming dog shows and events sanctioned by the organization, as well as results of past events.

dog clubs that represent large regions of the country. However, dog people love to traffic in information, and it shouldn't be too long before most clubs and associations are providing computer-equipped dog owners with online services.

This chapter covers some of the clubs and organizations that currently have a strong presence on the Internet, and runs the gamut from all-breed registries to larger breed clubs. Many organizations have Web sites that provide more information on their designated activity than on the club itself, and these sites can be found in the chapters within this book dedicated to that particular activity. The sites in this chapter focus on providing information on the actual organization and present wonderful opportunities for dog lovers to get very involved.

The Kennel Club

http://www.the-kennel-club.org.uk/

Before there was an American Kennel Club, there was a Kennel Club. This British organization was the first all-breed canine registry in the western world, and served as the model for the American Kennel Club's founders.

Started in 1877 in London by a group of dog fanciers, the Kennel Club compiled the first stud book in the history of purebred dogs. The organization now functions as the governing body for the sport of purebred dogs in the United Kingdom. The Kennel Club classifies breeds, registers pedigrees, handles transfers, and performs other administrative functions required to maintain a registry. The group also licenses shows, recognizes other clubs, and publishes its monthly publication, the *Kennel Gazette*.

A total of 188 breeds are currently eligible for registration with the Kennel Club. Divided among the Hound, Gundog, Terrier, Utility, Working and Toy groups, these breeds represent a wide variety of dogs.

The Kennel Club's online presence reflects thegroup's importance, and is an excellent source of information for dog owners who want to find out more about this influential organization.

The site starts with a description of the Kennel Club, and then leads into details on the Kennel Club Junior Organisation (KCJO). Designed to help children develop their skills with dogs, this program for those 8 to 18 years old includes a competition at the Crufts Dog Show, and conformation and agility events.

The Good Citizen Dog Scheme, described at length in the site, is similar to the American Kennel Club's Canine Good Citizen program. The primary difference is in the test itself, which presents different scenarios to dogs being evaluated. The end result is the same, however: passing dogs receive a decree that they are fit for life in modern society.

The site also includes information on the Kennel Club's Charitable Trust, events, publications, and other of the club's services. The area on the organization's library, featuring details on the collection and hours open to the public, is interesting, especially for dog lovers who may be planning a trip to London.

American Canine Association

http://www.he.net/aca/

The American Canine Association (ACA), located in Wilmington, Delaware, is David to the American Kennel Club's Goliath. A small, little known registry, the American Canine Association was started in 1984 to track and monitor the health, breeding, and performance of purebred dogs. Differing from the American Kennel Club in the way that its registration process emphasizes genetic health, the American Canine Association obviously considers itself an alternative to the older, more traditional registry.

The American Canine Association registers any and all breeds, judging from the list presented on the site, which includes not only the more common breeds but others such as the American Hairless Terrier, Azawakh, and Karelo-Finnish Laika. While it seems to embrace every purebred dog, the organization does not sanction or sponsor shows and events and serves solely as a registering body.

A detailed description of what the American Canine Association is all about appears early in the site, along with a history of the group. A persuasive argument on why dogs should be registered with the organization also appears here, along with details on how to actually register a dog with the association.

An area entitled Becoming an ACA Participating Club explains how the American Canine Association offers benefits to individual breed clubs that choose to maintain their own registries. The American Canine Association accepts the rules and restrictions dictated by individual clubs while serving as their registration arm. This is a unique service provided by this organization to the purebred dog community.

Dog owners can also download registration applications and other forms from this site, and send e-mails to the organization for more information.

Continental Kennel Club

http://www.ckcusa.com

Another alternative registry to the American Kennel Club and the United Kennel Club, the Continental Kennel Club bills itself as "the all-breed hassle-free kennel club." Founded in 1991, the organization claims to be growing at a rate that will make its registration figures top the one million mark within the next four to five years.

There's good reason for these high numbers: The Continental Kennel Club registers a whopping 423 breeds, including obscure dogs like the Abyssinian Sand Terrier, Majestic Tree Hound, and West Siberian Laika. A quick read of the club's Developing New Breeds area on its Web site shows why. Unlike the American Kennel Club and the United Kennel Club, the Continental Kennel Club encourages the development of new breeds. This controversial position is backed up by the group's statement that to do otherwise is to do "harm to the dog kingdom."

The Continental Kennel Club site provides a good means to learn about this organization, whether you agree with their policies or not. All 423 breeds are listed here, along with descriptions that include origin, height, group, weight, coat type, and color. In the Developing New Breeds section, there are details on the organization's unique policy of registering crossbreeds as a means of helping develop new breeds.

Other places on the site provide various other information on the club, including how to order a number of dog books published by various sources directly from the Continental Kennel Club and general advice on how to buy a puppy.

Pennsylvania Federation of Dog Clubs

http://www.paonline.com/pfdc

The Pennsylvania Federation of Dog Clubs is an organization of canine clubs throughout the Keystone State. Its purpose is to monitor state and regional legislation affecting dogs, and to educate the public about canine activities and responsible pet ownership.

Founded in 1970, the Pennsylvania Federation of Dog Clubs is composed of over 100 member clubs representing a variety of different dog-related activities, from showing to herding.

The group's Web site is primarily geared toward educating Pennsylvania dog owners about pending legislation affecting dogs and dog ownership. Considerable lobbying is done here on behalf of dogs, including strong encouragement for dog owners to write to their legislative representatives on a variety of dog-related subjects.

The Legislative area on the site points out pending legislation and provides news on recent rulings on local, state, and federal fronts. A section here also presents interesting information on dog ownership in Pennsylvania, including the fact that nearly 2 million dogs reside in the state, but only 800,000 are licensed.

The subject of puppy mills is high on the list of topics dealt with in this site, and there is an area devoted especially to it. Articles on the commercial breeding and sale of dogs, featuring reprinted pieces from the *Philadelphia Inquirer,* can be found here.

Detailed information on Pennsylvania Federation of Dog Clubs symposiums, dog licensing, dangerous dog laws, rabies, and how to get in touch with club officers as well as state officials is included in the site. There is even a complete draft of a proposed "puppy lemon law" available for perusing.

Jack Russell Terrier Club of America

http://207.69.134.171/jrtca.htm

The Jack Russell Terrier is a popular breed that so far has eluded American Kennel Club recognition. The reason for this is the strength and unity of the Jack Russell Terrier Club of America, an organization dedicated to fighting acceptance of the breed by the American Kennel Club.

The detailed reasons for the Jack Russell Terrier Club of America's resistance to American Kennel Club recognition are explained on its home page, part of the large Jack Russell Terrier breed site (see Chapter 1). Discussions about preserving the breed's working heritage are at the core of the explanation, which goes into considerable detail.

The Jack Russell Terrier Club of America site also provides information on club terrier trials, including results and details on upcoming events. A membership application, a list of the board of directors, and an explanation on how to join are also included.

There are several interesting areas in this site, including one link called Terrier Registration. Here, the Jack Russell Terrier Club of America's unique registration process is explained in detail. Unlike most registries, the Jack Russell Terrier Club of America does not register entire litters at birth. Instead, each dog is individually registered based on the animal's particular health and merits. A veterinary certificate stating that the dog is free from genetic defects is one of the more unusual requirements of registration.

Educational articles on the breed can be found at this site, along with personal stories about individual dogs submitted by Jack Russell Terrier owners. A page called Bad Dog Talk does everything it can to convince readers not to own a Jack Russell Terrier, since the breed is not right for everyone, but for those who can't be swayed, there is information on how to go about purchasing one of these small, high-energy dogs.

The American Rescue Dog Association

http://www.ardainc.org

Airscenting is the canine technique of locating quarry using air currents and the dog's incredible olfactory skills. The American Rescue Dog Association is the official organization for airscenting search dogs, animals whose talents are used to find humans in distress.

The American Rescue Dog Association was founded in 1972 by Bill and Jean Syrotuck, the couple who refined the concept of using airscenting search dogs for rescue work in wilderness situations. Subsequently, the organization has developed standards and training for airscenting dogs across the country.

The American Rescue Dog Association Web site features a description of the organization and information on how to become a member. Since membership in the American Rescue Dog Association requires extensive training in search and rescue using airscenting techniques, not just anyone can join. However, details on the type of education required can be obtained from the organization by individuals motivated to become involved in this rewarding activity.

A copy of the American Rescue Dog Association's award-winning book, *Search & Rescue Dogs: Training Methods,* released a few years ago by a major publisher, is also available for purchase online.

Frontier Belgian Shepherd Dog Association

http://www.critterschoice.com/fbsda/fbsda.htm

There are four different Belgian sheep-herding breeds: the Belgian Shepherd (or Groenendael), the Laekenois, the Belgian Malinois and the Belgian Tervuren. The Frontier Belgian Shepherd Dog Association represents all four of these breeds under one umbrella group.

Sanctioned by the United Kennel Club, and participating in United Kennel Club events, the Frontier Belgian Shepherd Dog Association is centered in the Rocky Mountain region of the United States. However, the group has members from around the country and includes anyone who loves the four Belgian herding breeds.

The Frontier Belgian Shepherd Dog Association Web site provides information on how to join the group and the benefits of membership, along with a list of current regional Belgian breed clubs and contacts. Links to Belgian dog-related pages are also included for those who can't get enough of these charming animals.

ARF!

http://critterschoice.com/arf/arfhome.htm

ARF! stands for Atlanta Recreation and Fun Club for Dogs, an unusual regional club headquartered in the South and dedicated to just having fun with dogs. ARF! doesn't register dogs or get involved in heavy political issues. It exists merely to promote social activities for dogs and their owners.

ARF! is a non-profit organization with an all-volunteer staff, who work to promote responsible pet ownership, raise funds for canine charities, educate the general public about dogs, and organize social events. The organization's Web site reflects this attitude, particularly in the ARF! Newsletter Online area. Here articles on the group's fun events, goings on, and other items can be found. A recent edition contained an article on a lost dog who was subsequently found, a report on coverage of the group by a local television station, and humorous instructions on how to photograph a puppy. Two issues of the ARF! Newsletter appear in each edition of the page.

A membership application and registration form are available online, as are other tidbits of canine interest. A list of ARF!-approved Web site links brings up the rear of the site.

The Ottawa Kennel Club

http://infoweb.magi.com/~okc

Canada is filled with dedicated dog lovers, and the Ottawa Kennel Club is just one of several organizations catering to them. Established in 1887, the Ottawa Kennel Club is the oldest continuously active kennel club in the Great White North.

The organization's objective is to promote the interests of purebred dogs. Boasting 450 members, the club promotes canine activities and provides a breeder referral service to the communities of Ottawa and Hull.

The Ottawa Kennel Club Web site reflects the activities of the organization, beginning with a detailed history of the club. A photograph of the founder and his family, along with information on the first dog show sponsored by the club can be found through the History hyperlink.

In the Ottawa Kennel Club Dog Shows area, information is provided on the club's six all-breed conformation shows and six obedience trials. Dates, judges, show secretaries, and judging schedules are all available online. Details on the Show of Shows is also presented here.

Upcoming happenings in the Ottawa Kennel Club's calendar can be researched online, along with details on the clubs executives and committees. Every committee from membership to publicity is listed in this area, along with names and phone numbers of committee chairs.

The Ottawa Kennel Club Breeder Directory section contains an article on purchasing a purebred dog along with the club's Code of Ethics for breeders. A list of breeds with corresponding member breeders in the Ottawa area is available, including names, addresses, phone numbers, e-mail and Web site addresses, if applicable.

Dog Writers' Association of America

http://www.prodogs.com/dwaa/contents.htm

Unlike other dog clubs listed here, the Dog Writers' Association of America is not specifically for those who own dogs, but rather for those who write about them.

The Dog Writers' Association of America is a professional organization for journalists who make a living writing about dogs, and those who aspire to. The club was started in 1935 by a group of reporters who found themselves spending a lot of their time covering dogs. Although only eight writers made up the founding party, the organization now boasts well over 400 members.

Every year in New York City, on the Sunday night just before the Westminster Dog Show, the Dog Writers' Association of America holds its annual banquet and awards competition for materials published on the subject of dogs the year prior. A monthly newsletter and scholarship program are also part of the organization's activities.

The Dog Writers' Association of America Web site is primarily devoted to promoting entry into the awards competition, featuring official rules, competition categories, special awards, and even a competition entry form. There is also considerable information on the profession of dog writing and what it takes to become a member of the association. An application for membership appears online, and can be printed and mailed in by qualified candidates.

The Guide Dog Association

http://www.world.net/Business/Charity/guide-dogs/
welcome.html

When it comes to training guide dogs for the visually impaired, the Guide Dog Association is one of the premier organizations in the world. It's Web site is small and simple, but provides basic information on the group and its projects. The presence of an adorable Labrador Retriever puppy on every page makes browsing here more enjoyable.

The first hypertext link, the Guide Dog Association, brings up a page with a brief description of the value of guide dogs and a testimonial from a guide-dog owner. Guide Dog Association Visits describes the actual speakers and their dogs who are available for school visits, or as pet therapy dogs for hospitals and nursing homes.

The organization also offers a list of videos on the subject of guide dogs. Details on the contents of each are given in the Guide Dog Association Videos area. This page provides an order form to that will enable you to obtain the video of your choice.

California Rescue Dog Association

http://yellow.crc.ricoh.com/carda/

The California Rescue Dog Association (CARDA) is known throughout the country for its team of 100 volunteer handlers and their specially trained dogs. Available 24 hours a day, 365 days a year, these volunteer searchers have helped victims and their families in a number of disasters over recent years, including the Northridge earthquake and the Oklahoma City bombing.

The California Rescue Dog Association was established in 1976, and is the largest search dog group in the nation. This non-profit organization trains search-and-rescue (SAR) teams for mission-ready status.

The group's Web site contains a lot of good information on how the organization works and how to become involved. The details begin with the CARDA Information Brochure hyperlink, which features data on how the group trains its members, what search-and-rescue dogs can do, and for whom the group works. Also here is an in-depth explanation of exactly what the organization does; its relationship to the California Office of Emergency Services Law Enforcement Division, FEMA, and other agencies; along with other information. Examples of actual searches done by the group are here as well, as are links to the Polly Klaas Foundation and Oklahoma City bombing sites.

There are certain techniques to training search-and-rescue dogs, and the California Rescue Dog Association site includes a collection of articles on working with and training a search-and-rescue dog. Experienced CARDA members also provide tips on training online.

The Pictures of SAR Dogs at Work area features color photographs of CARDA dogs at work on real searches and during training exercises, while Statistics! details the number of searches the group participates in each year.

Included here are areas on how to get in touch with the organization, how to send donations, and the latest news relating to the group's efforts.

National Association of Dog Obedience Instructors
http://www.kimberly.uidaho.edu/nadoi/

As stated in the National Association of Dog Obedience Instructors site, anyone can call themselves a dog trainer and go into business. This leaves the dog owning public with little means for determining that person's qualifications.

Because of the need for established qualifications in the profession, the National Association of Dog Obedience Instructors (NADOI) was formed. The group trains obedience instructors to ensure their competence, with the goal of the continued overall improvement of dog training.

The National Association of Dog Obedience Instructors Web site offers information to dog trainers and dog owners who want to learn more about this group's activities. For trainers interested in certification by NADOI, the Qualifications for Membership area clearly explains the requirements. Dog owners can also benefit by reading this section, as it provides information on the experience and expertise of any trainer who belongs to the group.

Other areas also spell out the benefits of using a NADOI trainer, including the What NADOI Means to an Instructor and What NADOI Means to the Dog Owner hyperlinks.

Also included here are the organization's Code of Ethics, information on the group's annual gathering and workshops, and a list of member trainers and their e-mail links.

Delta Society

http://petsforum.com/deltasociety/

In 1977, a medical doctor named Michael McCulloch began to work to understand the quality of the human-animal companion bond. The result was the formation of the Delta Society, an organization dedicated to the relationship between owners and their pets.

The Delta Society is a truly unique group, with a mission unequaled by any other organization in the canine community. The Delta Society's early years focused on funding the first credible research on why pets are important to their owners. The group has since grown to become a vital entity in the continued study of the relationship between humans and their pets.

The Delta Society's Web site begins with the Delta Society Overview, a section that details the group's mission and goals, history, accomplishments and organizational structure. It also provides an overview of the Delta Society's many programs.

On the subject of programs, there is considerable information to found in this site. The Pet Partners link describes this model pet therapy project, designed to train volunteers to visit nursing homes, hospitals and other places with animals in tow. Therapy dogs and other pets are screened through this program for temperament and training.

The National Service Dog Center is another Delta Society program. It helps people with disabilities achieve greater independence through the use of canine assistance. According to the site, this program combines the talents of those with expertise in the subject of service dogs to produce quality educational materials and information systems dealing with service-dog issues.

Another program that focuses on the Delta Society's original purpose at the time of its founding is People & Pets. Featuring activities that promote the human-animal bond, the motivation behind this program is the strongly held Delta Society conviction that pets are good for the physical and mental health of their owners. Information on the group's Animal Assisted Therapy Services is also included.

The Delta Society produces a wide variety of publications on the subject of the human-animal bond. Details on how to order and/or subscribe to this wide variety of materials are on the site. The group's special events and items for sale can also be accessed.

World Protection Dog Association

http://www.wpda.com

The subject of using dogs as a means for physical protection is somewhat controversial in the dog world. Some people believe that dogs who are violent toward humans—even in controlled situations—contribute to the negative image that dogs in general sometimes suffer from in our society. Other people, especially those who are involved in breeds developed specifically for guarding and attack purposes, feel that there is nothing wrong with owning and competing with a well-trained protection dog.

The founders and members of the World Protection Dog Association (WPDA) belong to this latter category. A relatively new organization created to establish guidelines for personal-protection–dog certification, the group intends to set standards by which dog owners who want their dogs to be trained in personal protection will be better able to choose a qualified trainer.

The World Protection Dog Association site discusses the benefits of the organization, as well as its various programs and activities. Geared primarily toward members, the site explains the group's rating system, gives information on upcoming events, and provides information on how to join. The thorough explanation of the organization's Pro Program can help dog owners understand how dogs are tested by the WPDA, and what kind of temperament and ability a dog needs to become a good protector.

North American Versatile Hunting Dog Page

http://www.navhda.org

The North American Versatile Hunting Dog Association (NAVHDA) is a nonprofit corporation whose purpose is to foster, promote, and improve what the group considers the versatile hunting-dog breeds. Functioning not only as a registry, but as a show-giving club, NAVHDA is made up primarily of individuals who hunt with their dogs.

NAVHDA defines a versatile hunting dog as one that is bred and trained to dependably hunt and point game and to retrieve and track wounded game on both land and water. Included in this definition are the German Shorthaired Pointer, German Longhaired Pointer, German

Wirehaired Pointer, Weimaraner, Vizsla, Wirehaired Vizsla, Small Musterlander, Large Musterlander, Brittany, Pudelpointer, Wirehaired Pointing Griffon, and several other miscellaneous breeds.

The NAVHDA Web site includes all this information and more. A calendar of events, a list of local chapters, feature articles on training, and even how to start your own NAVHDA chapter are here.

United Schutzhund Clubs of America/German Shepherd Working Dog Club

http://www.igateway.net/~usagsdog/

The activity of schutzhund was developed in Germany decades ago and is synonymous with the German Shepherd breed. It is for this reason that the United Schutzhund Club of America and the German Shepherd Working Dog Club are associated and have created a Web site to promote the sport.

Beginning with a detailed explanation of the United Schutzhund Clubs of America (which uses the sometimes-confusing acronym USA), the site starts out by describing the link between the group and the World Union of German Shepherd Dog Clubs. Along with sending an American team to the schutzhund World Championship event each year, the United Schutzhund Clubs of America also sanctions club trials, endurance tests, regional championships and two annual national championship trials. Information on the sport of schutzhund can be found at this site, as well as a membership application, lists of affiliated clubs, trial results, and even sportswear with the club's logo. A calendar of events, organized by region and date, is helpful, as is a list of trial judges' addresses and phone numbers.

United States Rottweiler Club

http://users.aol.com/USRCWEB/home.html

In Germany, dogs that were bred to work are required to demonstrate their capabilities before being thought of as quality breeding stock. Modeling themselves after the *Allgemeiner Deutscher Rottweiler Klub* of Germany, the United States Rottweiler Club (USRC) subscribes to this same philosophy and strives to encourage what they call "improved breeding" in American Rottweilers.

The United States Rottweiler Club conducts Breed Suitability Tests to determine a dog's breeding qualifications, based on its working instincts and skills. The group also holds an annual Rottweiler show as well as schutzhund trials.

The United States Rottweiler Club's site provides an array of information about the organization's activities. Membership information along with an e-mail address of the club's secretary are provided, plus a list of upcoming events that includes judges, classes and who to contact for more information.

Interested dog owners can obtain a list of provisional clubs, divided by region, along with e-mail links to the appropriate representatives. Details on the Breed Registry and Suitability Test can be found on the site, as can in-depth information on the Rottweiler rescue arm of the organization.

Old Dominion Kennel Club

http://members.aol.com/kblairh/odck.html

The Old Dominion Kennel Club is a prestigious, Virginia-based, all-breed dog club that was founded in the 1930s. The group holds two annual breed shows that are arguably the largest shows on the East Coast, boasting some 5,000 dogs per event.

The Old Dominion Kennel Club's Web site is small and simple, but provides solid information on the group's history and regular events. Dog socialization classes, fundraising events, monthly meetings, information on the club's breeder referral service, and, of course, information on the club's famous all-breed shows can be found here.

American Rare Breeds Association

http://www.arba.org

The mission of the American Rare Breeds Association (ARBA) is to promote and serve the rare-breed dog. By definition, this would be a purebred dog that is not eligible for full registration with the American Kennel Club, but which has a breed standard and is registered with a national or international kennel club.

The American Rare Breeds Association divides its recognized breeds into seven groups: Companion, Herding, Hound, Spitz and Primitive, Sporting, Terrier, and Working. The organization hosts a national rare-breed show each year that incorporates these seven groups. The club sanctions regional specialties as well.

The ARBA Web site is a good place to learn about rare breeds, since it provides information on each of the breeds it registers. And for people who want to purchase a rare breed dog, the listing of breeders featured here is invaluable since locating an uncommon breed can be incredibly difficult.

Since showing is an important part of ARBA, there is an extensive amount of material in the Show Catalogs area online, including lists of dogs that are pre-entered in shows (an unusual offering for any dog club), show entry forms, show schedules and lists of judges.

Rare-breed aficionados can purchase newsletters, T-shirts, and sweat shirts online, while breeders can find information here on how to advertise.

In order to find the bulk of aforementioned information, browsers must click on the hyperlink called Products & Services, which contains all the data on the group's recognized breeds, breeders, and activities.

Dog Shows

The dog show world is a phenomenon that knows few rivals. Decades old, the tradition of putting purebred dogs in the show ring and comparing their qualities is practiced the world over.

The hobby of showing dogs began in England in the mid-1800s, when dog-loving aristocrats came together to compare the appearances of their well-bred dogs. The practice soon spread throughout Europe and eventually the world.

In the United States, conformation dog showing (comparing dogs based on appearance alone) represents a large industry involving thousands of people and dogs. Many breeders work their whole lives toward developing winning show lines, and professional handlers, groomers, and kennel aides labor full-time as specialists in this field.

Dog shows in the United States are sanctioned by the American Kennel Club, the United Kennel Club, and the States Kennel Club. Events representing American Kennel Club member-clubs far outnumber the other organizations and run into the thousands each year. Each of these American Kennel Club shows features judging within each breed and breed group.

While dog registries sanction conformation shows, superintendents actually make the show happen. The superintendent's job is to accept entries, keep track of who wins what, and make sure the event runs smoothly and without problems. In the United States, there are currently

continued after the feature section

The Virtual Dog Show

http://www.dogshow.com

Real-life dog shows are exciting, but it takes a lot of work and knowledge to participate in one. Not so for the Virtual Dog Show, an online competition run by Idyll Mountain Internet that allows dog owners to present their canine companions for judging without asking their pooches to leave the couch.

Offering a variety of classes for both purebred dogs and mixed-breeds, the Virtual Dog Show combines the formality of a conformation show with the light-heartedness of a neighborhood party. Bright colors and pleasant graphics that are quick to load make the site enjoyable.

On the home page, where the concept of an online dog show is carefully explained. Dogs are judged through a series of photographs provided by the owner via e-mail or snail mail. Conformation classes are arranged by group and then by breed, and dogs are judged according to their respective breed standards. Mixed-breeds can also compete here in their own classes, and actually go head-to-head with the purebreds in the Best in Show competition, something unheard of in real dog shows.

Another area of competition, called the Variety Classes, consists of fun and unusual events. The largest category within this group is the Single-Dog Variety, which is made up of virtual classes for puppies, rescued dogs, old dogs, dogs who look like their owners, dogs in action, and others.

Because of the Internet's international scope, canines from all over the world are entered in classes at the Virtual Dog Show. In the Results area, photographs of the winning dogs from the most recent virtual show are displayed according to class. Here the Variety Classes prove to be especially entertaining to the casual browser.

The Show Schedule area lists upcoming virtual shows on the site. There are two full shows held each year, in the spring and fall, and smaller, specialized match shows (for puppies) in between.

The experts who volunteer their time to preside at the virtual show are experienced dog fanciers. Most are long-time breeders who show their dogs; a few are obedience trainers.

Judging and posting of results happen quickly. Judges award placements of first through fifth in the individual classes, along with awards of merit. The dogs who win get more than just their photos posted on the site. Prizes, donated by sponsor companies, are also awarded. A list of these gifts, appears in the Prizes area.

Just like a real dog show, this virtual happening is a social event. Participants can meet with judges, sponsors, staff, and other participants in real-time chats to discuss their dogs, the show, or anything they want.

While the chat area is only available to North American exhibitors, the Web masters assure us that European and Australian exhibitors will also be able to participate sometime in the future, making the Virtual Dog Show a truly international event.

17 annually licensed practicing dog show superintendents, each concentrating on a certain area of the country.

Dog show superintendents and fanciers alike are taking advantage of the Internet and providing dog lovers with information on how to enter, watch, and enjoy dog shows. Web sites on the subject of dog shows cover everything from superintendent pages to informational areas to virtual dog shows that any dog owner can enter.

Crufts Dog Show

http://www.crufts.org.uk/home.htm

The Crufts Dog Show is one of the oldest and most prestigious dog shows in the world. Started by Charles Crufts in 1891, the first Crufts show was held in London, England. Subsequent shows were managed and promoted by Charles Crufts until his death in the late 1930s. At this point, the Kennel Club took over the show and has run the event ever since.

The Crufts Dog Show moved from London to Birmingham, England, in 1991. With the exception of cancellations due to war, the Crufts show has been held annually for more than a century.

The Crufts Web site, managed by the Kennel Club, provides a variety of information of interest to the casual dog lover and the serious fancier alike. Beginning with the background of the show in the Crufts History area, the site details the beginnings of the event in the 1800s and talks at length about how Charles Crufts came to be the master of the occasion. Frames called "Did You Know?" appear throughout the site, featuring tidbits of historical information in less likely places.

If you are planning to attend the event in person, you'll want to check out the Show Information area, which contains invaluable facts about how to get there, places to visit, which show events will be judged in which rings, who the judges are, how to get tickets, and more.

Crufts is more than a conformation show, as is evidenced by other features on the site like the Good Citizen Dog Scheme (a demonstration designed to promote obedience training among dog owners) and KCJO (the Kennel Club's junior organization for 8–18 year olds).

Fans of the Crufts show can also purchase merchandise online at the site, including umbrellas, "hold-alls," body warmers, wallets, T-shirts, baseball caps and other assorted goodies bearing the Crufts logo. This opportunity is especially exciting for American and Canadian dog lovers who previously had to travel to England to buy one of these souvenirs.

And last but not least, Web browsers can find data on the most recent winners of the Crufts show, in the categories of Groups, Best In Show, Obedience, Agility, and Flyball.

Info Dog

http://www.infodog.com/main.htm

For many, the world of the dog show superintendent is a mysterious one. Dog shows just seem to happen; few people seem to know how.

Moss-Bow Foley Inc. (known as MB-F in the dog community) is one of several dog show superintendents that has made the move to demystify this element of the dog show world, and are using the Web to carry this out.

In existence since 1976, after a succession of mergers combining three different independent superintendents who had been staging dog shows since the turn of the century, MB-F puts on the majority of canine events in the Northeast United States. Among these shows is the prestigious Westminster Kennel Club Dog Show held in New York City every February.

Dog show exhibitors are familiar with the superintendents who run the events in their area because they must submit entries for the show through these organizations, previously by regular mail only. MB-F has made the process much easier for exhibitors by putting everything a dog owner needs to enter a show right there on the Web.

But Info Dog, the MB-F Web site, provides much more than just an entry form for exhibitors. Every year, results from the Westminster Kennel Club Show are posted on the site within minutes after they happen. Other dog sites strive to beat the MB-F site at its own game, and so the competition to get the results up on the Web is ferocious. During the Westminster Kennel Club Dog Show, the majority of die-hard dog fanciers around the country can be found glued to their computers, switching from the MB-F page to other sites, looking for the first results.

Because the Westminster show is so popular, Info Dog also includes links to other Westminster-related sites, despite the competitiveness on the two nights of the show. One of these is a connection to the show's television broadcast station, usually the USA Network.

If you want to find out who won what at just about any dog show in the Northeast, the Calendar of Shows and Results is the place to look. Results of shows over the past 150 days are posted, by date, as are lists of shows that are upcoming, according to event's state and date.

In addition to all-breed shows and national specialties, which cater to one breed only, match shows are also posted for those with puppies who need competition practice before they hit the big time shows. While these listings are invaluable to exhibitors, they are also great for dog lovers who just want to take in a dog show one weekend, but don't know exactly where to start.

The Judging Programs area is also invaluable to those who simply want to observe a dog show. Judging schedules, which break down the time and ring number for each breed of dog, are available here and are a must for viewing any show.

Many serious dog show exhibitors like to know who the judges are before they enter their animals in a show. Info Dog's Judges Directory is designed for these people.

Organized by group and breed, biographies of judges for each show are available for examination. E-mail addresses and phone numbers are also here for the viewing, presumably for club officials interested in hiring judges to preside at upcoming shows.

Thorough in its approach, Info Dog includes a chat area where dog fanciers can discuss shows, breeds, or anything they desire. The Pet & Show Dog Marketplace provides a listing of products geared toward dog owners, along with advertisements from breeders. The Bookstore allows browsers to select canine-related reading on topics such as kennel management, training, and showing.

As if this wasn't enough, links to other important dog sites appear on Info Dog, along with highlights of past shows (including photos of the dogs, in some cases). Most interesting is the Tour of MB-F, where the curious can find out exactly how a dog show is put together, complete with detailed text and photos of MB-F workers in action.

Onofrio Dog Shows

http://www.onofrio.com

Jack Onofrio and his wife Dorothy started superintending dog shows in 1968, and now run both large and small events in the South, lower Midwest and Southwest. With a staff of 60, Onofrio provides superintending services to over 400 all-breed clubs, 200 specialty clubs, and 20 obedience clubs annually.

The Onofrio Web site provides exhibitors with a way to enter their dogs in an Onofrio show through the Internet instead of by traditional snail-mail methods. With detailed instructions on how to prepare an online entry and information on how to enter in the old-fashioned way, should you prefer it, the site walks exhibitors through the process one step at a time.

Along with the history of the organization, other nonessential but informative data is provided on the site. The Premium Lists area provides a quick look at upcoming shows in the Onofrio territory, as well as the dates and the names of the judges who are officiating. The Current Judging Programs page lists shows happening in the current month, with access to the times the different breeds and groups will be judged.

An area for Frequently Asked Questions is furnished, with information on how to enter a dog show, plus more. A place called Little Known Facts About Jack Onofrio provides interesting tidbits here and there, like the detail that Onofrio has received over 500,000 total entries since its inception.

Actual Dog Show

http://www.neca.com/~szeder/dogshoh.html

Mary C. Wakeman, D.V.M., a Puli breeder and veterinarian with a practice in canine reproductive medicine, is the author of the Actual Dog Show site. Dr. Wakeman describes herself as a "Puli breeder first and a veterinarian second." This is a woman extremely dedicated to her canine passion and devoted to educating the public about the world of purebred dogs.

Dr. Wakeman's desire to teach people about dog shows motivated her to create the Actual Dog Show, a Web site designed to educate the novice and entertain the veteran. The site starts out with a hyperlink titled What Happens At A Dog Show, where Dr. Wakeman uses photos and descriptive text to describe the experience of attending a first dog show. Included are step-by-step instructions on what to do when you first arrive at the showgrounds; how to follow the judging; the difference between conformation, obedience, herding, and agility; and a description of junior showmanship. Also listed in chart form are the seven American Kennel Club groups and the breeds they encompass.

The I Want to Go To A Dog Show link features answers to novices' questions about how to get started in dog shows. There is information here on where to get a show quality puppy, along with a list of superintendents around the country. Links to American Kennel Club Web pages on dogs and events are also included, as is a link called What Is A Breeder, describing the qualities of those who responsibly breed purebred dogs.

The last link, Bitch Is Not A Dirty Word, features a glossary of dog show terms. Expressions such as "benched show" (a conformation event where dogs are assigned a space in a given area and required to stay in the area for the entire day) are clearly explained. The terms are organized in categories of General, Conformation, Obedience, Field/Sporting, Herding, Coursing, Agility, and Earthdog.

According to Dr. Wakeman, her sites (she has several others) are always under construction and she promises even more information in the future on the subjects of obedience, conformation, and grooming.

Higham Press Show Printers
http://www.globalnet.co.uk/~higham/index.htm

In the United States, show premiums, judging schedules, and show results are published by show superintendents and distributed by the American Kennel Club. In the United Kingdom, however, things work a little differently.

For example, Higham Press Show Printers is a British family business that has been printing dog show publications for the past 50 years. According to the company, they have printed every major United Kingdom championship show publication at one time or another, with the exception of Crufts.

The company's Web site is valuable to dog fanciers because it lists the most recent show results from the United Kingdom's top show events. The winners of the most recent U.K. Toydog, Birmingham National, Southern Counties, Windsor, Leeds, Welsh Kennel Club, Houndshow, Darlington, and LKA events can be found at this site. For those dedicated dog show enthusiasts who keep track of the goings on in shows outside the United States this site is a real find.

Show Dogs West

http://www.showdogswest.com

Conformation dog showing is big on the West Coast, particularly in Southern California. A large number of all-breed kennel clubs can be found in this area of the country, and a great many purebred dog owners in the lower portion of the Golden State participate in the sport of dogs.

Consequently, it makes sense that there would be an Internet resource that provides dog show exhibitors with information on where shows will be held, when, who will be judging and the like. This would be Show Dogs West. This nicely designed site provides dog show participants on the West Coast with the kind of information they need to get the most out of their show experience.

The site covers American Kennel Club all-breed and specialty shows, presenting premium lists, judging schedules, entry forms, closing dates and marked catalogs, all conveniently online.

In addition to this basic information, Show Dogs West also promotes the sport of dogs in the West by including lists of all-breed kennel clubs and breed specialty clubs, as well as a comprehensive listing of breeders and links to kennel home pages. A special section for junior showmanship

Newport Dog Shows

http://www.newportdogshows.com/index.htm

West Coast dog show superintendent William G. Antypas also uses the name Newport Dog Shows when he stages canine events in California. His company's colorful and attractive site promotes events that it manages and includes useful information for exhibitors.

At the time of this writing, details on upcoming show dates, judging schedules, directions to shows, hotel and motel accommodations, parking information, and results of past shows were available on the site, in addition to other tidbits of Newport Dog Shows information. The site is currently under construction and promises to provide users with even more of the information they need to plan their dog show activities in the future.

Canine Sports and Competition

There was a time when the only sanctioned competitive event a dog fancier could participate in within the United States was conformation showing. Sports like hunting and retrieving, obedience, and tracking were activities that dogs did on the side, either between dog shows or instead of them.

All this has changed. A movement in the early 1980s by purebred dog enthusiasts to legitimize performance events in the eyes of the American Kennel Club has led to an all-out explosion of canine sports and competitions.

The original obedience and hunting events sanctioned by the American Kennel Club several decades ago have recently been joined by agility, lure coursing, tracking, earthdog trials, and herding on the organization's list of approved competitive activities. One or more of these events can now be seen at just about any all-breed dog show or breed-specific show.

Participation in these kinds of activities is not limited to American Kennel Club registered purebred dogs, either. Other organizations such as the United Kennel Club, the United States Dog Agility Association, the American Sighthound Field Association, and the American Herding Breed Association provide competitive opportunities for active dogs.

Mixed breeds can also participate in a number of the same activities open to purebred dogs. Frisbee, flyball, certain

continued after the feature section

193

The Dog Agility Page

http://www.dogpatch.org/agility.html

The sport of dog agility just may be the fastest-growing canine event of the last two decades. Agility is fun to watch and even more fun to participate in.

Agility competition consists of a series of obstacles, laid out in a course. Each dog is expected to negotiate the course with its handler at its side, and to do it faster and more accurately than the other dogs in the competition. The obstacles include a tire jump, a dog walk (the canine version of a cat walk), a collapsible tunnel, an A-frame, and a number of other impediments. Just about any breed of dog can participate in agility, although some are better at it than others.

Just ten years ago, dog agility was strictly private sector competition, something not recognized by the large show-giving kennel clubs. Today, agility is sanctioned by the American Kennel Club and the United Kennel Club, just to name two groups who are encouraging this exciting sport.

The most comprehensive is the Dog Agility Page, authored by Mary Jo Sminkey, and is part of her expansive Dogpatch site. Sminkey has attempted to provide the most comprehensive agility site on the Web.

The Dog Agility Page starts out, with What is Dog Agility? Using a set of links to other pages and areas within the Dogpatch site, the author has created a thorough picture of the sport. A personal introduction to agility written by two Vizsla owners, an agility FAQ, and even an agility photo album are in this first area. (If you've never seen the obstacles in used in agility, a visit to the photo album is a must.)

Next is the Agility Lists section, featuring three different e-mail lists dedicated strictly to the subject of agility. The popularity of this sport can be gauged by the number of people already signed up to the original Agility List: 600, with a waiting list of one month!

The section on training is quite extensive, starting with articles detailing the basics of the sport. Anyone getting started in agility, or contemplating it, will have a complete overview of what's entailed by reading this section.

Also covered here are handling techniques, games classes, common problems at trials, score keeping, running a trial, and a huge list of other subjects.

The Agility Photos Pages area features no less than 13 dogs negotiating a variety of obstacles. The list of Online Agility Clubs includes training groups as well as businesses specializing in teaching agility. For links to organizations such as the United States Dog Agility Association and the North American Dog Agility Council, go to the Online Agility Organizations area.

Agility is not just popular in the United States; it has caught on with dog lovers all around the world. There are agility groups in a number of different parts of the world, and information on contacting organizations in England, Australia, Nova Scotia, Finland, Switzerland, and Norway is included here. There is also a reproduction of the Federation Cynologuque International rules and regulations for agility.

The site wouldn't be complete without agility-related products, a list of upcoming agility events around the country, and, of course, even more general agility links.

agility events, and some obedience trials allow dogs of unknown heritage to show their stuff.

As the pastime of competing in fun, athletic events with dogs continues to grow, more and more events keep cropping up in the dog community. Traditional sports like schutzhund and sledding are now part of a list of growing canine activities like flygility and skijoring.

If you want to learn about the various dog events out there, the Internet is the place to be. Nearly every dog sport is represented on the Net, in local, national, and international forums.

Almost every site in this chapter does a bang-up job of explaining the sport it covers, evidence of the dog community's desire to encourage newcomers to these events. The sites provide beginners with a good sense of what these sports are all about, and make apathy toward these games nearly impossible.

Dog Agility

http://cust.iamerica.net/dstar1/DogAgility.htm

Cool animated graphics of a Doberman Pinscher negotiating a hurdle and weave poles greet you as you open up the Dog Agility page. Authored by an HTML-literate agility enthusiast, the site strives to provide the basics on agility to newcomers to the sport.

The site's most substantial area is a place called The Elements, which describes each agility obstacle in depth and provides photos of dogs tackling each one.

Also included here are links to international and other agility sites, agility dog handler home pages, and agility clubs and training groups throughout the United States.

Finnish Agility Pages

http://lenkkari.cs.tut.fi/~tra/agility/english.html

Die-hard agility fans will want to check out the Finnish Agility Pages to find out what Nordic dog owners are doing in the sport. The English version of the site is still under construction, but what is there right now provides enough information to make a visit worthwhile.

The site includes a description of agility and details on how to get started in the sport. It also covers Federation Cynologuque International rules, the latest news in agility, a readers' photo gallery, a message board, and links to other agility pages around the world.

Flyball Home Page

http://www.cs.umn.edu/~ianhogg/flyball.html

Flyball has become one of the most popular canine sports in the dog community since its inception in the late 1970s. First seen by the general public on the *Tonight Show With Johnny Carson*, this team sport has finally come into its own.

Flyball consists of relay races with a team of four dogs. Courses are usually made up of a starting line, four hurdles placed 10 feet apart from each other, and a flyball box. The game is played when the first dog in the team jumps over the hurdles and then steps on a lever on the box that sends a tennis ball into the air. The dog catches the ball in its mouth and then runs back to the starting line, taking the hurdles again. As the dog crosses the line, the next dog in line repeats the procedure. The first team with all four dogs doing an errorless run wins the heat.

All this and more is covered on the Flyball Home Page. Subjects such as flyball in the media, quotes about flyball, flyball box designs, training forums and medical information pertinent to flyball dogs are just some of the areas touched on in this site. Information on the North American Flyball Association, the official titles given by the organization and even an analysis of the breeds competing in flyball can be found here.

Flyball

http://dspace.dial.pipex.com/town/square/tac61/flyball.htm

The British love flyball and this no-frills page, part of the U.K. Dogs site (see Chapter 18) has a lot of information on how to get started in the sport. History, rules, equipment, exercises, and Internet contacts are all included here. Great detail is given on a number of these subjects, especially equipment.

The United States Canine Combined Training Association

http://www.siriusweb.com/USCCTA

Dog people are often horse people too, which explains how the concept of combined training for dogs came to be. Combined training in the horse world (also known as three-day eventing) requires skill, discipline, endurance and athleticism.

Combined training for canines, which started only recently in England, is modeled after the equine version of the sport. Like the horse version, canine combined training consists of three phases held over a three-day period: dressage, cross-country and stadium jumping.

The United States Canine Combined Training Association (USCCTA) is the official organization for the sport, which the group describes as "the ultimate test of teamwork between handler and dog, demonstrating skills of precision, elegance, obedience, stamina, courage, jumping ability, endurance and all-around versatility."

The USCCTA Web site is designed to introduce newcomers to this intriguing sport. If you know little to nothing about canine combined training, start with the area "An Overview of the Sport," at the bottom of the home page. This clearly explains what canine combined training is all about.

From here you can learn about USCCTA eventing clinics, stadium jumping rule revisions, dressage point standings, judge's guidelines, and details about the three different phases of this exciting event.

The Tracking Page
http://www.cfw.com/~dtratnac

Daniel E. Tratnack, a German Shepherd Dog and Belgian Tervuren owner, and a tracking enthusiast, is the author of this site, devoted to the sport of tracking. Tracking requires a dog to follow a scent through a continuous course. Dogs have amazing scenting abilities, and tracking puts those talents to use in a fun and competitive way.

The Tracking Page has information about the details of tracking, the purpose of tracking tests, what kind of equipment you'll need to track with your dog, and what kind of dog you'll need to track with. Diagrams of tracks, AKC tracking regulations, organizations offering tracking tests and titles, and a glossary of tracking terms are all among the items of interest that can be found on this page.

Schutzhund.Com
http://www.schutzhund.com

The sport of schutzhund originated in Germany in the early 1900s. Originally to determine which German Shepherds should be including in breeding programs, schutzhund has grown into a popular competitive sport both in North America and in Europe.

Literally translated from the German, schutzhund means "protection dog." While protection is a large part of what schutzhund is all about, tracking and obedience are also included in the competition.

Schutzhund.Com is a multilingual site dedicated to promoting the sport and to providing information on it to interested dog owners. Text is available here in German, English, and Spanish, and includes an in-depth description of the sport. A variety of articles on competing, an option to search for local clubs, and a list of show results from around the world are available here.

Much of this site is still under construction, but promises to be the ultimate source of information on schutzhund on the Web.

DVG America

http://www.anet-stl.com/~dvgamer/

DVG stands for *Deutscher Verband der Gebrauchshund-sportvereine,* the oldest and largest schutzhund training organization in the world. The group was Germany's first police and service dog club and has now branched out to include members the world over.

DVG America is the only organization in the United States to offer Breitensport titles, according to the club. Dogs of any breed can participate, regardless of size.

The DVG Web site is a fun site complete with animated dog graphics. It does a good job of explaining the sport of schutzhund as well as outlining the complicated organizational structure of German dog sports.

Other areas on the site cover the club's programs, officers, and membership information.

Dog-Play

http://www.dog-play.com/

Dog-Play is a general canine sports and competition site, authored by active dog owner Diane Blackman. The site's goal is to provide a description of a wide variety of canine activities, along with links for each subject.

The sports covered here include agility, carting, lure coursing, racing, earthdog trials, eventing, flyball, herding, and hunting and field work. The links are extensive at this site and include some unusual ones.

Carting With Your Dog

http://www.bond.net/~warrickw/carting.html

Before mankind domesticated the horse, the dog was his only beast of burden. Consequently, dogs have been pulling carts for thousands of years.

The sport of carting became popular in the 1980s and the organized events taking place today test the skills of draft dogs. Obedience to the handler and an eagerness to pull are important assets in competitive carting events. The breeds seen most often in this activity are the Rottweiler, Collie, Newfoundland, Bernese Mountain Dog, Saint Bernard, and Bouvier des Flandres, all breeds that have carting deeply rooted in their heritage.

The Carting With Your Dog page was created by enthusiasts in the sport, and features an introduction to the world of carting, carting terminology, and a discussion of the different carting activities. FAQs on the sport, books, clubs, equipment vendors, and historical photos of dogs pulling carts are all included here.

International Weight Pull Association

http://www.eskimo.com/~samoyed/iwpa

Unlike the sport of carting, weight pulling is focused strictly on how heavy a load a dog can move. Large, strong breeds like Alaskan Malamutes, Samoyeds, and even American Pit Bull Terriers are usually seen in weight-pull competitions, where dogs are asked to outpull each other using a wheeled cart on an earthen or snow-covered surface.

The International Weight Pull Association's Web site is an excellent source of information on this canine sport, and provides detailed information on what happens at a weight-pulling contest and how to get involved in this activity.

Upcoming events around the country are listed so newcomers can attend a weight pull, and equipment resources are also provided. If you have a genuine interest in this activity, this site will get you started in the sport.

The Obedience Home Page

http://www.princeton.edu/~nadelman/obed/obed.html

Obedience competition is one of the staples of canine sport and has been a part of American Kennel Club sanctioned shows for decades. Dogs can earn a variety of titles based on their expertise. Beginner-level obedience classes consist of exercises such as heel, recall, and down. The higher level classes call for jumping and the location of scent objects.

Obedience competition is not widely represented on the Internet, although the Obedience Home Page does a good job of centralizing information on the sport. By putting together a series of links on different aspects of obedience competition, the site manages to provide a one-stop source of information.

Included here are links to American Kennel Club rules and regulations; upcoming obedience trials; show results from AKC, United Kennel Club, and Cycle events; and companies that produce obedience-related merchandise.

Lure Coursing

http://www.clak.net/pub/bdalzell/lure/lure.coursing.faq.12/html

Lure coursing is a sport that tests the instincts and skills of the sighthound breeds, dogs that were created thousands of years ago to chase game by sight. In lure coursing, Afghans, Salukis, Greyhounds, Basenji, Ibizan Hounds, Pharaoh Hounds, Borzoi, Irish Wolfhounds, Scottish Deerhounds, and Whippets can participate. They are placed on a course, three at a time, and asked to chase a lure. Each dog receives points for his or her run.

Lure coursing utilizes the ancient skills and modern-day training of these breeds, also known as gazehounds, and is a fun event to both watch and participate in.

Lure Coursing, the Web site, presents everything you could possibly want to know about this sport. Authored by American Sighthound Field Association and American Kennel Club lure-coursing judge Bonnie Dalzell, this site is short of graphics but tall on good, solid information.

The basics of lure coursing are all covered here. There are questions and answers on attending a trial, intermediate and advanced lure coursing, and personalities in lure-coursing. There are details on about the American Sighthound

Field Association, information about the Canadian Kennel Club's lure coursing program, a glossary, lists of publications, and more. It's impossible to browse through this site and not learn all about this sport.

Mushing Internet
http://www.readysoft.es/mushing/INGLES/HOME.HTM

Mushing is another term for sledding with dogs. Jack London made the tradition of mushing famous in *Call of the Wild* and *White Fang,* romanticizing this unique mode of transportation and bringing it to the attention of the world.

While there are still mushers in remote parts of North America who use their dog sled teams solely for transportation, a great many of the people involved in this activity today are in it for the fun of mushing. Which is not to say that they aren't incredibly serious about the sport. Entrants in the Iditarod, the famous Alaskan sled dog race, spend years in rigorous training just to complete the event.

The popularity of mushing is not limited to North America. Europeans enjoy it, too, as evidenced by Mushing Internet, a site originating in Spain that is devoted to dog sledding.

Authored by Spaniard and musher Charles Garcia, Mushing Internet contains information in Spanish and English. Browsers need to click on the Union Jack on the home page in order to be transported to a huge site with considerable information in English.

While the majority of information on this site is geared toward European mushers (activities, lodging, and clubs are all Spanish), there is still something to be learned by North American dog sledding fans. Breeders of mushing dogs advertise here and provide e-mail links, for those who would like to correspond with other involved in the sport. Under Mushing Material, a variety of different European mushing equipment companies can be found. In Software, mushing computer programs, dog games and other high-tech material relating to sledding can be found.

One of the best places on the site for those not located in Europe is the Mushers area. Here, a list of dog sledders around the world can be found, complete with links to their Web sites.

If you have an interest in mushing, this site is worth exploring in spite of its heavy European slant.

Mush With Pride

http://www2.polarnet.com/~pride/

Mush With Pride is an organization dedicated to enhancing the care and treatment of sled dogs in traditional modern use. The group was founded several years ago specifically to establish guidelines for proper sled-dog care.

The group's Web site is an excellent source of information on the management of sled dogs, starting with the Sled Dog Care Guidelines area. Housing, feeding and watering, exercise, training, whelping and puppy raising, and basic health care are all covered in this section.

The organization's most current newsletter is included online, and features articles on health, humane issues, and other topics of relevance to sled dogs.

Iditarod Trail Sled Dog Race

http://www.alaskanet.com/iditarod/

The Iditarod Trail Sled Dog Race is a 1,040-mile trek through the mountains, rivers, and forests of Alaska and is one of the most challenging sports events in the nation. Winning this race is an honor coveted by all serious mushers.

The official Iditarod Web site contains audio information from the latest race, which takes place each March, and includes interviews with competitors taped at the event. A list of the mushers for the race can be found here as well, along with checkpoint reports on competitors, current Alaskan weather conditions, official rules and regulations, names and times of past winners, and interesting facts and figures.

The most fascinating spot on this site is the area that contains the history of the race. The intriguing story of how this event began is worth the visit just on its own.

Skijoring

http://fytqm.uafadm.alaska.edu/dogs/skijoring.html

Skijoring is the practice of cross-country skiing with a dog. Anywhere from one to three dogs can be attached to a skier's waist with a wide belt and harness, using a 3 to 4 meter line. Any dog 30 pounds or over can participate in skijoring.

The Skijoring Web site, authored by dog lover Dianne L. Marshall, contains a description of the sport and the equipment needed to get started. Marshall points out here that you don't even need snow to go skijoring with your dog—you can run with him or her attached to your waist in the same way.

The site features step-by-step photographs of a harness being placed on a dog and hooked up, as well as advice on how to get a dog to run, where to skijor, where to get equipment, skijoring organizations, and more.

Mary Jo's Frisbee Dog Page

http://www.dogpatch.org/frisbee.html

Dogs who like to catch flying discs are known as Frisbee dogs, and there is a sport just for them. Made popular in the mid-1970s by Alex Stein and his dog, Ashley Whippet, the sport of Frisbee has grown considerably over the last two decades. Nowadays, Frisbee dogs compete in local, regional, and national disc-catching events. They also do it for fun, in parks, on beaches, and in their own backyards.

For Frisbee dog owners, Mary Jo's Frisbee Dog Page is the place to see on the Web. Part of the huge Dogpatch site (see Chapter 19), this page is devoted strictly to this exciting game. Links to various other Frisbee sites can be found here, along with information on how to join a

Frisbee e-mail list, photos of dogs catching Frisbees, places to order discs, a listing of dog and disc clubs, and information on the Alpo Canine Frisbee Disc Championships.

Dallas Dog & Disc Club

http://rampages.onramp.net/~friend/dddpage.html

The Dallas Dog & Disc Club is a local club for dog owners with Frisbee dogs. While their site is designed primarily for the club's members in the Dallas–Ft. Worth area, it also contains good general information on the sport.

The Interactive FAQ page provides a list of questions and answers on training, as well as other aspects of Frisbee. Photographs of members' dogs sailing through the air and catching discs are here, as well as informative articles from the club's newsletter.

National Capital Air Canines

http://www.discdog.com

A waving American flag greets you as you enter this site, along with photographs of dogs leaping in the air to catch flying Frisbees.

National Capital Air Canines is an organization formed in the Washington D.C. area by Frisbee-dog owners. The group's main purpose is to bring together fellow Frisbee enthusiasts and to have fun.

The group's Web site contains the usual club-related data, including upcoming events and a bimonthly newsletter. But what makes this site a real find is its FAQ area, which contains loads of great information on the sport of canine Frisbee. Here, you can learn about the various Frisbee events, basic training and equipment, and obtain a list of clubs around the country and various resources that can help you learn even more.

Canine Cycle Freestyle

http://www.woofs.org/cycle/freestyle/frstyl.html

The sport of canine freestyle is rapidly growing in popularity. A combination of obedience and dance, this event can be likened to figure skating. Music is used as a backdrop, and the presentations from handlers and dogs can only be described as artistic.

H.J. Heinz, makers of Cycle Canine Nutrition Products, sponsors a series of competitive canine freestyle events. The Canine Cycle Freestyle Web site explains the sport of canine freestyle and provides information on how to compete.

The history of this unusual sport is included in the site, as are a list of events and seminars, videos and tapes available for purchase, official rules and regulations, canine freestyle organizations and clubs, and details on how to get started.

American Working Dogs Association

http://ccwf.cc.utexas.edu/~donnell/Working/AWDA.html

The term "working dogs" can be applied to those canines who are involved in any number of activities. Decades ago, the notion of testing a working dog's abilities became popular in England, and the first working trial was held. At the time, the original purpose was to evaluate the basic skills of all types of working dogs in a realistic working environment.

Following in this tradition, the American Working Dogs Association (AWDA) was formed to promote and organize the sport of working sheepdog trials in the United States. Today, working trials are a practical test of a dog's knowledge, determining how well a dog functions in three areas: control, agility, and scent work.

The group's site, authored by dog owner Mark Donnell, provides announcements of upcoming herding events and links to additional pages on the subject of sheepdogs. It also describes the basics of working trials, how they work, and what they hope to accomplish.

Stockdogs

http://www.opus1.com/stockdog/into.htm

Traditionally, a stockdog is a dog that works livestock for a living, usually sheep. In parts of the world, stockdogs are still used extensively in pastures, and in some areas of North America, they can still be found working alongside ranchers from sunup to sundown.

Stockdog trials are those tests that challenge working dogs to determine their skills at driving and penning. Made famous in the movie *Babe*, stockdog trials are very popular in Europe, Australia, and the United States.

The Stockdogs Web site contains considerable information about stockdogs in general, provides a definition of the term "stockdog," details on stockdog trials, the history of the event, and much more.

A click at the bottom of the Stockdogs home page will take you to the Stockdog Server, a large site with 15 different areas to visit. Start at the bottom of the page for definitions of the icons, and then begin perusing. There is information here on stockdog breeds, stockdog breeders, trials, course and program descriptions, a library, training information, a list of trainers, and even an article on stockdog genetics.

Every herding organization imaginable is included here, as is an area showcasing stockdog merchandise for sale. Photographs of working stockdogs can be viewed and links to other stockdog sites are included.

The American Herding Breed Association

http://www.primenet.com/~joell/ahba/

The American Herding Breed Association is an organization devoted to promoting the skills and value of the herding dog. A number of herding breeds are represented by this organization, which sponsors tests and trials to determine herding instinct and skills.

The group's Web site contains details on these evaluations, plus an explanation of the herding titles granted. A list of herding clubs around the country is included, as well as a roster of the herding breeds included in the group.

Belgian Games

http://www.hut.fi/~mtt/belg_tricks.html

Merja Tornikoski is a Finnish Belgian Sheepdog fancier with her own Web site, Belgian Games. The site contains information on a plethora of miscellaneous canine activities that were designed for Belgian Sheepdogs but can be done by just about any dog from a somewhat athletic breed.

Divided into categories of Useful Tricks, Silly Pet Tricks, Problem Solving, Nose Work, and Balance Work, these simple activities provide mental stimulation for both dog and owner without the commitment required for most other canine sports.

Activities include heeling on the right instead of the traditional left, picking up toys and putting them away, the nose ball push, singing, opening boxes, and hide and find.

If you're at a loss as to how to teach these activities to your dog, don't despair. Tornikoski also provides a link to a training page that explains how to coach your dog into each of these activities.

French Ringsport

http://members.aol.com/FRENCHRING/private/ring.htm

This simple, all-text site authored by enthusiast Neal Wallis explains the 100-year-old European competition of French ringsport. The event, which utilizes the protection instincts of dogs, is the second most popular protection dog sport in Europe.

This activity, which is gaining acceptance in North America, is performed on four different levels. Unlike schutzhund, French ringsport does not include tracking, and involves bite work on the body and not on the sleeve.

The Web site does a good job of explaining the sport and distinguishing it from schutzhund. Breeds authorized by the French Society of Central Canine to compete in French ringsport are listed here, as is a description of the role of the decoy and the certification test for the event.

Workingdogs.Com

http://workingdogs.com

Billing itself as the "international cyberzine for working dogs and the people who work, train, breed, and love them," Workingdogs.Com is an electronic clearinghouse of information on working dog health, training, events, and news-making accomplishments.

Schutzhund, ringsport, herding, sledding, agility, and a number of other activities are covered in this site, which begins with a number of links to other Web pages containing information on working dogs. There is also a search option here, by word or phrase, to help you locate the exact working-dog subject needed.

An index of all articles and features linked to the site is included. Some of these are original pieces belonging to Workingdogs.Com, while others are pages on seperate sites. A wide variety of topics are covered.

A Working Dogs Bookstore can also be found at this site, featuring a large selection of titles on canine activities available online. Classified ads, FAQs on working dogs, health information, training and education, traveling with your dog, and other subjects are also linked at this site.

Earthdog/Squirrel Dog Hunting Homepage

http://www.zmall.com/pet_talk/dog-faqs/activities/edsdhp.html

Not more than a few years ago, the American Kennel Club sanctioned the activity of earthdog trials, and the sport has blossomed in popularity.

Earthdogs are Dachshunds and small terriers that were originally bred in Europe to chase down and kill rodents and other small animals, on farms and on large estates. Today, these same breeds have a primary job of being pets. However, in earthdog events, they can show off their age-old instincts.

Squirrel dogs are less known than earthdogs. The sport of squirrel-dog trialing is not recognized by the American Kennel Club or United Kennel Club. However, like the earthdog, the squirrel dog also had the job of hunting down small animals decades ago. While their earthdog cousins worked small game in Europe, squirrel dogs helped the pioneers survive in the wilds of a young America. Dachshunds and certain terriers are eligible to compete in modern-day squirrel dog trials.

Both earthdogs and squirrel dogs are covered in the Earthdog/Squirrel Dog Hunting Homepage, authored by enthusiast Dennis Reay. A thorough description and history of each dog is given here, plus explanations of earthdog den trials and squirrel dog trials. Clubs for each of these activities are listed here, as well as a calendar of upcoming events.

Wellington Hurricanines Flygility

http://homepages.ihug.co.nz/~mbutler/hurric.htm

A new sport that mixes elements of agility and flyball has been developed in New Zealand. Called flygility, the activity requires dogs to fetch a ball from a flyball box and then negotiate a series of obstacles when returning to the handler.

The Wellington Hurricanines is a local New Zealand flygility club, affiliated with the New Zealand Flygility Dog Association. The club's Web page offers interested dog fanciers basic information on this new sport and leads on how to get started.

While much of the site is obviously geared toward New Zealanders, there is one area where dogs from different clubs, in different regions, can compete with one another on a regular basis without meeting. This is done through the online publication of course scores.

Back Packing With Your Dog

http://www.zmall.com/pet_talk/dogfaqs/
misc.01.html#11_234117

Hiking and backpacking with dogs has become more popular of late. Dogs can be trained to carry their own back-
pack, which usually contains their own food and water, and
other items. Dog owners who like to hike have discovered
that having their dogs along not only makes the adventure
more enjoyable, but also more sociable: canine hiking clubs
are springing up all around the country.

There are aspects to hiking with a dog that everyone
should know before they attempt it. Dog owner Sue
Barnes has put together a simple but detailed page that discusses how to get started, how to condition your dog,
what kind of equipment to buy, and more. It's a must-read
before hitting the trail with a canine companion.

How To In-Line Skate With Your Dog

http://www.caryn.com/francis-blade.html

Just about any individual sport you can do without your dog,
you can also do with him. Caryn Shalita, an actress and dog
lover living in Los Angeles has proven that with her site, How
To In-Line Skate With Your Dog. Shalita rollerblades with her
dog Francis every day, and has dedicated her Web site to
teaching others to do the same.

Here you can find information on what kind of
equipment you'll need, how to start out, and how to handle a downgrade. You can also read about other people's
experiences with rollerblading with dogs, and see links to
traditional rollerblading sites.

As Shalita points out, dogs love rollerblading with their
owners because this is the only activity where the humans can
actually keep up.

Bird Dog News
http://www.Bird-Dog-News.com/

A great many of the sporting dog breeds were developed specifically to flush, point, and retrieve fowl. Many people keep this tradition alive by continuing to hunt birds with their dogs and by participating in field trials.

A publication for those who hunt birds with their dogs, *Bird Dog News* provides information for experienced bird hunters. The online version of the magazine reprints a number of these articles, and also presents products for sale and a national calendar of events. Season Pages, which give the dates for different species' seasons in each state, can be found here, as can bird counts and other relevant information. Hunting breeds are also included in the Dog Breed Pages, with links to their individual sites.

PAWS Working Dog Evaluation
http://www.gnofn.org/~malinut/paws.html

There are ways of determining whether or not a puppy will grow up to be a good working dog. One of those ways is the PAWS puppy evaluation test. Created by an obedience and agility competitor who was looking for a way to judge young puppies for their working instincts, PAWS is an acronym for Possessiveness, Attention, Willingness, and Strength.

This Web site, created and maintained by the originator of the test, describes the evaluation process in great detail, and includes an explanation of the seven parts of the test. After reading through this information, you will be able to apply the test yourself to any puppy that you meet.

Organization for the Working Samoyed
http://www.samoyed.org/ows.html

Samoyeds were developed in Siberia by indigenous peoples to help them survive in a harsh environment. Consequently, the Samoyed is a tough and rugged breed that thrives in demanding working conditions.

Professional writer and photographer Donna Dannen, a long-time Samoyed owner, is president of the Organization for the Working Samoyed, a group that was started in the late 1960s by a group of sled dog enthusiasts. At the time, Samoyeds were seldom seen at sled dog races and other working events. Now, however, that has changed.

The Organization for the Working Samoyed Web site contains information on the Samoyed as a working dog and photographs of Samoyeds functioning in a variety of activities: sledding, weight pulling, herding, skijoring and agility. Samoyed owners will be truly inspired to get active with their dogs after taking a stroll through this colorful site.

American Working Collie Association

http://mother.com/~catoft/awca/

The Collie is probably most well-known as a movie star, thanks to Lassie, but there was a time when Collies were expected to do just about everything from pull a cart to bring in the sheep. The American Working Collie Association is dedicated to promoting the working ability of the Collie and does a good job of it with its wonderful Versatility Program.

The American Working Collie Association Web site gives details on the Versatility Program, where Collies can earn Versatility Companion, Versatility Companion Excellent, and Versatility Champion titles. These honors are bestowed by obtaining honors in a variety of activities, including herding, obedience, tracking, protection, draft work, agility, flyball, Frisbee, and even conformation.

Also featured on this site are photos of Collies in action, working hard for their handlers.

Airedale Terrier Club of America Hunting and Working Committee

http://www.dvcnet.com/ataca/hwc

The Airedale Terrier Club of America was founded in 1900 to preserve the qualities of the popular Airedale Terrier. While most people know what an Airedale looks like, few are aware that the breed was originally used to work on farms controlling vermin, to retrieve birds during the hunt, and to work with hunters to bring down bears. This broad scope of duties makes the Airedale a generalist, as opposed to a specialist who can only function in one role.

The Hunting and Working Committee of the breed's national club is charged with the task of promoting these abilities in the Airedale. An Upland Bird Test, a Retrieving Test, and a Fur Test (using unharmed, caged raccoons) are all part of the club's program to encourage the working instincts of the Airedale.

The Committee's Web page explains the working heritage of the Airedale, and details the different tests designed to challenge the breed. The dates of upcoming events, a sign-in sheet for more information, and an explanation of the various titles awarded are all included.

C H A P T E R   1 1

Working Dogs

When it comes to discussion of the events that changed the course of human history, we hear plenty about the invention of the wheel and the harnessing of fire. Rarely within such groupings of revolutionary events do we find listed the domestication of the dog, even though it's a strong possibility that this had just as profound an effect on human progress as those other more obvious leaps. Had we never had the wisdom to invite the dog in to share our campfire, our food, and our lodgings, it's a safe bet we would not have advanced as far as we have in our dealings with the world around us.

Examples of the ways in which dogs have enriched our lives and simply made our many jobs, and hence our survival, easier, are almost too numerous to consider. These animals touched our lives and, almost like guardian angels, worked to please us and do our bidding. They have guarded and herded our livestock, helped us in our search for food, pulled our sleds and carts, rescued our lost and injured, guided and assisted our physically disabled, served in our armies, and protected our streets and homes. What a dour, pedestrian existence it would be without them.

The dog has made our mutual work all the more pleasant because of its very willing and companionable personality. That, plus our similar social structures, is why we chose this animal as our most trusted work partner in the first place. The work we face may seem daunting to us, the consequences of failure dire, but facing it side by side with a dog has always made the efforts all the more worthwhile—and no doubt inspires us to keep trying.

continued after the feature section

National Disaster Search Dog Foundation

http://www.west.net/~rescue/

Here is a site that tugs at your heartstrings from the moment you enter its home page. Opening with a vibrant black Labrador Retriever with a searchlight helmet on its head, the site proceeds to explain its reason for being: in a nutshell, the Oklahoma City bombing, the Northridge earthquake, and the many hurricanes that have hit our shores. "These incidents have shown a distinct need," the introduction explains, "for a dog with special training—called a Disaster Search Dog." It is this dog that is described in the pages that follow.

Tour this well-designed site by moving down the list of hyperlinks presented on the home page. Here you will find such subjects as: The urgent and critical need for Disaster Search Dogs; What is the National Disaster Search Dog Foundation?; and, in keeping with the educational spirit of this site and its sponsoring organization, a detailed list of links to other sites concerning search and rescue (SAR). Especially sobering is the section, "The rescue team is always ready to go! Anywhere!," for here we are told that the American Red Cross estimates that disasters occur somewhere every 10 minutes, and several serious ones can occur at one time.

Especially touching is the section "Oklahoma! The Heartland—Where we found our heart." Most of us can remember the televised images of dogs and handlers working tirelessly to find victims alive in the rubble in the aftermath of this tragedy. What we learn from this section is that those images made the Disaster Search Dog more of a publicly known entity and spurred efforts to increase the number of qualified teams that would be ready if such an unthinkable event ever transpired again.

Also unique is the section entitled "Firefighters and Disaster Search Dogs: A Life-Saving Partnership." Here we find a profile written by Barbara Neighbors Deal, Ph.D., administrator for the National Disaster Search Dog

The Oklahoma City bombing, the Northridge earthquake and recent hurricanes have all had something in common. These incidents have shown a distinct need for a dog with special training – called a Disaster Search Dog. The story of these dogs, the fascinating people who train and handle them, as well as the foundation which sports their name, is the content of these web pages.

Foundation, of a pilot program in which California firefighters are being trained to become Disaster Search Dog Handlers. They are learning to work with "a most valuable tool for finding people trapped in the rubble of collapsed buildings." One look at the opening photograph of three of the firefighting students and their Golden Retrievers, and you can see that this program can't help but be a success.

It is a shame that we must deal with situations in which people are in need of rescue in the wake of some of our most traumatic disasters. But the dogs love the work, and their handlers, often risking their own lives to save others, can think of no better way to contribute to society. These two facts emanate from every link of this site from the National Disaster Search Dog Foundation home page. Presented with energy and passion, this is a must-see site, which should make us all grateful that people and dogs like these are on alert at all times to help wherever and whenever help is needed.

While contemporary times have rendered some of the dog's traditional jobs obsolete, many continue to work in our service to this day. The following are Web sites, arranged by type of work, that promote and celebrate the working dog in all its many vocations, both those that are rooted in an honored past and those of more contemporary origin. The existence of these sites, and the enthusiasm and devotion that has gone into their creation, ensures that the public realize just what dogs have done for us in the past and what they continue to do for us today.

Black Paws Search, Rescue & Avalanche Dogs International

http://mama.indstate.edu/users/blkpaws/title.html

The reason the sponsor of this Web site is called Black Paws is because it is a breed-specific search-and-rescue organization based in Montana that uses a black-pawed dog: the Newfoundland. Founded by Susie Foley in 1985, this group chose the "gentle giant," as is explained in the Black Paws is Breed Specific section, because it was bred originally to save lives, and its kind temperament has a soothing effect on those it saves. The organization's Web site presents a great deal of information about the operations of its 15 chapters throughout the United States and New Zealand, its dogs, and the vocation of search and rescue itself in these clean, easy-to-navigate pages.

Take a tour of the site with the hyperlink menu on the home page, and you will gain access to such topics as Black Paws Training Standards (all volunteers must graduate from Black Paws National Newfoundland Search Dog Academy and vow to uphold the group's lengthy roster of standards), Black Paws FAQs, Suggested Reading List, Interested in Search and Rescue Dogs?, and Team Call-Outs & Locations. Unique in its focus and devoted to its calling and the skills of its breed, this site is designed both to promote its parent organization and to educate the public about search and rescue with Newfoundlands or any breed.

The California Rescue Dog Association, Inc.

http://yellow.crc.ricoh.com/carda/

While this site is dedicated to a specific organization, The California Rescue Dog Association, it provides a wealth of information on search and rescue in general and successfully draws browsers in to experience this calling firsthand. Let the Contents on the home page be your guide, beginning with the first choice presented: The CARDA Information Brochure. Here you will find a detailed Contents section that explains the training of CARDA dogs and handlers; descriptions of the kind of work CARDA dog teams can do; and information on how these teams, which are on-call 24 hours a day, 365 days a year, are called in by law-enforcement and emergency agencies.

Back on the home page, you may continue your journey of learning about search and rescue by exploring Training Techniques & Articles From Our Experts, Statistics! (information on the number of searches CARDA participates in each year), and Other Search & Rescue Sites (an excellent list of links to other local and national SAR sites). While you're here, don't miss Pictures of SAR Dogs at Work, accessible from the home-page Contents list. Here you will find pictures of training exercises and descriptions of how the dogs are being trained, as well as shots of actual rescues and the stories of the rescued individuals and the dogs that saved them. This unique element personalizes the site and celebrates these very deserving canine heroes for their tireless efforts.

Avalanche Rescue Dog's World

http://www.avalanche.org/ruff.htm

One of the most potentially disheartening jobs for a search-and-rescue dog is to search for victims of avalanche. The greatest reward for an SAR dog is to find people that are alive and grateful, but when the disaster that has led to the loss of those people is an avalanche, there is a strong possibility that the victims will not be alive. As part of the WestWide Avalanche Network, which is itself a part of the American Association of Avalanche Professionals, this site, as managed by avalanche rescue dog veteran Dan O'Connor, is dedicated to teaching SAR agency personnel and volunteers about establishing an SAR dog program dedicated to snow rescue and to keep those involved in touch with each other through a newly established news group.

O'Connor's overriding message is that though prevention by snow safety is preferable to situations in which rescue is in order, it is nevertheless imperative that those involved in rescue be prepared. This site acts as headquarters, providing not only a forum for the sharing of ideas and experiences for what is rightly referred to as the "Rrruf Work" of avalanche search-and-rescue dog teams, but as a valuable source of information, via excellent articles and seminar announcements. Perhaps the site's work will help ensure that these courageous dogs are able to rescue victims that are still alive and well.

Avalanche Dogs!

http://www.drizzle.com/~danc/avalanche.html

For in-depth background on the training of avalanche dogs and on basic canine search-and-rescue topics, as well, check out Avalanche Dogs!, presented by Dan Comden. While the human handlers of SAR dogs must approach their work with stoicism and a calm demeanor, the site conveys a tone of personal warmth and genuine respect for the dogs that share in this hazardous and emotional vocation.

Well-organized and simple in design, this site offers access to two distinct sections. The first of these, Avalanche Dog Training, offers access to various avalanche-dog–training topics and photos, as well as current records of avalanche finds by dogs in the United States (90 percent of avalanche victims, we learn, can survive if they are rescued within 15 minutes of the event). The second section is

General Canine Search and Rescue, offering more general-ized topics, including "Training tips," "Selecting a dog for SAR," and "An excellent dog behavior policy" (compli-ments of Marian Hardy of the Mid-Atlantic D.O.G.S. search group). Homespun and friendly in tone, this site offers browsers a view into the fascinating world of SAR dogs, and into the hearts and minds of the people with whom they work.

Alaska Search and Rescue Dogs

http://www.corecom.net/~asard/

One can only imagine the challenges that face the highly trained SAR dog-and-handler teams whose job it is to scour Alaska, a land of endless tundra and few roads, for lost people. Simple and unassuming, this site, composed by Mark Sickles of Alaska Search and Rescue Dogs (ASARD), greets browsers first with the group's logo—a Saint Bernard beneath the North Star and the big dipper—then invites them to explore three different areas: ASARD Information, Pictures of ASARD Dogs at Work (an eye-opening experience, to be sure), and SAR Links.

Choose ASARD Information, and you will discover at the next layer a list of hyperlinks to topics pertaining both to ASARD (How To Request ASARD Search Dog Teams, Volunteer Opportunities With ASARD, and Team Roster), and to the work of SAR teams in general. You can read about the history of the group and how the teams work, and read an account of life as an SAR handler written by Diane H. Sickles. Also of great value is the Frequently Asked Questions section, where browsers learn that this is a thankless volunteer calling; that it demands a great deal of time and training; and that it requires working in all kinds of weather, which in Alaska can mean just about any extreme. But for those at the core of this and other like groups around the world, there is no other way to live than, as the home page states, "Searching...To Save A Life."

National Association for Search and Rescue
http://www.nasar.org/

Though this is a short site, it does an admirable job of providing a sound background on "the humanitarian cause of saving lives" that is at the core of search and rescue. Under the guidance of Webmaster Robert Puffenberger, the site details the goals and activities of the nonprofit National Association for Search and Rescue (NASR). Members join this organization with the express purpose of saving people with the help of dogs. All one must do is witness the aftermath of such events as the Oklahoma City bombing and any of California's major earthquakes to see just how critical a mission this is. Also presented within this site is the NASR Code of Ethics to which members must commit. What you will learn in reviewing the tenets of this code is that an involvement in search and rescue is a vocation that is not to be taken lightly.

RiverBend Search and Rescue Dog Association Home Page
http://www.apci.net/~dchamb/rbsrda/

If you were lost within a forest where you could not find your bearings and your fear slowly crippled your ability to find the way out, imagine the joy you would feel if a big friendly German Shepherd suddenly appeared, ready to take you home. You would never forget that moment, never forget that dog. It is that moment for which the dog/handler search-and-rescue teams associated with RiverBend Search and Rescue Dog Association, based in Brighton, Illinois, exists.

Clean and crisp in design and easy to navigate, this site not only offers information on the group and its practices in searching for lost wilderness explorers, disaster and crash victims, and crime evidence, it also touches on the whole philosophy of search and rescue itself. From the top menu grid, it offers access to such topics as Using Search Dogs, How to Request a RiverBend Search, Volunteer Opportunities, and Why German Shepherd Dogs?, the answer to this latter question being the breed's intelligence, trainability, and physical endurance. When you look at the photographs of the RiverBend Shepherds, you will be thankful that dogs like this are trained to come to the aid of people in trouble.

RCMP Civilian Search and Rescue Service Dog Program

http://www.tgx.com/rcmpdog/

We typically associate the Royal Canadian Mounted Police (RCMP), known affectionately as the Mounties, with horses. But as this site tells us, dogs have their place amid this respected group as well, particularly with civilian handler/dog teams that meet rigorous RCMP standards to join in the noble mission of "Working Together So Others May Live." The RCMP site begins with a large grid of hyperlink options that lead browsers through the RCMP's Alberta, Canada-based operation, and in the process does much to explain the whole philosophy behind SAR dog teams.

Professional yet personal, this is a site that is as enjoyable to tour as it is informational. For instance, click on Search Dog Facts & FAQ, and you will find detailed bulleted lists describing SAR Dog Teams, Scent, and The SAR Dog. Also accessible from the home page are such topics as RCMP Role in Search and Rescue, RCMP-Civilian Dog Standards, RCMP-Certified Civilian Search Dog Teams and RCMP-Civilian Handler Standards. Review these sections and this privileged look inside the RCMP, and you will come to respect those few dogs and handlers who meet the required standards of this elite rescue group.

West Virginia K-9 Search and Rescue

http://wvit.wvnet.edu/~ablackwd/

Under the management of Andrew N. Blackwood, the West Virginia K-9 Search and Rescue site offers a unique voice in SAR cyberspace. This site is easy to navigate and almost deceptively rich with information. From the home page, browsers may use the block of hyperlinks to access inner layers that include Photo Gallery, Training Calendar (arranged month by month, with details on the type of training offered, when, and where), Information on the West Virginia K-9 Search and Rescue Amateur Radio Club, and Announcements. The Team Roster option presents all the group's team members (most with photographs), as well as information on what role each, dog and human alike, plays (i.e. handler, field support, air-scent, tracking/trailing). In the process of getting to know the teams and the organization, browsers may realize that they are also getting an education in search and rescue, all with an underlying tone of affection and respect for the dogs and pride in the work they do.

Puppyraiser Email List Web Site

http://www.iserv.net/~rugrat1/rsrs/

Before dogs enter the specialized training programs that prepare them for life as guide dogs, assistance dogs, hearing ear dogs or any of the other service vocations, they must spend their first two years or so of life getting to know the world. They do this with the help of special people known as puppy raisers. It is not easy to live so intimately with a dog for two years, training it, socializing it, loving it, taking it on every errand, and then give it up so it may go on to pursue its fate as "the arms, legs, eyes or ears for a fellow human being." This Web Site is a place for puppy raisers to share their experiences and their challenges.

Beginning with an introduction on what being a puppy raiser is all about, the home page then presents browsers with a boxed menu grid of options, including Puppy Raising—An Overview, "Puppyraisers" Info & Help, and A Puppy Raiser's Prayer. The home page also provides direct access to the Puppyraisers E-mail List. Also of value is the fact that in addition to fostering camaraderie among the community of puppy raisers, this site provides a great deal of information about a noble undertaking.

Service Dogs

http://www.zmall.com/pet_talk/dog-faqs/service.html

When you first enter this page written by Cindy Tittle Moore, you may only be looking for an overview of various service dog vocations. While it is indeed that, it is more, for it provides browsers with background information on such featured topics as hearing-ear dogs for the deaf, therapy dogs, and guide dogs for the blind (a great deal of information on the latter, as a matter of fact). It also provides names and addresses of many of the organizations that train the dogs and match them with the people who need them. Here you will find direct access to such organizations as Canine Companions for Independence and National Education for Assistance Dog Services, as well as detailed information on how these groups operate. Though this site is short on graphics and glitz, it is rich with information.

Wolf Packs Service Dog Directory

http://www.wolfpacks.com/catalog/serviced.htm

With few exceptions, organizations dedicated to service, assistance and therapy dogs are typically local in focus because of the intense and very personal nature of their work. Wolf Packs—maker of canine backpacking equipment, including items often used by service dogs—offers a fine service by providing this detailed list of names and addresses of service-dog organizations across the country. With the help of this site, in which these organizations are arranged by state, it is easy to locate and contact such groups by phone, snail mail, or e-mail, whether people want to volunteer time, offer financial support, become puppy raisers, or find out how to get one of these dogs for themselves.

The Seeing Eye

http://www.seeingeye.org/

America's first guide dog for the blind was a German Shepherd named Buddy, trained by the New Jersey organization The Seeing Eye for a gentleman named Morris Frank in 1929. The Seeing Eye Web site opens with a quote from Frank himself: "It was glorious—just the dog and a leather strap linking me to life." Today this site links browsers to the wonderful work that this pioneering organization continues to do, as the home-page introduction states, "to enhance the independence, dignity, and self-confidence of blind people."

A tour of this site begins at The Seeing Eye Information Center, which offers a long list of hyperlinked topics that address puppy raising, applying for a Seeing Eye dog, general information about the organization, blindness e-mail lists, and articles that chronicle dog guide history (accessible from the Dog Guide History Reading Room option). Also valuable is the Dog Guide Laws for the United States and Canada section. Choose this option, and you are asked to enter a U.S. state or Canadian province abbreviation, which subsequently calls up a detailed document on the laws of guide dog access in that given area. This site is thus not only informative in the rich history and general information it offers, but also in its role as a practical tool for those who share their lives with guide dogs.

The National Education for Assistance Dog Services, Inc.

http://chamber.worcester.ma.us/neads/INDEX.HTM

The Web site sponsored by The National Education for Assistance Dog Services, Inc. employs a homespun style and affectionate language as it introduces browsers to its

operation, which, as we learn from the home-page introduction, "trains dogs of all breeds, shapes, and sizes to help
people that are deaf or in wheelchairs." Following that
introduction, a visitor to this site may choose from several
options to learn more about this Massachusetts-based organization that has regional offices throughout the East
Coast and in the South. Choose Special Dogs for Special
People and learn all about the jobs for which NEADS
trains its dogs. Then, for a more personal account, check
out From NEADS to Miracles to see firsthand just what
those dogs bring to the human lives they share.

Independence Dogs, Inc.
http://www.ndepot.com/idi/

Opening with a logo that incorporates the Liberty Bell to
symbolize the liberty that service dogs can offer people with
mobility impairments, this site, sponsored by the
Pennsylvania-based nonprofit organization, Independence
Dogs Inc. (IDI), provides browsers with a great deal of information about its operation and the general concept of service
dogs. The site is designed as one long, well-illustrated, and
very informational home page with links to internal layers
that provide more in depth information. Together these
cover such topics as IDI's History and Founding (founded
by Jean King who held to the idea that her group would
graduate "a working team, not just a dog"); Types of
Independence Dogs (wheelchair dogs, walker dogs, and quad
dogs); Volunteering Your Time; and, in a very special feature,
IDI Success Stories, where browsers can meet the teams and
see just why such efforts as these are so worthwhile.

Guiding Eyes for the Blind
http://www.guiding-eyes.org/

The Web site for Guiding Eyes for the Blind welcomes
browsers in to learn about the operation of this New
York–based organization. This begins with a home-page

menu that offers browsers access to such topics as About Guiding Eyes for the Blind, All About Guide Dogs, FAQs, What's New, and How You Can Help. The pages employ a clean design of muted photographs of guide dogs and puppies that serve to remind browsers of the remarkable animals that make this organization work. Several layers of information present the group's history, training programs and services, and the challenges of meeting the $25,000 financial investment required "to breed, raise, and train each dog and prepare each team for their life together." But, of course, the independence and companionship such animals bring to their partners is priceless.

Canine Working Companions, Inc.

http://members.aol.com/DMauro5/cwc.htm

Simplicity and directness are the qualities that mark the Web site for New York–based Canine Working Companions. Dedicated to training dogs and placing them with people in wheelchairs and with hearing disabilities—as well as sponsoring therapy dog programs and educational seminars to "inform the public about the people, the dogs and their rights"—this nonprofit organization presents a home page that offers browsers direct access to their various areas of interest. A short menu grid offers hyperlinks to detailed sections on Hearing Dogs, Therapy Dogs, Service Dogs and Puppy Raising. Click on Hearing Dogs, for example, and you will learn all about these dogs that help to alert the hearing-impaired individuals with whom they live to the various sounds in their environment. With the reader-friendly language it employs and the depth of information it presents, this site is not only a powerful informational tool for its sponsoring organization, but for the world of service dogs at large.

Delta Society National Service Dog Center

http://petsforum.com/deltasociety/dsb000.htm

The Delta Society operates a Web site that addresses various topics related to the promotion of the human/animal bond. One of these topics, found on the page titled Delta Society National Service Dog Center (NSDC), is the role dogs play in assisting the physically challenged. This page offers browsers an informative overview of service dogs and their training through such subtopics as Mission of the NSDC, Why a Service Dog?, Service Dog FAQs, and various subjects related to the Delta Society training and advocacy programs. Such programs have helped service dogs, and thus the humans they assist, gain greater access to public places.

Hearing Dogs for the Deaf

http://www.htv.co.uk/wales/rhp/fshtm2/fshdogs.html

For a no-nonsense, informative overview of hearing dogs for the deaf, check into this British site, which opens with a quote from Helen Keller: "...you can touch a rose. You can smell it. You do not have to see it or hear it to know it, but not to hear a fellow human being's voice is the greatest of deprivations." This site is centered on the ways in which hearing dogs enhance their owners' lives by alerting them to "the everyday sounds which hearing people may take for granted," which, according to this site, include a crying baby, an alarm clock, a doorbell, a smoke alarm and a telephone. The site then provides information on how the dogs are trained and how people are trained to work with them as a team, illustrating the significance of these animals and the security they can lend to those who are hearing-impaired.

Paws with a Cause

http://www.ismi.net/paws/

For an enjoyable though informative service dog site, visit the Web pages of Paws with a Cause, a Michigan-based organization that sponsors the raising and training of dogs for people in need of help hearing, seeing, and getting around in wheelchairs. The brightly designed, well-illustrated home page offers browsers access to in-depth information on all of these types of working dogs, as well as information on the group's puppy-raising program (including a photo album of puppies in training), and on the PAWS program itself.

Unique to this site—and apparently to the program as well—are its sections on combination dogs and seizure-response dogs. The former are highly skilled dogs that can assist people with multiple disabilities; the latter are dogs that are trained to accept seizure behavior and remain with their owners should a seizure occur (some seizure dogs have also, because of their deep bond with their owners, been able to alert their owners of the onset of seizures). Much enthusiasm has gone into the creation and presentation of this site, highlighting an organization that is justly proud of its accomplishments and its dogs.

Tails of Joy Therapy Dog Program

http://www.geocities.com/Athens/2606/toj.htm

For a concise introduction to the work of therapy dogs, visit the Web site for the Tails of Joy Therapy Dog Program, a Northeastern U.S.–based chapter of the non-profit volunteer group Therapy Dogs International, which registers therapy dogs. Its members, in keeping with the traditions of animal-assisted therapy, visit people in hospitals, convalescent homes and other such institutions with their dogs. In a relatively short space, this site details the very sound philosophy behind animal-assisted therapy: to improve health and quality of life "through increased social stimulation, tactile stimulation (petting and touching), and improved morale and physical well-being. All of this can be facilitated by the unconditional affection of well-trained therapy dogs, which invariably adore their work and seem to sense they are part of a noble healing scheme.

Delta Society Pet Therapy Pages

http://petsforum.com/deltasociety/dsj000.htm

Earlier, we discussed the Delta Society's service dog pages. Another section of the copious Delta Society site covers animal-assisted therapy. Here you will find an overview of their program, which offers information and educational materials to people interested in volunteering for pet-assisted therapy programs, and facilities that would like to institute such programs.

Also a part of this site is a page devoted to the organization's Pet Partners Program (http://petsforum.com/deltasociety/dsa000.htm), a program that essentially certifies pets who visit hospitals, nursing homes, rehabilitation centers, and schools as therapy dogs. To become a Pet Partner a dog must be trained and evaluated in a workshop run by an instructor certified by the Delta Society, after which the animal will be viewed as more "official" in its work and may gain greater access to pet-therapy situations. Check out this page for a basic overview of the program, which, according to information presented here, is responsible for 2,000 Pet Partner teams that now operate in 45 states, "helping more than 350,000 people each year."

Lyn Richards' Therapy Dog Page

http://is2.dal.ca/~dcodding/therapy2.html

For an in-depth treatise on therapy-dog training, visit this site that showcases the Therapy Dog Team Training Program by Lyn Richards. This site is a must for anyone who believes his or her dog might be a strong candidate for therapy work and would like an overview on what preparing for that might entail. Here, presented in one long page, are those details, including Richards' own experiences with her dogs, to the actual training of dogs for therapy situations, to the health and cleanliness of the dogs, the American Kennel Club's Canine Good Citizen test, and the adjustments that Therapy Dogs International has made to the CGC test so it might better serve the needs of therapy work. This is a valuable site for therapy beginners, but also for veterans seeking a refresher or perhaps just some inspiration.

Furry Friends Pet Assisted Therapy Services

http://www.furryfriends.org/

Therapy-dog work is truly a labor of love, and that is reflected throughout the Web site sponsored by California-based Furry Friends Pet Assisted Therapy Services. From the relatively short home page for this site, browsers may click on to several hyperlinks, including "An introduction to our organization," which amiably presents background information on the Furry Friends volunteers who visit people in need of the kind of TLC only dogs can provide, and on why pet visits are important in the first place. Browsers may also access a section on frequently asked questions; a Furry Friends Photo Album that chronicles in vivid detail the group's volunteers, the dogs, and the facilities they visit; and even the Furry Friends Store. This site reflects the kind of people who choose to get involved with pet-assisted therapy and have made it such a success.

Livestock Guardian Dogs

http://www.lgd.org/

For thousands of years, people have enlisted dogs to protect their livestock. Bred for a natural instinct, size, and strength to protect sheep, cattle, and even poultry from predators, these dogs have for centuries proved more effective than all the firearms, poisons, and various other technological advancements that humankind has employed. That is why today, many people are realizing they can benefit from the same skills in contemporary farming and ranching efforts for environmentally friendly livestock care.

Check into the Livestock Guardian Dogs site managed by Julie A. Adams and sponsored by the Livestock Guardian Dog Association for a wealth of knowledge on this subject. Browsers may access an array of hyperlinks arranged by topics, including LGD Breeds (the Great Pyrenees, the Kuvasz, the Maremma, to name a few), Photos, Acquiring an LGD, FAQs, Training, Articles, and Health and Care. The pages presented in these sections have been contributed by people from all over the world, with all types of breeds, all types of experience, infusing this site with a thorough, in-depth and extremely broad-based pool of information.

On Guard!!!: Livestock Guarding Dog Magazine

http://www.terminus.com/~halpin/onguard1.htm

For a fun and informative view of livestock guarding dogs, check out this online 'zine presented by Julie and Pat Halpin.. Scroll down the home page, which is designed like the Table of Contents from a physical magazine, and you'll find access to information on the various breeds, personal stories, training tips, an excellent list of links to other livestock–guarding dog home pages, and a set of links to various mailing lists devoted to both livestock guarding dogs and to the various breeds (the Great Pyrenees, the Kuvasz and the Anatolian among them) that have for centuries made this work their vocation.

USDA-APHIS on Livestock Guarding Dogs

http://apollo.ahabs.wisc.edu/Individuals/Students/Lundberg/lgdinfo.html

Although the United States government typically prefers to handle livestock depredation by exterminating predators (with marginal results) through the controversial Animal Damage Control program, it has in recent years been willing to entertain the notion that perhaps the ancient tradition of protecting livestock with dogs is an alternative that farmers and ranchers should consider. As a result, the Animal and Plant Health Inspection Service of the U.S. Department of Agriculture has prepared this Web page to inform the public about the value and management of these dogs. It offers background information on livestock guarding dogs, as well as tips on raising one (minimize human contact, the dog may take two years to mature, provide for the dog's health and safety, etc.), and potential pros and cons. As is to be expected, it is straightforward in its approach and anything but a wholesale endorsement, but it's a start.

Livestock Guarding Dogs of the United Kingdom Homepage

http://ourworld.compuserve.com/homepages/Brian_Roberts/

For a complete, exhaustively researched round-up of the world's livestock guarding breeds, check out Brian Roberts' Livestock Guarding Dogs of the United Kingdom Homepage. Here you will find a long list of hypertext breed names, arranged by country. While some lists are still under construction, you can access most of these now to become an expert on some of the world's most intelligent and powerful dog breeds. No doubt there will be some names here that are unknown to even ardent dog lovers—the Aryan Molossus from Afghanistan, perhaps? Or maybe the Chien de l'Atlas from Morocco or the Owczarek Podhalanski from Poland? So take the time to scan this site and fill in the gaps in your education about livestock guarding dogs.

Vietnam Dog Handlers Association

http://www.vdhaonline.org/

Officially, the Vietnam War ended years ago, but there are some experiences that simply cannot be forgotten. Take a journey through the Web site for the Vietnam Dog Handlers Association (VDHA), managed by Steve Ball, and you'll soon understand just why those who served in Vietnam with dogs continue to honor their shared experience through this unique organization. Dramatically designed with vibrant colors and graphics against a black backdrop, the home page presents a menu of section options that offer information on membership in the VDHA, the organization's newspaper *Dogman*, a mailroom for member communication, a bulletin board of events, and several special features, the likes of which you won't find anywhere else.

Especially illuminating is the Archives section, which presents well-written articles, reflections, and memories of working with dogs in Vietnam written by those who did so. But perhaps the most touching experience within this site awaits those who access the Memorial section from the home page, a page designed "In Remembrance of Absent Friends. Their Sacrifices Are Not Forgotten." Here you will find an honor roll of handlers and dogs killed in action, and a poem by the late Donald E. Bowman, Sr., written for his scout dog, Phil. This poem defies anyone to leave this page with a dry eye. A tour of this site serves as a tribute to all 8,000 men and 4,000 dogs who served with K-9 units in Vietnam. It is an experience not to be missed.

Scout Dogs and Their Handlers

http://grunt.space.swri.edu/k9.htm

For more information on the courageous scout dogs and their equally courageous handlers that served in Vietnam, check out this informative, no-frills page that is part of a larger site devoted to Vietnam remembrances. A long list of hyperlinks offers browsers direct access to "Bibliography on Police and Military Working Dogs" (contributed by retired Air Force K-9 handler/trainer, Herb Mullican, Jr.), and "Another Mission" (a heartwrenching illustrated story by Tom Sykes about his experiences in Vietnam with his dog

Royal). Though compact in content, this site is of great value as a tribute to the Vietnam scout dogs and their handlers.

North American Police Work Dog Association

http://www.napwda.com/

Clean, crisp in tones of blue and gold, and to the point, the Web site for the North American Police Work Dog Association (NAPWDA) invites browsers to get to know this organization "Dedicated to Assisting Police Work Dog Teams Throughout the World." A wealth of information is presented here via a list of home-page hyperlinks to such topics as State Coordinator Roster, Master Trainer Roster, Workshop Information and NAPWDA Merchandise, and an Information Letter that presents details about this organization that supports officers who serve with dogs by their sides, and "strives to enhance the use of police work dogs by law enforcement agencies..."

You will learn all about membership (one need not be a law enforcement officer to be a member), canine standards and the group's overall goals. Though the language is professional, it belies an underlying respect and affection for the dogs at this organization's core, a respect most clearly summed up in the final statement on the NAPWDA home page: "They'll give you their life for a pat on the head and a kind word."

RCMP Police Dog Services

http://www.rcmp-grc.gc.ca/html/dogs.htm

Previously, we described the Royal Canadian Mounted Police's search and rescue dog pages. For a brief, though interesting, overview of the use of police dogs by the RCMP (which began when officers would use their own dogs to assist them in their work, and ultimately resulted in the formation of an official dog section in 1935), check into their page on Police Dog Services. Also covered are the breeds enlisted for this noble service (typically German Shepherds and Belgian Malinois), the handlers (those chosen must meet rigorous standards and "be capable of appreciating the known dog instincts"), and the duties (search and rescue, hostage situations, crowd control, etc.). It won't take you long to tour this page, but you're bound to find it of interest.

The Police K-9 Home Page

http://home.navisoft.com/k9officer/my-page.htm

For a friendly view of the police dog world, check into the Police K-9 Home Page presented by K-9 officer Randy Mucha and Randy's canine partner Marlo. Warm and respectful in tone, the home page provides hyperlink access to, among other topics, Training Events, Pictures, Books and other Police and Canine Web Sites. The home page also offers brief reflections on the relationship between officers and their dogs through a passage entitled "Why are we drawn to Canines?" and the true story of Gelert, a dog of the 13th century, who saved his master's infant from a wolf.

Check out the home page hyperlink Information on Police K-9 Associations, too. Here you will find links to several such groups listed, including the site for Dogs Against Drugs, Dogs Against Crime. Click on this hyperlink, and you will be greeted by a cartoon graphic of a German Shepherd in a police uniform pointing at you, the browser. This site represents a nonprofit organization founded by police officers "to fight the drug menace with the help of man's best friend," which it does by promoting the proper training of police dogs and officers, and by encouraging the establishment of canine drug units across the country.

The Police Dog Homepage

http://www.best.com/~policek9/k9home.htm

Impressive in both scope and design, this site sponsored by
The K9 Academy for Law Enforcement and operated by
Robert S. Eden is easy to navigate, despite its large, multilayered size. It has much to offer in the way of information
about every aspect of police dogs, their human partners
and their mutual training.

Your key to successful navigation is the menu bar on
the home page that covers such pertinent topics as Police
K9 Units (an extensive list of hyperlinks to various canine
units in the United States, Canada and abroad); K9 Case
Law (an overview of related laws); Training Calendar (a
listing of international seminars); Trainers Digest (a long,
well-organized list of articles covering such subjects as K9
Officer Survival, Scent & Tracking Related Issues, and K9
Care & Maintenance); and, a most touching feature, Valor
Rolls (a tribute to officers and dogs killed in the line of
duty). This site is aptly named, for it is indeed a headquarters to anyone involved with police dogs or those simply
interested in the subject.

British Columbia Municipal Police Dog Training Standards

http://www.best.com/~police9/bck9intr.htm

For a look into what goes into the making of a police dog,
check out this interesting site from the K9 Academy for
Law Enforcement (also the sponsor of the Police Dog
Homepage, above). Here, through the long hyperlinked
table of contents, you will find all the elements of this voca-
tion, including Training Philosophy (a focus on the "Praise
Reward" method), Obedience, Tracking, Criminal
Apprehension, Urban Searches, Building Searches,
Explosive Detection, Legal Aspects—the list literally goes
on and on. Also included are appendices on the Municipal

Police Dog Training Course and Police Dog Handler Selection Criteria. After a tour through this site, you'll never look at a police dog and its human partner in quite the same light.

K9 Sweden

http://home2.swipnet.se/~w-21278/

If you believe that police dogs are merely a North American phenomenon, think again. Police dogs are valued worldwide, evident in the colorful, affectionate site K9 Sweden, sponsored by Jan Bildtgard, a 20-year police veteran and the handler of a police Rottweiler. What makes this site stand out is not only its Scandinavian focus, but also the very personal style in which it is presented. Through home page hyperlinks to such topics as Helsingborg Police District (Bildtgard's turf), Training, and The Dogs, the site offers a unique insight into the Swedish way of doing things. What browsers gain is the message that police dogs, their training, and the respect and affection they receive from their handlers, are international.

Australian Police & Service Dogs

http://www.cops.aust.com/ap&sd/ap&sd.html

While the name of this site may suggest that it is devoted to the police dogs of Australia, enter its home page and you're in for a surprise. This site is actually the most complete resource of online police dog information you are likely to find, with a broad international collection of links to related sites. Divided into subject sections for ease of travel, the site does offer specific hyperlinks to Australian entities, but it also offers links from all over the world. The topics run the gamut from Competitions, to General Information, to K-9 Associations Overseas (in this case, of course, meaning North America), to Newsgroups, to Police Dog Sections, to Training/Aids. So if police dogs are your passion, make sure to bookmark this site. You'll be referring to it often.

Virginia Police Work Dog Association

http://users.aol.com/vpwda/private/p1.htm

In the unique relationship between a police officer and a dog, the two are partners in every sense of the word, which is evident in the opening photograph to the Web site of the Virginia Police Dog Work Association,depicting an officer in an affectionate pose with his canine partner.

After explaining on its home page that patrol/utility teams like the one that welcomes browsers to this site "are certified in obedience, aggression control, reasonable force, tracking, area searches, articles searches, and building searches," the site then offers hyperlinks to three more specialty sections: Narcotic Detection, Explosive Detection, and Search & Rescue Information. While the pages to which these links take you make quick work of introducing the subject at hand, the site offers more in-depth information through its extensive list of links to other police-dog-related sites via its home page.

National Police Bloodhound Association

http://www.westol.com/~npba/index.html

Here we find a variation on the police-dog concept, one that has been immortalized in books, movies, and television: the use, as we see stated on the home page for the National Police Bloodhound Association (NPBA), "of the man trailing Bloodhound in the field of law enforcement and search and rescue." This is not an elaborate site, but it offers the basics. Click on to the History option on the home page, for example, and you will learn all about the NPBA, which was formed in 1962, and the attention it has earned through the years thanks to the extraordinary scenting abilities of these dogs. While bloodhounds are often portrayed in film as baying predators out to trap falsely accused escaped convicts, most are pussycats at heart. Take the time to explore the Training Manual section, and you'll learn even more about bloodhounds and law enforcement.

Austrian K9-Handler Section

http://txk9cop.metronet.com/hotdogs/k9aust.html

Available in both German and English, the Austrian K9-Handler Section is a site that offers a glimpse of police dogs in Austria. Vibrant in design but simple and direct in language, the site includes K9 Handlers in Austria, a Photogallery and Best K9 of the Month—as well as a tour of Austria's police dogs, from the breeds that are enlisted into service on the streets of Vienna to actual photographs of the dogs in action. Once you have finished your tour, take advantage of the direct link to the International Military & Police K9 Information Exchange (located at http://txk9cop.metronet.com/interk9/interk9.hml), to access an extensive list of links to other canine-focused law-enforcement sites.

Texas K9 Police Association for Certification & Standards

http://txk9cop.metronet.com/index_2.html

For one of the most media-enhanced police-dog site experiences you are likely to have, check into the Web site for the Texas K9 Police Association for Certification & Standards. After the splashy welcome (the theme from the Cops television show and animated graphics), you may then explore the site's home page, which explains the purpose of this organization—to lend support to K9 officers throughout the state of Texas—and offers a detailed Table of Contents.

Choose from a variety of interesting, often interactive topics that include membership information and applications, the Virtual Trading Card Collection (computer-enhanced cards of members), newsletter articles, mailing lists and an online bulletin board. In the process it creates a community of dogs and their handlers who can find much camaraderie here within these lively, well-designed pages. Webmaster Kathleen Weaver has obviously had fun with this site, and in the process it succeeds in being an excellent source of information and an energetic tribute to law-enforcement dogs and the people who work with them.

Responsible Protection Dog Ownership

http://www.netpet.com/articles/protection.html

Before you consider bringing a protection dog into your home, you would be wise to read this page prepared by Timothy C. Minyard of Class Act K9 & Tactical Solutions. In the wrong hands a guard dog can be danger-ous, not to mention a legal liability, to its family as well as to would-be perpetrators. It is thus imperative than anyone interested in obtaining one take the time to do the neces-sary research. This long and very thorough document is a good place to start. It educates browsers on what a protec-tion dog is (and what it is not), the keys to a successful relationship between a trained protection dog and the peo-ple it protects; and how to find such a dog and a reputable, ethical trainer. Text heavy and devoid of graphics, it is nev-ertheless a valuable read on an extremely serious subject.

Bo's Nose Knows

http://ww2.netnitco.net/users/perrys/

Meet Bo, a 6-year-old black Labrador Retriever who, along with Officer Perry Stone, is assigned the duty of assisting in narcotics investigations for the Valparaiso, Indiana, Police Department. This site, dedicated as it is to Bo, uses the dog's viewpoint to instruct browsers on what a police nar-cotics dog does, in this case detecting as little as a half a gram of marijuana, cocaine, crack cocaine or heroin in a room or vehicle. From the home page, browsers may explore such topics as About Bo (as told by Officer Stone), Help Bo Take a Bite Out of Crime, Scrapbook (of Bo's successes), and Email Bo. Presented in a personal, reader-friendly style—with an ample collection of photos of its star canine—this site is unique in the ease in which it educates as well as entertains.

USDA Beagle Brigade
http://www.aphis.usda.gov/oa/beagle.html

If you happen to be at the airport and see a Beagle dressed in a bright green jacket sniffing about, be aware that that dog represents the cutting edge of law enforcement. It is a member of the U.S. Department of Agriculture's Beagle Brigade, a dog assigned to sniff through the luggage of people entering the United States from overseas in search of smuggled contraband, particularly illegal agricultural products that could, if allowed to enter, contaminate crops and livestock here in America. These talented dogs are featured prominently on this Web page from the larger USDA Web site.

Read on and you will learn all about the Beagle's extraordinary nose and the breed's work in a job that is tailor-made for this curious, friendly little hound that loves people and loves to work. Though this site is a quick read, it is quite interesting in the information it imparts, from the background of the Beagle Brigade, to a page of products that cannot be brought into this country, to a fact sheet that offers a more in-depth look. So next time you see a Beagle dressed in green, pay it the respect it is due for protecting America's crops and livestock.

WORKINGDOGS.COM: International Cyberzine for Working Dogs
http://www.workingdogs.com/

Enter this online monthly magazine dedicated to working dogs "and the people who work, train, breed, and love them," and you will find a plethora of information compiled and presented in a user-friendly manner by editor/publisher Monica Klinkam. It is dedicated to "canine athletes and duty-bound heroes," which includes sled dogs, Schutzhund competitors, police dogs, search-and-rescue dogs, herding dogs, and therapy dogs.

Well-designed and easy to navigate, the WORKING-DOGS.COM home page offers an illustrated Table of Contents that then segues into a list of hyperlinks that take browsers into such sections as the Quick Reference Index of All Articles and Features, Frequently Asked Questions, and the Working Dogs Book Store. This is a valuable, and very thorough, headquarters for those intent on preserving the working traditions of dogs.

Working Dogs

http://www.zmall.com/pet_talk/dog-faqs/working.html

For a thorough overview of many of the jobs in which dogs participate, read this well-written Web page from Cindy Tittle Moore. Arranged as one long page with a detailed Table of Contents to assist the browser in locating particular sections of interest, this document first covers various types of working trials, and then moves on to specific vocations, including search and rescue, sledding, herding, water-rescue dogs, and narcotics and evidence dogs. While this informative, though no-frills site is not entirely complete in subject matter (missing are therapy dogs and service dogs), it is a good launching pad for people interested in learning more about dogs that are gainfully employed.

PAWS Working Dog Evaluation

http://home.gnofn.org/~malinut/paws.html

Not every puppy is born to work, even if it comes from a long line of working dogs. This page, part of Jona Decker's The Malinut Page and derived from the Puppy Aptitude

Test developed by Jack and Wendy Volhard, presents the various attributes one should evaluate in a puppy to determine if it has the potential to someday be a working dog, whether in the recreational trial environment or the more serious vocations of police dog, search-and-rescue dog, or livestock guard. Decorated with cute canine caricatures that illustrate each concept being discussed, the page covers Prey Drive, Retrieve, Persistence, Tug, Possessiveness, Recall, and Attention, and then presents a case study of an actual dog that was evaluated in this way. Here, then, is a unique and practical addition to round out one's working dog education.

American Working Dog Association

http://ccwf.cc.utexas.edu/~donnell/Working/AWDA.html

With roots in an English tradition begun in 1924 of testing the skills of sheep, army, and police dogs and their relationships with their handlers, this newly formed organization is seeking to carry on that tradition in the United States. Check in to this Web site, sponsored by the American Working Dog Association under the guidance of Mark Donnell, for both as an informational resource and a headquarters for people interested in getting involved. It does this through several home page options that include a short FAQ, an overview of working trials past and planned, trial description and rules, and "An open letter to members of the American dog community interested in working trials." Appealing as it is, this activity that celebrates canine skills in service to humans should have no trouble attracting a devoted following.

Dog-Play

http://www.dog-play.com/home.html

This site, under the guidance of Diane Blackman, is devoted to all activities in which people may participate with their dogs. It includes several serious working activities. On the home-page list of hypertext options, you will find the pertinent headings, including Animal Assisted Therapy and Pet Facilitated Therapy. Click on these options and you will be treated first to a detailed explanation of the subject at hand, followed by lists of links to related sites. Well organized and simple to navigate with ample hyperlinks both in menus and within text, this is a valuable site.

PART IV

For Dog Owners

Services

As dog ownership has become increasingly sophisticated through the years, so have the services available to owners for the care of their dogs. Today, boarding kennels are more likely to be called pet hotels (and boast accommodations and services deserving of that name), some pet groomers have been known to charge fees approaching those charged by Beverly Hills styling salons frequented by big-name human clients, and canine day-care providers and summer camps have cropped up throughout the nation.

The existence of such services, the people who provide them, and the in-depth training required to help those people master the necessary skills, are all a testament to the great value we place on our pet dogs. Most owners at one time or another will choose to take advantage of the plethora of services available as part of the multi-billion-dollar "pet industry." Whether one simply wishes to take Rover in for a professional bath and haircut from time to time, or to enlist the services of a clean, well-run boarding kennel with a responsible, dog-loving staff when vacation time rolls around, how comforting it is to know that the professionalism of such endeavors has reached so high a mark.

That professionalism is evident in the Web sites below, sites dedicated to canine services. Some of these are universal in scope, while others are of a more local nature, yet even the local entities are valuable to the dog-owning population at large in that they, too, offer bits of wisdom that pet owners anywhere might find valuable. Some of these sites are

continued after the feature section

Camp Gone to the Dogs

http://camp-gone-tothe-dogs.com:80/index.htm

This site is introduced with the statement: "A Celebration of Dogs and All the Ways They Bring Joy into Our Lives." Since its founding in 1990, Honey Loring's Camp Gone to the Dogs in Putney, Vermont, has been attracting dog lovers and media attention alike in its efforts to help owners, as Loring tells browsers in her home-page greeting, whose "idea of a good time is having fun with your dog."

Apparently the concept behind Camp Gone to the Dogs, an actual camp that both dogs and owners attend together, has, says Loring "grown beyond my imagination." This site helps browsers understand why. Rooted in a philosophy of mutual learning in a noncompetitive atmosphere, the camp invites dogs and puppies of all ages, sizes, shapes, breeds and mixes of breeds—and owners of similar combinations—to discover "some hidden talents just waiting to be discovered at Camp."

The same affection for dogs and light atmosphere permeates this site, beginning with the portrait of two exuberant canine campers featured at the top of the home page. From there browsers may learn all about this camp and the upcoming sessions. Click on More Info, for example, and meet camp founder and director Loring, whose background includes tracking, agility, canine square dancing, lure coursing, sledding, pet-facilitated therapy, public education programs, and competitive obedience, experiences from which she has drawn in designing her camp's many programs.

The More Info section is also the place to find out the dates of upcoming camp sessions and the fees for attending camp, the latter depending on the type of accommodations one chooses (single occupancy, double occupancy, or bunk house). For even more information, click on to the home-page hyperlinks that take browsers into sections devoted to specific sessions and you will learn what is planned for them—i.e., agility exercises, a brush up on obedience, enjoyable walks

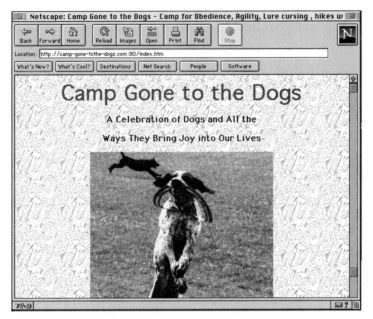

through the Vermont countryside, or the opportunity to "just sit around, kiss your dog and eat bon bons!"

Session pages are rich with detail, divided into sections that inform prospective campers about General Information (including guest trainers who will be available for special workshops); Classes, Clinics and Training (from Agility to Weight Pulling to Puppy Kindergarten to Swimming Lessons, the number of events available is astounding); Lectures, Demonstrations & Eventing Chats; Just Plain Fun; Extra Services (such as Canine Good Citizen, Therapy Dog Testing, and Tellington Touch—extra fees required); and Camp Staff.

Be warned that if this site inspires your interest in attending Camp Gone to the Dogs, you must make your reservations early, for sessions typically sell out quickly. Those who miss the window of opportunity are invited to sign up for a waiting list in hopes that something will open up before camp begins. If it doesn't, they'll just have to wait until next year.

sponsored by the service providers themselves who have chosen the Internet as an effective advertising and educational tool for their businesses. Other sites are dedicated more to the educational end of this equation, existing to help pet owners to understand what they should know about given service fields, and how they should go about choosing the best providers of that service for their pets, who are, after all, family members in every sense of the word.

American Boarding Kennel Association
http://abka.com/

As the non-profit trade organization that represents the boarding kennel industry, the American Boarding Kennel Association (ABKA) provides a valuable service to visitors to its Web site. Here within this professionally designed site you will find information on the organization itself, which strives to encourage and prepare member kennels to provide the best, most professional care possible to their boarders, and you will also find information that might help you choose a boarding facility for your pets.

From the detailed home-page menu bar, you may choose such options as Bulletin Board, Information (which provides information on the Facility Accreditation Program and the "nationally respected Ethics Program"), Education (which includes the Pet Care Technician Program and the Certified Kennel Operator Program), Pet Services Mall, and Calendar. But perhaps one of the most valuable services this site provides for non-member pet owners is found in the Member Kennels section. Here you are presented first with a map of the United States (as well as hyperlinks to Mexico, Canada, and other countries). Click on a state and you will find listed alphabetically ABKA member kennels that "subscribe to and must run their business in accordance with the ABKA Code of Ethics." Frequent travelers are thus wise to bookmark this site for future reference.

Home Away From Home

http://www.atbeach.com/services/homeaway/index.html

This Delaware boarding and grooming kennel has chosen a unique home-page design for the promotion of its many services—a design that makes the preliminary evaluation of the facility as quick and easy as possible for the prospective client. After a brief and friendly greeting from owner/operator Denise Irwin, the site presents two columns of information: the first entitled We Offer; the second, We Require. The pet owner can review the impressive roster of services Home Away From Home provides in a reader-friendly pawprint-bulleted format: heated and air-conditioned runs, daily playtime in two fenced yards, "soft, comfy bedding," soothing music, fire and security systems, a full-service grooming salon, and "plenty of treats and tender loving care," to name a few. In the next column required vaccines and the proof of same are outlined, as well as the message that "There are no exceptions to this rule!", a welcome warning to responsible pet owners who are seeking boarding services for their pets

Waldenway Canine Camp

http://www.escape.ca/~barryk/gloria/canine-camp.html

Though it is short on graphics and design, this site sponsored by Waldenway Canine Camp is unique in its clever approach to dog boarding. In referring to her Canadian facility as a camp, proprietor Gloria Delorme tells proprietors in her home-page greeting that Waldenway "strives not to be a kennel but instead a vacation facility." Read on and you will see that the design of the program at this "unkennel" revolves around making the visiting dogs' stay "a positive camp experience." The related Web site, which is actually one long home page, goes on to explain The Bunkhouse (where cleanliness and spaciousness are key), the Campground (dogs are allowed to frolic in a large enclosed area of grass and trees with a "camp counselor" four times a day), and Camp Services for You (rates and other services offered). Such a presentation would certainly soothe the uneasiness many dog owners experience when they must leave a canine family member behind.

Cactus Pryor's Canine Hilton (A Kennel)

http://www.Instar.com/canine/index.html

Before turning a pet over to the care of a staff at a boarding kennel, it is always wise first to tour the facility. The Web site for the Canine Hilton in Texas offers browsers an opportunity to visit this kennel online, beginning with the opening shot of the pleasant-looking facility. This is followed by additional home-page photos of various available suites and a bulleted list of information on the services provided by this unique six-acre boarding kennel, that also offers an obedience training program for boarders, grooming, and pet photography.

For even more information on this facility that was founded almost a quarter of a century ago by Cactus Pryor and John N. Ramsey (who continue to operate the kennel today), click on the cartoon-illustrated, home-page hyperlink "A Dog's Life." This section provides more in-depth information on the various Canine Hilton services and the facility's focus on companionship and health for its boarders. After an online tour of the well-illustrated, fun-to-navigate Canine Hilton, you will understand just why the home page states that this facility has been "recognized as one of America's finest."

Animal Resorts

http://www.ccconnect.com/animalresorts/index.htm

Animal Resorts, a Pennsylvania boarding kennel that states on its home page that it is a facility with "a warm heart for cold noses," has used the Internet as an effective tool for promoting its services. Well-designed and easy to navigate, it offers a home-page menu grid and a hypertext menu bar including such options as Boarding, Rates, Training, Required Vaccinations, Directions, and other links. Unique to this site are the many services that Animal Resorts provides. A full-service canine facility, in addition to boarding, it offers grooming, doggie day care, and is the home of a Rottweiler breeding program, information for all included within the site's pages. While those seeking a boarding kennel for their pets should always visit and evaluate the prospective facility ahead of time, access to such Web sites as this is a good place to start.

Positive Power Kennels

http://www.onr.com/user/bdqueen/index.html

Homespun and friendly is the Web site sponsored by the Texas boarding kennel, Positive Power Kennels. Browsers are bound to enjoy a tour through all of the home-page menu options, which, in the same warm and personal style, address such topics as About the Kennel (run by Bart and Courtney Emken and located on 15 dog-friendly acres where boarders are offered twice-daily fun runs), Pictures of our Boarders, Rules of the Game and What to bring when boarding, and Who is Dogboy? (this latter section being a delightful story of how Bart Emken came to realize his true calling with dogs and thus earned this affectionate nickname). Even a tour of the Positive Power Prices section is interesting, in that in a long boxed grid it explains the various services this facility offers. These services include obedience training and in-home boarding care for old or physically challenged boarders (a rather unique service), thus suggesting to browsers what perhaps they should be looking for in kennels within their own home towns.

RSPCA Australia—Operation of Boarding Establishments for Cats and Dogs

http://www.ezycolour.com.au/RSPCA/boarding_cop.html

For a technical account of what makes a boarding kennel efficient in its operation and ethical in its treatment of its charges, check out this site from the Royal Society for the Prevention of Cruelty to Animals (RSPCA) Australia. This page is taken from the RSPCA Australia Code of Practice, and though it may on its surface appear dry and text-heavy, it offers pet owners valuable information on what they should look for in a boarding kennel for their pets. It addresses all the important topics under the main headings: Staff; Husbandry (which includes Nutrition, Vaccinations, Hygiene, Exercise, Security and Housing); Records; Appendix 1—Sample Contract; and Appendix 2— [Nutritional] Daily Intake. All told, this page is a valuable resource for kennel operators and pet owners alike.

National Association of Professional Pet Sitters

http://www.petsitters.org/

The idea of pet sitting—hiring someone to come into your home to care for your pets when you are away—is gaining more and more credibility these days as some pet owners realize that their pets may be happier remaining at home in their absence. In response to this trend, is the Web site for the National Association of Professional Pet Sitters (NAPPS), a site that appeals both to pet sitters and to the pet owners they serve.

Pleasant to look at with softly colored cartoon animal designs and easy to navigate from a simple home-page menu, this site offers browsers a look into the NAPPS and provides information on what pet owners should be aware of when seeking a pet sitter. For example, click on to Why You Should Use a Pet Sitter, and you will find a page that seeks to convince browsers that "There's No Place Like Home." Also valuable to pet owners is the About NAPPS section, which details the organization's mission, its Code of Ethics and its development of a certification program, all of which serve to convince the pet owner that when seeking a pet sitter, one that is a member of the NAPPS is probably the safest choice.

The Circle of Cybersitters

http://www.petsitting.com/Web ring.htm

For quick and easy access to a variety of pet-sitting entities, check out The Circle of Cybersitters. Here you will find a group of Internet-advertising pet sitters and other pet-related site proprietors who have joined together to form a Web ring, all for the benefit of interested browsers and prospective clients.

Vibrantly designed and reader-friendly in the information it provides both about Web rings in general and the use of this one in particular, this home page is a door to several interesting sites, the tour of which you may begin by clicking on either Next Site or Next 5 from the home page. From here you may visit a variety of fun and informative pet sitter Web sites, including Happy Tails Pet Sitters in Texas, Dogs Luv Us in Toronto, Pooches and Plants in Arizona, and Spoiled Rotten Pet Sitting in Indiana, to name a few of the ring members. From each page you may move on to the next member of the Web, for your own convenience, as well as that of the ring members and their efforts to let their messages be seen.

Pet Sitters International

http://www.ols.net/users/psi/about.htm

As the vocation of pet sitting has gained more credibility—and clients—in recent years, Patti Moran created Pet Sitters International, an organization, this site's home page tells browsers, "Run BY Pet Sitters FOR Pet Sitters!" With more than 1,500 members in its ranks, this educational organization is working "to promote, support, and recognize excellence in pet sitting."

You may find out how PSI is pursuing this through a tour of its Web site. Though the home page lacks a traditional introductory home-page menu of options, its text is peppered with hyperlinks that carry browsers into subsequent layers dedicated to such topics as Quality Standards for Excellence (to which all members must adhere), Pet Sitter's Liability Insurance (available to members at group rates), Accreditation (which can bolster a pet sitter's credibility), Patti Moran's Products for Pet Sitters (books and videos), Nationwide Locator Line (a resource of members to which pet owners may refer to locate pet sitters in their areas), and online membership information. This site is thus a must for pet owners seeking pet sitting services, and pet sitters seeking professionalism in their position.

American Dog Trainers Network—Dogwalkers & Petsitters

http://www.inch.com/~dogs/dogwalkers.html

Opening with the title Dogwalkers & Petsitters: What To Look For, And What To Look Out For, this site sponsored by the American Dog Trainers Network is designed to help pet owners find a good "pet care person," who is "reliable trustworthy and cares about your pet's welfare." Scroll down this single-page document that is presented in a light, reader-friendly style, and you will find information on interviewing, terms and expectations, financial arrangements, the trial period—even how to handle the key situation and how to arrange a pet-supplies drawer in your home. Anyone looking for someone to watch his or her pet as dog walker or pet sitter is wise to stop here first, for the information presented on this site managed by Robin Kovary is as thorough as it can be and is thus of great value.

Pet Nannies

http://www.evansville.net/~ceegee/

A cute name and a cute presentation: That is what you will find upon entering the Web site for the Indiana-based pet-sitting business, Pet Nannies, owned by Cindy Gossett. Against a pale pink backdrop of heart and pawprint silhouettes, this site offers browsers a pleasant tour of its services, accessible from several home-page hyperlinks. Pet Nannies services are presented in thorough and rather comforting detail in both the "Our On-line Brochure" and A few of our fees and services..." sections. A rather clever feature is the Treat of the Month Club, in which "your pets receive special treats once a month, delivered to your door." And while you're on the subject of treats, check out the Critter Fritter Dog Treats section. While these pet sitters are apparently quite committed to ensuring their customers' peace of mind while traveling, so do they obviously believe that the quickest way to a pet's heart is through its stomach.

Pet Sitters Yellow Pages
http://www.petsitters.com/

A full-service pet-sitter site, the Pet Sitters Yellow Pages presents pet owners from coast to coast—as well as Canada and overseas—with a complete roster of pet-sitter names, numbers, and e-mail addresses, all arranged alphabetically by state and accessible from a Directory on the home page. But that's not all you'll find here on this yellow page. This site's home page also offers two additional menus that offer browsers access to selected pet-sitter sites and, in a unique feature, to a Pet Sitters Message Board, where those in the field may share their experiences and gain advice and support from their colleagues. Consequently, this site serves not only as a valuable resource to pet owners seeking pet sitters, but as a home base where those pet sitters can find camaraderie and an avenue by which they may promote their services.

Everything You Always Wanted to Know About Grooming... But Were Afraid to Ask
http://pages.ripco.com:8080/~pkansoer/evrythg.htm

One of the most common services sought by dog owners is that of the professional groomer. This unique site offers owners vital information on gauging what their pets might require in the way of grooming and the various issues associated with grooming, knowledge of which might help when it comes time to find a groomer for a pet dog. In many cases, grooming requires more than just brushing the dog. There are actually procedures that can be painful as well as controversial, and this page, written with compassion and affection for animals by Pat Kansoer as part of his larger C.A.T.S. by Pat site, addresses these issues (such as the pain and inhumanity of long dematting sessions), as well as such topics as Grooming Costs, Parasite Control, Grooming Older Dogs, and Dogs that Bite! Visit this site before choosing a groomer. It will help you both in choosing and communicating with this particular pet professional.

ABDog Grooming School

http://www.connect.ab.ca/~abdog/

Those considering a career in dog grooming may find a visit to the Web site of AB Dog Grooming School of interest. Though the school is located in Alberta, Canada, and thus not necessarily an educational option to all prospective grooming students, the information included in its Web site may be of research value to those who think they might want to attend a school of this kind. From the clean, crisp design of this site's home page, browsers may choose from hyperlinks that offer access to areas that provide information on the ABDog Grooming School, which is owned by Lois Friesen and offers a curriculum that teaches grooming of all breeds; Grooming Tips from Lois Friesen; and, a unique feature, a Picture Gallery, which presents photos from the school that emphasize all aspects of dog grooming and is expanded each month.

The Grooming Page from The Wonderful World of Poodles

http://www.geocities.com/Heartland/2826/groom.html

Needless to say, the Poodle is a dog that can require more grooming than any other breed, especially if a dog's owner is seeking one of the various powder-puff styles one sees featured in the show ring. This particular Web site is thus of great value to Poodle owners in that it offers them access to information and other pages and sites devoted to Poodle grooming. Essentially a long list of links, this page is divided into sections, including Links to Grooming Pages Specific to the Poodle, Links to Groomers Pages, Links to Suppliers, Links to Clipper & Blade Sharpening Services, Links to Learning to Groom, and Other Grooming Links. Given the broad scope of this site and the many grooming links it provides, it is thus of value to all dog people, those who own Poodles, and those who don't.

Perfect Touch Grooming

http://www.bnui.com/perfecttouch/

Much pride and affection has gone into the Web site for Valerie Shoemaker's California grooming shop, Perfect Touch Grooming. Presented with warmth and a very personal style, this site's home page, decorated with cute canine caricature illustrations, introduces Shoemaker and her 17 years of grooming experience that has ranged "from the giant Newfoundland to the tiny teacup Poodle, the lovable Mutts, the vocal Cats, and an occasional astonished rabbit." The site also includes a menu of hyperlink options that offer browsers information on two high-tech grooming tools in which Shoemaker has invested—the Clipper VAC and the Hydro Surge—as well as access to pet-sitting services and pet portraiture available from this full-service, very dog-loving business whose proprietor has succeeded in using the Internet as a valuable advertising tool.

Autumn Winds Dog Agility and Training Center

http://members.aol.com/agdog/home.htm

For a look into a unique angle on a training service, visit the Web site sponsored by Autumn Winds Dog Agility and Training Center run by Jan and Tom Santel in New Hill, North Carolina. With agility becoming a more popular event every year, this center targets those who would like to take advantage of the facility's "three outdoor agility rings and over 90 pieces of equipment" for the training of their dogs in this fun and lively event. But there is more to this site than simply information on the facility itself. Also offered on a detailed home-page menu is access to a variety of related topics, including Information about Dog Agility, Upcoming Trials, and Agility Equipment Catalog. Even prospective agility competitors who don't happen to reside in North Carolina can benefit from a tour of this site.

Camp Dances With Dogs

http://www.flyingdogpress.com/camp.htm

For a light, airy, and rather irresistible camp Web site, check in to Camp Dances With Dogs. Billing the unique summer camp it represents as "not your everyday dog camp," this site offers browsers a fun presentation of what the camp is (and what it is not), all to ensure that those who sign up understand what they are getting themselves into. Held each summer in the Hunterdon Hills of New Jersey, this camp, hosted by trainer and author Suzanne Clothier, focuses on various and rather unique aspects of living with dogs, including agility, tracking, animal communication, clicker training, behavior, tricks, and hypnosis. The curriculum is described here as humorous, unconventional, freewheeling, and noncompetitive; this short though enjoyable page targets a distinct type of dog owner, who, we learn here, may be inclined after an initial visit to keep returning "year after year after year."

Animal Camp: An Awesome Experience for Kids

http://www.adoptapet.com/alexandria/camp.html

The Animal Welfare League of Alexandria offers a unique camp experience, not for dogs this time, but for kids who love dogs. While summer camp for kids is hardly a unique idea, an animal-oriented summer camp for kids is. This site and the organization it represents sponsors a day camp open to small groups of kids ranging in age from 9 to 12, and 13 to 15 (depending on the session).

Designed to help children "understand and appreciate animals," the league's Absolutely Awesome Animal Awareness Camp curriculum consists of hands-on activities that teach young campers the art of dog training, the care of baby animals, the ins and outs of animal shelter operations, and it introduces them to various animal-related careers. The introductory information presented on this site's clean, easy-to-follow home page, is designed both to inspire and inform prospective campers. It is then complemented by hyperlinks to photos of the camp animals and the campers, and more in-depth information on how to sign up. Since space is limited, one can only hope that other organizations will follow this group's progressive lead and offer similar camps of their own for kids across the country.

Top Dog Training School

http://www.jaguNET.com/~spectrum/topdog/index.htm

Sponsored by renowned dog trainers Jack and Wendy Volhard, the Web site for the Volhard's New York–based Top Dog Training School details the various camps, conferences, and seminars at the root of this unique entity's efforts to get America's dogs trained. Focusing all of their efforts on their Motivational Method, the Volhards seek to attract, as their home page states, "people who like their dogs and have them first and foremost as pets and companions."

These people may in turn take advantage of several options introduced on the home page and discussed in greater detail in internal layers accessible from there. These include Instructor School Training Conferences ("A week of training fun with your dog"), Holistic Camp for a Healthy Dog ("A week long conference on canine nutrition and health"), and various single-subject seminars and lectures that address such topics as Aggression and Puppy Evaluation. Interspersed with information about Top Dog's conference/camp options and schedules, you will also find a great deal of background information designed to inform as well as motivate the browsing public.

International Association of Pet Cemeteries

http://www.petrest.com/iapc.html

You may have a little trouble figuring out how to get around within this site, but given its unique focus on the loss of a pet and how one might go about memorializing it, you may find the effort worthwhile. Here within one very long home page with very large print presenting information almost as a stream of consciousness, browsers can scroll down and learn all about the International Association of Pet Cemeteries (IAPC), which was founded in 1971, as well as options open to pet owners when they lose a beloved pet. Also included is detailed and very enthusiastic information on IAPC membership, activities, and seminars.

Take the time to explore this site and you will also find areas of a more traditional format, specifically the menu grid at the top of the home page with hyperlinks to such topics as About Burial Options, About Cremation and Where to Buy Pet Caskets. At the opposite end of the page is the IAPC Directory, consisting first of a list of hypertext state names one may use to locate member pet cemeteries in his or her area, followed by the names and addresses of the facilities themselves, some providing hyperlinks to their own home pages. While this is not the most pleasant type of pet-related service, it is nevertheless a vital one, and this site presents it with warmth, enthusiasm, and compassion.

Bubbling Well Pet Memorial Park

http://www.bubbling-well.com/

This site bills the park it represents as a place "For Those Who Care." Apparently those who care also contributed to the design of this site, which can only be described as peaceful and gentle—just the type of atmosphere one needs upon losing a trusted pet. The Bubbling Well home page opens with a lovely photograph of the California park, which is then followed by a Main Menu, each option illustrated with a soft pen-and-ink illustration. These options include Our History and Information, Memorial For An Important Friend, The Spiritual Side, and Grief Over The Loss of a Pet.

Also included is Photo Tour of Our Park, which allows browsers to visit a park that the Boston Sunday Globe called "the largest and most exotic" pet cemetery in the nation. Another impressive section is Grief Over The Loss of a Pet. Here browsers may find soothing information about this family tragedy, complete with a menu grid of related topics that include Euthanasia: The Difficult Choice, The First Stage: Denial, and The Proper Good Bye. This site is thus of value to all pet owners, for all will ultimately reach this point in their relationships with their pets, and it is comforting to know that some words of encouragement await within the Bubbling Well Web site.

The Hartsdale Pet Cemetery and Crematory

http://www.petcem.com/

An interest in history is reason enough to check out the Web site for New York's Hartsdale Pet Cemetery and Crematory. Founded it 1896, this facility, of which browsers may see a photo at the opening of the site's home page, has a long and illustrious past, and all of it is presented here.

Click on History from the menu bar that follows you throughout the site, and you will learn about the founding of Hartsdale, followed by a selection of hyperlinks to more in-depth historical information, including Famous People Who Have Buried Pets at Hartsdale, Notable Monuments (links to The War Dog Memorjal, The Oldest Monument, Oklahoma City Bombing Memorial, etc.), Famous Pets Buried at Hartsdale, and The History of Pet Burial & Memorialization. With a clean, crisp, easy-to-navigate design that presents current information on the Hartsdale facility and services as well as its history, this is a fascinating site devoted to a unique subject.

National Pet Registry, Inc.

http://www.nationalpetregistry.com/

It is indeed frightening to imagine waking up one day and realizing your pet is gone, that it has escaped from the yard, run away. That fear can, however, be allayed if you prepare for the unexpected and make sure your dog is properly identified. This is the underlying philosophy of the National Pet Registry (NPR) and the Web site it sponsors.

With a clean, easy-to-navigate design, the NPR home page informs browsers that this organization seeks "to provide a first class pet protection service at an affordable price." Explore the subsequent list of home-page options, and you will learn that NPR's method of identification is the oldest and still the most effective method: the pet tag. In the FAQ section, browsers learn that dogs are tagged with a special NPR tag and are registered with this national organization; then, should a dog be found, NPR is contacted and it then contacts the owner. There is even a Testimonials section, a forum for satisfied customers, of which it appears there are many across North America who took the time to identify and register their pets.

Lorna Barkey, The Pet Coach

http://www.interlog.com/~petcoach/

Clever creativity permeates the site of Canadian Lorna Barkey, which has apparently guided her career, as well. Barkey, it appears, has taken her passion for animals into several different service areas, all of which are offered here in this colorful, easy-to-navigate Web site. From pet sitting to house sitting to dog walking to pet transportation to pet workshops, this veteran all-around pet consultant offers all such services, and all under one roof. The most informational home-page link is entitled Lyon Petmobile Services, owned and operated by Barkey, who bills herself as "Your Pet's Travel Agent." Here she lists not only pet relocation and taxi services, but all of the services she provides. While geography will prevent most people from taking advantage of her services, a visit to her site is nevertheless of value to any dog lover who is looking for inspiration on how the all-around dog lover can channel that great affection in very positive, and perhaps lucrative, directions.

Dog Show Photography (Tom Di Giacomo)

http://www.DogShowPhoto.com/

For a different type of service that is just naturally cut out for advertising on the Internet, check out Tom Di Giacomo's Dog Show Photography site. As interactive and vibrant as Web sites can be, this is the ideal venue for a photographer to show off his wares, and Di Giacomo takes full advantage of this opportunity here. From the colorful home page, the browser may choose from several options presented in a boxed menu at the left of the screen. These offer access to such locations as Information, the American Kennel Club, and Order Form (which allows customers to order reprints online and to send copies to judges, handlers, breeders, or friends). But the most logical of these from the standpoint of the very visual medium of photography is the Sample Photos section. Here prospective clients can review Di Giacomo's work and see for themselves whether this is a photographer with whom they would like to work.

Publications

When it comes to reading about dogs, there is no shortage of sources available to the inquisitive dog lover, no matter what the category of publication. Magazines, newspapers, newsletters, books and special publications exclusive to canine subjects number in the hundreds. Several magazines covering all the breeds (including mixes) exist in the United States and Canada, and have a combined circulation of more than half a million. Nearly every breed club in North America publishes its own newsletter, and one publishing company exists primarily for the purpose of publishing breed-specific periodicals.

Canine newspapers are another phenomenon in the world of dog literature, and many are written primarily for the show community. Several publishing houses also specialize in books about dogs.

Since dog magazines and other canine publications specialize in informing dog lovers about their canine friends, it is only logical that these sources would provide some of the most comprehensive and informative sites on the Web. By using writers and photographers who specialize in covering dogs, many of these publications are able to present dog lovers with some of the most current and important canine information available on the Internet.

While the number of dog publications available to the general public is staggering, only a few general-interest dog publishers exist. The majority of these publishers maintain Web sites that serve as companions to the print versions of

continued after the feature section

Dog Fancy Magazine

http://www.petchannel.com/dogs/index.html

Dog Fancy magazine recently celebrated its 25th anniversary and boasts the highest circulation of any dog-specific publication in the United States. Published by Fancy Publications Inc., the largest publisher of pet-related magazines in the business, the print version of *Dog Fancy* covers everything from news to personal stories relating to man's best friend. Their Web is also a far-reaching resource.

The Newsline section of the site features reports on events, veterinary breakthroughs, and other time-sensitive subjects, special coverage of the Westminster Kennel Club Dog Show, and a calendar of American Kennel Club and United Kennel Club dog shows and events.

The Fido Finder, another feature on the master page, brings your browser to a directory of breeders, chosen by region and then by breed. The breeder listings, while not comprehensive, include active breeders who advertise puppies.

If you aren't sure what breed you want, the Fido Finder will take you to a complete listing of profiles of each American Kennel Club and United Kennel Club breeds. While the Breed-of-the-Month selection offers a photograph of the dog along with text on the breed's history and specifics, most of the profiles contain just enough information to get you started on your search for the right dog.

For general information on a variety of subjects, the Canine Library offers reprints from paper editions of *Dog Fancy* on a number of topics. Browsers can choose from Behavior and Training, Care, Health, and Nutrition. In the Behavior and Training section, for example, you have the option of learning about general behavior, training the dog at home, teaching kids how to behave around dogs, and housetraining puppies. If you choose to find out more, you'll be given the options of Children, Dogs and Biting, The Family Pet, and Dogs Meeting Kids.

One of the most exciting places on the *Dog Fancy* site is the K-9 Kids area. Dog-loving kids can view artwork created by other children and read poetry and essays about dogs

Departments

Newsline
Fido Finder
Canine Library
Canine Community
Bowser Browser
K-9 Kids
My Dog
Storefront
Members Area
Print Edition
Feedback

NEWSLINE AND CALENDAR
Study Offers Hope for Dogs with Cancer

FIDO FINDER
Looking for a new canine friend? You can find descriptions of breeds as well as a database of breeders in our Fido Finder.

CANINE LIBRARY
A library of information about caring for your dog. Articles include health, care, behavior, training and nutrition information.

BOWSER BROWSER
From personal dog pages to commercial sites, all you have to do is point and click and you're launched into dog land.

K-9 KIDS
Dogs and kids are cool! This portion of our web site is just for you: responsible, caring kids who love their dogs.

INTERACTIVE
Virtual Lucy
Our trusted friend Lucy seems to have misplaced her bones. Help her find them as you navigate our site and you can win a one year subscription to Dog Fancy Magazine. Requires JavaScript capable browser. Non-JavaScript browsers can start here.

For comments, suggestions or additional information, contact: editor@petchannel.com

written by fellow browsers. Kids can also submit their own poetry and essays by typing them directly into the site.

And what would a kid's area be without an interactive game? An elaborate doggy word scramble provides the opportunity for literate, canine-oriented children to fill in the blanks.

Kids are not the only ones who can read and submit essays to the *Dog Fancy* site. The My Dog area features personal stories about dogs submitted by readers of *Dog Fancy* and the Web site.

If you are in the mood to shop for products and services, you'll appreciate the Storefront area, which features classified advertising taken from the latest print edition of *Dog Fancy.*

As you navigate through the *Dog Fancy* site, be on the lookout for Virtual Lucy, a sad-eyed Basset Hound who has lost her cyber-bones. Lucy and her bones appear in various places throughout the site, and browsers who find just 6 of the 60 Lucy links are entered in regular drawings for subscriptions to *Dog Fancy* magazine—the paper version.

their periodicals. In addition to these online versions of print magazines, several book publishers specializing in canine works also offer Web sites.

This chapter focuses on the best, most informative sites authored by general-interest publishers of dog magazines, newspapers, and books. Each site provides valuable information on a variety of dog-related subjects, with information on how to obtain print versions of what these Web masters have to offer.

Canine Review

http://kamloops.netshop.net/caninerev/

It seems as though the entire Canadian dog show community reads *Canine Review* magazine, a publication devoted to the Canadian show scene. Established in 1978, the magazine provides information on what is happening in and around the show rings of the Great White North, and the Web site strives to achieve the same goal online.

The *Canine Review* Web site does not provide the in-depth information available in other online versions of popular dog magazines, but it does offer considerable breeder advertising. Recent show results from Canadian Kennel Club events are also posted on a regular basis, as are lists of upcoming Canadian Kennel Club events.

A sampling of features, columns, and departments from the most recent print edition are also offered online for those interested in subscribing to this niche publication.

Dogs in Canada

http://www.dogs-in-canada.com/

Much like the print version of *Dogs in Canada*, this Web site also offers articles and reports on a number of different topics in its Features & Articles area. Highlights from past issues, including stories on activities, breeding, grooming, health, judging, obedience, and other subjects abound. A detailed profile on a selected breed is also available each month.

The immediacy of the Internet is not lost on the *Dogs in Canada* site. An area called Webbits, featuring up-to-date news items on canine issues and events, is an important part of this magazine's home page.

Well-read and well-respected, *Dogs in Canada* has been published by the Canadian Kennel Club since 1889 and boasts a circulation of 30,000. The magazine provides a plethora of information for dog lovers, and the site is a wonderful companion to the paper version.

If you are looking for information on various dog breeds, the Breed Information area on the home page will provide you with details on 170 different kinds of dogs. Organized by breed group and listed alphabetically by name, each section includes a photograph of the breed in question plus history and particulars, along with a list of breeders who sell puppies in Canada. Not limited to Canadian Kennel Club breeds, this inventory of canine specimens also includes unusual dogs not recognized by the parent organization.

Hoflin Publishing Dogs Online

http://www.hoflin.com

In the world of purebred dogs, Hoflin Publishing serves a unique purpose. Publishers of annual and quarterly breed-specific magazines, Hoflin has its hand in nearly every remotely popular American Kennel Club breed.

The Hoflin Web site is a no-frills place filled with information on accessing Hoflin's extensive library of printed canine material. The site's Master Index by Breeds starts out with a list of breeds that each link to other areas within the Hoflin site and to other sites on the Net. You can use this area to find the most current standard for each breed, along with a directory of breeders and information on the top five dogs within the breed. Links to breed association home pages are also available here.

The Resources section of the site provides an inventory of doggy e-mail lists, which are postings by dog lovers interested in specific areas of dogdom sent directly to your e-mail box. The site provides the opportunity to join one or all of these specialized lists.

Another area within Resources, called the Dog Museum (not to be confused with the actual American Kennel Club Dog Museum in St. Louis, Missouri), features a collection of photographs of champion dogs and title holders, along with three-generation pedigrees for each dog. For dog owners wishing to research their purebred's ancestry, this is an excellent place to start.

A real-time dog chat, various articles on canine-related subjects, and doggy cartoons are all available on this site, as is information on how to order Hoflin books and periodicals. A section entitled Dog Prints is especially interesting. It provides images of selected dog art from the 1800s and 1900s, along with the option to order reasonably priced prints of these paintings and etchings.

Dog Lover's Bookshop

http://www.dogbooks.com

The Dog Lover's Bookshop, a tiny store for literate dog lovers founded in 1994 by Bern Marcowitz and Margot Rosenberg, specializes in hard-to-find dog books and out-of-print titles. This Web site, authored by the store's owners, provides browsers access to the tiny New York City shop's extensive inventory.

The Dog Lover's Bookshop lacks the graphic excitement so often associated with canine Web sites. But if you are looking for a certain dog book or just want to get an idea of what has been published on the subject of dogs, this is the place to visit.

Organized first by subject, then alphabetically by author, hundreds of dog books are listed in this site in a simple, text-heavy format. Information on how to order books from the Dog Lover's Bookshop by e-mail or snail mail is also included. New titles reviewed and recommended by the owners are another a nice treat.

Online, the Dog Lover's Bookshop has the same quirky atmosphere as the real store, which is located in midtown Manhattan above an Indian restaurant. A story about Potemkin, the dog who "founded" the store, is a good example of this.

By proclamation, the Dog Lover's Bookshop site is almost completely free of graphics. "We assume that photos of your dogs beautify your monitors, perhaps the dogs themselves are hovering nearby. We can't compete with perfection," state the authors, who say that they will continue to update the site with information but will keep graphics to a minimum.

Our Dogs

http://dspace.dial.pipex.com/town/square/tac61/dogsuk.htm

Our Dogs is a weekly canine newspaper published in the United Kingdom and read widely in Europe. It covers performance events, conformation shows, training, and other dog topics.

The online version of *Our Dogs* bills itself as "dedicated to British dogs and their owners." While the magazine and the site are targeted toward European dog fanciers, there are a lot of fun graphics and excellent articles here that any dog lover can appreciate.

The *Our Dogs* home page opens with a relatively tame look and a list of topics to choose from. The first option, Cool Site of the Day, takes you to a fun opening page that features tons of moving graphics that are worth the download wait. A flying saucer that zooms around, exudes a green beam of light, and subsequently deposits a little black dog is the best one of all. If you can tear yourself away from this page, go on to view the Cool Site itself, which can be anything from a Japanese dog fanciers club to an individual dog's own home page.

Within the Cool Site page is another area called Candid Dog Photos, containing a handful of genuinely funny pictures of European dogs doing goofy things—usually with the help of their human friends.

Other options on the home page include more serious subjects, including lists of training clubs in England and comprehensive articles on different aspects of training. Information on selected breeds of dogs, an article on a particular health issue, suggestions on how to choose a puppy, and an excellent piece on the mechanics of flyball are all accessible from the home page.

The authors of *Our Dogs* also promise to add a World Dog Magazine Gallery to the site in the future, featuring words and images from various canine publications around the world.

Pet View Online Magazine

http://www.petview.com

The *Pet View Online Magazine* is very much like the print edition of *Pet View*, a magazine published by National Pet Health and Care Network. The practical information featured in this site is of like content and quality to the paper version.

Dogs are only one of the many kinds of animals covered in this attractive, well-designed site. To find articles about dogs, you will need to browse through a variety of categories and skim for canine topics, which include Pet Clinic (veterinary question-and-answer), Nutrition, Dollars and Sense, and Natural View (holistic remedies and homeopathic medicine).

An area called Breed Showcase features profiles of two dog breeds that include photos and detailed information on history, personality, and grooming requirements.

Howell Book House
http://www.mcp.com/mgr/howell

One of the most visible publishers of dog books out there is Howell Book House, a division of Simon & Schuster Macmillan. Known for their numerous titles on the various breeds, training, behavior, adoption, and other doggy topics, Howell Book House produces quality books that are highly regarded in the dog world.

Howell's presence on the Web isn't flashy, but if you are looking for a book on just about any dog-related subject, you'll want to visit this site. The home page will take you to featured new titles (with descriptions of each book) and to the *Pet Newsletter*, which highlights books in the various departments within Howell Books. Since the company also publishes works on horses, cats, and other pets, you'll need to look around for the dog references.

The best feature on this site is the Search for Books page, where browsers can look for books on just about any dog-related subject by using words or phrases. If you aren't sure what you want, you can choose from a list of categories. A list of all the books published by Howell is also included in the site.

Dog World Magazine
http://www.dogworldmag.com

One of the front runners of the dog publishing field is 82-year-old *Dog World*, an all-breed magazine published by K-III Communications Company. The editorial slant of the print version of the magazine leans more toward the show community, while the online edition is more oriented toward average dog lovers.

Colorfully designed, the *Dog World* home page features several options for browsers, the most valuable of which is the Breed Spotlight. This area contains a detailed profile of a selected breed, broken down into several categories. The Bichon Frise was highlighted in one recent edition, and information on temperament, grooming, living with the breed, health problems, and the breed's surprising skills in the sport of agility was provided in article context.

The most valuable aspect of the Breed Spotlight is undoubtedly its Guidelines for Purchase section, which details how to choose a breeder and how to pick the right puppy. A list of where to obtain more information on the featured breed, including a list of breed clubs, books, and videos, provides the finishing touch.

Dog owners tackling behavior problems will find the Help the Canine Mind area particularly useful. An online trainer and behaviorist provides help in a question-and-answer format. A form for owners to fill out and send back to the site is available.

Contests, display ads from breeders and a bulletin board are also included in *Dog World* online. A comprehensive listing of American Kennel Club, United Kennel Club, and United States Dog Agility events fill up the calendar section. The inclusion of States Kennel Club shows in this area is a unique addition because States Kennel Club events are seldom publicized in the all-breed press.

Dog Owner's Guide

http://www.canismajor.com/dog/guide.html

The *Dog Owner's Guide* is an award-winning tabloid newspaper for dog owners. The electronic version of the publication could also stand to win some awards for its prolific collection of online articles covering a variety of canine subjects.

The topic list of articles includes Choosing the Right Dog, Breed Profiles, Food and Nutrition, Dog Sports, Health and Veterinary Information, Manners and Training, Behavior and Aggression, Kids and Dogs, Seasonal Travel and Vacation, Rescue, Canine Issues, Just for Fun, and Miscellaneous. Within each of these categories, there are numerous articles that are both accurate and well-written.

The index in this site also lists every article available, in alphabetical order. Each title has a hypertext link that takes you to the actual piece with a click of your mouse.

Amazon.Com

http://www.amazon.com

Of all the domestic animals, the dog has been written about most. Nonfiction is the most popular genre for canines, although there are several novelists who make their livings creating stories centered around dogs.

The Amazon.Com Web site is a huge resource for those who love books about dogs—or about anything. Calling itself the "Earth's biggest bookstore," Amazon.Com boasts 1.5 million books in print and 1 million out-of-print books.

There are hundreds of dog books available through this Web site, which contains a good intra-site search engine that will allow you to describe either the author, title, or subject of the book you are seeking. The search tool can be found on the opening page of the site. An entry of "dogs" alone as the subject will bring up a gigantic list of books.

Amazon.Com does more than just allow you to search for and order books online. It also provides readers with the opportunity to learn more about their favorite authors. A click on the In Their Own Words link takes you to a list of authors who have been interviewed by Amazon.Com, discussing everything from how they got into writing to discussions of their favorite food.

Good Dog!

http://www.prodogs.com/dmn/gooddog/index.htm

The print version of *Good Dog!* is a consumer magazine for dog owners. A bimonthly publication produced in Austin, Texas, *Good Dog!* is known primarily for its unbiased reviews of dog products.

The online version of *Good Dog!* provides a list of articles from recent issues of the magazine, covering veterinary topics, breeds, and, of course, reviews of products. A recent edition of the site included discussions by a veterinarian on dental care products and a head collar product test report.

Also available from Good Dog! are several books published by the magazine. Detailed descriptions of each book and information on how to order them are presented online.

Mushing Online

http://www.polarnet.com/Users/Mushing

Mushing is an international bimonthly magazine for those who enjoy the sports of dog sledding, skijoring, carting, dog-packing and weight pulling. Featuring articles on adventures, politics, training and other subjects relevant to these exciting outdoor canine activities, *Mushing* is published in Alaska, where dog sledding is a way of life.

Online, *Mushing* magazine features about 10 articles from recent editions of its print version, covering a range of topics. The page also contains an events calendar, a list of relevant books, a directory of supplies that selling mushing equipment, and links to other related Web sites.

CHAPTER 14

Products

Dog owners love to pamper their pets—and not just the owners with Toy Poodles, either. Evidence of this is easy to see at the cash register, where dog products are big business, representing an industry that runs into the hundreds of millions of dollars.

You could spend the rest of your life and all the money you've ever earned trying to buy all the goodies and gadgets that are out there for your dog, but you'd never succeed. There is so much merchandise being produced with canines in mind that it simply boggles the brain. Everything from dog bowls to toenail paint is available in every style and option imaginable. And when it comes to the basics like food and collars, the choices are even more overwhelming.

Items for the pooch himself are only part of the story. Merchandise for the people who love dogs is a growing segment of the industry, with new collectibles companies popping up all the time. Breed aficionados can cover their bodies (and even their homes) with items adorned with their favorite breed, and many of them do just that, as a trip to any dog show will prove.

Skeptics who say it's hard to make money from the Internet have never seen the products end of the canine Web. There are hundreds of Web sites catering to canine merchandise.

The Web sites appearing in this chapter are only a small sampling of what's out there. In some cases, we've tried to bring you examples of some of the more interesting sites or products, while with other sites, we've attempted to present

continued after the feature section

DOGZ!

http://www.dogz.com

There are dog lovers out there who, for whatever reason, do not have a dog in their lives. Whether due to living situation, health, age, or some other consideration, these individuals are deprived of canine companionship.

P.F. Magic undoubtedly had them in mind when it created Dogz, an intriguing software program that allows computer owners to raise a virtual puppy from weaning age to adulthood. Dogz are very much like their real counterparts: they eat, play, and get into trouble; they bark, scratch, and sleep.

But that's not all. Dogz is a very interactive program, and owners can do all kinds of stuff with their pets. By simply dragging your mouse, you can feed your dog, brush it, toss toys to it, and even spray it with flea repellent.

When purchasing a copy of Dogz, new owners can choose their pet from a group of puppies available for "adoption." Each one of these pups has its own unique appearance and personality. Once owners adopt a pup, they can change its appearance somewhat so the pet they own is an original that won't be found on other computers.

It is easy to get attached to these Dogz characters. Perhaps it's because so much personality has been programmed into each critter. Or maybe it's the result of the intensely interactive aspect of the software. Whatever the reason, it's not long before you feel as though your Dogz pet is a real creature that needs your care and attention.

The spirit of all this is captured beautifully on the DOGZ! Web site. Examples of the Dogz virtual canines appear right away on the opening page so browsers can get a sense of what this product is all about. There is also an option to download a sample of the software, which allows you to play with five puppies available for adoption.

If you already own a copy of Dogz, the rest of the site is made for you offering all kinds of opportunities to get

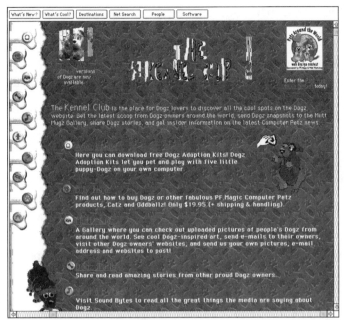

the most out of the program—and to live in the fantasy world of owning a virtual dog.

Dogz Tailz is an area devoted to stories written by Dogz owners about their virtual pets. E-mail links are included after each story, so owners can correspond with one another. Mutt Mugz is a place where "photos" of Dogz are displayed. These "photos" are actually screen captures of various Dogz in different owner-generated situations, and are quite creative. (The ability to preserve these images is a feature of the Dogz program.)

Owners of Dogz can join the Dogz Kennel Club online by filling out a form. Once owners join the club, they can submit stories of their own computer dogs, along with screen captures. FAQS are also available within the club (although nonmembers can access them), covering issues such as whether or not virtual dogs should live indefinitely, and how to teach them tricks.

The DOGZ! Web site is an ingenious way to involve product owners with their merchandise.

large or nearly complete offerings of specific or general merchandise.

If you are looking for a particular item and can't find it among the Web sites listed here, try using product links from other dog sites, or utilize some of the Internet's search engines to locate it. Chances are it's out there—you just have to know how to find it.

Telemark Productions Home Page

http://www.telemarkprod.com/

Telemark Productions produces CD-ROMs, and their venture into the dog world is titled *The Complete Guide to Dogs*. Winner of the Silver Apple Award for 1997 from the National Education Media Network, this program provides dog owners with information on choosing a dog, training, care and activities. Also included is a breed advisor using 40 different factors to help users identify the best breeds for their lifestyle.

The Telemark Web site contains extensive information on *The Complete Guide to Dogs,* an online version of the dog breed selector, technical support, and press releases regarding the release of the product and awards it has won.

Dog Saver

http://www.dogsaver.com/index.html

The Dog Saver Web site is a colorful and fun place to visit, especially if you are looking for a canine screen saver to add to your computer's software.

A Basset Hound wearing a T-shirt and writing a note with a moving paw and pencil, and a Dalmatian viewing the actual Dog Saver software at work on a cartoon computer are among the cartoons enlivening the home page.

The Dog Saver program consists of colorful pictures of a wide variety of breeds that flash on the screen. Other products available here are personalized itemsand custom screen savers, mousepads in 88 breeds, and free add-on modules for registered Dog Saver users. The site also offers a trivia contest with prizes and a series of FAQs about the product.

AHEAD Graphics

http://members.aol.com/ahead/aheadpg.htm

A drawing of a Doberman greets you as you open up the AHEAD Graphics home page, a lively, dog-loving site filled with colorful graphics and interesting text. A click on the Dobie takes you to another page featuring a drawing of purple poodles and an invite to purchase graphics of Poodles or any other American Kennel Club breed.

The next page asserts, "We have all American Kennel Club breeds of dogs," and has hypertext buttons linked to categories like Clip Art, Private Clips, Funstuff, Softball, Running Dobermans, and a number of other whimsical titles. There's even an area to view the dogs that belong to the owners of AHEAD Graphics. One is a beautiful Doberman Pinscher named Magnum who passed away and has his own page bearing a tribute poem.

The company's canine clip art is its strong suit, and there are over 300 pieces to choose from. All are done to breed standard and all are original artwork. Unfortunately, samples are not available online for proprietary reasons, but more information can be gleaned by contacting the company.

Wizard of Dogs

http://www.dog-e-zine

WildWood Interactive Inc. has produced an interactive CD-ROM to help dog owners with the training, care, and enjoyment of their pets. The product features videos, sound, music, and text.

The Wizard of Dogs Web site allows interested browsers the opportunity to view all 600 index entries in the book, see a full screen image of the main menu and "Socializing" openers, and of course, order the product online.

Corsini Original Dog Figurines and Art Gallery of Limited Edition Prints

http://dialspace.dial.pipex.com/corsini

Corsini makes dog-oriented original figurines, limited-edition prints, and other products designed in England. The company prides itself in producing images that are true to breed type, and works with breeders to ensure their accuracy.

The Company's Web site allows shoppers to view its vast collection of available breed figurines, prints, and miscellaneous products. Ordering information and an e-mail address for the company are also included.

Doggie Diamonds

http://www.primenet.com/~gillett/ddhome.html

Doggie Diamonds offers dog lovers a vast array of dog-adorned products, custom made for each buyer. Six different product categories, including Wearables, Around the House, Stained Glass/Crystal/Glass, In the Kitchen, Novelties/Personal Items, and Paper/Desk Images, head up the list of products available. Some of the more unusual items are clocks, birth announcements, decorator hand towels, luggage tags, appliance covers (which are hard to find even without dogs on them), and toilet tanks.

All of these items can be ordered with an image of the desired breed. Almost every American Kennel Club–recognized breed is here, plus a few rare breeds. Browsers can take a peek at the illustrations that are applied to the products.

Dog Lover's Gallery

http://www.computek.net/foheron/gallery/dogs.html

Gift items for both dogs and their fans are found at the Dog Lover's Gallery online. The variety of products is sparse, but each one gets special treatment on the Web site, where it can be seen in color and at a size and resolution that does it justice. Needlepoint kits for placemats, T-shirts, sweat shirts, calendars and posters, and of course Doggie Visors (for the dog to wear) are among the products.

Animal Krackers

http://www.halcyon.com/dianec/A-ZDOGS.HTML

The Animal Krackers site markets gifts and sculptures featuring a wide variety of breeds. Selecting your breed of choice on the opening page will bring you to a series of photographs of items they sell. Their products include bronze sculptures, note cards, wind chimes, holiday ornaments, jewelry and key chains. All items can be ordered online. Sculptures feature posed dogs as well as canines in action doing what they were bred to do.

Dog Figurines Online Catalog

http://www.pacprod.com/stone/dog.htm

A figurine of a yellow Labrador Retriever, which looks real at first glance, meets you when you open the Dog Figurines Online Catalog. Pacific Products Gallery produces this online catalog, which contains photos and information on a wide selection of canine statuettes.

Browsers have the option of choosing Adult Dog Figurines, Large Size Adult Dog Figurines, Large Size Puppy Figurines, Puppy Figurines and Medium Dog Figures. A description of each figurine is then provided, along with the option to view the photo and get ordering information if so desired. Not all breeds are represented in all sizes, but quite a few American Kennel Club breeds are available.

Attic Treasures Dog Collectibles Page

http://www.flash.net/~tslaton/animals/dogs.html

Aus-Ben Manufacturing has been creating wildlife castings since 1969 and is known for its cold-cast bronzes created by artist Charles Earnhardt. Other items are available through the company as well, and all are represented on the Attic Treasures Web site.

Included in the list of products are dog bumpers stickers (with sayings like "My dog doesn't have a single flea … they are all married with families"), and jewelry boxes. But the main foci here are bronze statues, pewter key chains, decorated drinking glasses, and planters. Not every items is available in every breed, but most common breeds are represented on the site.

For those who can't find what they want, Aus-Ben invites e-mail letters to the company detailing specific wants. The company will then try to locate the item for you.

Raining Cats & Dogs

http://www.dhinet.com/oldmystic/raining/cups.htm

Olde Mystic Village is a tourist attraction located in Mystic, Connecticut. In its midst, there is a store called Raining Cats & Dogs that boasts the area's largest selection of coffee mugs depicting all breeds of dogs and cats.

But the store has much more than that, as the Raining Cats & Dogs Web site demonstrates. A click on the Dalmatian on the opening page takes you to a screen with a picture of the store and selected hyperlinks with photos of some of the unusual items in inventory. The Cat & Dog Angel Statues are one such example.

There is no way to order products online from this site, but owner Shaun Regan provides the address and phone number of the store for those interested in what they see here.

Pegasus Originals

http://www.pegasusor.com

If you enjoy cross-stitch, needlework, and dogs too, the Pegasus Originals Web site has some beautiful canine patterns. Featuring a spectacular howling wolf design called

"Wolves Serenade," and a dog collection featuring a number of different breeds in very accurate renderings, the company boasts a collection of over 600 animal designs. The Web site provides large, color images of selected dog-related designs, along with a list of shops that sell Pegasus products, a catalog of craft books, upcoming needlepoint shows, and profiles on the different designers utilized by the company. A link to the company's Dogs page presents a list of all the canine designs available through the company. Nearly every American Kennel Club breed is represented.

Dannyquest
http://www.prodogs.com/dmn/danyqust/index.htm

Dannyquest Designs has been producing a collection of dog sculptures for the past 20 years. Proud of its attention to breed detail, the company has a wide variety of cold-cast sculptures to choose from. Wind chimes, jewelry, key chains, and specialty pieces are also available.

The company's Web site provides a virtual catalog that includes a history of the organization and images of many of the items for sale. Browsers can also order breed-specific catalogs online.

Golden Wonders Home Page
http://www.prodogs.com/dmn/GoldenWonders/index.html

Golden Wonders is a company run by Irish Wolfhound breeders specializing in dog jewelry. Boasting a selection of 120 breeds to choose from, Golden Wonders donates part of its profits to a local rescue organization.

Made from sterling silver, 24K gold plate over sterling, silver & gold two-tone and solid 14K gold, the pins, pendants, tie tacks, bolos, bracelets, earrings, money clips, and other items are also available in designs reflecting canine activities like agility, herding, and earthdog trials.

The Golden Wonders home page shows a few examples of the company's work along with an e-mail link to order the complete catalog.

P.M.L. Prints Home Page

http://www.prodogs.com/dmn/PMLPrints/index.htm

Breed-specific artwork produced by an unnamed artist is offered by P.M.L. Prints in Cleveland, Ohio. Only three prints are presented on the company's Web site, but each one is featured in a large size, with vivid color reproduction. The company must be contacted by mail or telephone, but prices, print sizes, and ordering information are all included on the site.

The Little Dog Laughed Home Page

http://www.thelittledoglaughed.com

The Little Dog Laughed is the catalog extension of the Reigning Cats & Dogs store in California. Specializing in gifts, collectibles, and unusual pet merchandise, the company is owned by Basenji lovers.

A click on the home page takes you to a list of the company's many products, including jewelry, ceramics, glasswear, greeting cards, bookends, and limoge boxes. If anything on the list strikes your fancy, go back to the home page and click on the hypertext link that offers instructions on how to use the site. This will take you to another page that lists the option to view products by dog breed or by product. Choosing a dog breed will bring you to a list of items specific to the breed, like different types of figurines. Some products feature links to photos of the items.

In addition to information on how to order, there are also links to an area featuring dog stories, tips, and American Kennel Club and rare breed rescue contacts.

Welcome to the World of Kong!

http://www.kongcompany.com/

In 1976, the Kong Company began production on an unusual rubber toy that dogs have gone completely wild over. Called the Kong Toy, the original version of this odd-looking product was based on a suspension part from a Volkswagon van. It has been embellished somewhat over the years: there are now Kong Toys available in a number of different sizes to accommodate different breeds of dogs.

The Kong Web site features the history of the Kong Toy, the product's features, information on how to use it, testimonials from happy users, a picture gallery of elated dogs with their Kong Toys, FAQs about Kong Toys, and where to buy the product.

Diamond Dogs

http://www.choicemall.com/diamonddogs/

The Buster Cube is an unusual item described as a "break-through toy" by its manufacturer, Diamond Dogs. Designed for dogs that are left alone all day while their owners are at work, and consequently experience separation anxiety, the company states that the cube provides good mental stimulation. The toy contains a hollow chamber that can be filled with food, keeping the dog busy as he or she tries to get it out. Shaped like a cube, as its name suggests, dogs can also push the Buster Cube around with their noses or paws.

The Web site for the Buster Cube provides photos of the toy in use, plus detailed descriptions on how it works and how to order it.

Planet Pet Naples Florida

http://www.planetpet.com/toys.htm

You've never seen dog toys that look like this. Akin to flying saucers, the Goodie Ship, Space Ball, and Goodie Grippers toys are designed to keep dogs minds and bodies occupied for hours.

Excellent photographs of these odd-shaped playthings are available on the Planet Pet Web site, along with descriptions of how the toys can be used to their best advantage. An e-mail link for more information is provided.

Captured by B. Walker—Litter I.D. Collars

http://www.prodogs.com/dmn/captured/index.htm

When a Weimaraner has a litter of 12 grey puppies that all look alike, it can be tricky for the breeder to tell them all apart. A company called Captured by B. Walker has sought to solve this dilemma by creating the Litter I.D. Collar. Each collar is adjustable, removable, and grows with the pup. Breeders order a set of the collars, the number in the set depending on how many pups were in the litter. Each collar comes in a different color, so one puppy can be told from the other.

The Captured by B. Walker Web site provides a photo of Rottweiler pups wearing the collar, plus information on how the collar came to be, how it works, and of course, how to order it. A color palette is also displayed, showing the different puppy-identifying tones available.

Changing Horizons Premier Dog Collar

http://www.chorizon.com/pet/precol.htm

There are a lot of dog collars out there on the market, but the Premier Dog Collar sets itself apart in its design. Touted as safer and more humane than a choke collar, the Premier Dog Collar also has quite a few other benefits, according to manufacturer Changing Horizons.

The Web site for this product features a photo and illustrations of the collar, a long list of advantages, sizing guidelines, a color chart, online patterns, details on payment options, and an order form. Matching leashes can also be purchased.

Wolf Packs Limited Slip Dog Collars

http://www.wolfpacks.com/catalog/collars.htm

According to Wolf Packs, LLC, the company's Limited Slip Dog Collar has an ingenious design that protects dogs from choking while on a tie-out. The Web site for the product features a photograph of the collar, a sizing chart, pricing, color swatches, and ordering information.

Fox & Hounds Collar and Leashes

http://www.marketsuite.com/foxandhounds/pet_supplies.html

Fox & Hounds Ltd. was started because company president Robin Kershner couldn't find a unique, well-crafted collar elegant enough to suit her Dalmatian. The result is a line of unusually patterned dog collars that will turn heads on the street.

The Fox & Hounds Ltd. Web site allows shoppers to view each collar in a large color image. Each item is accompanied by descriptive text. Sizes, pricing, matching leashes, and an order form can also be found online.

Canine Collars & Leashes at the Acmepet Marketplace

http://www.acmepet.com/canine/market/k9_col.html

The huge Acmepet Web site serves as home to many lists of canine product manufacturers, one of the largest being the collar-and-leash companies page.

Nearly 30 collar and leash producers are listed here, with photographs for many of the products included right on the page. All have links that will take you to the product's home page, where you can get detailed information on each.

Ruff Wear Home Page

http://www.ruffwear.com

Billed as "quality gear for dogs on the go," Ruff Wear produces items designed for dogs who do their fair share of traveling. Starting out a few years ago with a collapsible bowl, the company has branched out to include items like dog packs and dog boots.

The Web site provides information on each of the items, including photographs, details, and a way to order. For dog owners who like to travel with their dogs, this is a site to visit.

BowWow Fits

http://home.navisoft.com/alphamega/bowwow.htm

BowWow Fits is a provider of "elegant canine attire." Clothes for the dog, that is. The company's Web site offers browsers the opportunity to view the latest season's designs. Clicking on "Dogs are Having Affairs" will take you to a canine fashion show.

BowWow Fits doesn't mess around. The company makes holiday tuxedos, cocktail dresses, and exercise suits, to name just a few. There are pictures of canine models wearing these items online that have to be seen to be believed.

For those who want to order these fine duds, there is help online to make sure the size is right.

Personalized Retriever Clothing

http://www.us.pressline.com//dog

Only those who love the retrieving breeds need apply at the Personalized Retriever clothing site, maintained by Yellow Dog Designs, where T-shirts, polo shirts, and hats bearing the images of either Golden Retrievers or Labrador Retrievers can be found. The items can be personalized with a company, kennel, or family name. Prices and sizes are included on the site.

Petoria's Secret: Fashion Apparel For Dog Lovers

http://www.open-house.com/petoriasecret/index.html

Petoria's Secret makes clothes for people who are obsessed with dogs. Everything from dog-adorned bomber jackets, and dog-appliquéed handbags and vests covered with cavorting canines can be found in the company's inventory.

The Petoria's Secret Web site has photographs of all these items online, along with information on pricing and how to order. If you want the world to know how much you love dogs, check out this site and bring your credit card with you.

Tucker & Company Dog Biscuits

http://www.ashlandweb.com/dogtreats/company.html

All-natural treats and accessories are available through Tucker & Company, an enterprise started by Christy Davenport and her Beagle, Tucker. All products are hand-made and come in a variety of flavors.

The Tucker & Company Web site offers detailed information on the products, including package size, flavors, and price. Edibles aren't the only thing available here: T-shirts and aprons with the Tucker & Company logo can also be purchased.

Canine Country Kitchen

http://www.spidernet.ca/peacock/CCK/

Canine Country Kitchen is a Canadian company that offers all-natural dog food and treats available over the Internet. Unique feeding stations (also known as "feeding furniture") that feature designs not often seen in the United States are also for sale.

Their Web site presents Cookies, Mixes & Foods (two types of dog cookies or the mix to make them yourself, plus dog food), Feeding Stations, and Pricing (details on how much it all costs). Orders are accepted from the United States, and an e-mail link is here for those with further questions.

Whiskers Holistic Products for Pets

http://www.choicemall.com/whiskers/

Whiskers is a retail store in New York City known for its vast inventory of natural products for dogs, and its friendly and helpful atmosphere.

The online version of the store provides information about the purchase and use of holistic health-care products for dogs. Items in the categories of vitamins and supplements, pet food, flea relief, skin care and grooming, arthritis remedies, and books and videos can be ordered right off the site.

Program

http://www.programpet.com

When Novartis Animal Health's oral flea product Program came out a few years ago, it was a revolutionary concept that promised to change the lives of dogs and their owners everywhere. Years later, many people swear by it, and veterinarians recommend it heartily.

The Program Web site is well-designed and provides information on the product as it is applied to both dogs and cats (each one is addressed separately). If you are considering this product or just want to know what the hubbub is all about, pay a visit to this commercial site.

PetSage

http://www.petsage.com

On PetSage's opening page, the proprietors explain that the company blends the worlds of nature and science, using veterinarians, product specialists, biochemists, physiologists, and other animal care experts to provide health-care products and information to enrich the lives of companion animals.

The products the company offers are categorized by pet-owner need rather than product category. For example, the New Friends area of the site is designed for new pet owners, and features books, food supplements, and toys. The Old Friends section contains information and products to help in the care of older pets.

Other categories in the site include Remedies, Environment, Fleas & Ticks, Skin & Coat, Nutrition, and Exploring.

Home of Dog Stuff

http://www.lasernet.com/dogstuff

Dogstuff is a site that contains a wide variety of dog products. Organized in categories of Products by Breed, Calendars, Laura Rogers (a featured artist), Security Signs, Aluminum Signs, Rubber Stamps, Sculptures, Videos, and New Products, the site is not only a products-for-sale catalog, but a forum dedicated to disseminating information about pets.

Products listed on the site can be viewed by breed: click on the name of the breed you are interested in and products relating to that dog will show up. Under Australian Shepherds, prints, a T-shirt, coasters, a tote bag, a keychain, note cards, note pads, a magnetic pad with a pencil, a ceramic mug, a beer stein, and a baseball cap all show up bearing the Aussie's image. And these are only a few of the available products for the breed. A keepsake box, mouse pad, a calendar, security signs, freezer magnets, pins, earrings, figurines, rubber stamps, aluminum signs, and even a link to the American Kennel Club page on the breed can also be found here.

Gone to the Dogs Home Page

http://www.toltbbs.com/~accessicg/gone2dog

Proprietor "Liz" says she wanted to share her business at the Riverwalk in New Orleans with a larger audience, so she put a lot of her more popular doggy items online at the Gone to the Dogs home page.

Offered for sale here are breed-specific calendars (covering a lot of breeds), figures, crossing signs, sweats and T-shirts, and mousepads. Not every breed is covered in every product category, but the more popular pooches have made it to the store and can be ordered online.

SBM Products

http://www.prodogs.com/dmn/SMBProducts/index2.htm

SBM Products, based in Corona, California, produces an unusual variety of canine merchandise. A breath freshener for pets, a tail tamer, a tie-down strap and an all-natural supplement make up their short list of items for sale.

On the Web, these products are presented in detail, utilizing hyperlinks to pages devoted to each. A price list, order form, and e-mail link are all included, should one or more of these items strike your fancy.

Critters Choice Dot Com

http://www.critterschoice.com

The opening page of Critters Choice Dot Com is wildly designed and somewhat wacky. If you have the patience to wade through it and find the button that says "See our Web site," you'll be transported to something a little easier on the eyes.

On this page, the Critters Choice Online Catalog can be accessed, featuring a "sea of products," as the authors describe it. Included here are everything from the strange and unusual (cologne for dogs and wall pottery) to the basics (treats, beds, and collars). Photos of all of the products are not available here, but detailed descriptions are.

Fuzzy Faces

http://www.fuzzyfaces.com

Creativity is the name of the game at the Fuzzy Faces Web site, where a handful of interesting dog products are offered for sale. Included are such items as rubber pull toys, Fetch It Kits, fused glass pieces, jewelry, and a wide variety of other products. There's even a category online called Clumber Spaniel Stuff.

Clear color photos are available for each item, as are detailed information on the company, how the products are shipped, and even how they are made. An e-mail link is provided, as well as links to other dog-related Web sites enjoyed by the authors.

Bernard Basics

http://www.netviewinc.com/website_websites/bernard.htm

Bernard Basics is an online catalog of miscellaneous dog products. In addition to the list of inventory, the company's site includes a Fact of the Week, and hyperlinks to the various product categories.

Collars offered by the company include a hunting collar, a reflector collar, colorful kaleidoscope collars, and others. The leashes, not surprisingly, match the collars, while the T-shirts, mugs, and other gifty items also feature dog designs.

Photographs of all products mentioned are included in the site, as is information on price, color selection, and how to order.

Petmarket.com

http://www.petmarket.com/

The Pet Market is an online discount pet-supply source, selling a wide variety of canine merchandise. There are hundreds of products available through the company's Web site, including bedding, books, cages, carriers, cards, collars, bowls, grooming supplies and equipment, shampoo, toys, and treats. Color photographs and details are available for each product, which can be ordered online.

The Pet Market Web site is more than just a catalog of canine products. The home page also features links to cat items for sale, as well as a Pet Tip of the Month Club, a Cat & Dog Chat, a Pet Info Center, and Bulletin Board Discussions.

All Creatures Pet Supplies

http://www.allcreaturesonline.com/petsuply.htm

There are no product photos available on the All Creatures Web site, but there are a few shots of the company's "research committee," which consists of a few cats and a couple of dogs, on the opening page.

In lieu of the product photos, shoppers will have to make do with detailed descriptions of the merchandise available here, which includes a feeder tray, nylon chew bones, rope toys, and other products. All merchandise can be ordered online, and the company can be contacted for further information through an e-mail link.

K9 World

http://www.k9world.com/k9world./index.htm

Howard and Rhea Flint are the owners of K9 World, Internet distributors for two other companies that produce doggy products. As vendors seen frequently at dog shows in the Northwest, the Flints present four different products online: the Masterpiece Dog Beds, Plush Pile Fleece Blankets, TY Balls and Funny Toys (soft dog toys), and Pooper-Scoopers.

The site offers photos and details on each of the products, along with ordering information. An e-mail link is provided for those who need more product information.

Brown Kennel Supply, Inc.

http://www.bwci.com/clients/bksinc.htm

Brown Kennel Supply is run by dog show enthusiasts Don and Anna Brown, who sell a large selection of canine products at dog shows every other weekend. The company is a mobile business, consisting of "just a tent and two trucks."

Before the Internet, you would have had to run into the Browns at a dog show somewhere in the East to be able to purchase any of their products. Now, however, their extensive list of product categories can be accessed online. Their inventory includes arm bands (for showing), beds, breeding aids, bones, dog boots, bowls, brushes, car barriers, collars, treats, grooming products, obedience items, spray bottles, strippers, tack boxes, tie-outs, tools, toys, and ex-pens. Click on the product category, and you'll be taken to a list of products and prices. Unfortunately, photos are not included, but some of the Brown's favorite links are.

If you prefer to visit the company at a dog show instead of ordering by mail, a click on the Dog Show Schedule hyperlink will provide you with a list of where Brown Kennel Supply be in the upcoming months.

L.L. Bowsers

http://www.dotpets.com/llbowser.htm

As it states on the company's home page, the L.L. Bowsers Canine Emporium was created so dogs had a place of their own to go. What the authors really mean is that dog owners now have a place to go to shop till they drop! Nutritional products, recreational equipment, treats and snacks, beds and bedding, collars and leashes, dinnerware, and cages and carriers are just some of the products that can found in this site.

Hyperlinks for each of these categories will take you to company logos that you must click on to get details on different products. Photos, prices, and ordering information are all included.

DOGalogue

http://www.keytech.com/~dogalog/aboutus.html

DOGalogue describes itself as "accessories and accouterments for the cultured canine, dog lovers, and friends." This translates to an inventory of glitzy collars and leashes, fancy dogs clothes, dog bowls, placemats, and picture frames.

The DOGalogue Web site is very layered, and it takes a lot of persistence to get to the actual photos of the products. However, a number of these uncommon items are worth seeing. All are available to order online.

Canine Cryobank

http://www.prodogs.com/dsn/k9cryobk/orderfrm.htm

You really have to be into breeding dogs to appreciate Canine Cryobank Inc.'s products. All centering around the theme of canine reproduction, the product line consists of artificial-insemination kits and videos on how to perform the procedure. It also includes unusual items like earrings in the shape of sperm, T-shirts with sperm logos on the front, sperm-shaped candles, and even a "sperm bank" for storing loose change. Prints by canine artists featuring dogs with their puppies are available from the company as well.

All these items can be seen on the company's Web page, in living color. Prices and an order form also appear online.

Paul's Obedience Shop

http://www.paulsobedience.com

Enthusiasts in the sport of obedience, or those interested in getting involved in the activity, would do well to visit the Paul's Obedience Shop Web page. The site offers a huge variety of items necessary for obedience training and competition, and presents it in an attractive and very easy to use form.

Featured here are dumbbells, scent articles, training collars, jumps and gates, and lots of other products. Items for agility and flyball can be found here too. Paul's Obedience Shop even sells gift certificates for your obedience-happy friends.

Chihuahua Kingdom

http://www.3lbdogs.com/

"You've entered the realm of the Three Pound Dog." So says the opening line of the Chihuahua Kingdom Web site, devoted to those who love the little Mexican breed.

Run by Chihuahua fanciers, this site offers a lot of different items for Chihuahua lovers, including products in the Rescue Bazaar, where a percentage of proceeds go to Chihuahua Rescue. Items include *Chihuahua Kingdom: The Book*, Chihuahua Kingdom Logo Accessories (T-shirts, sweat shirts, and mugs), and a few other products.

If you appreciate this diminutive breed, you'll enjoy a visit to this entertaining Web site, and may even come away with a Chihuahua item or two.

Artistic Lasering's Tibetan Mastiff Catalog

http://www.tibetanmastiffs.com/merchandise/alcatalo.htm

Tibetan Mastiffs are not the most popular breed in the world. In fact, they are considered rare because they have not been recognized by the American Kennel Club.

However, that didn't stop Artistic Lasering from creating a series of gift items graced by the breed's image and making them available on the Internet.

Coasters, a glass treat jar, a glass canister, leather key fobs, a glass paperweight, a leather cinch dog collar, weather-treated maplewood house signs, a wall plaque, and a basswood clock make up the majority of products devoted to the image of the Tibetan Mastiff. The illustration that graces these products is attractive and certainly communicates the majesty of this breed.

Dachshund's Delights Badger Burrow Home Page

http://ourworld.compuserve.com/home pages/stemnock

The Dachshund's Delights Badger Burrow Home Page opens up with alternating graphics of Smooth, Longhaired and Wirehaired Dachshunds, followed by humorous text about the idiosyncrasies of the Dachshund in the human bed.

The company's list of featured Dachshund products, which changes from month to month, includes sweaters, harnesses, magnets, and mousepads.

Also found on this site are a Dachshund photo of the month, a Dachshund newsletter feature of the month, and other Dachshund goodies.

Dalmatian Delights

http://www.online-dogs.com/#bowltreat

If you are a Dalmatian lover, be sure to pay a visit to the Dalmatian Delights Online Gift Shop. This online catalog caters to fans of the spotted breed and features a wide variety of products.

Included here are Dalmatian end tables, a Dalmatian flag, a Dalmatian mug and food bowl, a Dalmatian dog bowl and treat jar, sandstone Dalmatian coasters,

Dalmatian-covered doormats and pillows, and much, much more. Products can be ordered online.

The Dal House

http://www.dalhouse.com

Dalmatian lovers can't get enough of their breed. Or so think the proprietors of The Dal House, another spot on the Web for Dalmatian products.

The Dal House Web site features books, clothing, custom photo products, general products, and stationery products, all in with the Dalmatian in mind. Spotted pooches adorn all this merchandise in a variety of ways, and each can be seen in its entirety online. (There's even a Dalmatian necktie.)

Ortho-Bean Pet Beds Home Page

http://www.prodogs.com/dmn/OrthoBean/index.html

Orthopedic beds are not just for people anymore. A company called Ortho-Bean has combined the dog bed principal with the orthopedic concept and created a bed designed for maximum canine comfort. Ortho-Bean claims the product may even help dogs with hip dysplasia and arthritis.

The Ortho-Bean Pet Bed Web site includes detailed information on the advantages of the bed, photographs of the product in use, ordering information, and links to other pet sites.

A Dog's Best Friend

http://www.dogsfriend.com

If your dog likes to receive birthday cards on his special day (and who doesn't), you'll want to pay a visit to the A Dog's Best Friend Web site. This company wants you to receive their catalog of dog products, and will entice you to ask for it by offering to send your dog a birthday card on the appropriate day.

Dog owners can fill out the form online, which requests their name and address along with the dog's name and birthday. A catalog will be sent right away and the card will come when your dog is ready to blow out the candles.

Canvasback Pet Supplies

http://www.sirnet.mb.ca/~cscramst/

Canvasback Pet Supplies, a Canadian outfit, was started in 1949 when a field trialer named John Sellen created his own canvas training dummy for his retriever, and realized it might have wider appeal. Almost 50 years later, the company stocks over 10,000 pet items, many of which are for dogs.

The items available on the Canvasback Web site include hunting supplies (dummies, whistles, scents, and starter pistols), basic equipment (kennels, collars, bowls, and dog beds), dog toys, grooming supplies, books, sledding supplies, and novelty items likes mugs and key chains.

None of these products are available online, but a supply catalog is in the works for those who want to order long distance. An e-mail link can connect you to Canvasback for your request or if you live in the province of Manitoba, you can visit the actual store.

Pet Supply Catalogs

http://members.aol.com/Drumguy/pages/catalogs.html

There are quite a few paper catalogs out there specializing in products for pets. They tend to carry items that are hard to find in pet-supply stores, are reduced in price, and cater to the serious fancier.

For those who like to catalog-shop for dog items, the Pet Supply Catalogs Web site, containing a simple, graphics-free list of just about every pet-supply catalog being published in America, is a major asset. The catalogs are listed alphabetically by name and toll-free numbers are included.

Pooch Pouch

http://www.interlog.com/~kellie/

The Pooch Pouch, offered by Bridgette Enterprises, fits into retractable leashes or can be worn on a dog walker's belt, wrist, or even on the dog's collar. A fanny pack of sorts just for dog owners, the Pooch Pouch can hold plastic baggies, keys, treats, tissues, and other small items.

The Pooch Pouch Web site provides detailed information on this handy accessory, and allows shoppers to order online. A photograph of the product is featured at the top of the home page.

Jones Trailer Company

http://www.prodogs.com/dmn/trailers/index.htm

We've all heard of horse trailers, but dog trailers? The Jones Trailer Company is making them, out of stainless steel, and in a variety of different styles. These trailers are pulled behind a vehicle, just as horse trailers are, but are naturally much smaller in size.

The company's Web site features photos of the trailers, details on basic features, and a virtual catalog for more in-depth information.

No Ants My Doggy

http://www.io.com/~gibson/leander/

For dogs who dine outdoors, ants can be a problem. There are several anti-ant dog bowls out there, one of which is the "No Ants My Doggy" Dog Dish, produced by Leander Mfg.

The principle is simple—put the dog food in the center of a moat, and ants can't get to it. There's a photograph of the dish on the page, plus details on what makes it good. A free brochure can be obtained via the company's e-mail link.

PART V

Puppouri

Individual Dogs

Dogs are hugely popular on the Internet, with all aspects of their care, character, and activities covered in detail in thousands of dog-related Web sites. But there is a special type of canine page on the Web that eloquently fills the gaps in the big canine picture with a personal viewpoint. These are the sites about individual dogs. Take a tour of such sites and revel in the affection and respect they exude, both for the dogs they represent, and for the canine species as a whole.

Web sites devoted to individual dogs present, in most cases, a unique brand of photo album created by owners who are proud of their dogs and literally want to show them off to the world. An affectionate narrative usually accompanies such a site, either presented from the dog's point of view or from that of its owner. Some of these sites are devoted to more than one dog, some feature the owner's other interests as well, most invite visitors to drop Rover an e-mail and thus expand his worldwide circle of fans and friends, and many also offer lists of the featured dog's favorite links.

The following is a selection of sites devoted to individual dogs—tributes to animals whose owners' affection is evident in the time and effort they have spent to honor their pets. Be warned, however, that the Web is rich with individual dog pages and touring them can become rather addictive.

Be warned, too, that the pages included here are by no means the only sites devoted to individual dogs, but they

continued after the feature section

Beau's Home Page

http://www.senate.gov/member/or/wyden/general/beau/beau.htm

Once upon a time, dogs were not allowed on the floor of the US Senate—dogs of any kind, including those who assist blind or otherwise physically challenged individuals. That is until Beau came along.

Beau is a guide dog who works for Moira Shea, an advisor to Oregon Senator Ron Wyden. Recently, Senator Wyden required Shea's help on the floor for a debate on energy legislation, only to discover that Beau would not be allowed entrance (in fact, an archaic Senate rule prohibited any tools for the disabled on the floor, including wheelchairs and canes). Inspired by the injustice of this event, Senator Wyden introduced a resolution to change this blatantly discriminatory policy. The resolution was passed, and Beau gained access to the Senate floor—and to media headlines nationwide.

And now, Beau has his own Web page. Occupying space within Senator Wyden's own site, Beau is now a celebrated cyber dog. His site presents several layers of information that introduce browsers to the details of Beau's Senate adventure and provide an online civics lesson.

Beau's home page opens with a photograph of its featured canine, a beautiful and very talented yellow Labrador Retriever. Scroll down for a synopsis of the events that transpired on the Senate floor regarding Beau's—and thus Moira's—right to be there. From there, you can access pages that provide in-depth coverage of Beau and his story.

Included within the site is a copy of Senate Resolution 71, Senator Wyden's resolution to allow individuals with disabilities to "...bring those supporting services (including service dogs, wheelchairs, and interpreters) on the Senate floor..." While it is hard to believe that anyone could possibly object to such a resolution, a debate did ensue, and a transcript of that debate is included here. Those unfamiliar with the language and format of Senate debates will find this transcript an illuminating window into the inner workings of

BEAU'S
HOME PAGE

Welcome to Beau's World Wide Web Home Page!

Click here for a high resolution, text-only version of this page for the visually impaired.

Beau recently made headlines when he became one of the first guide dogs allowed access to the Senate floor.

Beau works as a guide dog for Moira Shea, who in turn works for Senator Wyden as an advisor on energy issues. Moira has a genetic condition known as Usher's Syndrome, which significantly impairs her vision. Usher's Syndrome is the leading cause of deaf blindness in the United States.

Recently, Senator Wyden needed Moira's help during a debate on energy legislation on the Senate floor, but was confronted by old Senate rules that prohibited tools for the disabled of any type (guide dogs, wheelchairs, even canes!) on the floor of the Senate. (Click here if you want to read a transcript of Senator Wyden's request to allow Moira and Beau access).

Senator Wyden fought to rectify the situation, (click here if you would like to read the resolution he introduced), and convinced the Senate to change its discriminatory rules. (Click here for a transcript of the proceedings that allowed Beau to become one of the first dogs in history to be allowed on the Senate floor.)

This was an important fight that reaches far beyond Senator Wyden's office. As Senator Wyden pointed out, guide dogs are working dogs, not pets. Guide dogs are an integral part of a sight-impaired person's essential activities and professional

the US government—especially fascinating because the root of this very important debate is a dog.

The transcript takes browsers to the Senate floor, where they can almost hear Senator Wyden explain that "a guide dog is a working dog, not a pet.... I had hoped there would be no need to offer this resolution, but I am forced to because discrimination still persists here. Ms. Shea is being treated differently simply because she is visually impaired and needs to use a guide dog."

In the wake of Beau's victory, Senator Wyden's office was inundated with calls and letters from Beau fans. Establishing the dog's own Web site was the logical way to allow everyone a chance to voice their support and send e-mail to the canine object of their adulation. Browsers are invited to visit Beau's site and be inspired at just what can be accomplished within a democracy—even if the citizen in question happens to be a big yellow dog.

do provide a sampling of what is available both for the enjoyment of those browsers who know the featured dogs personally, and those simply seeking to make some new canine friends. Given the variety of styles, tones, and viewpoints represented within these sites, they may also serve as an inspiration for those contemplating preparing Web pages for their own pets. New individual dog pages are added to the Web all the time, and once browsers see these lively, fun, and friendly sites, they may be inspired to add their own to the mix.

Yahoo! Individual Dogs

http://www.yahoo.com/Science/Zoology/Animals_Insects_and_Pets/
Mammals/Dogs/Individual_Dogs/

If you want to get to know dogs who have their own Web sites, Yahoo! will help you satisfy that longing with ease. Visit the address above to access a list that offers you the opportunity to meet dozens of Internet-savvy dogs. The page comes up as a list of hypertext breed names. Click on one—say, Labrador Retrievers—to get to a long list of dogs' names arranged in alphabetical order, some with descriptions, some without; all waiting to get to know the browsers who have entered their breed section. Scroll down from the breed-specific list and you will find yet another list of featured individual dog sites. What a treasure to find so many dogs—and computer literate dogs, at that—in a single site. Beware, however, that once you have explored a few of these sites, it will be difficult to rest until you have explored them all—and perhaps added your own dog to the list, as well.

Foxbriar's Home Page

http://www.geocities.com/Heartland/Plains/1839/

Enter this site, and you will receive a warm greeting: "Welcome to Foxbriar, Home of Pepper, Foxfire, and Friends." This is actually a Web site belonging to two dogs: a female Toy Fox Terrier (Pepper), and a male Smooth Fox Terrier (Foxfire). The site is narrated by the older of the two, Pepper, who is eager to tell her smooth counterpart that "Mom does too like me best!" A grab bag of subjects highlight this fun, lighthearted page, including home-page hyperlink access to such topics as Go Hiking with The Fox and Pepper (photos of the playful pups on the trail), Pet Rescue (compliments of the Pet Action League), Pepper's Place (for Pepper's story), Diary of the Fox, and Pepper's and Foxfire's recommended books. Given the affectionate presentation of this site, these two terriers are obviously much loved by their "mom and dad," Mary and Ralph Beam.

Caesar's Home Page

http://www.geocities.com/Heartland/Plains/2579/

Caesar's Home Page offers browsers two opportunities. On one hand, it introduces them to a beautiful German Shepherd with an engaging personality reflected in the narration of his Web site. On the other, it takes them into the mind of a dog with a very important job. Caesar is a police dog who works with the Chattanooga, Tennessee, Police Department. As we learn from his home page, this dog, who was imported from the Czech Republic, lives with his handler and his family and is trained in both criminal apprehension and narcotics detection. Willing to share the spotlight with his canine colleagues, he introduces us to his fellow K-9 officers as well, and offers details about what their very important jobs entail. Those inspired by Caesar's story may take advantage of the links he provides to other police K-9 and German Shepherd Dog sites, all of which serve to pay tribute to those dogs who devote their lives to protecting people.

The Beau Page

http://www.teleport.com/~richards/bo.html

Beau is a beautiful Great Pyrenees from Oregon belonging to obviously very proud owners Susan and Eric Richards.

His very elaborate, multilayered site is rich with photos of this great white animal and information about his breed, a large dog bred to protect livestock from predators. The site is divided into sections that provide a list of photos and accompanying descriptions, along with hyperlink access to the photos. Sections include The Puppy Days... and Teenager!, with photos chronicling both Beau's show career and his more candid moments at home as a beloved pet. Also included for those who find themselves enamored of Beau's breed is a complete list of Pyrenees-related links.

Pictures of Our Dogs

http://www-hsc.usc.edu/~kit/scrapbk.html

Tinker Toy, Tippy O'Toole, and the late great Tinker Bell—Dick and Dee Neville's Dogs—are the stars of this Web site, which shines with the affection and devotion this trio has earned from its owners. This is a very sweet site, offering ample photos of its canine hosts (two Dachshunds and a furry toy moppet), as well as heartfelt tributes to each penned by their master. Together, this presentation, combined with an impressive, even dramatic, design, allows browsers to get to know the dogs and the great love they have enjoyed—the kind of love every dog deserves.

You Talking to Me?

http://www.silcom.com/~dphilip/Boo.html

Boo is apparently a movie buff. Just take a look at the name of his Web site, which is taken from the classic Martin Scorsese film *Taxi Driver*. But, as you'll see from the opening shot of his site, Boo looks nothing like the rather disturbed title character of that film. Rather, he is an adorable buff-colored Cocker Spaniel, who asks, "Who says a dog can't have a Web page?" While his home page presents a gallery of Boo shots and the opportunity to e-mail him, Boo is not content to hog the spotlight. Instructing browsers that while his owners are away he likes to "cruise the net," he then offers links to several of his favorite sites. He does ask visitors to his Web site, however, "please don't tell my owner I was on the computer."

Jeff and Teresa's Home Page

http://www.westworld.com/~fint/

Californians Jeff and Teresa present this page in tribute to their Border Collies, three dogs who in keeping with the very active heritage of their breed, participate in a variety of sports: agility, flyball, and scent hurdles. What makes this individual dog site of value is not only that it profiles these deserving animals, but also in that it offers valuable information to people who might be interesting in getting a Border Collie of their own. Within the home-page text, you will find hyperlinks to Border Collie information, as well as Jeff's and Teresa's own warning that though Border Collies are "wonderfully intelligent and we think they make great companions, they must be kept active." This breed requires more than just a weekly walk every Saturday. Jeff and Teresa then practice what they preach by offering additional links to information on the various activities in which their dogs participate.

Auggie's World

http://www.west.net/~ollybaba/index.shtml

Auggie is a Boxer, and, if his personal Web site is any indication, a very creative Boxer at that. Opening with a photo of Auggie sitting on top of the world (literally) in the company of his new roommate, American Bulldog Maude, this site presents a colorful home-page menu that follows browsers throughout the site, offering access to such topics as Skunked (a game section), Auggie's Friends (a section where browsers may submit their own pets' photos to Auggie's list of friends), Auggie Chat, Guestbook, and

Auggie's Bio (written by Auggie himself, of course). But perhaps the most clever feature is the Doggie Diaries section. These are illustrated diary entries from "Auggie the Doggie," detailing from his own very warm and personal point of view of his day-to-day activities. Auggie's mom and dad must indeed be proud of their pup for designing such a colorful, lively, and engaging Web page that other dogs would be wise to emulate.

Sara's Story

http://www.aimnet.com/~oaktree/sara.shtml

Sara's story, as told on this site, is troubled, though it has a happy ending. Check in to this sweet Mastiff's site to learn all about the circumstances that led to her being a shy, submissive dog, and now a beloved pet with a Web site all her own. What you will also learn from Sara's site is just how specialized the Internet can be. This site offers browsers direct access to Sara pictures and Mastiff information, but also to a mailing list for shy dogs, a shy dogs links page, and the doleful story of another shy dog, Belgian Shepherd Shaman, who was the original inspiration for the shy dogs mailing list. This site is thus not only a vehicle for getting to know Sara, but a source for help with your own shy dog. Sara would be pleased to know she could help.

Maui, Sabu & Trace's Homepage: The Three Dachshund Darlings

http://www.geocities.com/SoHo/9833/dachsie.html

If you love Dachshunds and just can't get enough of them, check into Sandy Lindsey's tribute to her three Dachshunds: Maui, Sabu, and Trace. The photos are abundant, accessible from a long list of well-organized homepage hyperlinks. Not only are these shots of fine quality, but they are presented with humorous captions (i.e., 'Maui and Sabu at work' depicts the two pups snoozing in ultimate comfort in the sun). Taken together, they capture explicitly the special character of this breed that has elevated it to a position as one of the world's most popular dogs. You will also find access to a section on Doggie Humor, which serves as the perfect complement to this lively, well-illustrated tribute to Dachshunds.

Ella the Dog

http://www.kissiloff.com/ella.html

A dog need not be a purebred to have a Web site of its own. Just ask Ella. She is part Labrador Retriever, part German Shepherd, part Husky and, according to her owner, Ari, 100 percent "very cool dog." This site offers browsers the opportunity to get to know Ella, beginning with her first photo at six weeks of age. Follow her through her development with a progression of photographs, most of which are introduced with cute descriptive titles. Also included is a list of links to other canine resources on the Web, covering such topics as health, obedience, hiking and other dogs of Ella's acquaintance. Given the breadth of this list, it appears that Ella is as smart as she is cool.

The Alaskan Husky Homepage

http://home2.inet.tele.dk/jens_eva/index.htm

Hailing from Denmark is this site devoted to Alaskan Huskies in general and to Lupus the Alaskan Husky in particular. Seeking to fill in the gaps in both online and offline sled-dog information that invariably provides "loads of information on Siberian Huskies or Alaskan Malamutes but not Alaskan Huskies," this site addresses that omission, introducing browsers to this breed that is almost universally considered the premier sled racing dog. You may get to know one particular Alaskan Husky by clicking on the home-page hyperlink, "Pictures of OUR dog, Lupus." This takes you to the Lupus Picture Page, where you will see

Lupus in various stages of puppyhood, as well as posing with cats and wearing a raincoat (hardly a necessity for a top-flight athlete like the Alaskan Husky). This site thus accomplishes two missions: introducing browsers to Lupus and to the Alaskan Husky.

Dino the Basset Hound

http://www.clark.net/pub/truffaut/dino1_1.html

Though he is a sad-eyed Basset Hound, Dino Bigfoot is a friendly fellow who is described by Lori, his owner, in the opening passage to his home page as "the greatest hound dog ever." We are then told that "like other Bassets, Dino spends the majority of his time eating and sleeping." To get to know Dino a little bit better, scroll on down his home page and see him engaged in all his favorite activities, including resting, sleeping, relaxing, waiting for Lori to come home, and frolicking at the annual Basset Bash with his fellow Basset friends.

Dog Agility: Fun for Man & Beast

http://cust.iamerica.net/dstar1/DogAgility.htm

If agility is your passion, or you are considering giving it a try, check out the list of personal agility-dog sites offered on this extensive Dog Agility information home page. Scroll on down the page to the Handler Home Pages section and you will find hyperlinks to a variety of home pages presented by dogs and their handlers who participate in this fun activity that is growing increasingly popular every day. Here you will meet, among others, Cardigan Welsh Corgis, English Shepherds, Border Collies, and Beagles, all of whom are eager to share their own love of this sport and links to further information for those who believe that they, too, would like to jump on the agility bandwagon.

Maggie's Homepage

http://www.txdirect.net/users/mpierce/dogs/maggie.html

Against a backdrop of muted Basset Hound illustrations, Maggie the Basset introduces herself to her cyber fans, and offers them an intimate glimpse into her life with "the person that feeds me," Mike Pierce. After a tour of Maggie's homepage, in which they meet Mike (about whom Maggie never passes up an opportunity to make disparaging remarks), view photos of this indomitable hound and her canine friends, and even hear what odd otherworldly sounds Bassets can emit when they feel so inclined, browsers will come to understand just why Bassets cast so profound a spell on their human admirers. If through her site and her dry sense of humor, she inspires others to join the Basset ranks, Maggie will know she has done her job right.

The Amazing Jessie Home Page

http://www.sure.net/~rfloto/alsation.html

Jessie the German Shepherd has earned the title "amazing" because, according to her Web page, Jessie is a time traveler. Sure, she has her more routine moments. Her room mate Robert Floto informs visitors to Jessie's Web page (which offers access to Jessie's Favorite Links and Jessie's Picture Gallery) that "when she isn't designing award-winning Web pages or intricate computer animation, she enjoys pizza and rice crispie treats." Yet when she isn't munching treats or surfing the net, Jessie enjoys traveling through time. Click on the home-page hyperlink to Jessie's Adventures Through Time and Space and witness Jessie's travels, which have included, among many other adventures, fraternizing with dinosaurs in 65,000,000 B.C., and spotting a suspicious someone on the grassy knoll in Dallas in 1963. Rarely will you find so well-traveled a dog—or so clever a site honoring one.

Emma's Place

http://www.geocities.com/Heartland/3537/

Against a soothing green backdrop, Windmere Labradors introduces Emma, known officially as Woodhaven's Emma of Windmere. Actually Emma introduces herself, informing browsers who have come for a visit that "this is my page." Visitors may scroll on down her page's vivid photographs and engaging text and read about this lovely black Labrador Retriever whose favorite hobbies are "sleeping, playing, sleeping, retrieving, sleeping, eating, sleeping, swimming, sleeping; well, you get the idea." She also offers links to her pedigree and to information about her "mom," the engineer. Also included are links to some of her favorite dog sites (i.e. The Rainbow Bridge and sites belonging to other Labs), and she has even set aside some space on her page for information on some of her mom's other hobbies: gardening and birding.

Murphy's World

http://lserver.aea14.k12.ia.us/SWP/mlippold/Mary.html

Murphy is a Bichon Frise. Visit Murphy's Web site and you will not only learn all about this rather talkative little dog (whose bark you are invited to listen to on the home page), but also about the Bichon breed. This fluffy white powder puff of a dog is often mistaken for a Poodle and often ends up with owners who are not prepared to provide the type of home it needs. Murphy was one of the lucky ones (and acknowledges this throughout the layers of this site) and attempts to inform the public so that all other Bichons will be lucky ones too. You may visit Murphy's World with the help of a menu grid that offers such topics as Adoptive Parents (an affectionate tribute to those humans Murphy calls Mom and Dad), History (the history of the Bichon), and Pics of Bichons (a gallery from the Doggie Diamonds Web site). Also unique to this home page is the Top Ten

List of Endearing Characteristics of the Bichon. Here, in a nutshell, browsers may learn that the Bichon is a security system, an attention seeker and extremely jealous. For the right owners, there is no other dog.

Holly's Six Border Collies

http://www.ntrek.com/~pubeditr/index3.html

Holly Hollan's Web site introduces her six Border Collies as "The Smartest Dogs in the World!" Indeed the Border Collie breed has frequently been proclaimed tops in intelligence, and Holly's dogs seem to be living up to that reputation. The home-page menu consists of photographs of each, along with his or her name in hypertext that, when clicked, will take browsers in to each dog's own personal page. Click on Bonnie, for instance, and you will find all her vital statistics (parents, date of birth, nicknames, etc.) as well as Special Facts About Bonnie. Once you have visited each of Holly's dogs, you will feel you know them personally, and that is why sites such as this exist in the first place.

Pepper's Page

http://www.zebra.net/~myrrh/pepper/

Most dogs with their own Web sites are there to promote their sociability, but Pepper, a Shih Tzu–Dachsund mix, offers a different viewpoint on his home page. As you will learn here, Pepper "hates and attempts to bite all living creatures" (except for those within his immediate family), yet he also "hopes to attend college one day so he can be known as Dr. Pepper." Nevertheless, Pepper, is presented affectionately (and honestly), within his Web site, where browsers may click on hyperlinks to areas that address such topics as Pepper's favorite television show, photos of Pepper (an adorable dog despite his propensity to bite), and Pepper's Guestbook (he is obviously not completely antisocial).

Ludvick's Homepage
http://www.idt.ntnu.no/~davclaud/ludde.html

Airedale lovers, or those who aspire to becoming Airedale lovers, will have a grand time within Ludvick the Airedale's home page. The menu bar that assists browsers throughout their tour of this site is designed not only to introduce visitors to Ludvick, a rather precocious dog from Norway, but also to introduce them to his breed, the largest of the terriers. Browsers will find such menu options as Origin of Greatness (rich in Airedale information), Hall of Fame (illustrated profiles of famous dogs), and Dogs in Space (links to Ludvick's favorite sites). Given the friendly tone of this site and the obvious effort that has gone into its creation, it would seem that Ludde, as his friends call him, is a much-loved dog indeed.

Labs in the Neighborhood
http://www.geocities.com/Yosemite/5000/labl.html

While thousands of dogs have joined the cyber revolution and been granted their very own Web pages, browsers seeking sites devoted solely to Labrador Retrievers need look no further than Labs in the Neighborhood from Eric Watanabe. Here you can access pages belonging to Labs of all colors from all over the world, from the U.S., Canada, Japan, Holland and beyond. The sites are beautifully designed and exude a friendly tone, and many, as an added bonus, promote Lab rescue. What this site teaches the browser who meets this international group of labs is that love for this people-loving breed knows no national boundaries.

Dogs in Culture

Dogs have had a huge impact on human lives for thousands of years, so it is not surprising that they should frequently be featured in expressions of our culture over time. Images of dogs were found on the tombs, walls, and artifacts of the ancient Egyptians, and their presence is seen in ancient Greek writings and artwork. The dawn of civilization broke with the dog standing at man's side, as evidenced by its persistent presence in ancient imagery.

Painting, sculpture, and literature are among the higher forms of culture that have featured dogs, while cartoons, advertising campaigns, and popular novels with dogs as their core subjects are evidence of the canid's influence in modern media. People love dogs, so dogs are used to sell products, television shows, and movies. More sentimental motives can be ascribed to artists, who portray dogs simply because the animal's trust, loyalty, and beauty inspires them.

The profusion of canine references in popular culture is, of course, reflected in the newest of media, the Internet. Almost all aspects of dogs in today's world are represented on the World Wide Web, from cartoons to photography to

The Web sites in this chapter represent a wide array of subjects in which the dog is seen in our culture today. Some of them strive to educate, while others have no purpose other than to entertain. Each is worth a look, since each one presents human creativity at its best form—when inspired by dogs.

Nipperscape

http://www.ais.org/~lsa/nipper.html

Ever since Linda Anderson was a child, she had a special love for Nipper, the little mixed-breed that appeared as the RCA trademark. Linda grew up and became a technical writer, but she never her lost her love for Nipper. Not long ago, she created the Nipperscape Web site in his honor.

Nipper has a long and fascinating history. Nipper was a real dog who belonged to English painter and photographer Francis Barraud, who came to own him after Nipper's master passed away. Barraud noticed that Nipper would attentively listen to his old phonograph and got the notion that the dog was waiting to hear his master's voice, and was inspired to paint the now-famous scene. The image was later repainted for the Gramophone Company, using a gramophone instead of a phonograph, and it became the company's trademark in 1900.

The Nipperscape Web site covers the history of Nipper as well as Nipper trivia, using photographs and well-written text to tell the story. Starting with a photograph of Elvis Presley singing to a statue of Nipper (Elvis recorded on the RCA label), the site leads browsers into a wonderful world of nostalgia and popular culture.

It is hard not to get caught up in the intriguing story of how this little dog became a huge corporate symbol, surviving an entire century of changes in advertising and modern culture.

Anderson does a good job of showing us how Nipper has become much more than just a trademark over time. For example, a huge statue of Nipper stands on Broadway in Albany, New York, and is so tall that an airplane beacon light had to be placed on his right ear. Plus, Nipper has made his name in the world of collectibles. Salt and pepper shakers in Nipper's image were produced at some point in his career, and they are now worth a lot to those who collect "Nipperie." Also out there are Nipper replicas made of papier mache, rubber, and plastic, as well as advertising

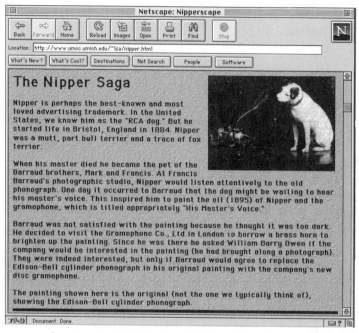

props of cardboard Nippers, along with posters, lighters, and other items, all bearing Nipper's image.

Nipperscape also presents other examples of Nipper's strong presence in our culture, including a humorous card showing a theater full of Nippers, a poster from a promotional campaign against drinking, and a picture of a Nipper-like dog model wearing 16th century boar hound armor from a museum in Massachusetts.

For those who are fans of the most recent real-life Nipper, and his companion, a puppy named Chipper, the site tells the story of the search that was conducted for the new Nipper, who was discovered by an agent as the dog was awaiting death at a research laboratory. The rags-to-riches story includes details on how the new Nipper likes his filet mignon served and how he travels in style from one assignment to another.

Anyone who loves dogs and appreciates their presence in popular culture should pay a visit to Nipperscape.

Index of Famous Dogs

http://www.evl.uic.edu/caylor/dogindex.html

If you have been struggling to think of the name of a dog you saw in a movie once, or want to name your new puppy after a well-known canine but you're not sure which one, a visit to the Index of Famous Dogs will most likely solve all your problems.

The names of hundreds of dogs that have appeared in advertising, cartoons, musicals, comedies, comic books, corporate logos, movies, newspaper columns, songs, toys, television, video games, and even throughout history are all listed at this site. Organized in alphabetical order, each name also includes the source (movie, logo, etc.) and a description of the character.

Every famous dog one can possibly imagine can be found on this site, authored by computer artist Misha Lee Caylor. Caylor also maintains an Index of Famous Cats and an Index of Famous Critters, both accessible from the Index of Famous Dogs page.

The Fame and Glory Hounds

http://velcome.iupui.edu/~bacaster/FAME.html

This simple page contains information on dogs throughout history and in the arts. Subjects include Great Dates in Dog History (Did you know the first pedigreed dogs were bred by Pharaoh Menes in 3,000 BC?), Dogs in the World of the Artist (including descriptions of important works of art featuring dogs), Dogs in the World of Literature (a short list of books about dogs and a list of famous authors' dogs), Dogs in the World of Music (popular songs about dogs), Politics (famous politicians' dogs), and Show Biz Dogs (dogs of stage and screen).

Jim's Puppy Quotes

http://www.metrolink.net/~lrice/quotes.htm

Dogs have played a large part in human history, and there's no better evidence of this than Jim's Puppy Quotes. This fun site, featuring an amusing animated dog named Tipsy, contains page after page of quotes about dogs. Included here are comments from Robert Louis Stevenson, Plato, George Bernard Shaw, Arnold Toynbee, Don Juan, *The New York Times Magazine*, Winston Churchill, and many, many others.

James Herriot Home Page

http://www.geocities.com/Athens/Acropolis/3907

When Heather Mazzaccaro was a child, she read her first book by James Herriot, and ever since then she wanted to be a veterinarian. Now a pre-vet student in Massachusetts, Mazzaccaro has devoted a good amount of her time to maintaining the James Herriot Home Page as a tribute to her favorite author.

Under the pen name of Herriot, veterinarian James Alfred Wight wrote a number of books celebrating the joys and sorrows of practicing veterinary medicine in a small British community. Wight's wonderful works inspired a whole generation of veterinarians, and brought him love and adoration from animal lovers everywhere.

When Wight died in 1995 at the age of 78, Mazzaccaro was inspired to create this captivating Web site, which includes photographs of Wight at work and several biographies of the veterinarian/author. An area called The Tribute to James Herriot Wall features personal tributes from his fans, and The James Herriot Chat Room allows his readers to discuss his works with other fans.

Some of Herriot's books are also reviewed here, and the author's comments about his own writings are included. For those who love the books of James Herriot—in which dogs feature prominently—this site is a real treat.

William Wegman on the World Wide Web

http://sjmusart.org/wegman/

You've probably seen his photographs. His images are hard to miss: a Weimaraner sitting stoically under a shower of powder; or several Weimaraners straddling a row of chairs.

Always featuring this greyest of sporting breeds in his work, William Wegman has obtained a level of recognition not often achieved by photographers.

Over the past 10 years, Wegman has become famous for creating unusual photographic portraits of his own Weimaraners in incongruous situations. In showings throughout the world, he has presented dog lovers and those who love photographic art with an abundance of whimsical images.

The San Jose Museum of Art, as part of its Web site, provides a page called William Wegman on the World Wide Web, with hyperlinks to various bits of information and imagery about this world-renowned artist. Starting with Wegman's resume, and winding down to an area called The Conceptual Fragmentation of the Work of Art, this site also includes a good number of Wegman's canine images, in both color and black and white.

Included here are lists of galleries, dealers and museums where Wegman's work can be viewed and sometimes purchased, as well as links to Weimaraner sites and other dog spots on the Web. If you enjoy William Wegman's work, this is the place to visit.

Snoopy's Doghouse

http://www.unitedmedia.com/comics/peanuts

No chapter on the canine in human culture would be complete without Snoopy, the most beloved Beagle to ever grace the pages of a comic book. An integral part of the Peanuts comic strip, Snoopy and the gang started in the 1950s when creator Charles M. Schultz presented a handful of drawings to United Feature Syndicate, who bought the cartoon. It has grown tremendously over the past 40 years, and now appears in 2,600 newspapers worldwide.

Snoopy is arguably the most popular character in the Peanuts strip, no doubt due to his un-doglike irreverence. His Web page, part of the United Media site, is called Snoopy's Doghouse, and provides Snoopy fans with a chance to learn more about Snoopy than they ever dreamed possible.

Snoopy fans can use this Web site to shop for clothing, stuffed toys, address books and other Snoopy items; read a profile on Charles M. Schultz; and see some Snoopy "first times," like the first time Snoopy appears in the strip (looking completely different), the first time he goes after Linus' blanket, and the first time he tries to sleep on top of his dog house, to name just a few.

Also on the site are a list of places around the country where Snoopy can be seen in person, general Peanuts information, games, milestones in Peanuts history, monthly TV lists and more.

Katharine Farmer: Dogumentary

http://www.envirolink.org

The Envirolink Vision Gallery, an online photo exhibition, features three artists on its Web site. One of these artists is Tennessee resident Katharine Farmer. An obvious dog lover and talented photographer, Farmer used a number of her own dogs as subjects for her black-and-white images that beautifully capture the essence of the rural dog.

The story in Farmer's artist's statement about how she came to acquire her many dogs lends even more charm to her photographs. A total of 12 images can be seen in this site, including "Dog Thought," "Lovers' Quarrel," "Good Dog," "Autumn Afternoon," and "Claudia's Reflection."

Official Blue Dog Site

http://www.mbay.net/~bluedog/

Several years ago, Cajun artist George Rodigue used his deceased dog Tiffany as the inspiration for a painting of a French-Cajun ghost dog. The reaction that Tiffany's image prompted among those who saw the painting led Rodigue to explore the possibility that Tiffany's spirit lived on in his canvas.

What followed was a series of paintings of the Blue Dog, based on Tiffany's haunting image. Popular among dog and art lovers alike, the Blue Dog works are easily recognizable for their eerie yet somewhat comical imagery.

The Official Blue Dog Site features examples of George Rodigue's art, along with a biography of the artist, a bibliography detailing his exhibitions and resume, and information about the four Blue Dog galleries located in California, Louisiana, Germany and Japan. Rodigue's Cajun-style restaurant in Lafayette, Louisiana, is also featured here.

The most interesting part of this site is the newer Kid's Take on Blue Dog area, featuring childrens' drawings of the Blue Dog. The young artists' skills at capturing the essence of Rodigue's Blue Dog is truly amazing.

The National Bird Dog Museum

http://www.net-source.com/birddog/museum.html

The National Bird Dog Museum Web site provides information on the museum, including hours, directions, and a calendar of upcoming events. The Bird Dog Boutique is part of this site, which includes a gift shop where prints of bird dogs in the field can be ordered online.

The actual National Bird Dog Museum is located in Grand Junction, Tennessee, home of the National Bird Dog Championship, and is a creation of the Bird Dog Foundation, Inc. The goal of both the museum and the foundation is to preserve the history of bird dogs. To this end, the museum displays paintings, artifacts, literature, photography, and other memorabilia relating to those sporting dogs that flush, point and retrieve. The Field Trial Hall of Fame is also part of the museum.

Rin Tin Tin

http://www.mdle.com/ClassicFilms/FeaturedStar/star48.htm

The canine Web would not be complete without a site for the most famous German Shepherd of all time, Rin Tin

Tin. Making his debut in 1922 in "The Man From Hell's River," Rinty earned nearly $1,000 a week in his prime.

Authored by Diane MacIntyre as part of the Silents Majority home page, an online journal for silent film buffs, the Rin Tin Tin site contains a profile of this beloved canine, a list of all his films, photographs to download and keep, and related links.

2 Stupid Dogs

http://home.sn.no/~tbk/2stupid.html

When Hanna Barbera created its "2 Stupid Dogs" cartoon, one has to wonder if they knew how many Web sites would sprout up in the characters' honor. There are no less than four on the Web at the time of this writing, with the most comprehensive being the site authored by Norwegian "2-Stupid-Dogs" fan Thore Karlsen.

The "2 Stupid Dogs" cartoon features the same two canines, neither of which has much going on upstairs. Popular with both children and adults, the cartoon also features a number of other regular characters who are equally as goofy.

Karlsen's Web site includes an Information section, with profiles of each regular character, and a Data area featuring pictures and sound clips from the cartoon. Browsers' favorite quotes from the 2 Stupid Dogs, along with e-mail links, can be found in the Quotes area, and links to the other "2 Stupid Dog" pages are also included.

Wiener Dog Art

http://www.ee.umanitoba.ca/~djc/wiener

Most people who love dogs also have a good sense of humor, and anyone with a good sense of humor can't help but love the work of cartoonist Gary Larson. While Larson's cartoons cover a broad range of subjects, his understanding and affection for dogs is one of the most obvious aspects of his work.

A fan of Larson's series of Wiener Dog cartoons (based on the Dachshund) has created an unofficial site called Wiener Dog Art.

The Wiener Dog Art page starts with Larson's humorous words about the Dachshund, and then presents links to eight exhibits. Each exhibit consists of a color reproduction of one of Larson's works of art featuring the Dachshund. Included here is "Cave Art," featuring the first cave painting of a wiener dog being discovered by an archeologist; "Through the Storm," a work showing the aggressive, seafaring warriors of the 1600s known as the Wienerkinds; the abstract, Picasso-esque "Wiener Dog With Head Turned"; and "The Whine," which bears a striking similarity to Edvard Munch's "The Scream."

It's hard to say which is funnier: the illustrations or the text that accompanies each. Anyone who loves art, dogs, and Gary Larson should pay a visit to this hilarious site.

101 Dalmatians Home Page

http://www.disney.com/101/_index.html

Walt Disney's *101 Dalmatians* was first released as an animated feature in 1961. The film's continued popularity throughout the past three decades prompted Disney Studios to produce a live-action version of the story. Seen in theaters in 1996 and released on home video early in 1997, the live action version of the film was a big success.

The movie starred Glen Close and Jeff Daniels, who worked with nearly 400 dogs in the making of the film. Almost half of those dogs were 8- to 10-week-old Dalmatian puppies, making the film's cuteness factor rather high.

While the live-action film is popular with children everywhere, responsible Dalmatian breeders were not very happy with its release. Despite an aggressive public education campaign by the Dalmatian Club of America, the film's success caused a sudden burst in the breed's popularity and eventually resulted in a large number of unwanted Dalmatians being dumped at the nation's animal shelters.

Seemingly oblivious to all this, Disney has maintained its *101 Dalmatians* Web site throughout the year in an obvious effort to promote sales of the home video. This colorful, graphics-heavy site features a game for children who can "find the puppy," which features characters from the film. Several special offers are also available online for those who wish to purchase the video for home viewing.

Wishbone

http://www.pbs.org/wishbone/

In October 1995, the Public Broadcasting System (PBS) began airing a children's series called Wishbone, featuring the adventures of a Jack Russell Terrier by that name. Designed to teach kids about classic literature and to encourage them to read books, the series features Wishbone in an ongoing list of adventures taken from fictional stories that have survived through the ages.

The Wishbone Web site is on the PBS server, and includes the latest press releases on the series, facts about Wishbone, titles and descriptions of all 40 episodes, and classroom and family activities from one of the shows.

Browsers can view a Quicktime promotional clip from the show, and can even learn all about the Jack Russell Terrier at this site.

Wile E. Coyote Page

http://www.eskimo.com/~wecoyote/wile_e/

It's hard to find anyone who grew up between the 1940s and now who does not know Wile E. Coyote. One of the most popular Warner Brothers cartoon characters ever created, Wile E. Coyote is a big hit on the Internet.

One of the many sites devoted to this single-minded canine is the Wile E. Coyote Page, authored by a computer-savvy fan. Loaded with lots of great graphics of the character, the site also includes a complete list of Wile E.'s film credits along with their dates of original release, a listing of all the videotapes and videodiscs that include the character, comments from the character's creator, Chuck Jones, and even interpretive names of Wile E. Coyote episodes in Latin!

Pictures of Wile E., the Road Runner, and Bugs Bunny are available to download, as are quotes and sound effects from the cartoons.

Q&A with Eddie the Dog

http://www.orangecoast.com/eddie.htm

Most dog lovers are familiar with the hit television show *Frasier* simply because of its charming and hilarious Jack Russell Terrier character, Eddie. In real life, Eddie is played by an actor dog named Moose.

Frasier fan Martin J. Smith decided to pose some questions to Moose, using an animal psychic to interpret the celebrity canine's answers, and the Q&A With Eddie the Dog Web site was born. On this tongue-in-cheek page, the author's questions and Moose's answers appear, along with a photo of this renowned dog. The subjects covered include everything from Kelsey Grammar's personal scent to Moose's opinions on O.J. Simpson's dog.

Snow Dog Festival (Inukko Matsuri)

http://www.media-akita.or.jp/akita/fuyu/004/WelcomeE.html

The dog is important not only in western culture; in Japan, the Snow Dog Festival originated in the early Edo era in that country and is still celebrated today. Ingrained in Japanese culture for the past 360 years, the Snow Dog Festival is practiced in the hopes of warding off evil and misfortune.

The Snow Dog Festival Web site, which originates in Japan, is a short, simple page from the Beautiful Akita site, Akita referring to the city in Japan. This page is part of Akita's winter festivals online area and explains the intriguing Snow Dog Festival. A photograph of the festival's snow shrines, with little nordic-type canines made from rice cakes, accompanies text that details the history and rituals of the event.

Big Dog Sportswear

http://www.bigdogs.com

Big Dog Sportswear is a product line that has reached considerable popularity in the West over the past few years. And now that the company has created a substantial presence on the Internet, this doggy-oriented clothing line could catch on all over the country.

Popular with fans of some of the larger breeds, Big Dog Sportswear features the company's well-recognized logo, an unidentified canine that looks very much like a St. Bernard. Dog lovers can often be seen sporting Big Dog t-shirts, caps and other items of apparel at dog shows and canine events. Consequently, the Big Dog company has embraced its popularity with dog owners, and now also offers a line of accessories for dogs.

The Big Dog Sportswear Web site tells the story of Big Dog, and has a link to its own Dog Lovers page, where stories about dogs, care tips, dog trivia, and links to other dog sites can be found.

Domestic Dogs on Stamps

http://www.philately.com/zoology/domestic_dogs.htm

Stamp collecting is a hugely popular hobby around the world, and since canine aficionados like to horde any and all things relating to dogs, it's only logical that there would be space on the Internet devoted to canine philately.

Part of the Study Unit of the American Topical Association site, the Domestic Dogs on Stamps page lists hundreds of stamps that have been produced featuring dogs of all shapes and sizes. The list includes occasional information about the stamp or breed of dog, and is organized by breed and type. The American Topical Association maintains a complete listing of all the dog stamps produced around the world, but only a partial listing is available on this site.

Wild Dogs

Within the past decade the popularity of wild dogs, particularly wolves, has soared. Thanks to an increasing sensitivity among the public toward the plight of endangered wildlife species, the charisma and human-like social structure of wild dog societies, as well as the popularity of such films as *Dances with Wolves* and *Never Cry Wolf,* many have found themselves enamored of these great beasts and have avidly joined the many efforts to ensure their survival.

Evidence of this can be found in events that 25 years ago would have been impossible. After much political wrangling, the gray wolf has been reintroduced with great success to Yellowstone National Park, and the park's attendance has increased dramatically. The fact that this ever came to pass is a credit to the public's willingness to write letters, and vote.

The popularity of wild dogs is also seen in the vast array of products that invoke their images. On any given day you can find someone walking down the street wearing the image of a coyote, the mischievous grin of the red fox or a howling wolf; art galleries are filled with detailed sculptures of wolf families and paintings that capture the wisdom of the wilderness within the yellow eyes of *Canis lupus*; and each year stacks of books are published on the folklore, biology, and social structure of wild dogs. Indeed the wild dogs have spawned a small industry.

Wild dogs have also found their way onto the Internet, having become a popular, sometimes controversial topic of chat rooms, e-mail lists, newsgroups, and Web sites. What follows are several of the latter, sites either devoted solely to

continued after the feature section

Defenders of Wildlife

http://www.Defenders.org/

Since 1947, Defenders of Wildlife has taken what many construe as an unpopular stand and worked to protect America's predators. The wolf is featured in the organization's logo, representing the belief that if it succeeds in protecting the wolf, it will protect the wolf's habitat and the many other species that share its space.

The Defenders Web site reflects its commitments to wolf reintroduction in Yellowstone National Park, the protection of wolves in Alaska, and pending efforts to reintroduce the endangered Mexican Wolf in the Southwestern United States. These issues, and many more, are presented in a user-friendly, highly detailed format, enabling those with a concern for wolves to enrich their knowledge dramatically.

The Defenders Web site is a good starting point for those who wish to become involved in wolf and wildlife protection. From signing petitions to volunteering at Defenders of Wildlife information booths nationwide to voicing their opinions to their elected officials, this site offers users the a number of ways to get involved. It has never been easier, for example, to write to your congressional representatives with concerns about the wolf and the environment. This site provides a complete listing of the e-mail addresses and telephone numbers of congressional representatives, the president, the vice president and all related agencies, as well as links to government Web sites.

Also available (within the What You Can Do section) is the Rapid Response Network, an e-mail list that disseminates Action Alerts of new developments to everyone on the network, who may in turn respond rapidly and easily to the parties involved.

You may keep abreast of these developments by touring articles on various subjects from *Defenders* magazine; by visiting the Endangered Species Learning Center, which offers a primer on biodiversity and endangered species in

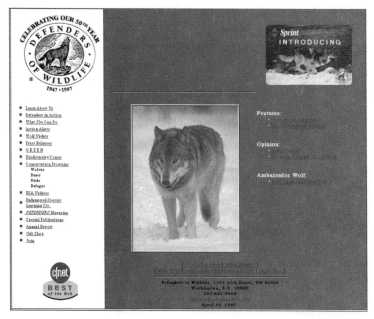

clear, concise terms; and by taking a quick trip through the What's New section, which keeps the public updated almost daily on what the organization is up to and how the animals and the environment are faring.

Webmaster Sajjad Ahrabi may be credited with maintaining a timely, well-organized site. The left-hand side of the home page shows a complete listing of departments. While some color contrasts here make for a difficult read, the overall organization of the site makes using it a breeze. Available with a click is a detailed treatise on this nonprofit group's history, mission, and focus, as well as its annual report and an online application form that makes "becoming a Defender" quick and easy. Visitors can also order wildlife viewing guides, stationery and even wolf-silhouette wallpaper from the online Gift Shop.

By focusing on education and action, Defenders' grassroots efforts to protect predators have been extremely effective. Judging by its Web site, the group seems to be putting its limited resources to the best use possible.

wild dogs or featuring them prominently amid a broader focus on wildlife at large. Such cyber-coverage can only serve to continue the public's education in this area, and in the process, perhaps increase the protection and understanding these animals, our dogs' beautiful wild cousins, so richly deserve.

International Wolf Center

http://www.wolf.org/

The prime directive of the International Wolf Center is to educate the public about what wolves are and what they are not, all guided by the belief that a public that understands the wolf is more likely to support its survival.

Presenting the wolf as an animal with a unique language, social structure, and biological attributes, the IWC Web site is an effective tool in the organization's educational mission. A user-friendly format highlighted by wolf-paw-print icons and elegant graphics of primarily blue, black, and white against a backdrop of gray wolf fur, contribute to the readability of the group's Mission and History, the IWC calendar of events, the Wolf Den Gift Shop Catalog, and Membership Information.

Also included is information about the IWC's Educational Programs and Resources and its internationally known education facility, the International Wolf Center itself, which has made its home in Ely, Minnesota since 1993. The center presents, as browsers learn here, not only a rich array of presentations and activities conducted by respected wolf experts, but also the internationally known "Wolves and Humans" exhibit, which once traveled the nation to educate the public about the close association our two species have always shared.

While this site is more informational than interactive, click on the Wolf Images icon and make a virtual visit to the IWC. Here you will find photos not only of the center itself, but shots of the Yellowstone reintroduction efforts, as well as shots from the National Biological Survey Study in the Superior National Forest, which tracks radio-collared wolves. Within the Telemetry Data section, browsers may actually collect information about those radio-collared wolves, and even learn how to track them via computer.

If wolves are your passion, you will find an abundance of IWC-sponsored activities, presentations, and events listed within this site that are sure to inspire your imagination, and perhaps prompt you to schedule a trip to Minnesota at your earliest convenience.

The Wolf Homepage
http://www.usa.net/WolfHome/

Everything you ever wanted to know about wolves can be found in this simple, no-nonsense site produced by Hippomedia Corporation.

The subjects run the gamut from the most basic factual information on wolves and their behavior (i.e. "Wolf Pups and Family Life" and "Are Wolves Endangered?") to technical updates on studies of radio-collared wolves and wolf recovery efforts throughout the United States.

Short on graphics but long on information, this site allows those with an interest in wolves to increase their knowledge quickly. For those who want some inspirational wolf images in the midst of their browsing, the site provides a Gopher link to Internet wolf photography, as well.

National Wildlife Federation
http://www.nwf.org

The preservation of America's wildlife is the focus of the National Wildlife Federation, and is the core of the NWF's site on the Web. With a friendly design that echoes the site's interactive character, the NWF site reflects a profound commitment involving and educating the public.

Kept up to date by Webmaster Ian Mishalove and assistant Webmaster Scott McGraw, the NWF home page first offers the opportunity to offer your two cents on recent environmental decisions and events. Also presented are Action Alerts that get people involved, by informing them about current environmental issues and instructing them on what they can do to help. Also timely is Hot News, the latest from the environmental front, a section that frequently features the very newsworthy wolf, a species often embroiled in one debate or another.

What truly stands out within this site, however, is its promotion of education. It offers young people ample access to educational games, activities, and publications, and teachers access to resource materials and training programs. In the Classroom, for example, offers teachers the opportunity to download "Animal Track Current Events Hotline," as well as the "Nature Quest" training program, designed to help educators "incorporate nature studies into the curriculum."

Kids and adults alike may also get a line on such NWF events and activities as Wildlife Camps, Teen Adventure, the NWF National Conference and various eco-adventures the organization sponsors throughout the country. These are located under the more educationally slanted headings as well as those listed under NWF Adventure and Entertainment.

And finally, if you enjoy wolf-related paraphernalia, check out the group's online catalog, which offers sweatshirts, shower curtains, stuffed animals, and the Sponsor a Gray Wolf Kit. Those impressed by what the NWF has to offer may then use the site to join this non-profit enviormental organization with an online application.

Kiopa's Side of the Jungle

http://www.geocities.com/Heartland/Plains/2373/frames.html

Rare, endangered, and often maligned, the Cape hunting dog (also known as the African wild dog) is fortunate to have Kiopa's Side of the Jungle representing its interests. Known as Africa's most endangered predator, this fascinating, large-eared canine receives the attention it deserves on this colorful, reader-friendly, and very informative site, which not only presents much-needed information, but does so in a presentation that actually invoke a jungle feel.

This site, as presented by Julie "Kiopa" Hedrick, effectively conveys the plight of this unique denizen of Africa, the victim of disease, habitat destruction, and misunderstanding in its perceived role in the predation of livestock. At the same time, the site engenders a genuine affection and respect for this animal, and offers people advice on what they can do to help it survive.

Kiopa's Side of the Jungle is complemented by colorful graphics, ample photos of this rare creature, and even an article on its social structure that is truly a testament to family values. Given the quality of this site and the passion of those working to save this animal, perhaps the wild dog has a chance at survival after all.

African Wild Dog Conservation Fund

http://personalWebs.myriad.net/theresa/

The message conveyed by the African Wild Dog Conservation Fund in this compact Web site is one that must be heard: Africa's wild dog is in trouble, and this non-profit organization needs help in trying to reverse that fortune.

Maintained by Theresa L. Stefancik, the purpose of this site is not only to inform the public about the nature and plight of the African wild dog, but also to outline what the AWDCF and its Italian sister organization, the Licaone Fund, are trying to do to help. The site thus provides information on the various projects to which it contributes in attempts to maintain and stimulate Africa's wild dog population.

Also included are a well-illustrated FAQ that serves as an excellent introduction to this animal first brought to public attention by Jane Goodall, and a short list of unique Web-site links. It's a start for a fascinating animal that does not deserve to meet an untimely end.

Adam's Fox Box

http://tavi.acomp.usf.edu/foxbox/

If foxes are your passion—or you would like them to be—check out Adam's Fox Box, presented by Adam Moss. Here you will find everything you ever wanted to know about foxes, all presented in a slick, well-illustrated, fun-to-read-and-navigate format.

Amid the many images of foxes that grace this page—cartoons, illustrations and photographs—you will find options that lead you to fox stories, fox articles, fox pictures, and even fox songs and poems. Devoted as it is to a creature of fable and folklore, the site is also rich with these tales. For instance, it opens with a tale from Aesop, and travels on to present various Native American tales as well as stories of the illustrious Reynard. This site thus pays tribute not only to the fox as a living, breathing, warm-blooded animal—with articles on fox trapping and news items—but also as an amazing, almost mythically intelligent creature that has never failed to capture the human imagination.

The home page also offers a section entitled Assorted Fringe-foxy Miscellany. Click on the hypertext options here and get information on newsgroups, other wildlife pages and the League Against Cruel Sports (i.e. fox hunting). You can even click on to a short film of a fox exhibiting its catlike hunting skills. All is presented in a friendly atmosphere that, has made this site a favorite among fox-loving browsers.

Wildlife Waystation

http://www.waystation.org/

For a different take on the plight of the wolf and its fellow wildlife species, check out the Wildlife Waystation Web site, which introduces itself with the statement "Where no wild animal in need shall ever be turned away!"

This energetic graphic-rich, site gets right down to business, presenting the facts about its facility and organization—a 160-acre rescue and rehabilitation facility in Southern California—and then inviting the browser to dive right in and learn the details. Click on Waystation Alert, for example, and learn about the latest animals in need of the Waystation's care, and what the public can do to help.

Click on The Animals icon (three reclining lions), and meet some of the 1200 animals that have found sanctuary at the Waystation. Here you will find a lengthy list of species. Click Coyotes on that list, and not only get to know Luna, a watermelon-loving coyote who is part of the Waystation's educational program, but also learn the facts about coyote character and social structure. Click on Wolves, and enjoy Waystation founder Martine Colette's treatise on the ten wolves that currently make her facility their home and on the nature, history and challenges of their species at large.

This site will also take you to Wildlife Waystation Current Events, Rescues, the Waystation Store, and into the Kids' Compound, the latter includes a visit to the Baby Animal Trailer, written to kids from the animals' points of view. In short, this is a site that an entire wildlife-loving family can enjoy.

Wolf Haven International

http://www.teleport.com/~wnorton/wolf.shtml

Founded in 1982 by Steve and Linda Kuntz as a sanctuary for captive wolves, as well as an educational organization targeted toward wolf conservation, Wolf Haven in Tenino, Washington, sponsors this informative site.

Though not particularly flashy in its presentation, this site, produced by Wade Norton, offers information about Wolf Haven (its educational programs, volunteer opportunities, hours of operation, and its summer Howl-Ins where participants can howl with the wolves), and also in-depth information on wolves themselves. While extremely text-heavy it does offer a unique inter-active opportunity, by inviting browsers to offer their comments by e-mail at the end of each internal subject link.

One aspect of its operation that has made Wolf Haven well-known among both wolf circles and the general public is its wolf adoption program, in which, for a fee, members of the public can sponsor one of the facility's resident wolves. Click on Wolf Adoption and get all the details of this program, as well as take a look at all the wolves available for adoption (their bios are available under Bio Sheets for Wolves of Wolf Haven). You may just fall in love and need to sign up right then and there.

The Ethiopian Wolf Home Page

http://www.scs.unr.edu/nncc/wolves/e_wolf.html

Think of wolves and you probably think of the classic wolf: North America's gray wolf. But wolves once roamed the entire planet, and though they have been eradicated from most of those environs, pockets still exist where you least expect them. One of these is occupied by the Ethiopian wolf in the African country of the same name.

Also known as the Simien fox, the Simien jackal, or the Abyssinian wolf, this rare creature even has its own Web site, with information compiled by canid specialist Claudio Sillero-Zubiri of the United Kingdom, and site maintained by Timothy Brogan. Within this short, attractive site, complete with an opening shot of this beautiful animal, you will learn all about a wolf that heretofore you might never have known existed.

Like virtually every other wolf in the world, the Ethiopian wolf faces the threat of extinction. Acknowledging this, the site offers browsers information on how they can help—and promises that the site will continue to be updated on an ongoing basis, preferably with good news about the health of the Ethiopian wolf's population.

The Virtual Zoo

http://207.71.29.70/zoo/dogs.html

The Virtual Zoo is not dedicated solely to wild dogs, but by using the address provided, you will be directed into the section—under Mammals, of course—that is. While wolf sites are relatively plentiful on the Net, those devoted to other wild dog species can be a bit more difficult to locate. The Virtual Zoo provides a one-stop shop of information on everything from wolves to foxes to jackals to coyotes.

Click on the Coyote section, for example, and with the help of "zookeeper"/Webmaster Amy Martin and the inspiration of Sean Garrity, this animal, which suffers from a much-maligned and undeserved reputation, gets full and very respectful attention. Here you will find sound information about the coyote's biology and habits, as well as about its fear of humans and the lack of harm it presents to us. Using a simple, bulleted format, the page paints a portrait of the coyote as a decent, hard-working wild dog that is simply trying to eke out a living. As an added bonus, this section also provides you with links to other coyote sites, which are few and far between.

The Virtual Zoo, a rich combination of solid information and artwork, is an animal-lover's paradise. After touring the Wild Dog section, you may want to take a gander at some of the other animals represented here, too.

Wolf Education & Research Center

http://www.wolfcenter.org/

Avidly involved in the gray wolves recently reintroduced in central Idaho and Yellowstone National Park, the Wolf Education & Research Center is working hard to see that the wolf survives. This fact becomes evident as soon as you visit the WERC Web site.

Simple and direct, this site consists of two primary parts. The first of these is an informative, no-frills home page outlining the group's various projects. These include their involvement in educating area school kids about the reintroduced wolves, and plans, in partnership with the Nez Perce Indian tribe, to establish a 20-acre "environmental and cultural education facility" in Idaho with a resident wolf pack.

The second part of this site is a section entitled "Meet the Reintroduced Wolves of Idaho!" Here browsers are provided with detailed biographical data on each and every one of the reintroduced wolves in that region, as well as the latest news on their progress (and related links). Though you may not be able to see the wolves themselves, you can follow their progress via computer.

The Wolf's Den

http://www.wolfsden.org/

When you first venture into The Wolf's Den, you are faced with a choice: either the Wolf Information Center or the Native American Resource Center. Of course those seeking wolf info will choose the former, but because those with an interest in the former often also have an interest in the latter, which is reflected in this site's Lakota Sioux comment "we are all related," it is nice to have both at one's fingertips.

Once within the Wolf Information Center, maintained by Webmaster Wolf McSherry, you will find a multifaceted page of information and options designed "to educate and inform the public about wolves as they really are."

Though it is somewhat slight on original material (the site is in a growth period), The Wolf Den is unique in that it offers the browser an ample list of links that originate in countries all over the world, thus bolstering the notion that a passion for the wolf, an animal that once roamed most of the globe, is universal in its scope.

CoyoteHowl

http://earth.simmons.edu/coyotehowl/coyotehowl.html

Subtitled "Tracking the Eastern Coyote," this highly interactive site, sponsored by Simmons College in Massachusetts, offers browsers an opportunity not only to learn about the coyote, but to become actively involved in studying them.

For instance, check out the discussion room where participants can chat about coyote facts, conflicts between coyotes and people, and tracking coyotes. Also offered are a variety of student activities, encouraging students to learn about these animals by writing stories from a coyote's point of view and studying the image of the coyote in various cultures. It also includes instructions on how to map where coyotes have been found.

As coyotes have been discovered throughout the Eastern United States, their population has become a topic of debate and interest in that region of the country. CoyoteHowl, maintained by Paul D. Colombo thus offers a section that is a real-life study of coyotes in New England: The CoyoteHowl Monitoring Project. New England participants can sign up via this Web site and actually contribute information on coyotes in their communities to this project, thus leading to an increased understanding of the behavior of eastern coyotes and the density and range of their populations. By the same token, those with an interest in *Canis latrans* who don't happen to live in New England may feel similarly inspired to implement some of these same projects in their own communities—all for the long-term good of this misunderstood creature.

WCSRC—The Wolf Sanctuary

http://www.wolfsanctuary.org/

The Wolf Sanctuary, states the opening to this site managed by Bridgette Daley, is working to provide "an alternative to extinction." Anyone with a passion for wolves, particularly the severely endangered Mexican wolf to which this site is primarily devoted, must hope that the Missouri-based Wild Canid Survival and Research Center, founded in 1971 by enviornmentalists including Marlin Perkins and his wife Carol, succeeds.

Follow the trail of wolf tracks that lead the browser through the home page, and you will come to understand just how the WCSRC hopes to educate the public and promote its collective support for the survival of the wolves that remain in the wild. First stop is the What's News section, where you will learn about all the latest happenings at the WCSRC's 50-acre sanctuary, which boasts captive breeding programs for both the Mexican and red wolves. Included here are news on resident Mexican wolves expecting pups and the sanctuary's calendar of events.

You can also learn about the sanctuary's Adopt-A-Wolf program, Volunteer Opportunities and basic information about wolves themselves, all presented in a format that is easy to navigate, fun, and informative.

Timber Wolf Information Network

http://www.coredcs.com/~twin/home.htm

Founded in 1989, the Timber Wolf Information Network is a non-profit collective of volunteers dedicated to forging the timber wolf's survival by educating the public. Toward this end, the group's Web site invites browsers to get to know TWIN and, more specifically, the wolves that run free, primarily in Wisconsin, one of the few states in the lower 48 that still hosts a natural wild population.

This site, maintained by TWIN volunteers, combines such hard-core information about the wolf as reading wolf body language, the ins and outs of lupine biology, and identifying wolf tracks, with timely reports on how the timber wolf is doing as a species.

One unusual feature is Population and Monitoring Updates for Wolves in Wisconsin, which provides users with an ongoing census of the wolves in the state's known packs. Also unique is the site's comprehensive and beautifully illustrated listing of links to other Web sites, including international and governmental sites.

Click on Scent Post from the home page, and meet other wolf-loving users on the Wolf E-mail Discussion Forum. Click on Lobo Lingo, and cruise through back issues of the TWIN newsletter, or check into Kids Only and find a rich collection of wolf-related activities, information and even a forum for young wolf lovers' artwork and poetry. Viewing the wolf portraits and poems that youngsters have contributed to this forum (the Kids Rendezvous Site), you can sense that a new generation will care about the future of the wolf.

Wolves of India

http://earthwatch.org/x/Xjhala.html

India is not often thought of as a haven, or even a home, for wolves, yet it does host a wild population of these large predators and, as an article in *The New York Times* recently pointed out, the ability of India's human population to coexist with their lupine neighbors is faltering.

Given the threatened status of their existence, it is a pleasure to be able to hit the Internet and discover a Web page devoted to the wolves of India. Thanks to Dr. Yakvendradev Jhala, of the Wildlife Institute of India, browsers may learn about these little-known creatures and an ongoing study being conducted in India's Velavadar National Park on what is described as "the last major predator in the Indian grasslands." The purpose of the study is to look into the conflict surrounding India's remaining wolves (estimated to be less than 2,000), in hopes that something can be done to save them from extinction.

This site outlines the study, and browsers are invited to join the team. It even provides some special insight into the project through the vivid memoirs of former team member Dorothy S. Conlon. Wolves of India is presented as part of a larger site sponsored by Earthwatch International, which sponsors scientific projects made possible by the contributions of volunteers.

Sinapu—Returning the Wolf to Colorado

http://www.sinapu.org/

For those not familiar with the word *Sinapu*, this home page explains that this is the Ute Indian word for wolves. Newcomers are invited to come in and learn more about the animal for whom this site is named and about the organization's purpose.

Festooned with graphics of gracefully running wolves, this site is devoted to efforts bring the gray wolf back home, as is being done in other regions throughout the West, to the southern Rocky Mountains of Colorado, a region where it once ran free.

As Webmaster Jose Alvistur explains in the About Sinapu section, this collective of volunteers has already succeeded in urging Congress to approve a feasibility study for wolf recovery and hopes to see more tangible success in the future.

In the meantime, Sinapu communicates its long-term plan, dispelling popular myths (i.e. Red Riding Hood) that threaten their goal, and even providing browsers with an on-line opportunity to "Cast your cyber-vote for wolves." And if you need wolf-related links, this is the place to find them. Click on Lots of Wolf and Other Environmental References on the Sinapu home page, and you will find one of the most complete listings of links to wolf and environmental Web sites on the Net. This feature alone makes the Sinapu site an invaluable resource to any browser with a passion for wolves.

Urban Fox Ecology

http://drycas.club.cc.cmu.edu/~furrball/urbanfox.html

The red fox, like the coyote, has the distinction of living quite successfully in close contact with humans in urban and suburban environments. While some humans find the fox's presence in their midst abhorrent, many more find this animal a charming addition to the urban and suburban landscape, and it is for them that this site is of great value.

Produced by Tim Susman, the Urban Fox Ecology page is a tribute to this sprightly animal, beginning with a home page that offers browsers choices including Contact Between Foxes and Humans, Fox Dens and Home Ranges, Fox Life History, and even the Webmaster's own master's study on the urban fox, which inspired him to feature the animal on the Net in the first place. Though arranged almost like an academic essay, this site's writing is warm and reader-friendly, and it offers links to Other Neat Foxy Stuff and easy access to The Urban Fox Bookstore from the home page.

Especially pleasing is the section on Foxes as Pets, in which the author makes the editorial comment right there on the home page "Bad! Bad!" As he states in the subsequent text, "Foxes are wild animals and are not accustomed, as are dogs, to living in a 'family' of humans." This is an important message to impart, especially when speaking of this small, adorable, seemingly lovable wild dog that seems so content in the human environment. Its presence reminds us that understanding a wild animal in our midst does not mean we should take it in as a pet.

U.S. Fish & Wildlife Service World Wide Web Site

http://www.fws.gov/

This government agency is familiar to wolf advocates in that it is the branch of the U.S. Interior Department charged with the duty of managing the nation's wildlife. While this site is not devoted exclusively to wolves, coyotes, foxes, and their brethren, it is of interest to those seeking information on governmental policies toward wild canids.

Maintained by the Fish and Wildlife Service's Division of Information Resources, the site's seemingly modest primary home page is actually the first step into an enormous network of topics. Click on the News section, for instance, and you will find a long list of the various FWS home pages.

For example, the Endangered Species Home Page is a well-organized page of hyper-texted topics, ranging from What's New? (excerpts from the Endangered Species Bulletin), to species-specific information (i.e., a complete listing of the status of every endangered species), to frequently asked questions ("Why do we have to protect endangered and threatened species on private lands?").

The site also offers browsers the opportunity to subscribe to the "fws-news" listserver. Sign up and you will automatically receive all "the latest news releases, bulletins, and other information about U.S. Fish and Wildlife Service activities." From the primary FWS home page, hit the hyper-texted "fws-news," and you will be transported to the area entitled "How to Subscribe to the "fws-news" Listserver.

With such a massive site, the Search feature is an invaluable tool. Click on Search, type in a name or concept in the search box presented, and the site will automatically call up related Fish & Wildlife sources for you to explore (which would otherwise take weeks to discover).

Desert Moon's Wolf Page

http://www.scs.unr.edu/~timb/desertm.html

Timothy Brogan has created a unique wolf site that practically brings the wolf into your living room. While it presents a great deal of information and artwork about wolves, it sets itself apart by offering browsers the opportunity to actually listen to a variety of wolf howls and to view them in action in a downloaded video, access to both of which is located on the home page.

The home page is well organized and inviting. The site boasts a Wolf Spirits section which explores the symbolism of wolves in various cultures, and a link to a newsgroup entitled "alt.wolves," the perfect informational supplement to this site.

Cochrane Ecological Institute (Swift Fox)

http://www.cuug.ab.ca:8001/~scholefp/swiftfox.html

The purpose of Alberta, Canada's Cochrane Ecological Institute is multifaceted. It seeks to educate the public about the plight of endangered species and to perfect methods of monitoring wildlife in their natural habitats. The organization is also involved in breeding endangered species in captivity with the intent of ultimately releasing them back into the wild. It is this latter mission that is of the utmost concern to the endangered swift fox, currently the target of such efforts.

Since 1983, the institute has been involved in the Canadian government's Canadian Swift Fox Re-introduction Programme, hoping someday to see this lovely creature—whose photo appears at the beginning of this site—enjoying health within a thriving population. Browsers may collect information on this project at the swift fox site, which also invites guests to donate to their cause if they feel so inclined. No doubt these wee foxes would be grateful.

World Wildlife Fund

http://www.wwf.org/

If you're seeking a flashy, colorful site rich in both graphics and information, this is it. An organization involved in the protection of hundreds of species from all corners of the globe, this site has its work cut out for it, and it succeeds in its mission with gusto.

With so broad a scope (a focus far broader than that solely of wild dogs), it is a relief to discover on the home page not only boxes that will take the browser to such areas as Species at Risk ("What, where, when, & why"), What's Cool ("Did you know...?"), Who We Are ("What we do &

where we work"), and What's New ("News and publications"), but also a box entitled Search WWF. By all means click that box and you will find an easy way to navigate through this site to the subject and species of your choice. As an added bonus, an additional Search feature appears in the What's New section, which allows browsers to search only that section.

The home page choices and the line-drawn graphics that illustrate them subsequently appear in each area, so you're never lost within this great maze, nor are you ever lacking in admiration for the artistry that went into the design of this site. Rarely will you find such vivid clever illustrations, and vibrant use of color in a Web site.

While those passionate about wild dogs may wish there was more concentration on the various canid species, it's difficult to resist this site that inevitably draws one in to the notion that all species deserve protection.

Consider the How to Help section, for example. This section, accessible from the home page, is unique in that it offers online information on membership (you may join right from the computer) and how-to advice on helping specific animals in currently critical situations, as well. From home page to finish, this site is a class act.

WWF Global Network

http://www.panda.org/research/facts/fct_dogfox.htm

The World Wildlife Fund for Nature (known as the World Wildlife Fund in the United States and Canada), concentrates on habitat and biological diversity throughout the world.

The World Wide Fund for Nature Web site which offers many of the same features as the primary WWF site, has text about endangered species throughout the world. You can use it's search function to learn about wild dogs all over the globe.

Typing in the site address provided here, for example, will transport you to an excellent article on the world's least known dogs (the dhole, the dingo, and the African wild dog) and many fox species that most people have never even heard of (the Bengal fox, the Cape fox, the Island grey fox). Also easily located through the Search function are articles on wolves, jackals, and African wild dogs. Listed at the end of each of these is the familiar bar of home page options that will take you instantly wherever you want to go.

The Searching Wolf

http://www.iup.edu/~wolf/wolves.htmlx

The Searching Wolf Web site, based at the Biology Department of Indiana University of Pennsylvania and administered by Webmaster Bill Forbes, Ph.D, is a vast collection of wolf-related resources.

Though simple in design—a plain, background with a single photo at the head of each section of a "searching wolf"—this well-organized site is rich with information, and it even offers a few surprises. For example, in the Wolves Howl and Growl section, browsers can listen to the mournful howl of a lone wolf or download the howling of a chorus of wolves.

This well-organized site's focus indeed runs the gamut, offering everything from Wolf Pictures to News to an incredibly complete listing of Interesting Wolf and Related Sites.

The latter section, which amplifies the title of the site, first offers a detailed listing of subjects. Clicking one of those subjects conjures up just about every related site on the Web—as well as individual articles presented in a concise, easy-to-access manner. Make your way through every nook and cranny of this site and you may just qualify for a doctorate in wolf studies.

Dingo Farm

http://www.wwwins.net.au/dog/dingofarm/01.html

Although it is part of a larger, all-dog-oriented site called Dogs Downunder managed by Denise Humphries (see Chapter 17), the Dingo Farm section of that site deserves special mention here. It's not every day that someone finds such a complete treatise on this unique wild dog of Australia.

This site focuses first on a dingo sanctuary in Australia operated by conservationist Bruce Jacobs, explaining first about what a dingo is and the valiant efforts being made to retain the purity of its gene pool. These pages are well-written and concise—and illustrated with excellent photos of these beautiful, though often misunderstood, animals.

After this introduction, the site offers the opportunity to explore the dingo further in sections that detail such issues as The Origins of the Dingo (thought to have arrived in Australia as long as 4000 years ago) and The Identification of a Pure Dingo (cross breeding with domestic dogs has made the pure dingo few and far between). Though the dingo is today rarely, if ever, seen in the wild, perhaps the Dingo Farm's efforts will see it returned to that niche someday.

The Predator Project

http://www.wildrockies.org/WildRock/ActiveOrg/PredProj/PredProj.html

There is nothing fancy about the Predator Project's Web site, but it has the potential of doing a lot of good for a lot of maligned creatures. One of those creatures is the animal that looks out from the top of the home page: the coyote.

The purpose of the Predator Project is to protect the forest and grassland habitat of animals that essentially compete with the human predator for survival. To see how they seek to accomplish this, simply follow the outline on the home page, and you will find several common-sense "initiatives." One of these, Conservation of Prairie Dog/Grasslands Ecosystem, holds that preserving the unique entity known as the prairie dog town would directly benefit a variety of species that are dependent on these fascinating creatures. One of those species is the coyote.

Crisp, clear, and to the point, this site, under the guidance of Carla Neasel, makes no attempts toward flash and panache, but it supplies vital information to those who share the vision of sharing the earth with our fellow predators—and thus perhaps preserving our own survival on this planet.

Swift Fox: Vulpes Velox

http://www.afternet.com/~teal/sfox.html

The swift fox is the smallest of North America's wild dogs, yet even it deserves an information site of its own, and here it has one. Presented in a very personal style that reflects the author's affection for this diminutive animal, this site from Ray Rasmussen offers browsers the opportunity to get to know the swift fox and to work toward preventing its extinction.

This page presents the swift fox's vital statistics in a clean and well-organized format. Within minutes you will know all about this small canid, after which you can browse through the many links listed to related Web sites on swift foxes and other fox species, other wild dog species, and organizations that are working to save this endangered animal.

A bonus on this page is a story written by the author's daughter, Terra. Click on "I Am a Swift Fox" on the home page, and read this tale of "one of the few swift foxes of Alberta." Beautifully written from the fox's point of view, it is no wonder that this story is what sparked the author's father's interest in the swift fox in the first place. It may do the same to any browser who comes across it.

Vulpinification

http://www.fysh.org/foxes/

Lest the name of this site be a source of confusion, it is derived from the scientific name for the fox, Vulpus. Once you understand that, it's clear that this site, the brainchild of Farthing W. Fox, is all about foxes and those who love them.

Indeed you will find all things vulpine here, although the site concentrates more on the mythical and spiritual existence of the fox, than it does on its biology and lifestyle, the latter of which is represented by the lovely collection of photos in the Gallery section. Focusing on the spiritual elements, author Fox implies in the introduction, is a natural for this animal, because the fox is what one would consider a "totem" animal in Native American cultures.

Short, and to the point, the home page leads the browser into a mythic world where foxes speak and often outwit seemingly weaker souls. Click on Fables and Stories, for example, and find a complete list of Aesop's fox tales (the fox was obviously a favorite of this storyteller), as well as Native American folktales and links to other fox-related titles.

Nebraska Wildlife—Coyotes

http://ngp.ngpc.state.ne.us/wildlife/coyote.html

Coyote sites are few and far between on the Net, perhaps reflecting the fact that this is one of the dog family's most maligned members. Despite its undeserved reputation as a bloodthirsty killer that wants only to decimate a neighborhood's cat population, the coyote is also the wild species that humans are most likely to spot in the wild, for this opportunist often lives in close proximity to humans in urban and suburban environments. Unbeknownst to them, the humans benefit from the coyote's propensity to hunt small rodents, keeping the mouse and rat population in balance.

While this site, an offshoot of a larger Nebraska wildlife site, seems to concentrate only on Nebraska's coyotes, the biological information presented is standard for all coyotes.

Being from a state agency, it is also understandable that the site would concentrate as well on livestock depredation by coyotes and the human desire to hunt the species. But what is unique about this site and makes it a valuable addition to a listing of wild dog Web sites is its direct link with a click on the headphone icon to a coyote howl—higher in pitch and even more mournful in tone than the wolf's howl. The opportunity to hear the coyote on the computer makes this site a valuable asset to those seeking knowledge about the world's wild dogs.

Ralph Maughan's Wolf Report
http://www.poky.srv.net/~jimrm/maughan.html

This site produced by Dr. Ralph Maughan, is so rich in text links that you will begin to think the entire page is printed in hypertext.

Clicking on every single one of those linked words and phrases and exploring what awaits beyond them would take days, if not weeks, but that is a tribute to the wealth of information contained in this site which is focused on the wolves being reintroduced to Yellowstone and central Idaho,

Enter this Web site and you will learn of the history of these wolves and the projects in which they are playing such key roles, including highly technical material, as well as that written with the layperson in mind. You will meet every wolf in every pack, and gain access to frequent Wolf Update Reports dating back to 1995. This site could keep the avid wolf advocate busy for a very long time.

Miscellaneous Dog-Related Sites

Despite the breadth of the other chapters in this book, there are canine sites on the World Wide Web that defy inclusion in any one of them. This is due in great part to the dedication, creativity, and computer expertise of dog lovers around the world.

We have tried here to bring you a sample of some of the more unique and unusual canine sites in a chapter all their own. They run the gamut from pages that will make you cry to sites that will make you laugh. Some might even disgust you, while others will provide you with valuable information not found anywhere else on the Web.

So sit back and loosen up your mouse for some unconventional dog-related browsing. And as you move through these sites, keep your eye out for links to even more singular pages.

Choosing a Dog Breed

http://www.cris.com/~ahendrix/choosing.html

A page devoted entirely to the subject of choosing a dog, Choosing a Dog Breed describes the reasons why taking the time to pick the right pet is so important. The author, Amy Hendrix, educates would-be dog owners with good, solid information.

Hendrix begins with Questions to Consider, which covers subjects like "What size is right for you?", "Where

continued after the feature section

Pet Loss & Rainbow Bridge

http://www.primenet.com/~meggie/bridge.htm

The price to pay for loving a dog is the pain of someday losing it. This is something that most people learn when they are children, after their first dog and closest friend passes on after years of devoted companionship. But the pain is often no less intense for adults.

Many people who grieve for their dogs feel alone and misunderstood. Comments like "Why are you so upset? You can just get another one," and "It was only a dog," drive grieving owners to keep their pain to themselves.

While the same insensitive comments may still be heard, mourning dog owners now have places to go where they *will* be understood. One of those places is the Rainbow Bridge Web site.

The Rainbow Bridge site is based on a story written by an unknown pet lover, describing what happens when a pet dies, leaving a devastated owner behind. The tale describes a beautiful place "just this side of Heaven," called the Rainbow Bridge. Pets go to this place of meadows and hills, and run and play with other animal spirits. Eventually, each pet is reunited with his or her owner, whose soul has come to this special place. Together, the two cross the Rainbow Bridge together into Heaven.

Many grieving dog owners find comfort in the story of the Rainbow Bridge when they are trying to cope with the anguish of never seeing their beloved pet again. The popularity of this site is testament to this.

The Rainbow Bridge Web site, run by a kind and compassionate animal lover named Kathie Maffitt with the help of volunteers, is a place for these saddened dog owners to come. Here they can post their own comments about the pet they've lost and even submit photos that are placed online as a tribute. This site is part of the Mourning Light Grief Support Webring, a group of pages, designed to link together in a virtual circle, for bereaved pet owners.

There is a lot to look at on the Rainbow Bridge site. The Tribute of the Month is dedicated to special pets that have passed away, and it recently included a list of pets that recently lost their lives in a tragedy at an Iowa animal shelter. Poems written by children and others close to the pets appear as somber and gentle music plays in the background.

The other tributes on the site are arranged by animal. Cats, birds, horses, rabbits, guinea pigs, and other pets are all honored here, with dogs having the greatest number of entries. Poems, stories, and photos abound for dogs of every breed, shape, size, and color.

A new feature on the Rainbow Bridge site is the Message Board, a bulletin board where grieving pet owners can share support and sympathy. For people who need someone to understand their loss, a place like this can make an incredible difference.

It's impossible to visit this site without feeling emotional. Be sure to have a box of tissues on hand.

will the dog live?" and "What past experience do you have with dogs?" She explains the reasons each one of these considerations is important and then tells readers what their answers should ultimately be.

Resources on choosing a dog are an important element at this site, and links to breed-specific FAQS, books on the subject, e-mail links and other places to learn more are included. After you read this site, you should have a pretty good idea of what kind of dog you should get—if any.

Bad Dog Chronicles

http://www.baddogs.com

The Bad Dog Chronicles Web site is dedicated to the misdeeds of dogs everywhere. Featuring stories submitted by average dog owners detailing the troubles their canines have caused, this site manages to poke fun at the irreverence of dogs without encouraging bad dog behavior.

Stories are organized by Hall of Fame tales, Newest stories, By Breed, and Recent Awards. The date of submission for each story is included, along with the breed of dog, the dog's name and, oddly enough, the price the owners paid for the dastardly critter. For those considering certain breeds, it might be wise to check out the antics of those particular representatives at this site. Photographs of each breed can also be found online.

Some of these stories are incredibly funny, and there are so many of them that you could spend all day just browsing through this entertaining site.

Bad Dog Humour Collection

http://geog.utoronto.ca/reynolds/humour.html

Harold Reynolds, a Ph.D. candidate in the Department of Geology at the University of Toronto, can appreciate the humor in owning pets. This is obvious after viewing his Bad Dog Humor Collection, which consists of funny comments about naughty and dumb dogs contributed by readers.

From Reynolds' home page, you can click on Bad Dogs or Dumb Dogs (or a list of other animal stories, if you are so inclined), where you will be transported to a page of phrases that dog owners would like to get their pets to write down and refer to on a regular basis. Because these comments are based on real-life situations, they ring funny and true.

The Bad Dog phrases cover topics like "[fill in the blank] is Not a Toy," and a variety of annoying and embarrassing habits. The Dumb Dog list features postings from dog owners with amusing stories of stupid stunts their dogs have pulled.

Traveldog

http://www.traveldog.com/homepage/homebase.htm

If you like to travel with your dog, then Traveldog is the place to be. The entire site is devoted to taking your dog with you when you leave home.

The site starts with the TravelDog Welcome Mat, featuring pet-friendly lodging around the country. The listings are organized by region, and then by state.

Next on the list is TravelDog Products and Services, featuring a few items that are of use to canines on the go. The TravelDog Tips area is most valuable, as it contains advice on how to choose a kennel, how to travel by plane with a dog, how to drive places with pooch in tow, and how to stay at a hotel without incident.

The Hotlinks area is useful too, as it links to other Web sites with relevant travel information.

Dean's Dog House

http://www.lynda.com/acwg/dsmith/home/

Dog owners usually have a good sense of humor (they have to) and love to share jokes that feature canines. Dean James is one of these people, and has created a Web site filled with drolleries concerning man's best friend.

Most of the jokes here are very funny, but quite a few of them are a bit off-color and for adults only. For people who have trouble remembering jokes, they are quick and easy to print.

Signs You Have a Dumb Dog

www.cbs.com/lateshow/lists/931019.html

Late night talk show host David Letterman is known in the dog community as a real dog lover who enjoys featuring canines on his show, *Late Night With David Letterman*, every now and then.

Aside from the Stupid Pet Tricks segment, Letterman's Top Ten Lists are one of the funniest parts of the show. In 1993, one evening's program featured the "Top Ten Signs You Have a Dumb Dog." The hilarious list, which includes comments like "Has suffered over two dozen concussions from toilet seat falling on his head," is posted as part of the CBS television network Web site.

NewPet.Com

www.newpet.com

Visitors to the NewPet.Com Web site are greeted by a dog named Ripley and a cat named Contessa. Each begs to be taken home, and Ripley's wagging tail is hard to resist.

The purpose of NewPet.Com is to assist new pet owners in learning to care for and enjoy their new member of the family. A sort of virtual hand-holder, NewPet.Com is a great primer for people who have never owned a dog before.

The MatchMaker area beckons first and starts off with questions to ask yourself before you choose a dog. Once you've established that you are ready and able to embark on dog ownership, you can move to the section covering where to look for a new pet. Much emphasis is placed here on getting a dog from an animal shelter or a responsible breeder.

Quick Tips, the next area in the site menu, details the kind of information pet owners typically need to handle their new arrival. Articles on bringing the pet home, house-breaking tips, and feeding and health care are included, as are words of advice on flea and tick control, grooming, and travel.

In the Best Friends category, a hodgepodge of fun and personal items appear, including a Pick-A-Name area, photos of browsers' dogs, and the story of Ripley, the site's spokespooch.

Overall, NewPet.Com provides an excellent public service to new pet owners, and every neophyte to the world of dogs should visit it.

The Dog Run/Dog Park Reporter

http://www.mindspring.com/~patmar/

The phenomenon of dog parks and dog runs is somewhat new, and is slowly catching on across the country. The concept arose from the frustration that dog owners in urban and suburban areas often experience over the lack of places they can safely let their dogs run free to play and be with other dogs. Through this frustration, the notion of enclosed areas used exclusively for dogs was born, and now a handful exist around the country. Examples of fenced areas can be found in city parks, piers, and beaches.

The Dog Run/Dog Park Reporter Web site is dedicated to providing information to dog owners about where and how they can enjoy dog parks and runs with their pets. Each listing contains the exact address of the place, who to contact for information, the organization that runs it, the approximate size of the area, the type of surface (grass, sand, dirt), and the facilities and amenities for humans.

An area for Dog Run Issues and News is also linked here, featuring discussions on waste cleanup, rules, problem, laws, and other subjects that related to the concept of dog runs.

As evidenced by the short list of states with official dog parks on this list, there are not as many of these places as dog owners might like. But that doesn't mean you can't work on starting one of your own with this Web site as your guide.

You Know You've Gone to the Dogs When...

http://www.dogpatch.org/gotodogs.html

Dog people are one-of-a-kind creatures who often drive their spouses, friends, and family to distraction with their passion for dogs. Mary Jo Sminkey, author of the huge Dogpatch site, is all too familiar with this unusual lifestyle. With the help of other dog owners, she has compiled a very funny list of ways you know you've gone completely berserk over dogs.

Some of the statements that can be found here are "You're more concerned with the dogs' needs that your own when the budget gets tight," and "At least three of your five weeks vacation are scheduled around grooming, vaccinations and dental cleaning for the dogs." If this sounds like you, visit this page and dicsover that you are not alone.

Stupid Pet Photos

http://www.digital-cafe.com/~webmaster/pets00.html

There are few things more hilarious than some of the goofy poses that dogs put themselves in (sometimes with human help). The popularity of the animal segments on the television show "America's Funniest Home Videos" is proof of that.

The still version of this phenomenon is funny too, and exists on the Internet in the form of Stupid Pet Photos, a gallery of hilarious shots of pets—many of which are dogs—doing incredibly silly things.

There were a total of 23 pages on this site at the time of this writing, all containing photos submitted by browsers. The pictures appear in a small size along with information about the pet, and clicking on an image will provide you with a larger format. There are pictures of dogs dressed up in absurd outfits, sleeping puppies piled up in heaps, and even a dog with its nose stuck inside a bottle of beer. (There is a lot of cat stuff here to wade through to get to the dog photos, so beware.)

You can stay with the photos and chuckle, or you can submit your own goofy shots.

The Dog Poo Page
http://www.1.bond.net/~keitht/

If you have a sophomoric sense of humor, then you may enjoy the Dog Poo Page, a site dedicated to the exploration of dog doo.

The crude Dog Poo logo on the opening page is a sign of things to come, and will certainly weed out the faint of heart. If you dare, click on it and get a main menu of items, starting with The Dog Body Parts game, a harmless and simple game that calls for putting a dog together one piece at a time. Cooking With Feces, the next option, contains five recipes using dog poo, including Golden Brown Pancakes, Lottas DungBalls, Swedish Carp Cake, Feces Pieces Pie, and Buffalo Pattie Chili. Reading the recipes will give you the distinct (and unsettling) impression that the author has actually cooked with dog excrement.

The Art of Dog Poo is next, and—you guessed it— features artistic renderings of dog doo. Also included is a poem about poo as well as song lyrics. And as if all this weren't enough, the Dog Poo Photo Album contains a selection of photographs of you-know-what, in disgusting color and resolution.

If all this has piqued your interest, go back to the home page when you are done and scroll down to the bottom so you don't miss the moving graphic of a dog going to the bathroom at the bottom of the page.

The Dog Hause
http://www2.dgsys.com/~hollyb/index.html

The Dog Hause is a fun site loaded with all kinds of dog-related goodies. Created and maintained by animal lover and webmaster Holly M. Burns, the site's description of itself as "a playground for pets and pet lovers" couldn't be more accurate.

On the Dog Hause home page, you will find 15 hyperlinks to some very enjoyable spots. The majority of them are specific to dogs, but cats and other animals are represented here as well.

The best places to visit are Funny Animal Stuff, where topics like "Reasons Dogs Don't Use Computers" and "You Know You're a Dog Person" can be found; Rule of Thumb (where myths are dispelled and truths are told); Quotes & Proverbs; Animal Trivia (where more myths are squelched); Free Graphics (filled with cartoon icons of dogs that you can download at no cost); Pet Photographs (containing pictures of various browsers' pets); Animal Sounds (with a couple of canine vocalizations included); and Dog FAQ (a link to the rec.pets.dogs FAQ home page, which contains loads of good information).

The dog-related material is mixed throughout the site, but almost everything is categorized by animal, so it is easy to find.

Kiva's Dog House

http://www2.huskynet.com/kiva/

In 1996, a Siberian Husky named Kiva was attacked and almost fatally wounded by another dog that was running loose in the street. While stories such as Kiva's are not uncommon, most dogs who suffer this tragedy don't have an entire Web site devoted to them.

Katrina Walden, a pet lover touched by Kiva's story, developed Kiva's Dog House to help raise funds for the Siberian's huge veterinary expenses. Even after enough money was raised, Walden kept the site going to address the issue of dog-on-dog attacks.

At the Newsstand area of the site, press coverage of Kiva's attack is posted. A progress report on Kiva, who by now has almost completely recovered from her injury, is updated monthly.

The Pawprints link takes you to a guestbook, while the Photo Album contains pictures of Kiva as a puppy as well as photos of her after the attack. An area for dog owners to converse on the issue of dog attacks is also here.

A fund has been set up by Walden to assist other dogs with severe attack-related injuries, and she promises more information on this in the months to come.

Pets in the White House

http://www.whitehouse.gov/WH/kids/html/pets.html

Not every pet who has lived in the White House has been a dog, but most of them have been. The White House Web site has a page devoted just to former First Pets, and dogs play a big part in it.

In order to find the dogs here, you'll need to scroll past the mocking images of Socks the Cat and wade through the occasional farm animal. But photos and short stories about pooches like Yuki, Lyndon Johnson's dog, and Fala, the Scottish Terrier belonging to Franklin Roosevelt, are worth the trouble. Ronald Reagan's King Charles Spaniel Rex and George Bush's Millie are also among the noteworthy canines on this site.

Allergic to Dogs?

http://members.aol.com/AHTerrier/allergies.html

There are many people who feel a deep need to be close to dogs, yet also suffer from terrible allergies caused by the dander in dogs' coats. Dog lover Kristina MacGregor understands this problem because she suffers from the same affliction, and has taken to time to create a Web site to help others with this dilemma.

If you are allergic to dogs but are determined to have one anyway (or already do), you will find this page extremely helpful. Based on Brown's personal experiences, the site contains valuable information on living with dogs, what kinds of breeds are best for allergy suffers (along with links to their sites), links to other pet-allergy pages, and connection to companies that sell products for allergy sufferers.

Cassie's 3-Legged Dog Club

http://lark.cc.ukans.edu/~kurdavis/doghome.html

There are a number of reasons a dog can end up with only three legs. Cancer surgery and injuries are just two of the tragedies can leave a dog with this permanent handicap. But this doesn't mean the dog's days are over. On the contrary, many three-legged dogs live full and happy lives.

Cassie's 3-Legged Dog Club site was created by Cynthia Davis, a warm-hearted dog lover who adopted a canine amputee from an animal shelter and named her Cassie. She created Cassie's 3-Legged Dog Club so other owners of three-legged dogs could come together and share stories about their special pets.

Davis' site is new and she is still gathering stories and photos to post. If you are the owner of one of these special dogs, drop in on the site and send her a note or a photo.

Canine Image Archives

http://www.nd.edu/~mbuening/dog_pics.html

If you enjoy looking at photos of other peoples' dogs (as many dog lovers do), then check out the Canine Image Archives, maintained by Michael G. Buening. Hundreds of jpeg and gif images featuring all kinds of dogs can be accessed at this site, accompanied by short biographies of each pet. It's easy to spend hours looking through here, taking in the adorable and sometimes humorous shots of canines from around the world.

Pet Name Pages

http://www.primenet.com/~meggie/petname.htm

If you are in the process of trying to come up with a name for a dog, then you should certainly pay a visit to the Pet Name Pages, a well-organized and well-designed site devoted exclusively to finding a great name for your pet.

Run by Webmaster extraordinaire Kathie Maffitt, author of the Rainbow Bridge site, the Pet Name Pages allow you to search for possible names from a huge list of categories. Names are organized according to Pet Type, Color, Origin, People Namesakes (famous people), Animal Namesakes (well-known dogs), Personality Traits, Food Reference, Signs of the Times (timely monikers), and Fun and Nicknames.

If you can't find a name for your dog after searching through this site, you'd best give up and just call him Rover.

Tale Waggers

http://www.ddc.com/waggers/

Most dog lovers enjoy reading stories about dogs, and if you are one of these people, take a look at Tale Waggers, a site made up of nothing but canine yarns.

There's a modest list of stories to read on this site, but they will keep you busy for a while. Pieces like Dog Humor, The Character, Doggie Carols, Meet the Kids, and even a few non-fiction articles on traveling with dogs and choosing the right pet are worth checking out.

A Dog's Prayer

http://www.chanton.com/prayer.html

This short, sweet and simple page will bring a tear to your eye if you love dogs as much as you think you do. Written by Beth Norman Harris, A Dog's Prayer is not meant for the ears of the Creator, but rather for humans. It gently asks for the love, kindness and compassion that every dog deserves, but not every dog gets. Dog owners should read this as a reminder of the great responsibility we have to our pets.

Hotel Search

http://www.travelweb.com/thisco/global/fast-search.html

Frequent travelers will want to check out this site, which features a hotel database and a search engine that allows you to look for accommodations that permit dogs.

This is how it works: Enter your travel destination, specifically the city, state or province, and country. Then, go down to the Property Features and Amenities Search and select "Pets Allowed," along with any other requirements you may have. Then start your search. You'll be provided with the names of facilities that meet your needs. Details on the hotel (including e-mail links where applicable) are another option, as is a photograph of the lodging.

Why Dogs are Better Than Men

http://home.cc.umanitoba.ca/~umorbeta/dogs.htm

A take-off on the "Why Beer is Better than Men/Women" lists, the Why Dogs are Better than Men Web site lists a huge number of humorous reasons why the female sex should prefer the company of canines over that of men. Including statements like "dogs are very direct about wanting to go out" and "you can train a dog," this is an amusing place to visit. There is also a list of ways that dogs and men are the same (both take up too much room in the bed and both are suspicious of the postman), and ways in which dogs fall down on the job (men can buy you presents and men can do math stuff). And just so men don't take all the heat, "How Dogs are Better than Women" follows, with comments like "dogs will listen to their masters," and "dogs don't get half when they leave you."

Dogs Down Under

http://www.wwwins.net.au/dog/downunder.html

The Australian authors of Dogs Down Under aim to educate the world about Australian dogs, and they do a good job. If you have an Australian breed, want to own one, or just have an interest in Australia's dog community, this site is the place to go.

Included here is a section called Australia's Own Breeds, which features breeds created in the land down under. Photographs and information on the history and characteristics of each breed are included.

The dingo, a wild dog that has been a resident of the Australian continent for thousands of years, receives a lot of attention in this site. In an area devoted just to dingos, a huge amount of information on this unique dog can be found, including coat color, temperament, ownership, registration, a bibliography, information on how to get involved in saving the dingo's purity, and a mailing address for the National Dingo Association.

Other areas of this site include a list of the most popular Australian breeds, information on the Australian show system, facts on importing dogs to Australia, and even a question and answer area for behavior problems.

CHAPTER 19

All About Dogs

There is so much to know about dogs, and there are a lot of Webmasters out there who want to spread the word. The category of general canine Web sites is a large one, good news for dog lovers who want to get an overview of what's out there. If you fit this description, the sites in this chapter are the ones you should visit first.

While each of the many general canine Web sites strives to be the most complete, there are only a few that come close. However, while a select few sites are able to provide massive amounts of information, it is impossible to include everything there is to know about dogs in one place. By exploring a number of different sites, you can put together a nearly complete library of information on dogs that you can refer back to again and again.

Each of the sites listed in this chapter has its own personality and style. Some are small and simple, others are complex and time-consuming. Certain sites provide information in small, condensed packages. Others try to be as in-depth and thorough as they can be. But despite their differences, there is one thing they all have in common: an expressed concern for the well-being of dogs. Not only do all these sites cover the technicalities of breed standards and other aspects of the hobby of purebred dogs, but they also strive to promote the best interest of dogs by providing information on rescue, adoption, and responsible ownership.

Some of the sites listed here also include information on other pets, although the canine areas within them are undoubtedly the largest. While a few require wading

continued after the feature section

Acme Pet

http://www.acmepet.com

Acme Pet is probably the largest general pet information site on the World Wide Web. Catering to lovers of dogs, cats, fish, horses, birds, reptiles, and exotics, Acme Pet specializes in links to other sites, organized by subject. In addition to these links, Acme Pet provides its own exclusive information for each of the designated animal species.

The Canine Guide is one of the larger areas on the Acme Pet site. Before you visit the Canine Guide, however, you may want to check out some of the areas listed on the home page. Dog information is scattered throughout.

The best spot on the home page is the Acme Pet Times, a virtual newspaper that contains in-depth features on many aspects of pet ownership, including health, ownership, training, and humane issues.

In the Multi-Media Gallery, browsers who have capabilities to view multimedia images can select sounds, movies, still pictures, software, and shared files.

Once you have finished investigating the links on the home page, move into the Canine Guide for dog specific areas. Begin with the Welcome Waggin', which will provide you with details on the Acme Pet site.

Club Acme is worth checking out if you like to interact with fellow dog-lovers. Here you will find Pet Chat Rooms, where you can talk to dog enthusiasts around the world; Pet Bulletin Boards regarding current pet-related topics; Pet Q&A, where browser questions are answered by a panel of pet experts; Cool Pet Site of the Day featuring the Webmasters' site *du jour*; and Acme's Pet Friends, where browsers can enter stories and photos of their own dogs for display in the site.

Back at the Canine Guide, you will find access to the Market Place, featuring classified ads covering doggy items like calendars, collars, urns, first-aid kits, and I. D. tags.

The Canine Library puts a wide variety of subjects at your disposal. The Grooming Resource provides articles on caring

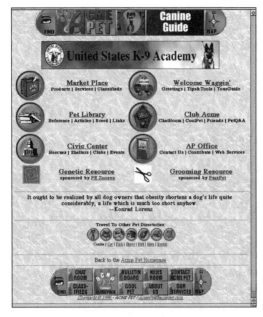

for your dog's coat, along with a bulletin board, a glossary of grooming terms, links to other grooming sites and a contribution area where you can add your opinions and experiences.

If you are a newcomer to the world of dogs check out the Canine Glossary, for dog-specific terminology in the area of anatomy, commonly seen abbreviations, and just about any other subject.

The Canine Forums area within the Canine Library is a variation on Club Acme. Listed here are dog-related chat rooms, links to newsgroups covering subjects like pet loss, dog behavior and canine activities, and e-mail lists for dog fanciers, who want postings to come directly to their mail boxes.

Also in the Canine Library, you'll find the Canine Genetic Resource, an incredibly in-depth area on the subject of genetic disease.

The Canine Guide also includes a Canine Civic Center, with links to shelters, rescue groups and dog clubs, along with a calendar of canine events. A lost-and-found classified section is also included here, complete with e-mail links to the individuals placing the ads.

through general pet information to find the canine information, they also provide an opportunity to learn about other domestic animals. If you are like most dog owners, you also own other pets and may find yourself unable to keep from wandering off the canine path while in some of these general sites.

WWW.Woofs

http://www.woofs.org

WWW.Woofs calls itself an online publication, and exists solely on the Web. This site bills itself as a "non-profit newspaper dedicated to the benefit of our best buddies."

The WWW.Woofs home page shows a listing of places to go, using a bare-bones format, but a click on Front Page takes you to a digital assault that is so full of graphics and moving images that it takes considerable time to load. Designed like the front page of a newspaper, the appropriately named Front Page features light news stories, flashing signs, and moving dogs.

A set of icons at the bottom of the Front Page takes you to Creative (a mix of images and text), a Chat room, and, most notably, the Adoption area. Adoption features separate pages within the site devoted to several rescue and placement organizations. Photos of dogs in need of homes are included in, along with information on how to adopt them.

The overall tone of WWW.Woofs is light and fun. A Hollywood theme seems to run throughout the site, including stories about celebrities' dogs and even a chance to talk to celebrities by signing the Guestbook.

Kahoos K-9 Line

http://www.iceinternet.com/kahoos/kk9hompg.htm

Kahoos K-9 Line is a modest site authored by Bull Terrier aficionados John and Shelley Ledfors that contains good general information on buying and keeping a purebred dog.

The home page features two options: the General Canine Information Index and Information about Bull Terriers. A click on the information index takes you to a page that offers a list of dog registries and organizations, plus options for general-interest articles, canine-site links, and more.

The most valuable information In this site concerns purchasing a purebred puppy. There is in-depth information on where to buy a dog, how to choose a reliable breeder, and even a "breeder selection questionnaire" to help prospective buyers choose a responsible seller. A section on paperwork also covers buyer/seller contracts, how to read pedigrees (including descriptions of canine titles and how to make sense of them), and an explanation of the registration process.

Ethical discussions of the lifetime commitment of dog ownership and whether to breed your dog are included, as is information about different aspects of training, how dog shows and other competitive canine events work, and, finally, how to purchase a show prospect.

All Pets Com

http://www.allpets.com

All Pets Com calls itself a "comprehensive pet magazine and encyclopedia," and it lives up to the moniker. Created by The Ayzenberg Group, the site features contributions from veterinarians and specialized writers.

While dogs are not the only pet included in this extensive Web site (there are also areas for cats, horses, fish, reptiles, and exotics), All Pets Com is big enough to give very extensive treatment to canine subjects.

From the All Pets Com home page, an icon called All Dogs takes you to an attractive, well-organized starting page for the canine section of the site. You can view an index of topics or conduct a search by topic of what you are looking for. Or, you can just browse through the vast number of categories covering dog-related subjects.

The first place to start your surfing is at Message Central & Chit n' Chat. Here you will have the option to read and write letters to the editors of the site, post messages to other dog lovers on the All Pets Com bulletin board, or look through the Photo Gallery of browsers' dogs.

Next on the list of spots to investigate is the Parade of Breeds. The title of this area makes it sound as if the information here will be exclusively on the different breeds. Not so. While the Pedigree Dogs section contains information and full-screen photographs of over 200 breeds of dogs, including hard-to-find information on diseases peculiar to certain breeds, there is a lot more here than might meet the eye.

Other sections within the Parade of Breeds category include Career Dogs, covering dogs who work with the handicapped, dogs who do search and rescue, dogs who pull sleds for a living, and other gainfully employed pooches; Mixed Breed Dogs, featuring Adopt-A-Pup, which encourages the adoption of mixed breeds and provides information on what to look for when searching for a mixed breed; Breed Rescue, explaining the concept of purebred dog rescue and information on how to reach local rescue clubs; and a Breeder's Listings, containing advertisements from breeders selling purebred puppies.

A return to the home page will provide you the option of clicking on something called Canine Care, where information on dealing with a new puppy, canine nutrition, traveling with your dog, playing with your dog, grooming, senior citizen dogs and how to choose a puppy can be found. An interesting and unusual approach to training information is located here too, under two categories: Training/Good Dog!, which covers basic obedience training, and Behavior/Bad Dog!, dealing with problems and negative behaviors.

If you are looking for information on canine health, The Clinic area has an Ask the Vet column and details on how to deal with emergencies. Most interesting are two places within this realm that break down the canine anatomy and provide basic information on canine genetics.

A listing of dog shows, along with detailed explanations of how shows work, are included in the Events area. Book reviews and products are featured in the Review section, and products and services relating to dogs can be found under the PetsMarket.

As if all this wasn't enough, there are quizzes, puzzles, and stories in the Fun Stuff area, and listings of articles, favorite links, and dog organizations in the Resources section.

All Pets Com strives to be a complete resource on dogs, and does a good job of it. This site is well worth the time it takes to peruse it.

Pet Station/Dog Domain
http://www.petstation.com/dogs.html#TOP

Pet Station is a huge site that caters to people who love pets. Within Pet Station, there are different realms, each devoted to a specific kind of animal. Birds, cats, horses, fish, reptiles, small mammals and of course dogs are all included in this vast area dedicated to promoting responsible pet ownership and the humane treatment of animals.

The opening page of the Dog Domain contains several areas of interest. The Breed Showcase features a highlighted breed, and includes a photo and a short piece of text. In Dogs We Love, stories from browsers about their own dogs, along with photos, are on display. The Vet Is In area features browser inquiries and answers from a veterinarian. Training tips, a library containing articles and listings of canine resources, an area to buy dog products and a photo gallery are all included in this site.

The Pet Channel
http://www.thepetchannel.com

Another general pet site, The Pet Channel features information on a variety of pets in addition to dogs. Unlike some of the other general sites, The Pet Channel does not separate the dog data from the rest, requiring browsers to do a little searching for canine-related subjects.

The areas containing doggy information include Pet Health, where vets answer medical questions; Pet News, covering updates and timely items about animals; Pet Fun, including horoscopes, contests, browsers' pets and other goodies; Find A Pet, featuring a lost-and-found and a list of shelters and rescue organizations; Pet Training, focusing primarily on dogs; Pet Shop, listing products recommended by browsers; and the User Forum, consisting of a bulletin board for animal lovers.

While the dog information in this site is scattered throughout, most of it is of a quality worth looking for.

Rec.Pets.Dogs FAQ Home Page

http://www.zmall.com/pet_talk/dog-faqs/homepage.html

The Rec.Pets.Dogs FAQ Home Page is a very low-key site, lacking the splashy graphics seen on other canine pages. However, its content is probably the most comprehensive of any dog area on the Web. Maintained by dog owner and computer whiz Cindy Tittle Moore, Rec.Pets.Dogs FAQ Home Page contains massive amounts of articles on just about any dog-related subject you can think of.

The opening page of this site presents you with a variety of search options. The Table of Contents area will present every article on the site in alphabetical order. Or you can choose articles on a huge number of subject titles such as training, nutrition, behavior, activities, and much more.

There is some valuable information in this site. For newcomers to the dog world, the list of canine acronyms is priceless, as it lists every single title granted to show and working dogs. Conversation acronyms used in everyday cyberspeak are also included. The list of the dog-related rec.pets newsgroups and what they cover is also a treasure.

Cyberpet

http://www.cyberpet.com

Using an outer space theme to emphasize the cyberspace aspect of the World Wide Web, Cyberpet strives to provide information to both dog and cat lovers. A click on Cyber-Dog, located on the colorful home page, will take you to the dog realm of this medium-sized site.

Throughout your journey through Cyberpet, you will be asked to "select a mission for Cyber-Dog," a masked cartoon dog and your constant companion throughout the site. He will lead you to a Breeders Showcase, where breeds are listed in alphabetical order. Choose the breed you are interested in, and see information and a photo. If you aren't sure which breed you want, go to the Breed Info section. You will be asked to list minimal criteria you are seeking in a dog. The database will take you to a breed that fits the bill.

The Articles section of Cyber-Dog has a lot of information on finding a puppy, health and nutrition, behavior, rescue, pet overpopulation, and more. While many of the articles reflect the personal opinions of the authors on certain subjects, there is some good information here that makes reading most of them worthwhile.

Products, services, and publications are also included, as is a bulletin board and selection of live chat rooms. A set of links to other canine Web pages tops off the site.

Canadian Animal Network

http://www.pawprints.com

The Canadian Animal Network was created for and by Canadians, but also offers some useful information to American dog lovers.

While sections such as the Pet Adoption Program, Vet Clinic Directory, Business Directory, and Retail Centre will only be of use to Canadian browsers, there are other areas that have international appeal.

Ask the Vet and Ask the Experts, two question-and-answer areas, provide dog owners with the opportunity to find out how veterinarians, trainer, and other animal professionals feel about certain subjects. The site's canine bulletin board is open to all dog lovers, and the CAN Features section contains articles on timely subjects, true stories about dogs, and more.

Don't let the Canadian slant scare you away from this site. The Canadian Animal Network has something to offer all dog lovers.

Adognet

http://www.adognet.com

Adognet is not a fancy site and, in fact, could use a design face lift. But despite its visual flaws, there is a lot of solid information here that is invaluable to dog lovers.

The site's primary value is as a resource guide. By using advertisements, lists, and links, Adognet manages to provide a comprehensive selection of hard-to-find contacts in the various areas of dogdom.

One of the greatest finds on this site is the listing of national breed clubs for nearly all the American Kennel Club breeds. The names, addresses and phone numbers of the corresponding secretaries are all here, and some even link to the club's Web site. Since the phone numbers of breed club secretaries are not even published by the American Kennel Club in its quarterly listing, this is a real gold mine for people doing in-depth research on specific breeds. The listing of national purebred rescue organizations is also comprehensive and hard to come by.

The remainder of canine listings on Adognet are in the form of advertisements. A good number of trainers, handlers, judges, pet sitters, groomers, dog show photographers, boarding kennels, and breeders all participate in this site, making it a good place to hunt around for doggy services.

Healthypet

http://www.healthypet.com

Although the American Animal Hospital Association is an organization of 13,000 veterinarians and hospitals, its

Healthypet Web site does not focus on veterinary issues alone. While there is a strong slant toward medical topics, dog owners can find good solid information on other dog-related topics at this site.

Since Healthypet covers all pets and not just dogs, the canine material needs to hunted out. However, it's worth the work. The greatest wealth of dog information is in the Pet Care Library. Categories such as Behavior (chewing, digging, crate training, housetraining), Common Health Problems (rabies, parvovirus, fleas, skin problems), Human Animal Bond (health benefits of owning pets, grieving, ownership survey results), Nutrition (overfeeding), and Preventive Care (choosing a vet, advancements in veterinary medicine) are loaded with wisdom for dog owners.

There are other places in the site where tidbits of dog info can be found. Interactive areas such as Tell Us About Your Pet and the Kids Coloring Page allow direct involvement with the site, and the Pet Care Library provides a big selection of books on a variety of dog and pet-related subjects, along with instructions on how to order.

PetNet

http://www.petnet.com

This site was developed by and for Australian dog owners, but there are several areas of interest to canine aficionados everywhere.

A place called SelectAPet allows you to choose the right dog for your living conditions. Browsers who fill out an online questionnaire are rewarded with a list of breeds that the authors believe are suitable for the respondent's lifestyle. While the selection process is based on Australian lifestyles and the breeds are based according to Australian National Kennel Council standards, the results are applicable for North American dog lovers. Keep in mind that because the list of breeds is drawn only from breeds recognized in Australia, certain dogs are missing from the list.

(The Australian Shepherd is one of these because, despite its name, it is a North American breed).

Another source of general information is the Dog Lover's Page, which can be found in the Petlover's area. Here, information on bringing home a new dog, feeding, health, ownership, urban dog ownership, and other topics are included. A list of breeds and their characteristics (again only those recognized by the Australian National Kennel Council) can also be found in this area.

If you happen to be curious about dog lovers in Australia, you'll want to peruse this entire site, which contains statistics and other information on dog ownership in Australia, as well as updates on veterinary research being done down under.

DogNet

http://www.colorado.net/dognet/home.html

This is a small, easy-to-navigate site containing both fun stuff and useful information.

If you are in the mood to play, visit the DogNet Pups Gallery, which features photos of browsers' dogs. A favorite from this group is chosen each month and crowned Pup of the Month by the Webmasters.

In It's a Dog Thing, which includes humorous and everyday tales of canine activity, you can read about other peoples' dogs and even submit your own stories.

If it's hard information you are seeking, the Canine Info area features articles on grooming, training, nutrition, and other topics. A handful of links in the Other Cool Dog Links area will keep you browsing for hours.

Just Pets

http://homearts.com/depts/pastime/00petsc1.htm

Just Pets is an area within the HomeArts site, an online general interest magazine. The site is small, but very attractive and contains a surprising amount of useful information on dogs.

The Pet Rescue Clearinghouse is dedicated to promoting the adoption of rescued pets. Using a list of shelters taken from the North Shore Animal League database, this area features a catalog of shelters by state. Some come complete with e-mail links for browsers who want to contact the shelters directly.

A section called Ask the Vet features a veterinarian who answers medical questions along with other miscellaneous queries. In Cybershopping, a click on the Gifts for Dogs area takes you to a place where advertisers' products are featured, including color photos and a lot of text.

Selected features are also included in this site. An in-depth article on the hows and whys of pet health insurance was posted as of press time.

Professional Dog Networks

http://www.prodogs.com

According to the authors of Professional Dog Networks, this is the "largest dog breeder site in the universe." Run by dog fanciers with extensive experience in showing and breeding, this site features a lot more than just dog breeders. Consisting primarily of advertised services, the Professional Dog Networks site provides a large database of dog-related information.

Each area of interest is clearly separated, starting with Dog Merchandise, which features publications, gifts, breeding supplies, food, catalogs, dog schools and other items and services. Advertisements from the companies offering the merchandise or service are accessible, with links to their sites.

In the Dog Breeders section, browsers can choose among breeders around the world. Selection by breed or by kennel name are available, as are a list of Hall of Famers (dogs with considerable titles, chosen by the Webmasters) and Litter Announcements. The breeder information available here is in-depth and includes photography.

Other categories with advertisers offering services include Boarding Kennels, Dog Handlers, Canine Health (featuring organizations involved in dog care), Breed Rescue, Kennel Clubs (miscellaneous canine organizations), and Dog Trainers.

In the Education and Information section, articles from various paper dog magazines are reprinted. Love My Pet features stores and photos of browsers' pets.

Purina Pet Care Center

http://www.purina.com

This massive, beautifully designed site is authored by Ralston Purina, giants in the dog and cat food industry. However, despite Purina's allegiance to the subject of nutrition, the Purina Pet Care Center is well-rounded in its approach to dog care.

There are seven main areas of the site, each with considerable detail within. In Pet Care, you can find answers to common questions, as well as advice on everyday dog care. Topics here include selecting a vet, training and behavior, bathing, nutrition, and when to vaccinate.

In the Training Yard, there are various articles on different topics such as puppy rearing and correcting problem behaviors. For dog owners with troublesome cats, there is also information here on feline misbehavior.

Purina is famous for its computerized Select-A-Dog program, which it exhibits to the public at dog shows and other canine events. The program is available on this Web site, too, in the Breeders & Champions area. In the online version of Select-A-Dog, browsers are asked to input the canine traits they are seeking directly into the search engine. Another option is to use the Personality Test, which asks around 25 questions about *your* temperament. If you want to take a look at all the breeds in the database, select View All Dogs and go through the list alphabetically.

Characteristics, photos and information on temperament are all included.

Other areas within the Breeders & Champions area include a question-and-answer section, and a listing of upcoming events and shows.

Young dog lovers can find enjoyment in the Fun & Games area, which features trivia, canine horoscopes, stories about dogs, and cartoons. The Bulletin Board, containing information on how to throw your dog a birthday party and the Great American Dog Contest, are fun for grown-ups too.

For serious canine researchers, the Library features an article index with access to features on various subjects relating to dogs.

Talking Dogs

http://www.tetranet.net/users/homedog/

Talking Dogs is a canine site with a unique angle. Created and maintained by dog writer Janine Adams, the site is designed specifically to allow dog lovers to communicate with one another.

First-time visitors to Talking Dogs can get help with the site by stopping by the First Visit area, which includes a Welcome message and information on how to use the site. From there, you can move to the Question of the Week, the first interactive area in the site.

The Question of the Week is posed to browsers, whose answers are posted online. Questions include queries such as "What are dog's most unusual fears?" and "What is the funniest or silliest thing your dog has ever done?"

Responses to these questions appear in the next area, Response to Last Week's Question. If you are a dog lover, you will no doubt enjoy reading about the trials and tribulations of other owners. The stories are often humorous and are always enlightening.

If you want to read some reviews on the hundreds of dog books on the market, The Library section will be of use to you. A list of the author's favorite Web sites and an In Search Of for dog lovers will introduce you to other browsers who want to correspond via e-mail on the topic of dogs.

The Dogpatch Doghouse
http://www.dogpatch.org/dogs.html

The Dogpatch is a beautifully designed general-interest site covering a variety of doggy as well as non-doggy topics, and is authored by Mary Jo Sminkey, a dog trainer and Webmaster extraordinaire. While the Dogpatch site covers a little bit of everything, Sminkey's passion for dogs is evident. The Doghouse, the title for the Dogpatch's canine area, is the largest section of the vast Dogpatch site.

If you know what you want to look up, you can start with the Dogpatch Search Engine, which will take you to specific dog-related areas. It's more fun to just browse the Doghouse, however, in order to discover its wealth of information.

The hodgepodge of doggy stuff at this site includes information about dog books, along with ways to order books online. A list of the author's favorite Web sites, the opportunity to add your own site link and a bulletin board are all here.

Many Webmasters of canine sites have a breed preference, and Sminkey is no exception. The Doghouse features a huge Shetland Sheepdog area containing nearly everything you would ever want to know about Shelties.

The site's activity pages are also noteworthy and cover a variety of performance events. Descriptions of the different activities, along with information on how to get involved with them are included.

As if all this wasn't enough, the More Dogpatch Specials area contains information on canine mail-order catalogs, rescue groups, poisonous plants, humor, photography, and much more.

World Wide Woof

http://www.worldwoof.com

World Wide Woof contains an expansive collection of canine resources, with a focus on purebred and adoption information.

The Adoption Network is the first area browsers come upon in this colorful site, and lists of dogs that need homes can be found here. Organized by breed and by geographical location, this area also allows browsers to post their own information about dogs they are trying to place.

In the Animal Shelters and Humane Societies area, browsers can click on the state of their choice and get the names, addresses, and phone numbers of shelters, alphabetically by city. The only thing missing here are e-mail links.

On the topic of purebred dogs, there is the Breeder Directory, listing a large number of kennels and individuals by both state and breed. Names, addresses, and phone numbers are listed for each breeder. An area containing the American Kennel Club breed standards for each recognized breed is also useful.

One of the best places on this site is an area called the Sporting Dog. The name is somewhat misleading, as this area does not cover the Sporting Dog group, but actually provides detailed information on competitive canine activities such as flyball, agility, mushing, Frisbee, and schutzhund.

A listing of upcoming American Kennel Club shows and events is included, as are links to a number of other canine sites. Advertisements for dogs at stud and products for sale also have their own areas.

Pet Path

http://pathfinder.com//twep/petpath

The small site provides "the latest in pet news, information and entertainment for a healthy and happy pet," according to its authors. Covering both cats and dogs, the site is easy to navigate and has some good information.

Structured like a magazine, Pet Path features an area for regular features on a variety of subjects. Topics are usually general (message therapy, artists, adoption), applying to both dogs and cats. While the Pet News and VetPedia sections don't offer too much in the way of articles, the Bulletin Board area makes up for it. Arranged by topic, bulletin board postings feature considerable dog activity and are worth visiting.

K9NetUK

http://www.k9netuk.com

Self-described as the dog lover's window to the British dog scene, K9NetUk is produced by Britons Barrie and Sue James. Dog trainers who are aiming for a site that will give a complete picture of the British dog scene and encourage responsible dog ownership.

A click on a doghouse graphic on the welcome page takes you to a contents site with no less than 15 categories to choose from. Even though this site was created by and for British dog owners, there is plenty here for North American browsers.

The many areas in this site include results of the huge Crufts Dog Show in England, links to other United Kingdom dog sites, selected overseas sites that are organized by country, and a shopping mall filled with British dog products—especially books—not normally available in the United States. A section on British quarantine regulations written for those outside the country who may be contemplating a move to the United Kingdom is especially valuable.

Two areas of particular interest include the Problems Page, where browsers can ask questions of a canine behaviorist, and the Training area, which contains a number of articles on how to train along with essays on training issues.

While the remaining areas containing upcoming British seminars, a list of canine charities and rescue clubs, and an assortment of European breeders may not have practical uses outside of the United Kingdom, browsing through them will give you a good sense of what the international dog community is all about.

K9 Web

http://www.k9Web.com

Labrador Retriever breeder and Web page designer Liza Lee Miller developed the K9 Web to provide dog owners with a quality source for canine information on the 'Net. She has succeeded in creating a small but good general site that covers several areas of importance to dog lovers.

The best area on the K9 Web is the Breeder's Directory. Containing a catalog of breeders who are online along with links to their Web sites or e-mail, browsers are offered the option of viewing all the breeders listed, searching by breed or simply by state or country. Other breeder directories online are also included.

A separate area containing links to breed pages is also available here, as are link pages to kennels, dog club and canine publications.

The Pet Project

http://chtrib.Webpoint.com/pets/

The Pet Project site is unusual in that it is a syndicated Web page that is located within Web sites sponsored by several newspapers across the country, including the *Chicago Tribune*. A virtual syndicated column, it is written by Steve Dale, author of "My Pet World," a column appearing in real-paper newspapers around the country. Dale's style lends this page a particularly upbeat tone not seen in most other general Web sites.

The Pet Project covers everything from dogs to iguanas, but an entryway on the opening page will allow you to go directly to the canine area.

Here you will find several areas to choose from, each containing well-written and entertaining stuff about dogs. A good place to start is The Kennel, which offers a database of breed descriptions and photographs. The Buying Guide provides facts and suggestions for people looking for a new dog. Care and Gear features advice on purchasing dog supplies, while Pet Peeves touches on behavior and other problems. A bulletin board called The Doghouse is also available to dog lovers who want to correspond with others.

Dog-e-Zine!

http://www.dog-e-zine.com

The Dog-e-Zine! site works as a clearinghouse of sorts for canine Web sites, providing reviews and easy-to-use categories for browsers. Dog-e-zine! features around 100 sites at a given time, rating each with a one through four "bone system." The best sites receive four bones, and the worst, only one.

Reviewed sites are categorized by topics, including All About Dogs, Rescue Associations, Breeds, Competitions & Exhibitions, Health Tips, Dog Clubs, Training, Contests, Special Dogs, and Store.

Regular visits to the Dog-e-Zine! can keep you up to date on the latest and best canine sites coming onto the Web.

Dogs Northwest

http://www.dogsnw.com

This site was created by Washington state resident and Web designer Craig Siegman specifically for dog owners in the Pacific Northwest. If you are planning to travel with your dog to Alaska, British Columbia, Oregon, Washington, or Idaho, there is plenty of information here to make your stay more enjoyable.

Topics here include free-run dog areas in the Northwest, specifically, parks that allow dogs to roam supervised off-leash. Links to information on the individual parks are included. Other areas include contact info on veterinarians, boarding kennels, animal shelters, dog clubs, shows, breeders, lost dogs, trainers, as well as local dog-related news.

If you live in the Pacific Northwest, your dog is eligible to be included in the Gallery, which features photographs of browsers' dogs.

Canine Home Page

http://www.cheta.net/connect/canine/default.htm

The Canine Home Page provides a variety of information for current and would-be dog owners, and is a good stop to make in your dog-related surfing.

Included in this site are monthly features on a number of subjects like dog food, rescue, breeds, training and veterinary medicine. The Article Archives provides a list of several hundred articles available on this site.

A Breeder Directory is also a part of this site and stands out among many of the other breeder listings on the Web. It not only provides information on how to contact breeders, but also details the genetic tests done, the guarantees given; and whether or not the breeder sells puppies and adults, provides stud service, and works in breed rescue. Information on national breed clubs is also included here.

The Canine Home Page contains a chat room and bulletin board, a Breed Information Index with links to sites for each individual breed and a list of rescue groups with Web pages. The Breed and Kennel Clubs area allows browsers to locate local kennel clubs in three ways: by breed, by state or country, and by activity.

A unique area called Recipe Exchange features postings of recipes for homemade dog food and treats.

Kirby's Korner

http://www.TheArray.com/kirby.htm

Kirby's Korner is a fun and memorable site with a slant toward dog ownership in San Francisco. Authored by San Franciscan Ed Cosentino, who created it after discovering the dog-friendliness of his town, Kirby's Korner takes a while to load because of all its colorful graphics. Even if you don't live in the City by the Bay, it's still worth the wait. There is good information here for all dog owners, and Cosentino plans to include even more in the future.

While this site contains a lot of details on dog-related places and services in San Francisco, such as dog-friendly parks, local veterinarians, rental properties that allow dogs, and restaurants where dog owners can dine with their pets, there is also general information here on a number of subjects.

Short pieces on a variety of medical problems appear in the Medical Information area, and details on how to get rid of external parasites appear in the Fleas section. The Dog Foods area is unusual in that it provides ingredient charts for several of the major premium dog food product lines, along with addresses and phone numbers for each of the companies that produce these products.

Fun areas such as Dear Kirby, where browsers send in letters and photos of their dogs, and Kirby's Friends, with photos and information on individual dogs who help inspire the site, add to the fun feeling of Kirby's Korner.

Bestdogs.com

http://www.bestdogs.com

A truly international site, Bestdogs.com is maintained by Belgian dog breeder Jean-Claude Michiels. With a variety of canine information available in English, French, German and Spanish, Bestdogs.com strives to educate dog lovers the world over.

The most interesting place on this site is the Canine Breed Standards area, which features breeds recognized by the Fédération Cynologuique Internationale (FCI), an international dog registry headquartered in Belgium. Organized according to the FCI groups (which vary some-what from the American Kennel Club groups), a number of breed types are listed, with links to the specific breeds. For information on the Norwegian Elkhound, for instance, browsers must select the Spitz breeds, then Nordic Hunters. Once in this area, clicking on the flag representing the desired language will produce information on the breed in question, along with the FCI standard.

Also available in this site is a list of breeders by country, upcoming international exhibitions (including a link to the World Dog Show), and a list of FCI member countries.

Because there are no North American all-breed clubs that belong to the FCI, information on American and Canadian breeders and shows are not available here.

According to the author, the site is still under construction and will eventually list the breed standards of every FCI breed, in the four official languages of the organization.

NetPets

http://www.netpets.com/compinfo.html

A small site with some interesting bits of information, the NetPets site is meant to educate pet owners to help improve the lives of pets everywhere, according to its authors. NetPets also has a literary feeling to it, with several areas containing special essays on dogs.

The first area available on the site is called Shop for Pet Products Online, and provides information on various products along with links to the product's home page. Next comes Our Dog Breed Reference, an area that discusses only a few breeds, including mixed breeds, but covers them completely.

The NetPets Image Gallery is a somewhat non-doggy area on this site, and features photos of landscapes and a variety of domestic animals for downloading purposes. A Special Tribute includes an interesting excerpt from a speech by a lawyer in 1870 who was prosecuting a defendant for killing another man's dog. Those Amazing Animals also touches on the creative, featuring dog-related poems and excerpts from literary classics. Browsers are also invited to submit their own works.

Pet Care Tips and Information provides pieces on preventive health care, introducing new pets, taking your dog to work, and other miscellaneous subjects. And a link to Bad Dog! takes you to stories of the antics of naughty dogs, written by fellow browsers.

Pet Vet

http://www.pet-vet.com

Despite its name, Pet Vet has a lot more to offer than just medical information. Authored by noted veterinarian and writer Lowell Ackerman, Pet Vet provides original articles on a number of canine topics, as well as links to pages on other sites.

The subject of choosing the right dog receives considerable attention on this site, with two areas devoted exclusively to this topic. Articles on choosing a breed, finding a breeder and the characteristics of the American Kennel Club breeds are plentiful.

Other areas within the site include Basic Care (feeding and nutrition, bathing, raising a puppy), Health Care (by topic or by body system), Training (basic, behavior problems, trainer associations), and Organizations (lost-and-found groups, rescue, search-and-rescue, etc.). Most of the health-oriented articles are written by Dr. Ackerman, as are some of the other items.

But Pet Vet is more than just an informational site. An area called Fun Stuff features a pet/owner look-alike contest, photos of browsers' pets and links to lighthearted sites.

I N D E X

A

Abyssinian Sand Terrier, 164
Afghan Hound, 4, 141, 202
African Wild Dog, 346-348, 361
African Wild Dog Conservation Fund,
   347-348
aggression, 2, 73, 77, 81, 86
agility, 66, 78, 185, 188-189, 194-197,
   200, 207, 210, 211, 214, 251,
   253, 264, 291, 305, 318, 319,
   322, 399
aging, 29, 57
Airedale Terrier, 326
Airedale Terrier Club of America, 215
Akbash Dog, 5-6
Akita, 6
Alaska Search and Rescue Dogs
   (ASARD), 223
Alaskan Husky, 321
Alaskan Malamute, 6-7, 30, 134-135,
   201, 321
Alaskan Malamute Club of America, 7,
   135
Alaskan Malamute Protection League
   (AMPL), 134-135
allergies to dogs, 377-378
ALPO Canine Frisbee Disc
   Championships, 206
AKC Gazette magazine, 161
America Online Pet Care Forum, 54
American Animal Hospital Association
   (AHAA), 45, 392-393
American Association of Avalanche
   Professionals, 222
American Association of Food Hygiene
   Veterinarians, 45

American Boarding Kennel Association,
   254
American Boxer Club, 156
American Bulldog, 7
American Canine Association (ACA),
   163-164
American College of Veterinary
   Behaviorists, 45
American Eskimo Dog, 8
American Hairless Terrier, 164
American Herding Breeds Association,
   193, 208-209
American Holistic Veterinary Medical
   Association (AHVMA), 47
American Humane Association (AHA),
   147-148
American Kennel Club (AKC), 16, 27,
   35, 159, 160-161, 162, 163, 165 ,
   166, 181, 188-189, 190, 193,
   194, 199, 201-202, 210, 269,
   272, 275, 280, 288, 289, 291,
   292, 299, 305, 392, 399, 404-
   405, 406
American Kennel Club Dog Museum,
   276
American Pit Bull Terrier, 16, 201
American Rare Breeds Association
   (ARBA), 178
American Rescue Dog Association
   (ARDA), 167-168
American Shih Tzu club, 37-38
American Sighthound Field Association,
   193, 202
American Society for the Prevention of
   Cruelty to Animals (ASPCA),
   143-144
American Topical Association, 340
American Veterinary Dental College, 45

American Veterinary Medical
  Association (AVMA), 44-45
American Working Collie Association,
  214
American Working Dogs Association
  (AWDA), 207
Amory, Cleveland: 138
Animal Protection Institute (API), 137-138
Animal Resorts, 256-257
animal shelters, 141, 142, 385, 390,
  395, 399, 403
Animal Welfare Act, 141-142
Animal Welfare League of Alexandria,
  265
Antypas, William G.: 190-191
arthritis, 47
Association of Pet Behaviour
  Counsellors (APBC), 84
Atlanta Recreation and Fun Club for
  Dogs (ARF!), 168-169
Aus-Ben Manufacturing, 289
Austin Humane Society and SPCA,144
Australian Cattle Dog (ACD), 8-9, 126
Australian Kelpie, 9-10
Australian National Kennel Council,
  393-394
Australian Shepherd, 299, 394
Autumn Winds Dog Agility and
  Training Center, 264
Ayzenberg Group, The: 387
Azawakh, 164

B

backpacking with dogs, 212, 282
  see also hiking with dogs
barking, 85, 86
Basenji, 202, 292
Basset Hound, 136, 141, 272, 286,
  322, 323
Beagle, 10-11, 138, 245, 322, 332
Bearded Collie, 117
Bear Paw Kennels, 116
Belgian Groenendael, 11-12, 168
Belgian Laekenois, 11-12, 168

Belgian Malinois, 11-12, 168
Belgian Shepherd, 11-12, 168, 209
Belgian Tervuren, 11-12, 168, 199
Bergh Memorial Animal Hospital, 143
Bernese Mountain Dog, 12, 201
Best Friends Animal Sanctuary, 135
Bichon Frise, 280, 322
Bide-A-Wee, 142
Big Dog Sportswear, 339
Bird Dog News magazine, 213
Black Paws National Newfoundland
  Search Dog Academy, 220
bloat, 25, 26
Bloodhound, 242
Blue Dog, 334
boarding kennels, 251, 255, 256-258,
  371, 392, 396, 402-403
books: available for purchase, 29, 31,
  32, 41, 44, 46, 48, 61, 64, 65, 68,
  71, 100, 143, 165 , 168, 187,
  210, 239, 246, 260, 276-277,
  279-281, 298, 299, 302, 305,
  307, 308, 317, 370, 393, 398-399, 400
book reviews, 389
bordatella, 60
Border Collie, 13, 319, 322, 325, 326
Border Terrier, 13-14
Borzoi, 202
Bouvier des Flandres, 201
Boxer, 14, 156, 319
Boxer Rebound Inc., 156
Brainstem Auditory Evoked Response
  (BAER), 58-59
Brittany, 176
Brown Kennel Supply, 303
Bull Terrier, 15, 386-387
Buster Cube, 293
buying a puppy, 18, 19, 59, 109, 111

C

Cairn Terrier, 15-16
California Office of Emergency Services
  Law Enforcement Division 172

California Rescue Dog Association (CARDA), 171-172, 221
Canadian Kennel Club, 203, 274-275
cancer, 61, 378
Canine Companions for Independence, 227
Canine Cryobank, 304
Canine Eye Registration Foundation (CERF), 47-48
Canine Good Citizen Test (CGC), 85, 163, 234, 253
Canines of America Center for Dog Training & Clinical Behavior Therapy, 70
Canine Review magazine, 274
Canine Working Companions, 230
Canvasback Pet Supplies, 308
Cape Hunting Dog, 346-347
  see also African Wild Dog
Cardigan Welsh Corgi, 322
cardiomyopathy, 93
carting, 200-201, 282
cats, 44, 52, 53 58, 90, 92, 95, 135, 146-147, 263, 298 , 302, 364, 369, 372, 375, 376, 384, 387, 389, 396, 399
Caucasian Ovcharka, 136
Cavalier King Charles Spaniel, 377
Changing Horizons, 294-295
chat rooms, 23, 29, 31, 36, 39, 341, 384-385, 386, 388, 403
Chesapeake Bay Retrievers, 118
chewing, 74, 81, 393
Chicago Tribune, 401
Chihuahua, 16, 117, 305
children, 15, 26, 27, 44, 57, 77, 85, 87, 126, 127, 139, 147-148, 265, 272, 280, 335, 337, 346, 349, 368, 393
choosing a dog, 9, 41, 44, 112, 115, 151, 160, 280, 367, 372, 379, 387, 388, 391, 396, 402, 406
Chow Chow, 106-107, 141
clicker training, 71-72, 264
Clumber Spaniel, 301
Cochrane Ecological Institute, 359

Cocker Spaniel, 17, 136, 318
College of Veterinary Medicine at University of Illinois, 55
Collie, 17-18, 36, 113, 201, 214
Collie Club of America, 18
Companion Animal Rescue and Education Service (CARES), 152
Continental Kennel Club, 164-165
copper toxicosis, 54
Covey-Tucker Hill Kennels, 121
coyote, 337-338, 341, 351, 353, 356-358, 364-365
craniomandibular osteopathy (CMO), 61
cross-country, 198
Crufts Dog Show, 184-185, 400
Cycle Canine Nutrition Products, 98, 207

D

Dachshund, 18-19, 210, 306, 318, 320, 325, 336
Dallas Dog & Disc Club, 206
Dallas/Ft. Worth Shelter Rescue Inc., 138
Dalmatian, 19-20, 124-125, 141, 286, 295, 306-307, 336
Dalmatian Club of America, 336
deafness, 57-59
Defenders magazine, 342
Defenders of Wildlife, 342
Delta Society, 173-174, 231
dental care, 29, 46, 52, 57
dhole, 361
Diamond Dogs, 293
digging, 71, 393
dingo, 9, 361, 362, 381
Disney Studios, 336-337
distemper, 45
DNA, 53, 54
Doberman Pinscher, 20-21, 287
dog camps, 251-253, 265-266
doggy day-care, 251, 257, 264
Doggie Drive-Thru, 95

Dog Fancy magazine, 272-273
dog food: making at home, 99
Dog Lover's Bookshop, 276-277
Dogman newspaper, 237
dogs on stamps, 339-340
Dog Owner's Guide newspaper, 280
dog parks/runs, 373-374, 402, 404
dog show photography, 269, 333, 392
Dogs in Canada magazine, 118, 274-275
Dog's Prayer, A: 379-380
Dog Training Clubs of Great Britain, 78
Dog World magazine, 279-280
Dog Writers' Association of America (DWAA), 170-171
Dogz, 284
Domino Chow Chows, 106
Doris Day Animal League, 151, 154
dressage, 198

E

ear cropping, 21, 25, 84
Earthdog trials, 189, 200, 210-211, 291
Earthwatch International, 355
E. coli, 52
Eddie, 338
elbow dysplasia, 48
electronic mailing lists, 18, 19, 68, 385
    animal-related, 56
    deafness, 58
    Doberman Pinscher, 21
    English Setter, 21
    Frisbee, 206
    German Shepherd Dog, 23
    Golden Retriever, 23
    puppy raisers, 227
    Samoyed, 34
    Shetland Sheepdog, 37
    training, 72
    wild dogs, 341
    wolf, 355
English Setter, 21

English Setter Association of America, 21
English Shepherd, 322
English Springer Spaniels, 21-22
entropian, 7
epilepsy, 47
euthanasia, 44, 267
eventing, 200
event listings, 68, 78, 397, 398, 399, 403
Excite, xxvii
eye disorders, 53, 60

F

famous dogs, 330, 377, 386
Fancy Publications Inc., 272
Farmer, Katharine: 333
feces, eating of: 82
Federation Cynologuque International (FCI), 195, 197, 404-405
FEMA,172
first aid, 44
fleas, 29, 52, 61, 298, 299, 393, 404
flyball, 185, 193, 197-198, 200, 211, 214, 305, 319, 399
flygility, 196, 211
Food and Drug Administration Center for Veterinary Medicine (FDA CVM), 50
fox: 348, 351, 357-358, 364
    red fox, 341, 356-357
    Simien fox, 350
    swift fox, 359, 363
Fox & Hounds Ltd., 295
fox hunting, 2
Fox Terriers, 141, 317
freestyle, 207
French ringsport, 209-210
Frisbee, 66, 193, 205-206, 214, 399
Fund for Animals, 138-139
Furry Friends Pet Assisted Therapy Services, 234

G

genetics, 31, 47, 388
genetic: disease, 43, 46, 48, 49, 51, 53, 54, 60-61, 110 , 385
German Longhaired Pointer, 175
German Shepherd Dog, 22, 64, 69, 121-122, 176, 199, 224-225, 228, 239, 317, 321, 323, 334-335
German Shepherd Working Dog Club, 176
German Shorthaired Pointer, 175
German Wirehaired Pointer, 175
Giant Schnauzer, 35
Golden Gate Labrador Retriever Club (GGLRC), 150-151
Golden Retriever, 23-25, 113-115, 153-154, 219, 296
Gone to the Dogs, 299-300
Good Citizen Dog Scheme, 163, 185
Good Dog! magazine, 281-282
Great Dane, 25, 100, 110, 141
Great Dane Club of America, 25
Great Pyrenees, 25-26, 235, 317
Great Pyrenees Club of America, 26
Greyhound, 52, 66, 75-76, 202
Greyhound Rescue & Adoption Inc., 145
grieving, 44, 142,144, 368, 393
grooming, 124, 255, 256-257, 261-263, 384-385, 388
  Bichon Frise, 280
  Collie, 113
  Golden Retriever, 115
  Shih Tzu, 37-38
  supplies, 298, 302, 303, 308
  Yorkshire Terrier, 41
Guide Dog Association, 171
Guiding Eyes for the Blind, 229

H

hair loss, 30
Heinz Pet Products, 98
Herriot, James: 331

Hill's Pet Nutrition, 56
Hippomedia Corp., 345
heart disease, 45, 48
heartworm, 29, 59
heat exhaustion, 52, 57
hemophilia, 60
herding, 9, 66, 124, 125-126, 188-189, 200, 207, 208-209, 210, 214, 246, 291
Higham Press Show Printers, 189
hiking with dogs, 212
hip dysplasia, 7, 43, 48, 49-50, 52, 59, 60
H.J. Heinz, 207
Hoflin Publishing, 275-276
Home Away From Home, 255
horoscopes for dogs, 390, 397
horses, 44, 53, 369, 384, 387, 389
housetraining, 29, 64, 68, 71, 77, 115, 373, 393
Howell Book House, 279
Humane Society of the United States (HSUS), 86, 132-133, 154
humor, 370-371, 372-373, 374-376, 380, 397-398
hunting: 49, 193, 213, 215, 334
  supplies, 308

I

Iams Company, 90-91
Ibizan Hound, 202
Iditarod, 203, 204-205
incontinence, 57, 81
Independence Dogs Inc. (IDI), 229
Indiana University of Pennsylvania, 361
Institute for Genetic Disease Control in Animals, 51
International Association of Pet Cemeteries (IAPC), 266
International Weight Pull Association, 201
International Wolf Center, 344-345
Irish Wolfhound, 115, 202, 291
Italian Greyhound, 119

J

jackal, 350, 351
Jack Russell Terrier (JRT), 2-3, 120, 166, 337, 338
Jack Russell Terrier Club of America, 166-167
Jack Russell Terrier Club of Canada,120
Jerky Treats, 98
junior showmanship, 119, 188

K

K9 Academy for Law Enforcement, 240
K-III Communications Company, 279
Kal Kan, 94
Kansas State University School of Veterinary Medicine, 52
Karelien Bear Dogs, 116
Karelo-Finnish Laika, 164
Katwala Australian Cattle Dogs, 126-127
Keeshond, 30
Kennel Club Junior Organisation (KCJO), 163, 185
Kennel Club, The: 162, 184
kennel cough, 52
Kinlayke Kennels, 118
Kong Company, 293
Kong Toy, 293
Kuvasz, 141, 235

L

Labrador Retriever, 26-27, 136, 150-151, 218, 244, 289, 296, 316, 321, 322, 326, 401
Lakeland Terriers, 118
Large Musterlander, 176
Larson, Gary: 335-336
Lassie, 17-18, 36, 37,113, 125, 214
League Against Cruel Sports, 348
Legg/Calv Perthes, 60
legislation, 33, 165
Leonberger, 27-28

Letterman, David, 372
Lhasa Apso, 119
Liacone Fund, 347
Litter I.D. Collars, 294
Little Shelter Animal Rescue, 146
livestock guarding, 5, 25, 38-39, 41, 234-236 , 247
L.L. Bowsers Canine Emporium, 303
Louisiana State University, 58
lurecoursing, 189, 200, 202, 251
luxating patella, 30, 48, 60-61
Lyme disease, 45, 60

M

Majestic Tree Hound, 164
Maltese, 28-29
Maremma Sheepdog, 41-42, 235
Marin Humane Society (MHS), 155
Massachusetts Society for the Prevention of Cruelty to Animals (MSPCA), 149-150
Mastiff, 1, 320
Meaty Bone dog food, 98
Mexican Hairless: *see* Xoloitzcuintli
Mexican Kennel Club, 123
Michigan State School of Veterinary Medicine, 53
Mid-Atlantic D.O.G.S., 223
military dogs, 236-238
Miniature Schnauzer, 35
mixed breeds, 388, 405
Monks of New Skete, 64, 73
Moss-Bow Foley Inc., 185-187
mushing, 203, 204, 282, 399

N

Nadelhaus German Shepherds, 122
National Animal Poison Control Center, 25, 55
National Association of Dog Obedience Instructors (NADOI), 172-173
National Association of Professional Pet Sitters, 258-261

National Biological Survey Study, 344-345
National Bird Dog Museum, 334
National Capital Air Canines, 206
National Dingo Association, 381
National Disaster Search Dog Foundation, 218-219
National Education for Assistance Dog Services, 227, 228-229
National Pet Health and Care Network, 278
National Pet Registry (NPR), 268
National Police Bloodhound Association, 242-243
National Service Dog Center, 174
National Wildlife Federation, 345-346
neutering, 57, 59, 115, 144, 147, 151, 154, 155
Newfoundland, 29, 201, 220, 263
newsgroups, 25, 36, 341, 385, 390
Newport Dog Shows 190-191
New Yorkers for Companion Animals (NYCA), 148
New Zealand Flygility Dog Association, 211
Nez Perce Indian tribe, 352
Nipper, 328
North American Dog Agility Council, 195
North American Flyball Association, 197
North American Police Work Dog Association (NAPWDA), 238
North American Versatile Hunting Dog Association (NAVHDA), 175
Northridge earthquake, 171, 218
North Shore Animal League, 395
Norwegian Elkhound, 404-405
Novartis Animal Health, 298
Nuez Kennels, 123

O

obedience:
  accessories, 303, 305
  competition, 68, 78, 185, 188-189, 193, 199, 201-202, 207, 214, 251
  training, 21, 160, 172, 185, 240, 256, 257, 388
obesity, 93, 99,101
Oklahoma City bombing, 171,172, 218, 224, 268
Old Dominion Kennel Club, 177-178
101 Dalmatians, 336-337
Onofrio, Jack: 187-188
Organization for the Working Samoyed, 34, 214
Orthopedic Foundation for Animals (OFA), 7, 48, 50
O'Serenity Shetland Sheepdogs, 125-126
Ottawa Kennel Club, 169
Our Dogs newspaper, 277-278

P

parvovirus, 45, 61, 393
Pedigree dog food, 94
pedigrees, 12, 54, 128
Pekingese, 117
PennHip Method, 49
Pennsylvania Federation of Dog Clubs, 165
People for the Ethical Treatment of Animals (PETA), 153
pet sitting, 258, 269
Pet View magazine, 278-279
Perpetual Pet Care, 52
pet cemeteries, 266-268
pet-facilitated therapy, 70, 142, 227, 230, 233-234, 246, 248, 253, 388
pet health insurance, 395
pet loss, 71
  see also grieving
Pet Products Plus, 97
PetSage, 298-299
P.F. Magic, 284-286
Pharaoh Hound, 202
phosphofructokinase deficiency, 54
P.M.L. Prints, 292
poetry, 19, 30, 37, 369
police dog, 68, 69, 238-247, 317

Polly Klaus Foundation,172
Pomeranian, 1, 30, 117, 141
Poodle, 31, 263, 287, 322
Pooper-Scooper, 302
portosystemic shunt, 60
Positive Power Kennels, 257
Predator Project, 362
professional dog handlers, 396
Program, 298
protection dog, 68, 199, 214, 244
Public Broadcasting System (PBS), 337
Pudelpointer, 176
Pug, 32
Puli, 123, 188
puppies: hand rearing, 118
puppy mills, 105, 109, 166

Q

quarantine, 400

R

rabies, 45, 393
racing, 200
Ralston Purina, 92-93, 396
Ravenwood Dalmatians, 124
recipes, 30, 94, 96-97
Reigning Cats & Dogs, 292
rescue organization listings, 17, 24, 108, 110, 117, 134, 140-141, 145, 156, 292, 385, 386, 388, 390, 392, 396, 398, 400, 402, 406
Reward dog food, 98
Rhodesian Ridgeback, 59
ringworm, 52
Rin Tin Tin, 334-335
Riverbend Search and Rescue Dog Association, 224
Rodigue, George: 333-334
rollerblading with dogs, 212
Rottweiler, 32-33, 127-128, 150, 177, 201, 241, 257, 294
Rouse Hill Boarding Kennel, 119

Royal Canadian Mounted Police (RCMP), 225, 238-239
Royal Society for the Prevention of Cruelty to Animals (RSPCA), 258
Russia, 116
Russo European Laika, 116,
    see also Karelien Bear Dogs

S

Saint Bernard, 33-34, 201, 339
Saluki, 202
Samoyed, 30, 34-35, 139-140, 201, 213-214
Samoyed Club of America, 34
San Francisco SPCA, 146
San Jose Museum of Art, 332
SBM Products, 300
schutzhund, 176, 196, 199, 200, 210, 246, 399
Scottie Cramp, 60
Scottish Deerhound, 202
Scottish Terrier, 377
search-and-rescue (SAR), 29, 171-172, 218-226, 238, 246, 388, 406
Seeing Eye, The: 228
Select-A-Dog, 396
Sensible Choice dog food, 97
service dogs, 226-234, 314
Shar-Pei, 36
Shetland Sheepdog, 36-37, 125, 138, 398
Shih Tzu, 37-38, 325
shock collars, 85
Siberian Husky, 149, 321, 376
Siberian Husky Club of America, 149
Simmons College, 353
Simon & Schuster Macmillan, 279
skijoring, 196, 205, 214, 282
skin problems, 30, 47, 57, 393
sledding: 203, 204, 210, 214, 246, 251, 282, 388
    supplies, 308
    see also mushing
Small Musterlander, 176

Smooth Fox Terrier, 317
Snoopy, 10, 332-333
Snow Dog Festival, 338
Solid Gold Health Products for Pets, 100
spaying, 57, 59, 115, 144, 147, 151, 154, 155
Spuds MacKenzie, 15
socialization, 68, 70, 78, 85
squirrel dog trials, 210-211
stadium jumping, 198
Standard Schnauzer, 35
States Kennel Club, 159, 181, 280
Stone Fort Rottweilers, 127
Superstar Irish Wolfhounds, 115-116
Switzerland, 34
Szeder Pulik Kennel, 124

T

Tamaron Collies, 113
Telemark Productions, 286
temperament testing, 110, 213
Texas K9 Police Association for Certification & Standards, 243
Thai Ridgeback Dog, 128-129
thyroid disease, 48
Tibetan Mastiff, 38-39, 305-306
Tibetan Spaniel, 39
Tibetan Spaniel Club of America, 39
Timber Wolf Information Network, 354
Timberline Retrievers, 113-114
Timmery Pet Care, 97
Tom DiGiacomo's Dog Show Photography, 269
Top Dog Training School, 265-266
Toto, 15
toxoplasmosis, 45
Toy Fox Terrier, 317
tracking, 193, 199, 209, 214, 240, 252, 264
traveling with dogs, 44, 210, 280, 296, 371, 379, 380, 388
2 Stupid Dogs, 335

U

urinary stones, 59
United Kennel Club, 123, 159, 164, 165, 168, 181, 193, 194, 202, 210, 272, 280
United Schutzhund Clubs of America (USA), 176
United States Border Collie Club, 13
United States Canine Combined Training Association (USCCTA), 198
United States Dog Agility Association (USDAA), 193, 280
United States Rottweiler Club, 177
University of California at Irvine, 46
University of Pennsylvania, 50
University of Toronto, 370
USDA-APHIS, 235-236
U. S. Department of Agriculture's Beagle Brigade, 245
U.S. Department of Interior, 357
U.S. Fish & Wildlife Service, 357
U.S. Senate, 314-315

V

vaccinations, 57, 59, 60, 396
Velavadar National Park, 355
veterinarian: career as, 44, 56
  choosing a, 44, 54, 393, 396
  holistic, 47
veterinarians: organizations for, 45, 56
Veterinary Information Network, 54
veterinary: journals, 46
  education, 52
  ophthalmologists, 53
  schools, 46, 56
  specialties, 56
VetGen, 53-54
videotapes, 61, 65, 68, 260, 280, 298, 299
Vietnam Dog Handlers Association, 236-237

Virginia Police Dog Work Association, 242

Vizsla, 176

vomiting, 57

von Willebrand's disease (VWD), 54, 60-61

W

Waldenway Canine Camp, 255-266

Walkoway Beardies, 117

Waltham, 68, 94-95

Warner Brothers, 337

Wegman, William: 331

weight pulling, 201, 214, 253, 282

Weimaraner, 176, 294, 331

Welsh Terrier, 40

Welsh Terrier Club of America, 40

West Highland White Terrier, 40-41

Westminster Kennel Club Dog Show, 121, 170, 185-186, 272

West Siberian Laika, 164

West Virginia Canine College, 69

West Virginia K-9 Search and Rescue, 226

WestWide Avalanche Network, 222

Whippet, 202, 205

Whisker, 298

White House, The: 377

Wild Canid Survival and Research Center, 354

Wildlife Institute of India, 355

Wildlife Waystation, 348-349

Wile E. Coyote, 337-338

Wirehaired Pointing Griffon, 176

Wishbone, 337

Wolf Education & Research Center, 351-352

Wolf Haven, 349-350

Wolf Sanctuary, 353

Wolf Spitz, 30

wolf, 59, 341, 344, 350, 352, 358-359, 361

   designs, 290-291

   protection, 342, 353-355, 357-358

reintroduction, 341, 342, 351-352, 356, 365; rescue, 348-350

World Wildlife Fund, 359-361

worms, 57

World Dog Show, 405

World Protection Dog Association (WPDA), 174-175

X

Xoloitzcuintli, 123

Y

Yahoo!, xxvii, 316

Yellowstone National Park, 341, 342, 351-352, 365

Yorkshire Terrier, 16, 41